D0087725

EAST ASIAN HISTORICAL MONOGRAPHS
General Editor: WANG GUNGWU

The Origins of an Heroic Image:
Sun Yatsen in London, 1896–1897

EAST ASIAN HISTORICAL MONOGRAPHS
General Editor: WANG GUNGWU

When this series was first introduced in the late 1960s studies of Asian history were still seen to be too closely identified with Western activities and enterprise and to reflect too little either Asian viewpoints or the economic and social factors which lay behind political events.

As the series moves into its second decade, a new generation of historians has emerged who by their researches have opened up entirely new perspectives and charted new courses in the study of the historical process in the region.

It is the hope of the publishers that the East Asian Historical Monographs series will, against this background of innovative scholarship, continue to play a role in meeting the need and demand for historical writings on the region, and that the fruits of the new scholarship will thus reach a wider reading public.

Other titles in this series are listed at the end of the book.

The Origins of an
Heroic Image:
Sun Yatsen in London,
1896–1897

J. Y. WONG

HONG KONG   OXFORD   NEW YORK
OXFORD UNIVERSITY PRESS
1986

Oxford University Press

Oxford New York Toronto
Petaling Jaya Singapore Hong Kong Tokyo
Delhi Bombay Calcutta Madras Karachi
Nairobi Dar es Salaam Cape Town
Melbourne Auckland

and associated companies in
Beirut Berlin Ibadan Nicosia

First published 1986
Published in the United States
by Oxford University Press, Inc.
New York

British Library Cataloguing in Publication Data

Wong, J.Y. (John Yue-wo)
The origins of an heroic image: Sun Yatsen
in London, 1896–1897.—(East Asian
historical monographs)
1. Sun, Yat-sen 2. Kidnapping—England—London
I. Title II. Series
364.1'54'0924 HV6604.G7259/
ISBN 0-19-584080-1

Library of Congress Cataloging-in-Publication Data

Wong, J. Y.
The origins of an heroic image.

(East Asian historical monographs)
Bibliography: p.
Includes index.
1. Sun, Yat-sen, 1866–1925—Exile, 1896–1897—
England—London. 2. China—Presidents—Biography.
I. Title. II. Series.
DS777.W66 1986 951.04'1'0924 [B] 86–21779
ISBN 0-19-584080-1

Printed in Hong Kong by Golden Crown Printing Co. Ltd.
Published by Oxford University Press, Warwick House,

To Marjorie Jacobs,
Emeritus Professor
University of Sydney

Foreword

It is hard to believe that there is more to know about the kidnapping of Sun Yatsen in London in October 1896 and what he subsequently did there before his departure in June 1897. After the extensive researches of Luo Jialun (1930; 1935), Harold Schiffrin (1961; 1968), and Wu Xiangxiang (1962–4; 1970–2; 1982), one might conclude that the subject has been laid to rest. But there remained a number of disagreements between scholars and also some doubts about interpretation which have left readers uneasy. Was Sun Yatsen really kidnapped or did he voluntarily walk into the Chinese Legation? How important was the kidnapping to his image as a revolutionary hero? How much did the London stay influence his major political views, especially those concerning the Three Principles of the People?

I was surprised some three years ago to learn from Dr John Wong that he was about to embark on a thorough re-examination of this subject. Dr Wong's international reputation has come from his remarkable study of Viceroy Yeh Ming-ch'en (1852–8) and from his contributions to our knowledge of the Chinese documents (1839–60) in the British Foreign Office Records. And he was engaged in another major monograph on Sino-British relations during this period of history. Why did he interrupt that work to turn to the end of the century in order to write another book on a subject so fully explored? He explained that his several visits to China during the recent resurgence of Sun Yatsen studies (including conferences on the 1911 Revolution on both sides of the Taiwan Straits), had led him to wonder if Sun Yatsen was not being subjected once again to myth-making on a large scale. In particular, he was concerned to see how some dubious assertions about Sun Yatsen's London experiences in 1896–7 were entering into the realm of historical fact, assertions which he personally knew were at variance with the sources available to him. He was sufficiently moved by this development to offer to explore the subject again. He is at home in London and familiar with the archives and various libraries there. He has access to a wide circle of scholarly friends around the world. What is more, he has had experience, through his full portrayal of the tragic and much-maligned career of Viceroy Yeh, with the taxing task of historical revisionism. It was something he knew he could do as a contribution to Sun Yatsen scholarship. Little did he know how much more demanding this task was to turn out to be than expected. I know how much time he has had to take to re-examine every source exhaustively. He has certainly needed his 'stout pair of boots' to walk the streets of London and trudge from library to library in many cities to follow up every lead he could find wherever it might take him. As for the hard thinking necessary to challenge received views and to reconstruct a better set of interpretations, only Dr Wong knows how much that has cost him in concentration and energy.

Now that he has completed the job, I am surprised not only by the amount of new material he has been able to find but also by what he has discovered in the known sources which others had either mis-read or failed to see. This book is, of course, not simply a piece of investigation. The historian as detective, prosecutor, judge, and defence lawyer all rolled into one is common enough, but how many who have attempted to be all four have forgotten to be an historian as well! It is in the end the act of reconstruction, after the data have been picked to shreds and analysed almost beyond the reader's endurance, that marks the successful historian. After his work on Viceroy Yeh, we have come to expect Dr Wong to be able to reconstruct with both skill and elegance. He has not failed us here.

Dr Wong has throughout the book noted his great debt to his predecessors, especially to Luo Jialun and Harold Schiffrin. He has modestly suggested that he has merely taken the story a little further than they had. Indeed there are still matters of which we remain uncertain. Despite Dr Wong's efforts in uncovering new material that illuminates aspects of Sun Yatsen's political views while he was in London, it is still very hard to determine how much his London experience contributed to his maturity as a revolutionary thinker. On the other hand, there is no doubt that many issues are now clearer than ever before. For example, it is likely that Sun Yatsen did not enter the Legation voluntarily; Sir Halliday Macartney was probably less of a villain than he has been made out to be; Dr James Cantlie does seem to have been the real author of *Kidnapped in London* and was the first person consciously to project an heroic image of Sun Yatsen, although Chen Shaobai in Japan was not far behind; and Sun Yatsen was not slow to cultivate this image of himself soon afterwards and did so with a keen sense of his destiny. There are many more insights and discoveries in this closely-woven book. They remind us that there is no subject in history of which we can say we now know enough.

WANG GUNGWU
Australian National University
Canberra
30 May 1986

Preface

I am indeed fortunate to belong to a large and scholarly Department, in which colleagues are friendly, understanding, and helpful. Whether it be in the common-room or in the corridor, I can always draw on a great range of expertise. My retired colleague, Marjorie Jacobs, to whom this book is dedicated, has taken an active interest in my work. She has read my manuscript with meticulous care and has asked searching questions. I must thank her not only for this, but for the personal kindness and scholarly support she has given me over the years that I have known her. Special thanks are also due to Grahame Harrison, who has seen this project emerge, develop, and grow into its present form, sharing with me *my* agonies over conflicting pieces of evidence and *his* wide knowledge and long experience. He has read numerous drafts of my initial chapters. He has been a source of constant encouragement and support. He, Jim Waldersee, and Ken Cable have also read the entire manuscript and made valuable suggestions. Deryck Schreuder and other colleagues, with whom I teach several courses jointly, have been most co-operative in making alternative arrangements to enable me to participate in two important Sun Yatsen international conferences. He, Ken Macnab, Bruce Fulton, Richard Waterhouse, and others have lent me books and offered kind advice. Successive heads of the Department cannot have been more helpful.

My University has been most supportive in granting me leave to undertake research on numerous trips overseas. For this, in view of the financial stringencies of today, I am particularly appreciative.

The combination of field-work and archival research undertaken in an attempt to reconstruct a well-known but very patchy story, and to unearth and interpret the numerous bits and pieces of new evidence as well as to reinterpret old ones, means that I have involved a large number of people and institutions, and incurred endless debts. I do not know how I can ever thank them adequately; nor would space allow me to mention all of them here. In specific cases, therefore, acknowledgement is made in a footnote.

Mr Colin McLaren, archivist at Aberdeen University, and his colleagues, Professor Peter Ramsey, Mr Donald Withrington, and Dr Dorothy Johnston, were of great help in my attempts to find out more about Dr James Cantlie and his family.

Archivists at the Beijing Palace Museum (now the First National Historical Archives of China), Mr Liu Guilin, Ju Deyuan, and others, have offered me every assistance during my various trips there; so has the staff of Beijing Library (now the National Library of China). Historians in Beijing, particularly Professor Jin Chongji, have always been prompt to answer my queries.

Miss Janet Wallace, archivist at the British Museum, ploughed through the Central Archives and located valuable information for me about Sun Yatsen's activities in that famous institution. Mr Howard Nelson and Dr Frances Wood of the Department of Oriental MSS and Printed Books have never failed me whether I was physically in the British Library or thousands of miles away. Mr Nelson is an old friend, and our correspondence in the course of my research is one of the longest on file.

Dr Joseph Needham, Dr Carmen Blacker, and Dr Chris Andrews at the University of Cambridge have helped me clarify some technical points crucial to an understanding of the kidnapping incident.

Professor Wang Gungwu in Canberra has taken an active interest in my project ever since its inception, has read all the chapters, and has favoured me with the Foreword.

Members of the Cantlie family, in particular, Kenneth, James, Audrey, and Colin, have been most generous in sharing with me their family history and papers. Their hospitality is also fabulous.

Chinese Embassy and Consular staff in both London and Sydney have gone out of their way to help me locate materials not normally available to historians. The tracings of the Legation building in London have been indispensable in my attempts to reconstruct that part of the story encompassing the days when Sun Yatsen was inside the building.

The librarian of the Mitchell Library in Glasgow, Mr Paul Duffy, has answered my queries promptly.

Greater London Council Record Office staff, especially Miss Cobern, Mr John Philips, Mr R. Hart, and Miss Susan Snell, took great pains to search for old maps and photographs which have played an important role in sorting out certain puzzles, clarifying certain points and demolishing some common beliefs.

The Hong Kong Public Records Office archivists, Mr Ian Diamond (formerly) and Mr Lau Yun-woo (currently), and their colleague Ms Robyn McLean, and the deputy librarian of the University of Hong Kong, Mr Malcolm Quinn, and his colleague, Mr Peter Yeung, have provided me with primary and secondary sources crucial to an understanding of Sun Yatsen's activities there.

Professor Ramon Myers, at the Hoover Institution, was most hospitable and helpful when I used the Boothe Papers at Stanford.

The librarians of the Inns of Court, Mrs Theresa Tom (Gray's Inn), Mr Roderick Walker (Lincoln's Inn), and Mr W. Breem (Inner Temple), as well as Mr J.A. Tomlin of the Senate of the Inns of Court and the Bar, and Mr C.L.Fisher, librarian of the Royal Courts of Justice, have all gone out of their way either to check the sources available to them, or to put me in touch with people who might help.

Miss Patricia Methven, archivist of King's College, London, has supplied useful information about Professor R.K. Douglas, who befriended Sun Yatsen in London.

Archivists in Liverpool, Miss Janet Smith, Mrs N. Evetts, and Miss E. Organ (Liverpool Record Office), Miss Deborah Lindsay (Modern Records Centre), and Mr Gordon Read (Merseyside County Record Office), have all done more than their fair share to clarify minute details about Sun Yatsen's short sojourns in that city. Mr William Calveley of Telecom rescued me from potential disaster on 6 March 1984, and offered me princely hospitality during my own equally short stay.

Archivists in Manchester, Dr Frank Taylor and Miss Glenise Matheson (John Rylands University Library of Manchester), and Miss Jean Ayton (Central Library), have helped me pursue clues that had their origins in London. Dr Taylor is another old friend and helps me in every way whether or not I am in Manchester. Our correspondence in the course of my research is also one of the longest on file.

New South Wales Parliamentary Library staff, particularly Mr David Clune, have generously given me access to their collections.

Professor Nicholas Tarling in New Zealand has read the entire
manuscript and has saved me from at least one significant blun-
der.

Oxford don and fellow St Antonian, Dr Mark Elvin, suggested
to me on 17 March 1984 that I might consider investigating the
origins of Sun Yatsen's heroic image. To him I owe an intellectual debt. Mr Keith Eddey, lecturer in Law, spent hours talking
with me about the various legal aspects related to Sun Yatsen's
kidnapping in London. The Revd Ian Thomson of All Souls
College told me much about the relationship between his grand-
father and Sun Yatsen in the Canton Hospital.

Professor Geoffrey Martin, keeper of the Public Record Office
in London, and his colleagues, Dr Roy Hunnisett, Mr Norman
Evans, and Mr John Walford, have, as always, been friendly,
considerate, and helpful. Mr Pat Coates and his old friend, Mr
Joe Ford, have shared with me their knowledge and experience
in the Consular Service in China. Mr Ford lent me his copy of
Fengling's diary, which he believed was one of only two copies in
the West. Fengling was the naval attaché at the Chinese Legation
when Sun Yatsen was kidnapped. I have seen the diary quoted in
secondary sources, but it is not the same as reading the entire
diary myself.

The librarian of the School of Hygiene and Tropical Medicine
(London), Mr R.B. Furner, has supplied valuable information
about Dr Patrick Manson.

Officers of Scotland Yard, Mr John Back, Gwyn Jones, and
others, have provided me with much insight into the organization
and working of that famous institution, and how the case of Sun
Yatsen's kidnapping would have been dealt with in those days.

Mr Wu Deduo (Institute of History, Shanghai Academy of
Social Sciences) lent me his rare copy of Wu Zonglian's memoirs.
Wu Zonglian was an attaché in the Legation and was actively
involved in assisting the minister in handling Sun Yatsen's case.
Again, I have seen his memoirs quoted in secondary sources, but
reading the memoirs word for word puts their contents in the
proper perspective. Professor Tang Zhijun of the same Institute
has been most generous in sharing with me his vast knowledge
about Sun Yatsen's contemporaries, particularly about Zhang
Binglin.

Dr Lee Lai-to, Kwan Siu-hing, and their colleagues at the
National University of Singapore have given me the Singapore

perspective on Sun Yatsen. I am also grateful to Dr Lee and Mr and Mrs Tan Boon Chiang for their princely hospitality each time I go to Singapore to do research.

Professor Junji Banno of Tokyo University has been exceptionally kind and hospitable whenever I have visited Japan. Without his help, and that of his research students, the Japanese sources in this book would have been sadly inadequate. His colleague, Professor Hiroshi Watanabe, and Mr Azusa Tanaka of the National Diet Library, as well as Hisako Ito of the Yokohama Archives of History and Professor Ichiro Yamaguchi of Kansai University in Kobe, have all attempted to locate for me the pertinent issues of the *Kobe Chronicle*. Professor Naoki Hazama of Kyoto University and Professor Bunji Kubota of Nihon Joshi University (Tokyo) have helped with other Japanese sources. The unflagging support which my colleage Mr Toshihiko Kobayashi of the Department of Oriental Studies in the University of Sydney has offered me will always be remembered.

The records officer of University College, London, Mrs C.M. Budden, has patiently checked various references in relation to Edwin Collins and the College.

Zhang Kaiyuan, Peng Yuxin, and Xiao Zhizhi in Wuhan have compared notes and exchanged views with me, which have proved thought-provoking.

Zhongshan University has a long-standing friendship with me. I wish to thank Professor Hu Shouwei in particular for his warm reception. He has given me every assistance each time I have visited the University.

Finally, my lifelong friends, Dr Andrew Purkis, Dr Janet Hunter, and Dr Stephen Hickey, have been a source of tremendous intellectual stimulation and support each time I have visited London. I also wish to thank Mr Richard Hawkins, who has helped me check a few things in London at Dr Hunter's request. Dr Lance Eccles has given me valuable assistance throughout. Miss Meran Gluskie typed my manuscript. She has been wonderful in every way, and without her help, I do not think that the typescript would have been submitted to the publisher in time. My family, too, has been a source of great support and encouragement. My parents have borne with good grace the burden of the enormous physical distance that separates them from their son.

To all others, too numerous to mention, I offer my most grateful thanks.

I have presented papers on various aspects of my research almost as progress reports and as a means of stimulating discussion and canvassing views. Therefore, the opinions and interpretations expressed therein may not be entirely the same as those contained in the present work. Scholarship is a living thing. It continues to change and develop. I hope that my readers will appreciate my position.

In the text, I have adopted the following conventions. In Chinese and Japanese, the surnames come first, unless the authors write in English. Therefore, in citing their works written in their own languages, their surnames come first. In citing their works written in English, their surnames come last. *Pinyin* is used in transliterating Chinese names, with some exceptions, such as Sun Yatsen, Hong Kong, and Chiang Kaishek.

Works that are cited regularly have had their titles shortened. English works have had their titles shortened in English; Chinese and Japanese works have had theirs shortened in transliteration. Thus, the reader may know that the citation is from a source originally written in a Western or an Oriental language.

There are numerous editions of Sun Yatsen's collected works. I have decided to use the latest one, although only the first three volumes have been published to date. For those not yet published in this latest edition, I have used the other editions.

When I published my first book, a reviewer twisted my story and then attacked the twisted story. I hope that this book will have better luck.

On the other hand, my thanks are due in advance to any reader who may be kind enough to forgive errors in this the ninetieth year since Sun Yatsen was kidnapped.

J.Y. WONG
Department of History
University of Sydney
Australia
26 June 1986

Contents

 IV The Help of Translators   193
  V The Help of Lord Salisbury   196

5   SUN YATSEN AS NATIONALIST   203
  I Widening Horizons: Through the Cantlie Connection   203
 II Widening Horizons: Through the Kidnapping
      Sensation   220
III Attempts to Accommodate British Might   230
 IV The Hong Kong Connection   235
  V The Cultivation of the Heroic Image   240

6   SUN YATSEN AS OBSERVER   247
  I The Power   247
 II The Glory   255
III The Poverty   269
 IV The Hope   273
  V The Projection of the Heroic Image   285

    CONCLUSION   292
  I The Farewell   292
 II Sun Yatsen, the Man   293
III The Creation of the Heroic Image by Others   295
 IV The Cultivation and Projection of the Heroic Image   296
  V The Hero's Image of Himself   296

    Selected Bibliography   299
    Glossary   320
    Index   323

Plates

Tables

宇和 黃先生大著

分析孫中山倫敦被難及其影響

一九八五年 秦咢生署岩時年八十五

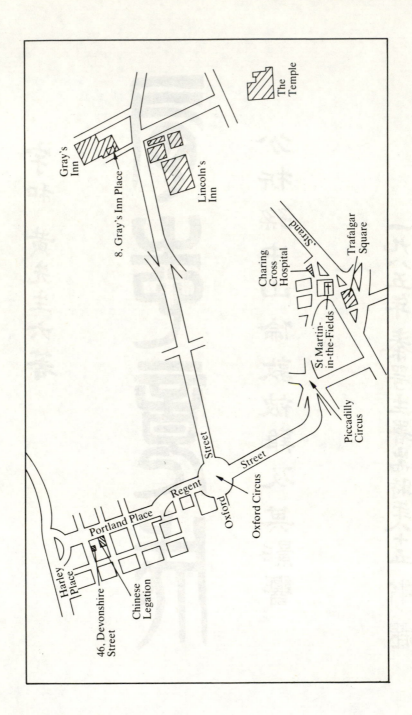

The Temple

Gray's Inn

8. Gray's Inn Place

Lincoln's Inn

Charing Cross Hospital

Strand

Trafalgar Square

St Martin-in-the-Fields

Piccadilly Circus

Street

Street

Regent

Oxford

Oxford Circus

Portland Place

Harley Place

46, Devonshire Street

Chinese Legation

Introduction

I The Origins of the Heroic Image

Sun Yatsen was born in China in 1866. He went to school in Hawaii and Hong Kong. He read medicine, also in Hong Kong, under the direction of Dr James Cantlie and Dr Patrick Manson among others, graduating in 1892. He plotted to overthrow the provincial government at Guangzhou (Canton) in 1895, as a prelude to toppling the Manchu regime in China. The plot failed. He fled first to Hong Kong, then to Japan, Hawaii, and America, reaching London in the autumn of 1896.[1]

It was while he was in London that a tremendous legend about him arose, to which may be attributed the origins of an heroic image. This legend has two aspects: his kidnapping by the Chinese Legation, and his subsequent claim that he gained wisdom about the Western world during his stay in London. This book attempts to deal with both aspects.

First, the kidnapping in London. This international incident elevated him from the position of a malcontent, of whom there were many in China at this time, to that of a global figure. His name and his cause were printed in many languages in the major newspapers throughout the world.[2] The incident, and the publicity that followed it, was to have a profound effect on the Chinese agitators in both Japan and China, and appears to have played an important role in his being elected the overall leader of the Revolutionary Alliance which was to be formed in Japan in 1905 and which was instrumental in the overthrow of the Manchu regime by the 1911 Revolution.[3] It is perhaps not far-fetched to suggest that even his election as the first president of the Chinese Republic was related to his international reputation which began with the kidnapping in London. Shortly after his death, there were pamphlets issued and public gatherings held on the anniversaries

---

1. Details of Sun Yatsen's life up to 1896 may be found in Harold Z. Schiffrin, *Sun Yat-sen and the Origins of the Chinese Revolution* (Berkeley & Los Angeles, University of California Press, 1968), pp. 10–97 (hereafter cited as *Origins*).
2. See Chapter 1, Section V.
3. See Chapter 4, Section IV.

of the kidnapping, urging the Chinese to emulate his unusual courage and perseverance as exhibited during the saga.[4] By this time he was well on his way to being sanctified as the *Guofu* (Father of the Nation).[5]

Second, the wisdom he gained from the West during his stay in London. In a grand plan for the regeneration of China, drafted between 1917 and 1919, he wrote that, after his release in London, he remained in Europe to observe the politics and customs there. He made friends with distinguished intellects and heroes. What he saw and heard in these two years provided him with much food for thought. And he began to realize that rich, powerful, and democratic though the European Powers might be, not all of the people were happy, giving rise to social revolutionary movements. Consequently, his answer for China was that the questions of the people's livelihood, national independence, and democracy had to be solved simultaneously. This realization enabled him to finalize his Three Principles of the People.[6] When Sun Yatsen was later sanctified as the *Guofu*, his Three Principles of the People became the orthodox state philosophy.

I suggest, therefore, that the origins of Sun Yatsen's heroic image may be traced to the time he spent in London in 1896–7. But how much do we know about the kidnapping saga, and what exactly did he learn about Europe at this time?

II The Kidnapping in London

Apart from the newspaper reports of the time, the first published account of the incident may be found in a booklet entitled *Kidnapped in London: Being the story of my capture by, detention at, and release from the Chinese Legation, London* (Bristol, 1897).[7] This booklet alleged, as did Sun Yatsen at the time, that he had been kidnapped. The booklet was subsequently translated into Russian, Japanese, and Chinese. For the sake of clarity, one

---

4. See, for example, Wan Xin (ed.), *Zongli Lundun beinan gailue* (Guangzhou, 9 October 1928).
5. It is not clear exactly when he began to be called *Guofu*; but it is obvious that he had not yet been given this title when the pamphlet mentioned in the previous footnote was printed.
6. Sun Yatsen, 'Jianguo fanglue zhiyi', in *Sun Zhongshan xuanji* (Beijing, 1981), p. 196. The translation is mine.
7. Hereafter cited as *Kidnapped in London*.

of my conclusions may be anticipated here. Although the authorship of *Kidnapped in London* was attributed to Sun Yatsen himself, I have established beyond reasonable doubt that Dr James Cantlie was the real author.[8]

Dr Cantlie's version was generally accepted without question until Professor Luo Jialun challenged it in 1930.[9] Luo was the first historian to do serious research on the topic, using documents he had discovered in the central government archives in Beijing, and copies of the relevant papers in the Chinese Legation in London, including the reports prepared by Slater's Detective Association, which had been employed by the Legation to shadow the fugitive. He also used the published memoirs of the French interpreter of the Legation, Wu Zonglian,[10] and the published diaries of the naval attaché, Fengling.[11] In addition, he relied on oral evidence given by some of Sun Yatsen's subsequent close comrades, Hu Hanmin and Dai Jitao. Then, in the second edition of his book, he quoted Chen Shaobai, who had been associated with Sun Yatsen's revolutionary activities from the beginning, and who had asserted in writing that he had heard afterwards from Sun Yatsen himself that the hero had walked fearlessly into the Legation.[12] Luo Jialun's research enabled him to suggest very strongly that although Sun Yatsen had certainly been detained in the Legation, he had entered it of his own free will; that is, strictly speaking, Sun Yatsen had not been kidnapped at all.[13] Luo emphasized, however, that he was merely speculating and that a conclusion would have to await the emergence of further evidence.[14]

Professor Harold Schiffrin turned this suggestion into a conclusion.[15] He drew heavily on the results of Luo's work, and enriched them with the fruits of his own meticulous research in additional primary sources (principally the British Foreign Office records, classification FO 17/1718).[16] But what enabled Schiffrin

---

8. See Chapter 4, Section III.
9. Luo Jialun, *Zhongshan xiansheng Lundun mengnan shiliao kaoding* (Shanghai, 1930; second edition, Nanjing, 1935) (hereafter cited as *Shiliao*).
10. Wu Zonglian, *Suiyao biji sizhong* (1902) (hereafter cited as *Biji*).
11. Fengling, *Youyu jinzhi* (1929) (hereafter cited as *Jinzhi*).
12. Luo Jialun, *Shiliao*, p. 43.
13. Luo Jialun, *Shiliao*, pp. 42–3.
14. Luo Jialun, *Shiliao*, pp. 42–3.
15. See Schiffrin, *Origins*, pp. 112–13.
16. Schiffrin, *Origins*, pp. 106–13.

to come to such a conclusion was not the new English information which he used, but the old Chinese evidence which Luo had produced.[17] Furthermore, Schiffrin's text, footnotes, and bibliography all seem to indicate that he did not scrutinize the original Chinese sources which Luo had unearthed, but simply quoted Luo's findings.

He went further. Whereas Luo merely suggested that Sun Yatsen's possible motive for allegedly twisting the story was to denigrate the Manchu regime,[18] Schiffrin stated categorically that this was the explanation.[19] Luo's other suggested explanation was Sun Yatsen's unusual courage as an outstanding revolutionary;[20] Schiffrin asserted positively that it was this audacity that prompted Sun Yatsen to venture into the Legation.[21]

At a time when everybody believed that Sun Yatsen was the true author of *Kidnapped in London* (in which had been told the story of his kidnapping and his subsequent news conferences about the same), the mere suggestion by Luo Jialun in 1930 that Sun Yatsen could have lied appears to have upset the Guomindang authorities greatly. It is said that the confidential secretary and aide to Chiang Kaishek[22] applied to the Central Committee of the Guomindang Party to have Luo's book banned; but in view of the fact that the book was already in circulation, and that the author heaped praise upon Sun Yatsen for his great courage in having walked into the Legation, no action was taken.[23] In addition, numerous popular writers had already joined in eulogizing the hero's courage.[24] This episode indicates that the heroic image of the *Guofu* may have been firmly established by 1930.

---

17. Schiffrin, *Origins*, p. 112.

18. Luo Jialun, *Shiliao*, p. 43.

19. Schiffrin, *Origins*, p. 113: 'That the truth would have to be modified in order to achieve this end was something Sun intuitively grasped when he told his story to the British'.

20. Luo Jialun, *Shiliao*, p. 42.

21. Schiffrin, *Origins*, p. 111. I shall evaluate in more detail his treatment of the subject in Chapters 2-4.

22. See 'Shao Yuan-chung', in Howard L. Boorman and Richard C. Howard (eds.), *Biographical Dictionary of Republican China* (New York, Columbia University Press, 1967-71, 4 vols.), Vol. 3, p. 94.

23. Wu Xiangxiang, '"Lundun mengnan" zhenxiang bixu chengqing', in *Lianhe bao* (Taipei, 12 November 1964); reprinted in Li Yunhan (ed.), *Yanjiu Sun Zhongshan xiansheng de shiliao yu shixue* (Taipei, 1975), p. 231 (hereafter cited as 'Mengnan').

24. Wu Xiangxiang, 'Mengnan', p. 231.

But others remained unhappy at the suggestion that the *Guofu* could possibly have lied. Professor Wu Xiangxiang was one of them. In 1959, he went to the Public Record Office in London, studied the British Foreign Office records, and had parts of FO 17/1718 photographed. He was particularly interested in the printed report prepared by the Treasury solicitor, Mr H. Cuffe, who had been commissioned to hold an official inquiry into the kidnapping incident. These papers convinced him — though they failed to convince Schiffrin later — that Sun Yatsen had indeed been kidnapped.[25] They also enabled him to point out, in an article in 1962, some of the inaccuracies in Wu Zonglian's memoirs, upon which Luo Jialun had relied so heavily for his hypothesis.[26] In 1964, Wu launched a fierce attack on Luo's thesis, accusing him of attempting to shake the confidence of the Chinese people in the integrity of the *Guofu*, which was detrimental to the political well-being of the nation.[27] In 1970, he published the first volume, and in 1972, the second, of a biography of Sun Yatsen, in which he again attacked Luo.[28] In 1982, he published two large volumes of a total of 1,783 pages on the life of his hero,[29] in which he once more tried to prove that Sun Yatsen had not lied.

When he published the 1964 article, Wu was still addressing Sun Yatsen as *Guofu*. But when his first biography of Sun Yatsen appeared in 1970, he switched to *Xiansheng* (Master). His enthusiasm for defending his hero, however, remained unabated. In his 1962 article, he seized upon the Treasury solicitor's words, 'Having found Sun truthful on material points', to prove that Sun Yatsen had been kidnapped.[30] Repeating this in his 1964 article, he added that since the law reigns supreme in Britain, the findings of the legal authorities there cannot be doubted.[31] Furthermore, he argued that since *Kidnapped in London* had been published in Britain, its contents could not, under the circumstances, have been

25. Wu Xiangxiang, 'Haiwai xinjian Zhongguo xiandaishi shiliao', in *Zhongguo xiandaishi congkan* (Taipei, 1962), Vol. 1, pp. 55–6 (hereafter cited as 'Haiwai').
26. Wu Xiangxiang, 'Haiwai', pp. 57–8.
27. Wu Xiangxiang, 'Mengnan', p. 233.
28. Wu Xiangxiang, *Sun Yixian xiansheng* (Vol. 1, Taipei, 1970; Vol. 2, Taipei, 1972).
29. Wu Xiangxiang, *Sun Yixian xiansheng zhuan* (Taipei, 1982, 2 vols.) (hereafter cited as *Sun Yixian zhuan*).
30. Wu Xiangxiang, 'Haiwai', pp. 55–6.
31. Wu Xiangxiang, 'Mengnan', p. 230.

fabricated.[32] He denounced Luo for having used the Manchu central government records blindly, on the grounds that the Manchu authorities could do absolutely nothing else but maintain, even in their own confidential papers, that Sun Yatsen had gone to the Legation voluntarily.[33] These sweeping statements, assumptions, and denunciations testify to the wonders of which the heroic image is capable.

In his two-tome work of 1982, Wu went to extraordinary lengths to defend his case. For example, the Treasury solicitor had observed that Sun Yatsen might have thought of visiting the Legation before the actual kidnapping incident, on the grounds that Sun Yatsen had spoken to Dr Manson about it.[34] Wu Xiangxiang retorted, 'Sun was in England on his way to France to study agriculture. He had a passport issued by the Manchu Foreign Office. To enquire about a French visa, a trip to the Chinese Legation was inevitable. Of course, he never dreamt that the Manchu net for him was spread overseas as well. Consequently he unreservedly asked [Dr Manson] the question [about going to the Legation]'.[35] Every sentence in this quotation is an assertion. To date, nobody knows for certain if Sun Yatsen was actually on his way to France. Nobody knows for sure if he intended to study agriculture there, if he did go. Nobody knows exactly what kind of passport he held, if any. We do know, however, that he did not go to the Chinese Legation in Washington to enquire about a British visa before setting sail for Britain; and common sense suggests that enquiries about a French visa would have been directed to the French Embassy, not the Chinese Legation. In fact, until the First World War, visas were unknown in Europe, and people could move freely among most European countries except Russia and Turkey without a passport.[36] Furthermore, if Sun Yatsen felt so confident about his safety once he left China, why

32. Wu Xiangxiang, 'Mengnan', p. 232.
33. Wu Xiangxiang, 'Mengnan', pp. 228-30.
34. FO 17/1718, pp. 113-16, Cuffe to Home Office, 16 November 1896, para. 9. See, also, FO 17/1718, p. 112, Manson's statement at the Treasury, 4 November 1896, para. 2.
35. Wu Xiangxiang, *Sun Yixian zhuan*, Vol. 1, p. 153. The translation is mine.
36. I am grateful to my colleague, Mr Grahame Harrison, for this information; and to another colleague, Professor D.M. Schreuder, for drawing my attention to the following passage in A.J.P. Taylor, *English History, 1914-1945* (Oxford, Oxford University Press, 1965), p. 1: 'Until August 1914, a sensible, law-abiding Englishman could pass through life and hardly notice the existence of the state,

did he undergo a complete change of appearance as soon as he arrived in Japan from Hong Kong?[37] Indeed, why did Wu Xiangxiang try so hard to discredit the Treasury solicitor's observation when he had also asserted that the findings of the same lawyer must not be doubted?[38]

Wu wrote in 1982, 'For ten days, Mr Sun had been taking the same route every day from his lodgings to visit the Cantlies. The detective shadowing him must have taken note of it.... The Chinese Legation, on receiving such information from the detective...':[39] but Luo Jialun had already pointed out that there was absolutely no information of this kind in the detective's reports, and even reproduced these reports fully in his book.

III The Hero and the Villain

Whatever their differences, all four authors mentioned in the previous section agree that Sir Halliday Macartney[40] was the villain of the piece. This is extraordinary. It seems that a hero cannot exist without a villain, even if only to provide a contrast. And all four are unanimous in their denunciation of Macartney, although the severity with which they condemn him varies.

Dr Cantlie was the first to accuse Macartney of having been the 'head centre of all this disgraceful proceeding'.[41] This accusation went far beyond what Sun Yatsen had told journalists at the time of his release from the Legation;[42] and consequently beyond all the newspaper reports and editorials, which merely expressed dismay that Macartney should have been involved at all.[43] Cantlie may have had certain motives for singling out Macartney for

---

(36. *continued*)
beyond the post office and the policeman. He could live where he liked and as he liked. He had no official number or identity card. He could travel abroad or leave his country for ever without a passport or any sort of official permission.... For that matter, a foreigner could spend his life in this country without permit and without informing the police'. My colleagues, Dr Bruce Fulton and Dr Mark Hayne, also inform me that the French government did not require visas from Chinese visitors at this time.

37. See Schiffrin, *Origins*, p. 101.
38. Wu Xiangxiang, 'Mengnan', p. 230.
39. Wu Xiangxiang, *Sun Yixian zhuan*, Vol. 1, p. 154. The translation is mine.
40. See Chapter 2, Section II, for a brief outline of Macartney's career.
41. Sun Yatsen, *Kidnapped in London*, pp. 63–4.
42. See Chapters 2–3.
43. See Chapters 2–3.

special treatment, one of which was to gain more sympathy from
the British public for a hero who had been grievously wronged by a
Briton.[44] But Cantlie did not make this accusation without reason,
as it was based on the account of Macartney's role in the affair
provided by George Cole, the warder at the Chinese Legation.[45]

The second author under review, Luo Jialun, presents a
different line of argument. He begins by saying that Macartney
went to find a private detective to shadow Sun Yatsen.[46] On the
basis of this, he asserts that 'because Macartney was the man in
charge of the affair, therefore he received a telegram from the
private detective in the afternoon of 3 October 1896'.[47] Employing
a private detective was only part of the operation, and cannot be
used to prove that the person who did so was in charge of the
entire operation. The lack of logic in Luo's argument is obvious.
One can only assume that he read and then used the Chinese
translation of Cantlie's account without acknowledging it. If so,
the absence of such an acknowledgement in what is otherwise an
extremely meticulous piece of work may be taken as an indication
that, by 1930, it was common knowledge and generally accepted in
China that Macartney was the villain of the piece.

The third author, Harold Schiffrin, has given more detail than
anybody before him about Macartney's activities *after* Sun Yatsen
was already inside the Legation building. As for the part
Macartney played before the entry, Schiffrin points out that
Macartney was called in on that Sunday morning.[48] This is an
important piece of information which merits more attention than
Schiffrin has given it, for it may suggest that Macartney was not
party to what appears to have been a snap decision in the
Legation. But instead of pausing to assess its implications,
Schiffrin goes on to suggest that Macartney was one of the
conspirators by asserting that somehow *Macartney* might have
obtained the intelligence about Sun Yatsen's routine visits to the

---

44. See Chapter 4, Section III.
45. Sun Yatsen, *Kidnapped in London*, p. 67: Cole said, 'Sir Halliday is in
town, he comes to the Legation every day; it was Sir Halliday who locked Sun in his
room, and placed me in charge, with directions to keep a strict guard over the door,
that he should have no means of escape'.
46. Luo Jialun, *Shiliao*, p. 17.
47. Luo Jialun, *Shiliao*, p. 20. The translation is mine.
48. Schiffrin, *Origins*, p. 110.

Cantlies and therefore 'decided to ensnare him'.[49] This is an assertion which neither Cantlie nor Luo Jialun makes. Thus, the picture of the villain has progressed from that of the man in charge of Sun Yatsen's detention after the latter's entry into the Legation, to that of a man who participated in a plot which was intended to get him inside.[50]

The fourth author, Wu Xiangxiang, goes even further. Without giving any evidence, he repeatedly accuses Macartney of having initiated the plot to kidnap Sun Yatsen, and of having masterminded its operation.[51] Such an accusation obviously contradicts the evidence given by George Cole, and mentioned by Harold Schiffrin,[52] that Macartney had been 'fetched' from the comfort of his home on that fateful Sunday morning.[53] Wu Xiangxiang's solution to this blatant contradiction is as unusual as his accusation. He simply states that Macartney made a special trip to the Legation on that Sunday morning,[54] thus giving the impression that the trip had been arranged beforehand. Of course he does not quote the source which he had had photographed in the Public Record Office in London in 1959, and which includes Cole's evidence.[55]

He then concludes his treatment of the entire episode by saying that Macartney was forced to leave his position (*quzhi*)[56] in the Legation; while Mrs Howe, who was the first to alert Dr Cantlie to Sun Yatsen's plight, kept her job in the Legation, where she worked for a total of forty years.[57] Typically, Wu Xiangxiang gives no evidence to support his statement about Macartney. But since he mentions Boulger's biography of Macartney in his preceding paragraph, I presume that he is quoting Boulger. However, upon

49. Schiffrin, *Origins*, p. 110.
50. This is one of Schiffrin's hypotheses, which does not necessarily contradict his conclusion that Sun Yatsen eventually walked into the lion's den (see Schiffrin, *Origins*, pp. 112–13).
51. Wu Xiangxiang, *Sun Yixian zhuan*, Vol. 1, pp. 156, 164, and 168.
52. See previous paragraph.
53. FO 17/1718, pp. 116–19, Cole's statement at the Treasury, 2 November 1896, para. 5.
54. Wu Xiangxiang, *Sun Yixian zhuan*, Vol. 1, p. 156.
55. Wu Xiangxiang, 'Haiwai', pp. 55–6.
56. This term can mean either dismissal or resignation. I have given it a neutral translation here, namely, 'to leave his position', in order to give Professor Wu the benefit of the doubt.
57. Wu Xiangxiang, *Sun Yixian zhuan*, Vol. 1, p. 178.

checking the biography, I find that Macartney continued to work without interruption for about ten years in the Legation until his retirement in 1905.[58] Boulger's story is corroborated by documentary evidence I have found in Beijing.[59] Wu Xiangxiang does not substantiate his statement about Mrs Howe's tenure in the Legation either. But his moral is clear: the just are rewarded, and the wicked punished.

It seems, therefore, that the image of the villain, like that of the hero, has become sharper and sharper in the minds of some people, as time goes by. And again like that of the hero, the image of the villain seems to have been taken for granted in some historical writing.[60]

IV A New Approach

In history, as in other disciplines, we build on the knowledge of our predecessors. Whatever my assessment of the work of those before me, particularly the four authors mentioned above, I am deeply grateful to all of them for having done pioneering work, without which I could never have hoped to present my own research in its present form.

It is, however, of some historical significance to try to find out more about the kidnapping in London, to which one may trace the origins of Sun Yatsen's heroic image. It is also important to determine whether he was actually kidnapped, as he maintained when he was in London in 1896-7;[61] or whether he walked into the Legation to preach revolution, as he is alleged to have claimed.[62] For it is upon the answer to this question that we must

---

58. Demetrius C. Boulger, *The Life of Sir Halliday Macartney, K.C.M.G.* (London, John Lane, 1908), p. 485 (hereafter cited as *Macartney*).

59. Beijing Palace Museum Records, Waiwubu 871, Macartney to Zhang Deyi, *circa* January 1905. In this document, Macartney outlined his career in the Chinese service up to 1905 and asked for permission to retire with a pension.

60. See, for example, Li Enhan, 'Qingmo Jinling jiqiju de chuangjian yu fazhan', in *Jindai Zhongguo shishi yanjiu lunji* (Taipei, 1982), p. 295, in which the author accused Macartney, when manager of the Nanjing Arsenal in China in the 1870s, of tyrannical and insulting behaviour towards the Chinese workers. No evidence was given to support this accusation.

61. See the pertinent British Foreign Office records, as contained in FO 17/1718; the major London newspapers of 23-4 October 1896; and Sun Yatsen, *Kidnapped in London*.

62. See Luo Jialun, *Shiliao*, pp. 42-3; and Schiffrin, *Origins*, pp. 112-13.

depend for our judgement of the man who lay behind the heroic image: was he an open and honest revolutionary leader whom generations of young Chinese have been urged to emulate; or was he a foolhardy agitator who lied for reasons of expediency? For the sake of the record, too, it is of interest to find out if Macartney was the villain that he has been accused of being.

My approach is threefold. In addition to 'research' in the conventional sense of the word, I have also engaged in field-work, and I have tapped oral sources.

In terms of the use of Chinese-held sources, Luo Jialun's book was a breakthrough. He discovered twenty-eight documents in the archives of the central government pertinent to the kidnapping, including cyphers between the Chinese Legation and Beijing.[63] I have unearthed eleven more in Beijing, including the annual financial reports of the Legation, which give a good picture of that establishment during the period under review. Luo borrowed from Wang Chonghui the copies of the Legation's papers which the latter had had made in London in 1929. I toured the Legation building in 1969, and acquired copies of the tracings of the entire building in 1984, both of which have enabled me to obtain a concrete idea of the setting.

Luo Jialun's other *coup* was to have gained access to the limited editions of the writings of two members of the Legation staff. They were the memoirs of the French interpreter, Wu Zonglian, and the diary of the naval attaché, Fengling.[64] In assessing the value of these two private sources, Luo criticized the diary for its confused presentation, but came to the conclusion that the 'sequence of events [described in the memoirs] does not look as though it had been fabricated'.[65] Indeed, Luo relied heavily on the memoirs to make the suggestion that Sun Yatsen walked into the Legation of his own free will.[66] I have studied these two sources. While agreeing with Luo's verdict on the diary, I find that the memoirs are full of inexplicable gaps, assertions, and an illogical sequence of events when viewed in the context of the other materials which I have discovered.[67]

---

63. Luo Jialun, *Shiliao*, Preface.
64. Luo Jialun, *Shiliao*, Preface.
65. Luo Jialun, *Shiliao*, p. 35. The translation is mine.
66. Luo Jialun, *Shiliao*, pp. 34–5.
67. See Chapters 2–3 for my assessments of the various points of interest raised by the memoirs.

Luo placed a good deal of importance on the oral evidence given by Hu Hanmin, Dai Jitao, and Chen Shaobai, all of whom alleged that they had subsequently heard from Sun Yatsen's own lips that the hero had gone to the Legation of his own accord.[68] Unfortunately, I have not been able to interview these three gentlemen, as they are now dead. I have, however, found one interesting aspect to this oral history. When Sun Yatsen was still in London recovering from his ordeal, and therefore long before his reunion with Chen Shaobai in Japan and many years before he came to know either Hu Hanmin or Dai Jitao, someone in Japan wrote an article claiming that Sun Yatsen had gone voluntarily to the Legation to preach revolution.[69] Who was this mysterious person in Japan, who showed intimate knowledge of Sun Yatsen when he wrote?[70]

In terms of British-held sources, Wu Xiangxiang and then Schiffrin achieved another breakthrough by discovering FO 17/1718 among the British Foreign Office records, although Schiffrin used the collection much more meticulously and accurately than Wu. The way in which Wu abused this source has been noted. As for Schiffrin, I have noticed only one inaccuracy, when he wrote, 'Up to the last, Macartney tried to keep his staff in line, and on the 22nd gave Cole and the other English servant a sovereign each with a promise of a better reward when "all this is over"'.[71] Upon checking his reference, it is clear that, according to Cole, it was in fact the minister who sent Deng Tingkeng to bribe the two English servants — Macartney was not involved at all.[72] A subconscious preoccupation with the villain may well have accounted for this error, and for the insufficient attention paid to the role played by the minister. After all, the minister was the source of all authority in the Legation.

I have added to FO 17/1718 other Foreign Office papers.[73] These records are not directly relevant to the kidnapping itself. But, when used in conjunction with the other materials which I

---

68. Luo Jialun, *Shiliao*, pp. 42–3.
69. See Chapter 3, Section I.
70. See Chapter 4, Section I, for further details.
71. Schiffrin, *Origins*, p. 122.
72. FO 17/1718, pp. 116–19, Cole's statement at the Treasury, 2 November 1896, para. 23.
73. They are FO 17/1158, FO 17/1286, and FO 17/1327.

have found, they provide much information about the minister himself: his family, his official career, his sympathies, and even his health.[74] Thus, the minister is no longer a shadow in the background, but a being of flesh and blood, with hopes and fears and, of course, ambitions. Consequently, I have been able to ascribe to him a more active role in that international incident than did Schiffrin, who used mainly FO 17/1718.

Luo Jialun regretted that he did not have access to the biography of Macartney.[75] Schiffrin had such access, but does not seem to have used it extensively.[76] Wu Xiangxiang consulted it too, but only to misuse it.[77] I went over the same ground as a matter of course, and found some interesting information. For example, shortly after Macartney returned to Britain in 1877 as the interpreter of the newly formed permanent Chinese Mission to London, the then minister ordered the execution of a delinquent servant in the back kitchen. Macartney did his best to save the man's life, and succeeded, his main argument being that diplomatic immunity would not cover such an act.[78] This incident anticipated the Legation's threat to have Sun Yatsen executed on the spot if he could not be shipped back to China.[79] What could have been Macartney's true attitude in the kidnapping affair?

Luo Jialun did not use any newspapers. Schiffrin consulted some of the London newspapers: *The Times*,[80] the *Daily Telegraph*,[81] and the *Globe*;[82] as well as the *Overland China Mail*,[83] which was the overseas edition of the Hong Kong *China Mail*. As for the *China Mail* itself, Schiffrin used only extracts from it which had been reprinted in *Kidnapped in London*.[84] It was by checking the original version, as published in the *China Mail*, that I discovered

74. See Chapter 2, Section III.
75. Luo Jialun, *Shiliao*, pp. 35–6. He said that he managed to read extracts which Wang Chonghui had had copied.
76. See Schiffrin, *Origins*, p. 105, n.6, and p. 108, n.34.
77. See the previous section of this chapter.
78. Boulger, *Macartney*, pp. ix–x and 286. This source is corroborated by Guo Tingyi, *Guo Songtao nianpu* (Taipei, 1971, 2 vols.), Vol. 2, p. 694 (hereafter cited as *Guo Songtao*).
79. Sun Yatsen, *Kidnapped in London*, pp. 46–7.
80. See, for example, Schiffrin, *Origins*, p. 108, n.35.
81. Schiffrin, *Origins*, p. 123, n.87.
82. Schiffrin, *Origins*, p. 125, nn.90 and 92.
83. Schiffrin, *Origins*, p. 127, n.98.
84. Schiffrin, *Origins*, p. 127, n.99.

the fact that it was a mysterious person in Japan who made the claim in 1896 that Sun Yatsen had walked fearlessly into the Legation — a discovery which has proved crucial in the study of the origins of Sun Yatsen's heroic image.[85] Wu Xiangxiang appears to have limited his use of English newspapers to those extracts reprinted in *Kidnapped in London*.[86] But he was the first to quote a Chinese newspaper, the *Shiwubao* of Shanghai.[87] For my part, I have consulted all the major London newspapers, if only to gain some idea of the magnitude of the sensation and the nature of press opinion, as well as some of the newspapers outside Britain to see how far his name had spread.[88]

One crucial private source, which has not been used systematically by any historian,[89] is Mrs Cantlie's diary. I am extremely fortunate to have been granted access to it. The diary has enabled me to gain further insight into the kidnapping incident. The descendants of the Cantlies, particularly Colonel Kenneth Cantlie (Dr James Cantlie's fourth and youngest son, now in his mid-eighties), Dr J. Cantlie and Dr A. Cantlie (Dr James Cantlie's two eldest grandchildren, both in their sixties), have been extremely generous in agreeing to share with me the tradition of their family.

An entirely new approach, which I have adopted, is field-work. As far as possible, I have tried to locate, identify, and visit the places pertinent to the kidnapping incident. Where was 8, Gray's Inn Place, Sun Yatsen's address? Where was 46, Devonshire Street, the Cantlies' address? Where was the Legation? When Sun Yatsen went to visit the Cantlies, which side of Portland Place would he have gone up: the left-hand side, and thus past the front door of the Legation? I found that the Cantlies lived on the left-hand side of Portland Place, just around the corner from the Legation. The likelihood, therefore, is that Sun Yatsen would

---

85. See Chapters 3–4.
86. Wu Xiangxiang, *Sun Yixian zhuan*, pp. 172 and 174–5.
87. Wu Xiangxiang, *Sun Yixian zhuan*, pp. 172–3.
88. See Chapter 1, Sections IV–V.
89. It has been used by Neil Cantlie and George Seaver in *Sir James Cantlie: A Romance in Medicine* (London, John Murray, 1939) (hereafter cited as *Sir James Cantlie*); and by Jean C. Stewart in *The Quality of Mercy: The Lives of Sir James and Lady Cantlie* (London, George Allen & Unwin, 1983) (hereafter cited as *Quality of Mercy*). But none of these authors were historians. Besides, I have found some most interesting information about Sun Yatsen in the diary, which all three authors have overlooked.

have passed the front door of the Legation each time he went to see the Cantlies. Macartney was fetched from his home on Sunday, 11 October 1896, the day on which the kidnapping took place. Where did he live? How long would it have taken the messenger to reach him, having started the journey at about 10 a.m., and how long would it have taken Macartney to arrive at the Legation? I have found that Macartney lived within walking distance of the Legation, and could have been inside the building within minutes. Why, then, were the servants ordered as late as 11 a.m. to clear a room for the purpose of detaining Sun Yatsen? Did Macartney spend all that time in trying to change the minister's mind about not bringing Chinese justice to bear upon an offender, as he had done some twenty years before?[90] It is field-work of this kind that has enabled me to obtain some insight into what may have happened.

Field-work has also enabled me to avoid perpetuating the misinformation that some of my predecessors have produced. For example, I have found that Regent's Circus was not a 'circus', where monkeys jumped and lions danced,[91] but was a synonym for Oxford Circus.[92] I have also found that there was no such thing as a Shishi tushuguan (Stone Building Library).[93]

In Chapter 1, I attempt to reconstruct the story of Dr Cantlie's relentless efforts to rescue his former student, and to recapture some of the sensation generated by the scandal. In other words, the chapter is a narrative of the role played by the third party — Dr Cantlie and the British government. It sets the scene for an analysis in Chapter 2 of what might have been going on inside the building occupied by the Legation — the second party. Chapter 3 deals with the first party — Sun Yatsen himself. Chapter 4 examines the origins of Sun Yatsen's heroic image, which slowly emerged in the wake of the saga. All the narrative, analyses, arguments, and speculations in these four chapters are so interwoven that reading any one chapter in isolation may not make much sense, particularly in terms of speculation as to whether Sun Yatsen was in fact kidnapped or not. I realize that this presents

---

90. See my reference earlier in this section to the incident of 1877.
91. Wu Xiangxiang, *Sun Yixian zhuan*, Vol. 1, p. 187.
92. For the written word about this, see *The Queen's London: A pictorial and descriptive record of the great metropolis in the last year of Queen Victoria's reign* (London, Cassell, 1902), Vol. 1, p. 189 (hereafter cited as *Queen's London*).
93. See Chapter 6, Section II.

difficulties to my readers. I can only plead forgiveness for not having found a better way of doing it. Chapters 5 and 6 look at Sun Yatsen's activities during the rest of his sojourn in London with a view to assessing his claim that what he saw and heard helped him to finalize the formulation of his Three Principles of the People. These last two chapters present problems of a different kind. I have decided to include details about the places and people visited by Sun Yatsen, details which normally I would have preferred to leave out. But so imperfect is our understanding of the environment in which Sun Yatsen finalized his Three Principles of the People that any information which seems relevant should not be allowed to remain buried. These details may be too familiar to some people, and too burdensome to others. I can only plead that in the present state of Sun Yatsen scholarship, such details probably deserve a place in this book.

V The Three Principles of the People

The Three Principles of the People are generally translated as Nationalism, Democracy, and the People's Livelihood. A systematic exposition of these principles was not undertaken by Sun Yatsen until 1924, twenty-seven years after his kidnapping in London and one year before he died. It took the form of a series of lectures in Guangzhou, the notes of which were taken and then published subsequently. On the other hand, it was in 1919 that Sun Yatsen claimed in writing that what he saw and heard during his two years in Europe helped him to finalize the formulation of his Three Principles of the People.[94] Thus it may be assumed that Sun Yatsen acknowledged the continuity between the initial formulation of his ideas and their eventual exposition. I am not proposing that one can use the 1924 version to gauge accurately the thoughts of Sun Yatsen in 1896-7. I am merely suggesting that his sojourn in London deserves more attention than it has so far received.

For a long time, historians had to rely almost exclusively on two accounts for information on Sun Yatsen's time in London. One was written in 1912 by Dr Cantlie, who said that Sun Yatsen was

---

94. See Section I of this Introduction.

'forever at work, reading books on all subjects which appertained to political, diplomatic, legal, military, and naval matters; mines and mining, agriculture, cattle rearing, engineering, political economy, etc, occupied his attention and were studied closely and persistently'.[95] The other account is contained in a brief autobiography by Sun Yatsen, published in 1919.[96] In it, he simply stated that after his release in London, he remained in Europe for the time being so as to observe the politics and customs there, and to make friends with distinguished people whether they were in power or not.[97]

Schiffrin has done much to find out more specific details. To begin with, he points out that Sun Yatsen 'was not in England for two years nor did he visit any other European country',[98] alleging that Sun Yatsen's memory had failed him.[99] I shall deal with Sun Yatsen's claim, and Schiffrin's assessment of it, in Chapter 6. Schiffrin also identifies one of the close friends that Sun Yatsen made in London. He was Rowland J. Mulkern, a British soldier who later took part in the Huizhou (Waichow) Uprising of 1900.[100] Other contacts, which Sun Yatsen made and which Schiffrin has pinpointed, included the famous British missionary, Timothy Richard,[101] and the Russian exile, Felix Volkhovsky.[102] Perhaps Schiffrin's greatest *coup* was to have unearthed an article which Sun Yatsen had written 'with the assistance of one Edwin Collins'.[103] The article was entitled 'China's Present and Future: The Reform Party's Plea for British Benevolent Neutrality', and was published in the *Fortnightly Review* in London on 1 March 1897.[104]

Schiffrin points out that the private detective's reports frequently refer to Sun Yatsen's lengthy visits to 12, Albert Road, from the end of October to December 1896.[105] But the reports

95. Schiffrin, *Origins*, pp. 134–5, quoting James Cantlie and C. Sheridan Jones, *Sun Yat-sen and the Awakening of China* (London, Jarrold & Sons, 1912), p. 242 (hereafter cited as *Sun Yat-sen*).
96. Sun Yatsen, 'Jianguo fanglue zhiyi', p. 115 n. and p. 196.
97. Sun Yatsen, 'Jianguo fanglue zhiyi: youzhi jingcheng', p. 196.
98. Schiffrin, *Origins*, p. 137.
99. Schiffrin, *Origins*, p. 137.
100. Schiffrin, *Origins*, p. 128 and n.103.
101. Schiffrin, *Origins*, p. 128.
102. Schiffrin, *Origins*, p. 135 and n.124.
103. Schiffrin, *Origins*, p. 130.
104. Schiffrin, *Origins*, p. 130.
105. Schiffrin, *Origins*, p. 134, n.120.

themselves throw no light whatsoever on the occupant of the premises. I note that the same reports mention Sun Yatsen's regular, though briefer, visits to 5, South Square. Where was 12, Albert Road? Where was 5, South Square? Who lived at these addresses? These questions are particularly important in view of Sun Yatsen's claim that it was what he saw and heard that had had a great influence on his way of thinking. I shall attempt to provide some answers in Chapters 5 and 6.

While I was in Cambridge in May 1983, trying to find out more about Professor Herbert Giles, who had requested Sun Yatsen to prepare a short entry about himself for the *Chinese Biographical Dictionary*[106] which Giles was compiling,[107] I again met Dr Carmen Blacker. She told me that a book on a Japanese botanist, Minakata Kumagusu, contained some references to Sun Yatsen while he was in London.[108] This opened a new line of enquiry, in the light of which the view put forward first by Marius Jensen and then by Harold Schiffrin, that Sun Yatsen's friendship with the Japanese Pan-Asianists began in Japan itself and subsequent to his sojourn in London, may have to be reconsidered.

When I visited Tokyo in August 1983 to find out more about Minakata Kumagusu, Professor Banno Junji drew my attention to the existence of Minakata's recently published diary.[109] I found that the diary complemented the reports of the private detective who had been shadowing Sun Yatsen in London. Then Professor Banno introduced me to Professor Kubota Bunji, who gave me a copy of No.3 of the journal *Shingaikakumei kenkyu*, in which was reproduced an article written by Sun Yatsen in collaboration with Edwin Collins, entitled 'Judicial Reform in China'.[110] Thus, we know now that Sun Yatsen wrote at least two articles jointly with Edwin Collins while he was in London. Who was Edwin Collins?

Yet another important source, which complemented both the private detective's reports and Minakata's diary, was Mrs Cantlie's

106. This was published subsequently in 1898.

107. Sun Yatsen, *Sun Zhongshan quanji* (Beijing, 1981–4, 3 vols.), Vol. 1, p. 46.

108. The reference she gave me was Kasai Kiyoshi, *Minakata Kumagusu* (Tokyo, 1967).

109. Minakata Kumagusu, *Minakata Kumagusu zenshu* (Tokyo, 1975), Supplement 2, Diary (hereafter cited as *Zenshu*).

110. The article was originally published in a London quarterly called *East Asia*, No. 1, July 1897, pp. 3–13.

diary. I obtained access to her 1896 diary in February 1984, which
was a great help in my efforts to gain some understanding of the
puzzling question as to whether or not Sun Yatsen was kidnapped.
But it was not until January 1986 that I finally had the opportunity
to scrutinize the entire 1897 diary, which enabled me to give more
specific details about Sun Yatsen's activities during his sojourn in
London.

On the basis of his research findings, Schiffrin suspected that the
Three Principles were not so clearly formed in 1896–7 as Sun
Yatsen thought more than twenty years later.[111] My own work has
not put me in a position to say anything more specific than that.
But my main concern is not to gauge precisely what Sun Yatsen's
thoughts were at that time, which is an almost impossible task.
Rather, I am more concerned with Sun Yatsen's heroic image. In
this regard, what Schiffrin went on to say aroused considerable
interest in me: 'When he became famous, he found it much more
attractive to attribute his political ideas to direct Western
influence'.[112] How famous he was in 1919, or to what extent he
viewed himself as being famous in 1919, is an open question. If
anything, 1919 probably represented one of the lowest ebbs in his
political life, with the May Fourth Movement surging to the front
of the Chinese public scene, and he and his followers being forced
to the sidelines. Indeed, if it were true that he attributed his ideas
to direct Western influence, the motive could have been to boost
his heroic image both within his own party and without.

Here, I may be allowed to anticipate some of the conclusions I
have arrived at in Chapters 1–4. It appears to me that although the
origins of Sun Yatsen's heroic image may be attributed to the
kidnapping episode, I have not found Sun Yatsen actively creating
such an image for himself. Rather, it was his friends and comrades
who were responsible. And some of their motives were principally
political: to make him a hero so that he might command more
respect from both friend and foe, in the hope that this might help
the revolutionary movement that he led. During the rest of his
sojourn in London, which is dealt with in Chapters 5–6, I found
him actively cultivating and projecting an heroic image of himself.
He did so, not on the basis of the kidnapping sensation, but by

111. Schiffrin, *Origins*, p. 137.
112. Schiffrin, *Origins*, p. 137.

writing articles and attempting to widen his circle of friends, among other activities. This image was based not on the kidnapping incident, but on his attempts to impress on the world that he was indeed the man destined to regenerate China. The subsequent 1911 Revolution failed to realize his dreams, and Yuan Shikai's monarchical designs forced him to flee China once again.[113] Determined to have a more disciplined political party, Sun Yatsen insisted that every member swear allegiance to him personally. It is against this background that his attribution in 1919 of his political ideas to direct Western influence in 1896–7, if true, should be viewed.

The heroic image was one created by men out of the revolutionary needs of the time. This book attempts to verify the origins of this image in the light of my research findings on Sun Yatsen's activities in London between 1896 and 1897.

---

113. See Ernest P. Young, *The Presidency of Yuan Shih-k'ai, 1859–1916* (Ann Arbor, University of Michigan Press, 1977). See, also, Jerome Ch'en, *Yuan Shih-k'ai, 1859–1916: Brutus Assumes the Purple* (London, George Allen & Unwin, 1961).

1 The Sensational Kidnapping in London

Extraordinary rumours have been in circulation within the past few days as to the kidnapping and imprisonment of a prominent Chinese gentleman at the Chinese Embassy in London.

The *Globe*[1]

I The Thunderbolt

Sun Yatsen landed at Liverpool on 30 September 1896. He proceeded to London on the same day, arriving there at 9.50 p.m.[2] The detective who had been hired by the Chinese Legation to watch him took great care to note his movements, including the fact that he had landed in Liverpool at 12 noon, that he had had his 'luggage placed in the van of the 2.50 p.m. express for London', but that somehow he had missed the train and 'left by the 4.45 p.m.' He even jotted down the number of the cab which took Sun Yatsen from St Pancras Station to Haxell's Hotel in the Strand.[3]

But the detective lost his subject for a good part of the next day, until he spotted him again at 4.30 p.m. emerging from the hotel for a walk 'along the Strand, Fleet Street, to Ludgate Circus'.[4] The weather report described London as having been engulfed in a 'thick mist' on that day.[5] On this occasion, therefore, the efficiency of the detective might be given the benefit of the doubt. Actually, what happened on this first day of October 1896 was that Sun Yatsen went to see Dr Cantlie at 46, Devonshire Street, Portland Place, in the morning.[6] He spent a good

1. *Globe*, 22 October 1896, reprinted on 23 October 1896, p. 5, col. 2.
2. Chinese Legation Archives, Slater to Macartney, 1 October 1896, in Luo Jialun, *Shiliao*, p. 111.
3. Chinese Legation Archives, Slater to Macartney, 1 October 1896, in Luo Jialun, *Shiliao*, p. 111.
4. Chinese Legation Archives, Slater to Macartney, 6 October 1896, in Luo Jialun, *Shiliao*, p. 113.
5. *The Times*, 2 October 1896, p. 9, col. 6.
6. FO 17/1718, pp. 121–2, Cantlie's statement at the Treasury, 4 November 1896, para. 2. See note 7.

part of the day there,[7] before Cantlie took him to 8, Gray's Inn Place, the landlady of which, Miss Lucy Pollard, agreed to let him a furnished room for ten shillings a week.[8] He moved in the next day.[9]

'He told me he proposed to go about and see the sights of London',[10] said Dr Cantlie. 'He saw me nearly every day, and told me from time to time how he had been passing his time'.[11] The visits stopped on Sunday, 11 October 1896, when Sun Yatsen disappeared into the Chinese Legation.[12] What is so remarkable about the reports of the private detective shadowing him is that no mention whatever was made about his trips to 46, Devonshire Street, nor indeed about his ever going, prior to or on that day, anywhere near Portland Place where the Chinese Legation was located at No. 49. Thus, the world is denied the most direct and independent evidence as to whether Sun Yatsen was decoyed into the Legation, or whether he walked into the Legation of his own free will. The English secretary to the Chinese Legation, Sir Halliday Macartney, went to see the manager of Slater's Detective Association first thing on the morning of Monday, 12 October 1896. The atmosphere of the interview may be glimpsed from the note which Henry Slater, the manager, put to paper immediately after Macartney had left, for the sake of the record. He solemnly declared, 'Yesterday, Sunday, observation was renewed and continued throughout the day, but the party in question was not seen to leave, no doubt owing to the inclement state of the weather'.[13]

The key word in the report, as in other reports prepared by

7. Cantlie's signed statement to the Central News, as printed, for example, in the *Daily Graphic*, 24 October 1896, p. 13, col. 1.

8. FO 17/1718, p. 123, Pollard's statement at the Treasury, 5 November 1896, para. 2.

9. FO 17/1718, p. 123, Pollard's statement at the Treasury, 5 November 1896, para. 2.

10. FO 17/1718, pp. 121–2, Cantlie's statement at the Treasury, 4 November 1896, para. 3.

11. FO 17/1718, pp. 121–2, Cantlie's statement at the Treasury, 4 November 1896, para. 5.

12. FO 17/1718, pp. 119–20, Sun Yatsen's statement at the Treasury, 4 November 1896, para. 8.

13. Chinese Legation Archives, Slater to Macartney, 6 October 1896, in Luo Jialun, *Shiliao*, p. 115.

Slater, is 'renewed'.[14] This shows that the detective was not keeping a twenty-four-hour watch over Sun Yatsen, but rather that the watch was renewed every day at the place where the detective had left him the day before. Indeed, I have checked all the available Sunday reports by Slater and have found that although the detective insisted that he had renewed observation on these days, all his reports were either vague or couched in evasive terms, such as 'the party was not seen to leave the house throughout the day', or 'nothing of importance occurred',[15] while on most weekdays he had something substantial to report.[16] I suspect that the detective never worked on Sundays, despite his claims to the contrary. Sometimes, the detective arrived at Sun Yatsen's lodgings too late to catch him before he went out: but when he did manage to keep him within sight, his reports are normally corroborated by independent sources.[17]

The Cantlies were not unduly disturbed initially by Sun Yatsen's failure to appear. After all, Sun Yatsen had told Dr Cantlie on the very first day of their reunion in London that he simply 'called to say that he was in London and was going to stay two or

---

14. Neither Luo Jialun (*Shiliao*), nor Schiffrin (*Origins*, Ch. 5), the two scholars who have contributed most to our knowledge of the episode, appear to have considered this feature of the detective's reports. Therefore, although their annoyance with Slater is understandable, their frustration over the lack of an explanation continues to trouble them.

15. See Slater's reports for the Sundays of 11 and 25 October 1896; 1, 8, 15, 22, and 29 November 1896; 6, 13, 20, and 27 December 1896; 3, 10, 17, 24, and 31 January 1897; 7, 14, 21, and 28 February 1897; 7, 14, 21, and 28 March 1897; and 4, 11, and 18 April 1897. See also Table 1.

16. See Table 1.

17. For example, Slater reported that on 7 December 1896, Sun Yatsen went to the Reading Room (for the first time) of the British Museum (Chinese Legation Archives, Slater to Chinese minister, 16 December 1896, in Luo Jialun, *Shiliao*, p. 129). According to the *Registers of Readers' Signatures, 1896–1897*, among the British Museum Central Archives, there is an entry for Sun Yatsen, whereby he was issued a reader's ticket for six months. (I am grateful to Miss Janet Wallace, archivist of the British Museum, for her help in this matter.) Again, Slater reported that on Tuesday, 13 April 1897, Sun Yatsen went with another Chinese and a Briton to Tilbury Docks. (Chinese Legation Archives, Slater to Chinese minister, 7–15 April 1897, in Luo Jialun, *Shiliao*, pp. 158–9. In this source, 'Tuesday 15 Apr 1897' is a misprint: 'Monday 12 Apr 1897' should be followed by 'Tuesday 13 Apr 1897', and not 'Tuesday 15 Apr 1897', as printed.) Minakata Kumagusu's diary (p. 80) corroborates this. In addition, the so-called 'Chinaman' referred to in Slater's report was none other than Minakata Kumagusu himself, showing that Slater had mistaken a Japanese for a Chinese. Furthermore, we learn from the diary that the said Briton was R. J. Mulkern, Sun Yatsen's friend.

three months, and was afterwards going to Paris'.[18] On the fourth day subsequent to the fateful Sunday of 11 October 1896, Mrs Cantlie noted in her diary, 'Miss Pollard [Sun Yatsen's landlady] came and I gave her 10 shillings for trimming two hats'.[19] Still, there was nothing in the diary that showed signs of alarm. Dr Cantlie did recall subsequently that the landlady had told him on that occasion about her lodger not having 'been home since the Sunday'.[20] Even then, the doctor was not overly troubled, apparently trusting that nothing as incredible as Sun Yatsen's disappearance into the Chinese Legation could have happened.

On Saturday, 17 October 1896, Mrs Cantlie had already written her diary of the day and the whole family had gone to bed. In another half an hour, two more days would have slipped by since the visit of the landlady. But, at '11.30 p.m.', wrote Mrs Cantlie across her diary, as there was no room for a further entry, they 'got a note to say that Sun Yatsen has been taken prisoner by the Chinese Legation, an anonymous note ...'.[21] Dr Cantlie also recalled, 'A ring at the doorbell brought me from my bed. I found no one at the door but observed and picked up the letter which had been pushed in below the door'.[22] The letter was from the English housekeeper of the Chinese Legation, Mrs Howe.[23] It read:

There is a friend of yours imprisoned in the Chinese Legation here since last Sunday; they intend sending him out to China, where it is certain they will hang him. It is very sad for the poor man and unless something

---

18. FO 17/1718, pp. 121–2, Cantlie's statement at the Treasury, 4 November 1896, para. 2.
19. Mrs Cantlie's diary, 15 October 1896.
20. FO 17/1718, pp. 121–2, Cantlie's statement at the Treasury, 4 November 1896, para. 5.
21. Mrs Cantlie's diary, 17 October 1896.
22. Cantlie and Jones, *Sun Yat-sen*, p. 61.
23. FO 17/1718, pp. 116–19, Cole's statement at the Treasury, 2 November 1896, paras. 20–1. Not having access to this primary source, the author of *Kidnapped in London* might be forgiven for calling the writer of the letter Mrs Cole (p. 63). In the same vein, Cantlie and Jones might be pardoned for having referred to her in general terms as 'the wife of one of the English servants in the Legation' (*Sun Yatsen*, p. 60). But Mrs Jean Stewart, having claimed to have used the British Foreign Office records, has no excuse for writing the following: 'Sun in his book *Kidnapped in London* calls her Mrs Cole, the wife of his gaoler and later benefactor. Cantlie and Seaver in their biography of Sir James call her Mrs Howe. That she was a female European housekeeper employed in the Chinese Legation is all that is known for certain' (*Quality of Mercy*, p. 88).

is done at once he will be taken away and no one will know it. I dare not sign my name, but this is the truth, so believe what I say. Whatever you do must be done at once, or it will be too late. His name is, I believe, Sin Yin Sen.[24]

The doctor sprang into action. He had practised in Hong Kong for almost ten years and had travelled widely in China. He was quite familiar with the Qing mode of justice. He appears to have known that Sir Halliday Macartney was the English secretary of the Chinese Legation. His first thought, therefore, was to seek help from this gentleman who he believed would not have tolerated such an outrage had he been aware of it. Quickly, he located Sir Halliday's address — 3, Harley Place — which was within walking distance of 46, Devonshire Street.[25] He found that the house was deserted. While he was busy knocking on the door and peering through the windows, a policeman who was on night-duty in the area watched him suspiciously. Apparently, an attempted burglary had been reported to the police three nights previously. Undeterred, Cantlie approached the somewhat hostile policeman and managed to find out from him that the Macartney family had gone to the country for six months.[26]

II The Disbelief

From Harley Place, Cantlie took a cab[27] to Marylebone Lane

---

24. Sun Yatsen, *Kidnapped in London*, p. 63. The same quotations also appeared later in Cantlie and Jones, *Sun Yat-sen*, pp. 60–1.

25. With a modern map of London in hand, I went to 'Harley Place' in May 1983. None of the houses there I regarded as becoming to the social status of Sir Halliday. Then I discovered an old street plaque, on which the engraving was still faintly recognizable. It read, 'North Harley Mews'. I am greatly indebted to Mr R. Hart and Mr John Phillips of the Greater London Record Office for having spent a whole afternoon with me in an attempt to locate the place, which was eventually pinpointed at the north-west corner of Harley Street and Marylebone Road (Map 143 J.St.M. 1864). The premises have been pulled down and replaced by high-rise buildings. The full significance of finding out the exact location of Sir Halliday's address will be seen in the next chapter, particularly in connection with his being summoned to the Legation on the fateful morning on Sunday, 11 October 1896.

26. Sun Yatsen, *Kidnapped in London*, p. 64.

27. Sun Yatsen, *Kidnapped in London*, p. 64. The original text reads: 'Mr Cantlie next drove to Marylebone Lane Police Office'. But as 46, Devonshire Street, never had a mews, and as Dr Cantlie's youngest son, Colonel Kenneth Cantlie, has assured me that his father never had a carriage of his own, it is unlikely that the doctor literally drove to Marylebone Lane himself. The word

Police Station.[28] The inspector on duty was apparently at a loss as to what action to take in such an extraordinary case. Cantlie proceeded to Scotland Yard, near Westminster Bridge.[29] The detective inspector politely listened to his story and took down his evidence, but confessed that he could not initiate any action.[30] The frustrated doctor recalled, 'The chief difficulty was to get anyone to believe the story. The police even at Scotland Yard said it was none of their business, and that I had done my duty when I reported the matter to them, and that I ought to go home and keep quiet'.[31] The language of the police officer who took down his evidence is understandably more discreet:

I explained to him that it was not a matter in which Police could interfere even if it was known that he [Sun Yatsen] was detained there. I advised him if he thought fit to pursue the inquiry farther, to call at the Embassy and make inquiry respecting him. This he said he would do and should he not get satisfaction he would communicate with the Foreign Office and the public press. He then left.[32]

Scotland Yard began taking Cantlie's evidence at 12.30 a.m.[33] It would have been well into the small hours by the time all this was written down, and the niceties exchanged. The agitated doctor then found himself in the street again not knowing what else he could do before dawn.

When the dawn of Sunday, 18 October 1896, did come, he went 'first thing to see Judge Ackroyd. Then Mr Hughes'.[34] The latter

(27. *continued*)
'drove' in nineteenth-century usage probably means that he 'was driven'. Finally, a primary source puts the matter beyond doubt. In Dr Cantlie's own words, he 'got into a cab and drove away'. (FO 17/1718, p. 121, Cantlie's statement at the Treasury, 4 November 1896, para. 6.)

28. Sun Yatsen, *Kidnapped in London*, p. 64. The building has been pulled down and replaced by a modern office block. I am grateful to Scotland Yard for showing me an old map as well as an old photograph of the building, which gave me some idea of the distance Dr Cantlie had to travel from Harley Place and of the atmosphere of that old police station.

29. The present-day Scotland Yard has also moved from its premises by Westminster Bridge to a new building in Victoria Road.

30. Sun Yatsen, *Kidnapped in London*, p. 65. Cantlie's evidence may be found in the British Foreign Office records. See note 32.

31. Cantlie and Jones, *Sun Yat-sen*, p. 62.

32. FO 17/1718, pp. 47–8, Chief Inspector Henry Moore's report, 12.30 a.m., 18 October 1896.

33. FO 17/1718, pp. 47–8, Chief Inspector Henry Moore's report, 12.30 a.m., 18 October 1896.

34. Mrs Cantlie's diary, 18 October 1896.

was the head of the Chinese Customs in London.[35] Cantlie was
hoping that Mr Hughes would

approach the Legation privately, and induce them to reconsider their
imprudent action and ill-advised step. Not receiving encouragement in
that direction, he went again to 3, Harley Place, in hopes that at least a
caretaker would be in possession, and in a position to at least tell where
Sir Halliday Macartney could be found or reached by telegram. Beyond
the confirmation of the policeman's story that burglary had been attempted, by seeing the evidence of 'jemmies' used to break open the door, no
clue could be found as to where this astute orientalised diplomatist was
to be unearthed.[36]

Then Cantlie met the rest of his family in St Martin-in-the-
Fields, where they had 'taken sittings'[37] for the Sunday service.[38]
They went home for lunch, after which the doctor was on the
move again, this time to see his old colleague, Dr Patrick
Manson,[39] who had taught Sun Yatsen in Hong Kong.[40] No
sooner had he left Devonshire Street than a second messenger
came from the Legation. He was one of Sun Yatsen's warders, by
the name of George Cole. For a whole week, Sun Yatsen had
persistently pleaded with him to take a note round to the
Cantlies.[41] When he finally agreed, and entered 46, Devonshire
Street, with Sun Yatsen's message in his pocket, he was petrified.
'Among Cantlie's collections of curios from the East was a life-
sized and very life-like figure of a Chinaman, so placed as to be
the first object visible on opening the hall-door'.[42] It was just as
well that Cole did not run away in terror. Mrs Cantlie quickly
calmed him down and sent him on to Dr Manson's, at 21, Queen
Anne Street, which was also within walking distance. The poor

35. Sun Yatsen, *Kidnapped in London*, p. 65.
36. Sun Yatsen, *Kidnapped in London*, p. 65.
37. Mrs Cantlie's diary, 20 September 1896. In those days there were pews
with high partitions which families could rent for their exclusive occupation during
church services. I am grateful to the authorities of St Martin-in-the-Fields for
having explained to me, in person as well as by correspondence, the various
traditions and features of the church.
38. Mrs Cantlie's diary, 18 October 1896.
39. Mrs Cantlie's diary, 18 October 1896.
40. FO 17/1718, p. 122, Manson's statement at the Treasury, 4 November
1896, para. 4.
41. FO 17/1718, pp. 116–19, Cole's statement at the Treasury, 2 November
1896, paras. 12–21.
42. Cantlie and Seaver, *Sun Yat-sen*, note on p. 104.

man must have still been quite nervous, and subconsciously quickened his pace to such an extent that he overtook the brisk-walking Cantlie. While he was ringing the doorbell, Cantlie came up from behind.[43]

Cole's story, and Sun Yatsen's visiting-card with a message for help in his own hand, written on its back,[44] left no room for doubt. Immediately Cantlie, this time with Dr Manson by his side, again went to Scotland Yard.[45] There, Cantlie was told 'that a man had called in the middle of the night with the same statement, and that the inspector on duty could not make out whether he was drunk or a lunatic'.[46] Thereupon, 'I told the inspector now on duty I was the same man, and again he gave me the advice to go home and keep quiet'.[47] The police file was no more flattering. Donald Swanson, one of the superintendents of Scotland Yard, minuted Cantlie's evidence which had been taken in the small hours of the day in the following terms: 'I think it is just possible that the Dr has [blank space] himself, for there are no Chinese vessels trading between England and China and such a prisoner could hardly be sent by a British ship'.[48] It would be most intriguing to know what word or words the superintendent had intended to insert in the space that was left blank.

The two doctors took counsel together, and decided 'to invade the precincts of the Foreign Office. They were told the resident clerk would see them at 5 p.m. At that hour they were received, and delivered their romantic tale to the willing ears of the courteous official. Being *Sunday, of course* [sic] nothing further could be done, but they were told that the statement would be laid before a higher authority on the following day'.[49]

On their way home, and being apprehensive that something might happen to Sun Yatsen that very night, Manson suggested

43. FO 17/1718, pp. 116–19, Cole's statement at the Treasury, 2 November 1896, para. 21.

44. FO 17/1718, pp. 116–19, Cole's statement at the Treasury, 2 November 1896, para. 21. For an analysis of the text of this message, see Chapter 5.

45. FO 17/1718, pp. 121–2, Cantlie's statement at the Treasury, 4 November 1896, para. 6; and FO 17/1718, p. 122, Manson's statement at the Treasury, 4 November 1896, para. 4.

46. Cantlie and Jones, *Sun Yat-sen*, p. 62.

47. Cantlie and Jones, *Sun Yat-sen*, p. 62.

48. FO 17/1718, p. 48, Swanson's minute on Cantlie's evidence [18 October 1896].

49. Sun Yatsen, *Kidnapped in London*, pp. 69–70.

that the Legation should be paid a visit 'to let them know that anything they might be doing would not be done altogether in a hole'.[50] As Cantlie appeared to be known to the Legation, it was decided that Manson might stand a better chance of gaining admittance. Manson rang the doorbell, was allowed in by the butler, and was later received by the English interpreter, Deng Tingkeng.

'Is Sun Yatsen here?'
'Who?'
'Sun Yatsen.'
'There is no such man here.'
'Well, I know that he is here; I have got information that he is here, and
     moreover, the police and the Foreign Office are aware of the fact, and
     I would like to see Sun Yatsen.'
'No Sun Yatsen here.'[51]

But the obliging interpreter did leave the doctor for a moment and went to a back room in order to give the impression that he was making enquiries there, even if only to return with the answer, 'No; no Sun Yatsen here.'[52]

Obviously the interpreter was an extremely good actor. The apparent openness and frankness with which he spoke so impressed Dr Manson that when the doctor rejoined Cantlie in the street, he began to express reservations about Sun Yatsen's story. But when the two doctors discussed the matter further, it became clear that their former student could not possibly have played a trick of this kind. They parted company at 7 p.m.[53]

However, the more Cantlie reflected on the matter, the more restless he became. Manson's visit to the Legation could have prompted the instant removal of the captive that very night,

---

50. FO 17/1718, p. 122, Manson's statement at the Treasury, 4 November 1896, para. 4.
51. FO 17/1718, p. 122, Manson's statement at the Treasury, 4 November 1896, para. 4.
52. FO 17/1718, p. 122, Manson's statement at the Treasury, 4 November 1896, para. 4. At least two Chinese scholars have alleged that it was the Chinese minister, Gong Zhaoyuan, who received Dr Manson. See Shao Chuanlie, *Sun Zhongshan* (Shanghai, 1980), p. 38; and Shang Mingxuan, *Sun Zhongshan zhuan* (Beijing, Beijing Press, 1982), p. 44. They are obviously unaware of the fact that Gong Zhaoyuan had had a stroke in August 1896 (FO 17/1286, pp. 232–3, Medical report, 28 August 1896) and had been confined to bed since. For more details, see Chapter 2.
53. Sun Yatsen, *Kidnapped in London*, pp. 72–3.

when the streets were quiet; and 'if immediate embarkation were not possible, a change of residence of their victim might be contemplated'.[54] He could hardly wait for dinner to finish before he went off again, this time to find a private detective to have the Legation watched. He called at a friend's place and obtained the address of Slater. Off he went to the City. But he found 1, Basinghall Street, entirely locked up. Neither 'shouting, bell-ringing, nor hard knocks could elicit any response' from that granite building.[55]

The irate doctor took his friendly cabman into his confidence. The two consulted a policeman passing by. The trio decided that help should be sought from the nearest police station. But the City police felt utterly helpless in a case in the West End; and 'got rid of the persistent doctor'[56] only by giving him the address of a retired policeman who might be willing to earn a little bit of money by staring at 49, Portland Place.

Before proceeding to Gibston Square in Islington to find this retired policeman, Cantlie thought of *The Times* office not too far away. He got there at 9 p.m., and was told that no one would be in until 10 p.m. Off he went to Gibston Square, and after much peering in the dimly lit streets, found the place and the man. But the man could not go; instead, another man who was then watching a public house in the City was suggested. A message was sent to the man's house, while Cantlie went back to the City to look for him, in vain. So he set off again for *The Times* office. By the time his statement was taken down, it was already 11.30 p.m. When the hopeful Cantlie passed Portland Place at midnight, however, his heart sank. The man who was supposed to have finished his duty at the public house at 11 p.m. had not yet arrived. 'He [Cantlie] said good-night to his wife, and set out to observe the Legation, ready to interfere actively if need be'.[57]

He met his man in the street and put him in a hansom cab under the shadow of a house, ready to give chase should Sun Yatsen be smuggled out of the Legation in the small hours. The doctor turned in at 2 a.m., convinced that the life of his former student was 'practically saved'.[58] Little did he realize that the

54. Sun Yatsen, *Kidnapped in London*, p. 73.
55. Sun Yatsen, *Kidnapped in London*, pp. 75–6.
56. Sun Yatsen, *Kidnapped in London*, pp. 76–7.
57. Sun Yatsen, *Kidnapped in London*, pp. 78–80.
58. Sun Yatsen, *Kidnapped in London*, pp. 81–2.

man he had paid to keep vigil over the Chinese Legation was none other than a Slater agent.[59]

The doctor was woken up at 6 a.m. the next morning, Monday, 19 October 1896, by the arrival of 'a third communication concerning the matter'.[60] The 'matter' was obviously about Sun Yatsen, but it is not clear who sent it.[61] Probably, it was from the 'night watchman', who finished his vigil at 6 a.m., to say, 'Nothing was observed during the night'.[62] 'Cantlie had always been an early riser since his student days, and 6 a.m. was the usual hour for him to be [already] at work in his library',[63] but on this occasion he had to be woken up. 'Breakfast at 8 o'clock was preceded by morning prayer which all the maids attended, and 9 o'clock would often see the first patient arrive'.[64] One can imagine that on this morning his time in the library and over breakfast was spent eagerly scanning *The Times*. But however hard he searched, he could find no trace of his story.

He hurried to the City, again to ask Slater for detectives. They gleefully came, and were quite happy to be posted 'with instructions to watch the Legation night and day'.[65] Thereupon, Slater

---

59. See next two paragraphs.

60. FO 17/1718, pp. 8–12, Cantlie to Foreign Office, 19 October 1896, para. 12.

61. Cantlie was quite specific about this third communication. The full paragraph reads: 'This morning 19 Oct 1896 at 6 a.m., I received a third communication concerning the matter, and left it at the Foreign Office' (FO 17/1718, pp. 8–12, Cantlie to Foreign Office, 19 October 1896, para. 12). The first communication was no doubt the one from the Legation housekeeper, Mrs Howe, at 11.30 p.m. on 17 October 1896; the second was a card from Sun Yatsen brought by Cole on 18 October 1896. Cole did not bring another message to Cantlie until the evening of 19 October 1896 (FO 17/1718, pp. 116–19, Cole's statement at the Treasury, 2 November 1896, para. 21). Unfortunately, the Foreign Office did not keep this 'third communication' which Cantlie had left there. Thus, one can only guess, from the context of Cantlie's letter to the Foreign Office, that it was from the 'night watchman'.

62. FO 17/1718, pp. 8–12, Cantlie to Foreign Office, 19 October 1896, para. 11. The full paragraph reads: 'I employed a private detective recommended by the City Police and had the house watched from 12 midnight until 6 a.m. this morning. Nothing was observed during the night'.

63. Cantlie and Seaver, *Sir James Cantlie*, pp. 134–5.

64. Cantlie and Seaver, *Sir James Cantlie*, pp. 134–5.

65. Subsequently, in a signed statement dated 23 October 1896 which Cantlie provided to the Central News and which was therefore printed in all the major newspapers in London, Cantlie said that he had reported the matter to a London newspaper, 'asking if they thought it better to delay publication of the news until it was seen how things would turn out'. (See, for example, *Echo*, 23 October 1896, p. 3, cols. 2–3.) It is difficult to believe that Cantlie took so much trouble to

sent a telegram to Macartney in the following words: '*Fresh* [*my italics*] instructions from doctor to rescue party; any further instructions?'[66] The 'night watchman' had finished his vigil at 6 a.m.,[67] and apparently reported back to Slater's office. It seems that Slater had immediately apprised Macartney of this new development. Thus, when Cantlie later arrived with a request for private detectives, Slater telegraphed Macartney about having received *fresh* instructions from the doctor.

After Cantlie had been received by Slater in the City on Monday morning, he went to the office of *The Times* again, ostensibly with 'additional information'[68] to offer but obviously with the intention of making some discreet enquiries as to the fate of his story. But once more he was to be disappointed: *The Times*, in fact, never published his story. It was the *Globe* that eventually made the scoop.

From *The Times* office he went straight to the Foreign Office again. 'Mr James Cantlie (of Charing + Hospital) called this morning with reference to some papers and cards etc. he left here yesterday with the R. Clerk' began a Foreign Office memorandum.[69] Apparently, Cantlie was told then that yet another verbal message was not good enough. 'At 12 noon, by appointment at the Foreign Office, Mr Cantlie submitted his statement in writing'.[70] Having encountered so many incredulous faces, he was beginning to describe his own statement as 'improbable'[71] and his story as 'hearsay'.[72] But he persevered. Throughout his statement, he made no reference to *The Times*. Then he remembered the Legation's denials to Manson. Envisag-

(65. *continued*)
give his story to *The Times* so that it might not be published. More likely, he intended it to be a face-saving exercise for that influential newspaper.

66. Apparently Macartney had kept this telegram himself, because it was not in the Legation Archive. However, the Treasury solicitor investigating the case was aware that some telegrams had passed between Slater and the Legation. He applied to the Home Office to issue a warrant for those telegrams to be produced by the Post Office, and subsequently saw them. (FO 17/1718, pp. 113–16, Cuffe to Home Office, 12 November 1896, paras. 23 and 26.) He did not quote the other telegrams, which, therefore, have sunk into oblivion.

67. FO 17/1718, pp. 8–12, Cantlie to Foreign Office, 19 October 1896, para. 11.

68. Sun Yatsen, *Kidnapped in London*, p. 86.

69. FO 17/1718, pp. 3–5, Foreign Office memorandum, 19 October 1896.

70. Sun Yatsen, *Kidnapped in London*, p. 83.

71. Sun Yatsen, *Kidnapped in London*, p. 84.

72. Sun Yatsen, *Kidnapped in London*, p. 83.

ing that a similar enquiry by the Foreign Office would meet with the same misleading answer, he penned another note to the Foreign Office in the afternoon. 'In the event of the Legation denying the presence of Sun Yatsen in their premises', he wrote, 'I can see no other way of bringing the matter home than to hand the facts to the Press for publication'. This was a thinly veiled threat, the blow of which Cantlie quickly sought to soften by adding, 'This might help the Foreign Office in the event of the Chinese denying the presence of Sun in their Legation. This I am prepared to do with that intent'.[73] He did not say that he had already told *The Times*.

Towards the evening, Cantlie received another message from Sun Yatsen, brought to him personally by the English porter of the Chinese Legation, George Cole.[74] Cantlie immediately penned his third communication of the day to the Foreign Office, enclosing the written message from Sun Yatsen, if only to keep up the pressure. It also seems that he tried to add some moral pressure by singling out Sir Halliday Macartney, a Briton, for mention. 'Sir Halliday Macartney has been in the Legation every day during the past week — the messenger tells me. He also says again that Sir Halliday conducted Sun to his room when he was taken'. As if that was not enough, he wrote a postscript, 'His guard at his room door has been doubled tonight. Sir Halliday Macartney has told all the servants he is at home to nobody'.[75]

III Official Intervention

Without himself knowing it, Cantlie's efforts were in fact abundantly rewarded on Monday, 19 October 1896. After his visit in the morning, and even before his written submission at 12 noon, the Foreign Office contacted the Home Office.[76] The Home Office sought advice from a superintendent of the CID in Scotland Yard. The superintendent reported that he had no control over a foreign Legation, and that the matter was 'one for diplomatic action to ascertain the truth or untruth of the

---

73. FO 17/1718, pp. 13–15, Cantlie to Foreign Office, 19 October 1896.
74. FO 17/1718, pp. 116–19, Cole's statement at the Treasury, 2 November 1896, para. 21.
75. FO 17/1718, pp. 19–21, Cantlie to Foreign Office, 19 October 1896.
76. FO 17/1718, pp. 3–5, Foreign Office memorandum, 19 October 1896, para. 5.

allegation'.[77] But the Home Office had much wider responsibilities than those of a policeman. Indeed, 'there might be a great outcry if the circumstances got out, and it was known that the government had had information of what was taking place'.[78] Although thinking, like the police superintendent, that the Chinese Legation could not be entered, the Home Office thought that 'a discreet police officer might be told off to communicate with Cole, and that a detective might be stationed outside the legation with orders to watch and communicate with Sun if an attempt is made to remove him against his will'.[79] Before taking any such action, however, the Home Office asked the Foreign Office to think it over and contact them again in the afternoon.[80]

In the afternoon, the papers reached the desk of the assistant under-secretary of state, the Honourable Francis L. Bertie.[81] Bertie minuted as follows: 'Ask the Home Office to take steps at once to watch the Chinese Legation and to prevent the deportation of Dr Sun if any attempt should be made to put him on board a ship against his will'.[82]

When Cantlie's second communication of the day reached Whitehall, it was immediately submitted to Bertie with the comment, 'We have communicated privately with the Home Office. The police are ready to take steps to have the Legation watched and to communicate with Cole — the guardian'. Bertie ordered that the Home Office be communicated with formally at once.[83] Thereupon, a letter marked 'Pressing' was drafted in the name of the foreign secretary, Lord Salisbury, to the home secretary, Sir Matthew Ridley.[84] Meanwhile, Bertie sent a Queen's courier to Lord Salisbury's country residence at Hatfield with the relevant

77. FO 17/1718, p. 42, Swanson's report, 19 October 1896.
78. FO 17/1718, pp. 3–5, Foreign Office memorandum, 19 October 1896, para. 5.
79. FO 17/1718, pp. 3–5, Foreign Office memorandum, 19 October 1896, para. 7.
80. FO 17/1718, pp. 3–5, Foreign Office memorandum, 19 October 1896, para. 8.
81. FO 17/1718, p. 12, Foreign Office memorandum and Bertie's minute, 19 October 1896.
82. FO 17/1718, p. 12, Foreign Office memorandum and Bertie's minute, 19 October 1896.
83. FO 17/1718, p. 12, Foreign Office memorandum and Bertie's minute, 19 October 1896.
84. FO 17/1718, pp. 1–2, Foreign Office to Home Office [draft], 19 October 1896.

papers and a note of his own. The note read: 'I have told the Home Office that I am sending this minute down to you. If you approve what is suggested will you please telegraph "Yes"'.[85] Salisbury's reply was 'Given in at Hatfield at 6.30 p.m. Received at Whitehall at 6.47 p.m. Sent out for delivery at 6.48 p.m.' It read: 'Yes'.[86]

When George Cole finished work at the Chinese Legation in the evening, he took another written message from Sun Yatsen to Dr Cantlie,[87] as mentioned. When he got home, he found a policeman in plain clothes waiting for him. This was Chief Inspector Frederick S. Jarvis, who had instructions to interview Cole and to report direct to the chief constable in charge of the CID in Scotland Yard.[88] Cole requested that his name be kept secret,[89] and upon Jarvis' solemnly agreeing to do so, disclosed all he knew.[90]

After the interview, Jarvis reported the result to his chief as directed. Then he went to the Marylebone Division[91] of the Metropolitan Police under whose jurisdiction Portland Place fell. He saw the commanding officer, Acting Superintendent Robert Shannon.[92] Arrangements were immediately made for a twenty-four-hour watch over the Chinese Legation by six detectives in

---

85. FO 17/1718, pp. 6–7, Bertie to Salisbury, 19 October 1896.

86. FO 17/1718, p. 7, Salisbury to Bertie [telegram], 19 October 1896.

87. FO 17/1718, pp. 116–19, Cole's statement at the Treasury, 2 November 1896, para. 21.

88. FO 17/1718, pp. 38–41, Jarvis' report, 20 October 1896, para. 7. The original text was: 'reporting the result of my interview with Cole to C. C.' The abbreviation stood for 'Chief Constable', who was Melville L. MacNaghten at the time. There were four chief constables in London, directly under the police commissioner; the other three being in charge of three districts into which the capital was divided. A district was subdivided into divisions, each headed by a superintendent. Because of the importance of the CID, however, Melville Mac-Naghten had three superintendents, of whom Donald Swanson, mentioned before, was one. The next rank down the hierarchy was chief inspector. I am greatly indebted to Scotland Yard for explaining to me the organization of the Metropolitan Police and the usage of some of their language, both of which proved to be of great help in my attempts to read the intricate reports. See the next few notes.

89. FO 17/1718, pp. 38–41, Jarvis' report, 20 October 1896, para. 2.

90. FO 17/1718, pp. 38–41, Jarvis' report, 20 October 1896, paras. 2–5.

91. FO 17/1718, pp. 38–41, Jarvis' report, 20 October 1896, paras. 2–5. The original text referred to 'D Division', which stood for the Marylebone Division.

92. FO 17/1718, pp. 38–41, Jarvis' report, 20 October 1896, paras. 2–5. Robert Shannon was, like Frederick Jarvis himself, a chief inspector; but being posted to a division, he was the only chief inspector of that division. In the absence of the head of the division, Charles W. Sheppard, Robert Shannon became acting superintendent.

three shifts. Their instructions were to follow Sun Yatsen and his escort should he be taken out of the Legation, to telegraph the particulars direct to Scotland Yard, and to await further instructions. Observations began at 10 p.m.,[93] an hour or two after Cantlie had dispatched his third communication of the day to the Foreign Office.[94] Although only six detectives were directly involved, one might assume that the entire police force of the Marylebone Division was alerted.[95]

It must have been quite a scene, with official detectives and private agents both keeping a night vigil over the Chinese Legation and, presumably, over each other as well: Cantlie was not told about this government move, and therefore did not stop the services of Slater until the next day.[96]

The following morning, Tuesday, 20 October 1896, the day on which, according to Sun Yatsen, he was supposed to be shipped out of the country,[97] Chief Inspector Jarvis visited 46, Devonshire Street. He told Cantlie of the police action taken. The doctor gave a photograph of Sun Yatsen to the policeman, who lost no time in handing it over to his fellow officers engaged in observing the Legation.[98] Cantlie withdrew his private detectives.[99] While Slater lamented the end of such a lucrative sinecure, Cantlie congratulated himself on no longer being regarded as a lunatic or a drunkard by the police. Had he known what Slater had been up to, he would also have congratulated himself on no longer being treated like a fool. Above all, he was relieved to know that the government was now on his side, and that the chances of his former pupil being smuggled out of Britain would be minimal. The vision of the prisoner being poisoned in

93. FO 17/1718, pp. 38–41, Jarvis' report, 20 October 1896, paras. 2–5. Without the advantage of advice from Scotland Yard, Schiffrin wrote that Jarvis 'sent six officers to watch the Legation' (*Origins*, p. 121), giving the impression that they were detectives from Scotland Yard. Even the London newspapers, without access to police files, assumed that the detectives were from Scotland Yard. In fact, they were all from the Marylebone Division.

94. FO 17/1718, pp. 19–21, Cantlie to Foreign Office, 19 October 1896.

95. Sun Yatsen, *Kidnapped in London*, p. 84.

96. Cantlie's signed statement to the Central News, 23 October 1896: see, for example, *Echo*, p. 3, col. 2. See, also, notes 97 and 98.

97. FO 17/1718, pp. 8–10, Cantlie to Foreign Office, 19 October 1896, para. 13.

98. FO 17/1718, pp. 38–41, Jarvis' report, 20 October 1896, para. 8.

99. Cantlie's signed statement to the Central News, 23 October 1896: see, for example, *Echo*, 23 October 1896, p. 3, col. 2.

the Oriental fashion, however, continued to haunt him. Thus, when he received the following message from Cole during the course of the day, he was tempted to act on it. The message was: 'I shall have a good opportunity to let Mr Sun out on to the roof of the next house in Portland Place tonight. If you think it advisable, get permission from the occupants of the house to have someone waiting there to receive him. If I am to do it, find means to let me know'.[100] Cantlie went with the note to Scotland Yard and requested that a constable be posted with him to carry out the operation. Not surprisingly, the police thought it an undignified proceeding, dissuaded him from it, and assured him that Sun Yatsen would 'walk out by the front door in a day or two'.[101] Meanwhile, Chief Inspector Jarvis continued to busy himself with the schedule of the day, interviewing Dr Manson, making enquiries as regards any steamers leaving for China, and going to see the commanding officer of the Thames Division of the Metropolitan Police, Superintendent Hawes. The two police-men devised ways and means of keeping all ships (passenger or cargo) that were about to leave for China under surveillance.[102]

On Wednesday, 21 October 1896, Chief Inspector Jarvis had 'a private interview with Mr McGregor [of] one of the firms owning the Glen Line of Steamers'.[103] By 'private interview' Jarvis must have meant his going to see McGregor in the office of McGregor, Gow, and Company, situated at 1, East India Avenue, in the

100. Sun Yatsen, *Kidnapped in London*, p. 92. The date given here was 19 October 1896 which, from the reconstruction of events so far, is clearly a day too early. In this regard, Mrs Cantlie's diary is more accurate. She referred to Cole's note and her husband's approach to Scotland Yard in her entry on 20 October 1896. However, the entry itself contains errors: 'A note today to say that Coles the warder will let Sun out tonight onto the roof of the Embassy. Hamish consulted Scotland Yard Police, but decided not to allow the risk. It is not the right way'. The name of the impromptu warder was Cole, not Coles. No. 49, Portland Place, had five storeys (not counting the basement) and 51, Portland Place, had four. Sun Yatsen was detained on the third floor of the Legation, which was about the same level as the top floor (part rooms, part patio) of 51, Portland Place. Sun Yatsen's room looked over the skylight of the Legation, from which it was possible to descend 1.2 metres on to the patio of the neighbouring house. Hence, there was not much point in letting Sun Yatsen on to the roof of the Legation. I am grateful to the engineer attached to the Embassy of the People's Republic of China, Mr Wang Fengchang, for having shown me the tracings of the two buildings (which no longer exist) and for having explained to me most patiently the set-up of the two places when I was in London in May 1983.

101. Sun Yatsen, *Kidnapped in London*, pp. 92–3.

102. FO 17/1718, pp. 38–41, Jarvis' report, 20 October 1896, para. 9.

103. FO 17/1718, p. 94, Jarvis' report, 23 October 1896. See note 104.

docks area of East London,[104] instead of summoning McGregor to Scotland Yard to make an official statement. McGregor said that 'his firm had been approached'[105] by the Chinese Legation respecting the conveyance to China of a *lunatic*. Their steamer, the *Glenfarg*,[106] had not kept her time so could not be dispatched on the date advertised[107] and would not be ready to sail until the middle of November.[108] Under these circumstances, the negotiations fell through. McGregor promised, continued Chief Inspector Jarvis in his report, 'should anything further transpire in this matter he would immediately communicate with me'.[109] As for the other shipping companies, which the Chinese Legation might have approached, but about which there were no clues to follow, Jarvis reported, 'As regards shipping generally a watch is being kept by Thames Division on all craft leaving London for China'.[110]

Jarvis' interviews with Cole and with McGregor established beyond doubt that Sun Yatsen was being kept a prisoner in the

---

104. Jarvis' report, and indeed all relevant documents on the subject, refer only to the Glen Line, which was not listed in *Kelly's Post Office London Directory, 1897* (hereafter cited as *Kelly's*). The explanation lies in the fact that the registered name of the company was McGregor, Gow & Co. (*The Times*, 14 October 1896, p. 2, col. 2). It is of some importance to find out the exact location of the firm, even if only to obtain some idea of the trouble the detective, and hence the British government, were prepared to take in the matter.

105. Jarvis' report does not specify when McGregor was approached by the Legation, and by exactly whom in the Legation. The Treasury solicitor subsequently found out that it was Macartney who had telegraphed McGregor on 14 October 1896, asking for an appointment on that day. (FO 17/1718, pp. 113-16, Cuffe to Home Office, 12 November 1896, para. 24.) See Chapter 2 for more details.

106. The *Glenfarg* was built in 1894, of 3,647 gross tons. She subsequently struck a rock one mile north-west of Shirose, Japan, and sank on 14 August 1914. (E. P. Harnack, 'Glen Line to the Orient', *Sea Breezes*, new series, Vol. 19 [April 1955], p.285.) I am grateful to Miss E. Organ, Miss N. Evetts, and Miss Janet Smith, all of the Liverpool Record Office; Miss Deborah Lindsay and Mr Gordon Read of Merseyside County Council; and Dr Frank Taylor of the John Rylands Library and Miss Jean Ayton of the Central Libraries, both in Manchester, for their help in my research on the *Glenfarg*.

107. McGregor had put in a special advertisement for the *Glenfarg*, saying that she was scheduled to sail for the Straits and China sometime in October (*The Times*, 13 October 1896, p. 2, col. 2). See Chapter 2 for more details.

108. The *Glenfarg* was finally advertised to set sail on 14 November 1896 (*The Times*, 28 October 1896, p. 2, col. 2). But according to her voyage record, she did not actually leave London until 21 November 1896. I am grateful to Miss Deborah Lindsay of Merseyside County Council for drawing my attention to this record (Lindsay to Wong, 14 November 1984, encl., copy of the voyage of the *Glenfarg*).

109. FO 17/1718, p. 94, Jarvis' report, 23 October 1896.

110. FO 17/1718, p. 94, Jarvis' report, 23 October 1896.

Chinese Legation, and that there was every intention of smuggling him out of the country under false pretences. Having taken the necessary precautions, such as keeping a continuous surveillance on both the Chinese Legation and all China-bound shipping, the British police now went over to the offensive. Although it was already night-time on Wednesday, 21 October 1896, Chief Inspector Jarvis was instructed by Scotland Yard to contact both Dr Cantlie and Dr Manson, requesting that the two doctors make themselves available the next day.[111]

On Thursday, 22 October 1896, Chief Inspector Jarvis was directed[112] to take Dr Cantlie and Dr Manson to St Paul's Chambers at 19–23, Ludgate Hill.[113] There, the two doctors gave sworn statements in front of a lawyer, Mr Stephen A. Jones.[114] Then the party went to the Old Bailey, entered the Central Criminal Court and there, at the Queen's Bench Division, applied to Judge R.S. Wright for a writ of habeas corpus to be taken out against the Chinese Legation.[115] At the end of the day, Mrs Cantlie wrote in her diary, 'The Chief Inspector of Police took Hamish to a judge to get him to swear Habeas Corpus but it could not be done for some reason'.[116] Apparently, this was what she was told by her husband, who could not have been offered more information in court by Judge Wright. The written judgment by His Honour, which was not divulged to the public at the time, is much more revealing. He wrote,

I hesitate to make any order in this matter, partly because I am not the Vacation Judge, partly because I doubt the propriety of making any order or granting any summons against a foreign Legation. But the affidavits appear to me to make out a sufficient case for using diplomatic pressure to obtain an explanation and an undertaking that the man shall

---

111. FO 17/1718, p. 94, Jarvis' report, 23 October 1896.
112. FO 17/1718, p. 94, Jarvis' report, 23 October 1896. It is not clear who directed him, probably his immediate superior.
113. FO 17/1718, pp. 22–32, Affidavits by Cantlie and Manson, 22 October 1896.
114. FO 17/1718, pp. 22–32, Affidavits by Cantlie and Mason, 22 October 1896.
115. FO 17/1718, pp. 22–32, Affidavits by Cantlie and Mason, 22 October 1896. The affidavits were simply entitled 'In the matter of an application for a writ of Habeas Corpus'. They did not specify to whom it was to be served. However, the judge's minute left no doubt that it was intended for the Legation. The significance of the vagueness in the title of the affidavits will be seen later.
116. Mrs Cantlie's diary, 22 October 1896.

not be removed until there has been an opportunity of further consideration.[117]

But no harm was done. The result seems to have been expected. It has been mentioned that Chief Inspector Jarvis had been directed to conduct the two doctors to have two affidavits prepared. It has also been mentioned that Jarvis' immediate superior, Superintendent Donald Swanson, had reported that Scotland Yard could not interfere with the affairs of the Legation. Therefore, even if Swanson had instructed Jarvis to have the two affidavits taken, the instruction itself must have come from higher authorities. The higher authorities appear to have known what they were doing. With extraordinary speed, the two affidavits, together with Judge R. S. Wright's minute, were conveyed from the Old Bailey to the Home Office. Equally swiftly, the Home Office wrote to the Foreign Office; indeed, so swiftly as to have left no time for copies of the affidavits to be made and enclosed in the letter.[118] In the normal course of events, an official dispatch of this kind would have been drafted initially by a clerk, amended by the senior clerk, and read and amended further if necessary by the permanent under-secretary of state or his assistant, before it was submitted to the home secretary for his approval. Once it was approved, it would have had to have been copied out in a fair hand by a clerk and signed by the appropriate authority before it was dispatched. While all this was taking place, there ought to have been more than enough time for the two affidavits to have been copied out. The fact that the Home Office was unable to enclose copies of these two documents seems to indicate that the official letter had been prepared beforehand and was instantly dispatched upon the arrival of the affidavits.

The contents of this important letter from the Home Office, marked *Confidential and Pressing*, are equally revealing. Part of it read:

I am directed by Secretary Sir Matthew Ridley, to acquaint you, for Lord Salisbury's information, that he has received affidavits sworn by two registered medical practitioners to the effect that a man of the name

---

117. FO 17/1718, p. 32, Judge Wright's minute, 22 October 1896.
118. FO 17/1718, pp. 51–3, Home Office to Foreign Office, 22 October 1896. The postscript read: 'Copies of the affidavits above referred to will be sent you in the course of to-day'.

of Sun Yatsen is at the present time confined against his will at the Chinese Legation, Portland Place ... The truth of the affidavits has been corroborated by inquiries made by the Metropolitan Police. Sir Matthew Ridley will therefore be glad if you will bring these facts to the Marquis of Salisbury's notice and move His Lordship to take such action as he may deem proper to secure Sun Yatsen's immediate release from custody.[119]

This letter was put on the desk of the permanent under-secretary of state, Sir Thomas Sanderson, of the Foreign Office. Sanderson, in turn, and without waiting for copies of the affidavits to arrive, consulted the attorney-general.[120] When the copies of the depositions did arrive, therefore, Sanderson was in a position to ask 'Sir Halliday Macartney to call at once'.[121]

It is quite obvious that the entire proceeding was a well-planned operation, and that the official letter from the Home Office was intended for the record only. To begin with, the two doctors were taken to Ludgate Hill to give sworn statements and then to apply for a writ of habeas corpus without being told specifically to whom it was to be served:[122] Dr Cantlie said afterwards that 'a writ of Habeas Corpus was made out against either the Legation or Sir Halliday Macartney, I know not which'.[123] What he did not know, either, was that Chief Inspector Jarvis had alerted the lawyers even before he contacted Cantlie

---

119. FO 17/1718, pp. 51–3, Home Office to Foreign Office, 22 October 1896. See note 102.

120. FO 17/1718, pp. 51–3, Home Office to Foreign Office, 22 October 1896. Schiffrin thinks that it was Lord Salisbury himself who consulted the attorney-general (*Origins*, p. 122). The source given is FO 17/1718, p. 94. Upon checking this source, which is a record of an interview between Macartney on the one hand, and Sanderson (in the company of Bertie and Davidson) on the other, it is clear that Sanderson was telling Macartney in the name of Salisbury that the attorney-general had been consulted. Foreign Office practice, as with that of other government departments, is for less senior officials to do all the homework and suggest a course of action for the approval of the head. Even the most important official dispatches are handled in this way. It is most unlikely, therefore, that Salisbury and not Sanderson was the person who had consulted the attorney-general. In any case, Salisbury was away from London, in his country home at Hatfield.

121. FO 17/1718, p. 35, Sanderson's minute on the Home Office letter of the same day, 22 October 1896.

122. As mentioned before in a footnote, the affidavits were simply entitled 'In the matter of an application for a writ of Habeas Corpus'. (FO 17/1718, pp. 22–32.)

123. Sun Yatsen, *Kidnapped in London*, p. 85. As for my view that Dr Cantlie was the true author of the booklet, see Chapter 4, Section III.

and Manson, 'having made all the arrangements the night previous'.[124] Even Judge Wright seems to have been unaware of the real intention of the exercise. The day after he had heard the case, he wrote to Lord Salisbury elaborating on his decision not to issue the order.[125] By the time this letter reached the Foreign Office, Sun Yatsen had been released.[126] The true objective of acquiring the two affidavits and Justice Wright's endorsement appears to have lain in their value as written evidence to wave in front of Sir Halliday Macartney, since the written reports by Chief Inspector Jarvis on his interviews with both Cole and McGregor were by their very nature 'private'. Even the depositions could only be used to wave at Macartney, if necessary, because, as Sanderson put it at the time, 'they mention the man Cole, who does not wish his name to appear'.[127]

However, the messenger whom Sanderson sent out to ask Macartney 'to call at once in order to speak to him in the sense addressed by the Attorney-General'[128] failed to find his man.[129] At once Sanderson drafted a diplomatic Note addressed to the Chinese minister, asked two senior colleagues to look at it and obtained their concurrence, and got a clerk to copy it out in a fair hand, ready to submit both the draft and the 'signature copy' to Lord Salisbury for action.[130] In a docket which was to accompany the two documents, Sanderson wrote, 'We ought not to lose time as we are told that the two doctors have sent a letter to *The Times* office which is withheld from publication, pending action by us, but which they may at any time decide to put forward. If the affair is published there may be a considerable scandal particularly if we have done nothing'. Then, as an afterthought, he added, 'Unless you see reason to the contrary, I propose, on your returning the Note signed, to send it at once to the Chinese Legation'. At this very juncture, Macartney turned up, and Sanderson finished his docket with the following words: '7 p.m. Macartney

124. FO 17/1718, p. 94, Jarvis' report, 23 October 1896.
125. FO 17/1718, pp. 64–7, Wright to Salisbury, 23 October 1896.
126. Sanderson's minute on FO 17/1718, pp. 64–7, Wright to Salisbury, 23 October 1896.
127. FO 17/1718, pp. 33–5, Sanderson to Salisbury, 22 October 1896.
128. FO 17/1718, p. 35, Sanderson's minute on the Home Office letter of the same day, 22 October 1896.
129. FO 17/1718, pp. 33–5, Sanderson to Salisbury, 22 October 1896.
130. FO 17/1718, pp. 33–5, Sanderson to Salisbury, 22 October 1896.

at this moment arrived but I send the Note as it may be required'.[131] By that he probably meant that he was still going to submit the Note for Salisbury to sign in case the interview with Macartney did not go well and the Note then became imperative.

Indeed the interview, conducted between Sanderson and his two senior colleagues, Bertie and Davidson, on the one hand, and Macartney, on the other, could have gone better. Sanderson began by referring to the 'sworn affirmations by two medical men of respectability', and requested that Sun Yatsen be released immediately. Macartney admitted that 'the man was detained in the Legation', but added that Beijing would have to be telegraphed for instructions. Bertie demurred at the delay which was implied; and Sanderson spoke about *The Times*, 'If the matter came out in this manner the scandal would be great'. Macartney gave the assurance that 'the Minister would telegraph at once', that very evening. Bertie again expressed his unhappiness about the delay, and Sanderson threatened to take 'very serious steps'. Macartney replied that he would inform the Chinese minister at once of what had passed, and left.[132]

It was just as well that Sanderson had submitted the diplomatic Note to Salisbury for his signature. After the interview with Macartney, and subsequent to further consultation with his colleagues, Sanderson dispatched a special courier to Portland Place with the Note. The Note was delivered at the Chinese Legation at 9.50 p.m.[133] It was short and pungent:

I have the honour to state that I have been informed by Her Majesty's Secretary of State for the Home Department that two sworn depositions by medical men of respectability residing in London have been communicated to him affirming that an individual named Sun Yatsen recently resident in Gray's Inn Place has been for the last few days detained against his will in enforced confinement in the Chinese Legation.

The detention of this man against his will in the Chinese Legation is, in the opinion of Her Majesty's Government, an infraction of English law which is not covered by, and is an abuse of the diplomatic privilege

---

131. FO 17/1718, pp. 33–5, Sanderson to Salisbury, 22 October 1896.
132. FO 17/1718, pp. 54–61, Sanderson's record of his interview with Macartney, 22 October 1896.
133. FO 17/1718, pp. 24–5, Salisbury to Gong Zhaoyuan [draft], 22 October 1896.

accorded to a foreign Representative. I have, therefore, the honour to request that Sun Yatsen may be at once released.[134]

British newspapers invariably referred to a peremptory Note which effected Sun Yatsen's release. Little did they realize that an enormous amount of homework lay behind that Note: first the investigations, then the preventive measures, and finally the acquisition of two affidavits from the two doctors on the basis of which the Note was formulated.

In spite of the remarkable speed with which all this was done, partly with a view to beating the press towards the final stages,[135] the Note was delivered at 49, Portland Place, just a little too late. An evening newspaper, the *Globe*, got wind of the story and printed a supplement to their regular editions which had already been published, thereby launching a sensation.[136]

Before we examine this sensation, it may be useful to put the foregoing reconstruction and assessment of the sequence of events in an historical perspective. Chinese accounts have alleged for a good part of this century that the British government intervened on behalf of Sun Yatsen only under the pressure of public opinion, believing that the British government took action only after the newspapers had published the story. This allegation even found its way into school textbooks,[137] and has re-emerged in two recent biographies of Sun Yatsen.[138] In view of what the Foreign Office, the Home Office, and Scotland Yard had done up

---

134. FO 17/1718, pp. 24–5, Salisbury to Gong Zhaoyuan [draft], 22 October 1896.

135. Sanderson's docket, written shortly before 7 p.m. on 22 October 1896 (FO 17/1718, pp. 33–5), was the first indication of the Foreign Office's being aware of *The Times*' possession of the story.

136. This supplement, entitled 'Special Edition', cannot be found in the British Library. The full text, however, was reproduced by all the major London newspapers the next day, including the *Globe* itself (*Globe*, 23 October 1896, p. 5, col. 2). Thus, the error in the following statement is obvious: 'Early in the morning of 21 [October 1896], Dr Cantlie bought a copy of the *Globe* in the street and found on its front page the startling title of "The Kidnapping in London of the Revolutionary Sun Wen"'. (Shao Chuanlie, *Sun Zhongshan*, p. 38.) The *Globe* was an evening newspaper, not a morning paper. In addition, the date of the relevant publication was 22 October 1896, late in the evening; not the morning of 21 October 1896, as alleged.

137. I have not read such textbooks myself. I am grateful to older scholars in China, who told me during a conference on Sun Yatsen in November 1984 that they had been taught with such textbooks in their school-days.

138. Shang Mingxuan, *Sun Zhongshan zhuan*, p. 44; and Shao Chuanlie, *Sun Zhongshan*, pp. 38–9.

to the point when the *Globe* published its supplement on the evening of 22 October 1896, one can safely conclude that the allegation is groundless. It would have been more accurate to say that worry about the possible publication of the story prodded the British government into even more rapid action. As for the actual role of public opinion which subsequently emerged as a result of the *Globe's* action, it was in expediting Sun Yatsen's release by the Chinese Legation, as we shall see in the next section of this chapter.

IV The Sensation

It is not clear when and how the *Globe* got wind of the story.[139] But by the afternoon of 22 October 1896, the newspaper felt confident enough to send a special correspondent to knock on the door of 46, Devonshire Street.[140] The reporter asked Cantlie if 'he knew anything about a Chinaman that had been kidnapped by the Chinese Legation. Well, he thought he did; what did he know about it?'[141] Even at this stage, Cantlie still regarded *The Times* as the proper place for the story to make its first appearance.[142] It seems that the journalist was able to convince the cautious doctor that 'the oldest evening paper'[143] might do just as well. 'Read over what you have written about the circumstance, and I will tell you if it is correct', said Cantlie.[144] 'The

139. Schiffrin suggests that the *Globe* 'got wind of the case through the Old Bailey proceedings'. (*Origins*, p. 23.) However, the footnote to Schiffrin's statement makes no reference to its source of information. The full text of this note reads: 'The "Special Edition" of 22 October is not available but the story was reprinted in the 23 October issue'. The *Globe* (23 October 1896, p. 5, col. 2) referred to rumours having been in circulation during the previous few days. Another contemporary source also revealed that 'some two or three hundred people' had known of the story by the morning of Tuesday, 20 October 1896 (Sun Yatsen, *Kidnapped in London*, p. 86). It is quite possible, therefore, that the *Globe* had heard about the story in some detail before 22 October 1896.
140. Sun Yatsen, *Kidnapped in London*, p. 85.
141. Sun Yatsen, *Kidnapped in London*, p. 85.
142. Sun Yatsen, *Kidnapped in London*, pp. 85–6.
143. *Globe*, 24 October 1896, p. 4, col. 2.
144. Sun Yatsen, *Kidnapped in London*, p. 86. The *Globe's* report, as printed, was in fact not entirely accurate. For example, it referred to Saturday, and not Sunday, as the date of Sun Yatsen's disappearance. It was also vague about Sun Yatsen's address, mentioning only 'the neighbourhood of Gray's Inn Road', thus sending (as we shall see later) at least one reporter to the wrong place in search of information.

information the *Globe* had received proving correct, the doctor endorsed it, but requested his name not to be mentioned'.[145]

As stated before, the supplement to the *Globe* of 22 October 1896, which broke the news, is not available. The reproduction of the same report the next day by the *Globe* and the other newspapers did not include the headline. Hence we have to trust that the author of *Kidnapped in London* reproduced the correct heading, which was 'Strange Story! Conspirator Kidnapped in London! Imprisonment at the Chinese Embassy!'[146] The opening paragraph read:

Extraordinary rumours have been in circulation within the past few days as to the kidnapping and imprisonment of a prominent Chinese gentleman at the Chinese Embassy in London. It is only this afternoon, however, that we have been able to confirm these rumours, and to gather some facts bearing on the matter.[147]

The report then went on to describe in some detail Sun Yatsen's plot to subvert the Chinese government the year before, his 'arrest in the streets of London', and the journeys made by his friends to Scotland Yard and the Foreign Office in an attempt to rescue him. The concluding paragraph is nothing short of inflammatory:

The strangest feature of the affair is that, in answer to inquiries by his friends at the Embassy, the officials deny that the man is here [*sic*]. His friends, however, possess conclusive proof that this denial is absolutely false.[148]

The publication of the news 'immediately aroused the greatest public interest', wrote the *Globe* proudly. 'Inquiries were at once set on foot by the London morning newspapers'.[149] Within two hours,[150] both the Central News[151] and the *Daily Mail* had their men inside 46, Devonshire Street. Cantlie was still 'too reticent to please them, but the main outlines were extracted from

145. Sun Yatsen, *Kidnapped in London*, p. 86.
146. Sun Yatsen, *Kidnapped in London*, p. 94.
147. *Globe*, 23 October 1896, p. 5, col. 2.
148. *Globe*, 23 October 1896, p. 5, col. 2.
149. *Globe*, 23 October 1896, p. 5, col. 2.
150. Sun Yatsen, *Kidnapped in London*, p. 87.
151. The Central News was one of the major news agencies in London.

him'.[152] As reporters continued to arrive in force,[153] Cantlie subsequently prepared a written statement for those who came;[154] and for those who had yet to come, he gave a copy to the Central News for dissemination.[155]

One after another, the journalists also knocked on the door of the Chinese Legation just around the corner. Their excitement was evident in their subsequent reports, which in turn generated a still greater sensation. It appears that the *Daily Telegraph* was the first on the scene, to make 'inquiries as to the accuracy of the story of the alleged kidnapping. The only official accessible was the translator to the Legation, and the gentleman professed to have no knowledge of the affair, and said he "thought" there was no such person as Sun Yatsen detained there. Our representative then asked to see Sir Halliday Macartney, and was informed that he was not in the building. A visit to Sir Halliday's private residence in Harley Street was equally fruitless'.[156] But resourceful and persistent as reporters generally are, the perseverance of the *Daily Telegraph* was rewarded with the information that the English secretary was hiding in the Midland Hotel.[157]

Meanwhile, the Central News and the *Daily Mail*, having had their interview with Cantlie, turned up at 49, Portland Place.[158] 'At the Chinese Embassy', wrote the *Daily Mail*, 'the official Interpreter absolutely denied ... any knowledge of anyone being detained at the Embassy, and stuck to his statements with a firmness and a protestation of innocence that would have convinced anyone but a journalist'.[159] The Central News was less

---

152. Sun Yatsen, *Kidnapped in London*, p. 87.

153. Among them was a representative of the Press Association, whose report was printed, *inter alia*, in the *Daily Telegraph* (23 October 1896, p. 6, cols. 6–7) which, as we shall see, went direct to the Chinese Legation without his first approaching Cantlie for more facts.

154. The *Globe* (23 October 1896, p. 4, col. 5), for example, paid another visit to Cantlie on 23 October 1896, copied the signed statement and published it on the same day. See, also, the *Morning Advertiser* (24 October 1896, p. 5, col. 6), which wrote, 'We have been favoured with the following signed statement by Dr James Cantlie ...'

155. The *Morning Leader* (24 October 1896, p. 7, col. 4) wrote, 'The Central News yesterday received a signed statement from the Doctor'. The *Evening News* (23 October 1896, p.3, col. 2) also wrote, 'The Central News has been favoured with the following signed statement by Dr James Cantlie ...'

156. *Daily Telegraph*, 23 October 1896, p. 7, col. 6.

157. *Daily Telegraph*, 23 October 1896, p. 7, col. 6.

158. Sun Yatsen, *Kidnapped in London*, p. 87.

159. *Daily Mail*, 23 October 1896, p. 5, col. 5.

restrained, and 'said it was no good denying it, and that if Sun was not given up, he might expect 10,000 men here [sic] tomorrow to pull the place about his ears'.[160]

Then the *Morning Leader* arrived, asking to see Macartney. 'He was out — at the Midland Hotel, said the porter'.[161] Not knowing how lucky he was in having this valuable piece of information thrust upon him, the journalist requested to see an official of the Legation.

Presently he was ushered into the presence of a bland Celestial, who unlocked the door of an apartment which was half office, half bedroom, and then read the report which had been handed to him with charming innocence. 'Absurd!' laughed Mr T. H. Tang [Deng Tingkeng], the Interpreter of the Legation, when he had finished reading the paper. No, there was no such person there; it was the first he had heard of it. It was easy to disprove the report. Would he show the *Leader*'s representative the rooms of the Embassy? Well, the inquisitor had better call and see Sir Halliday Macartney at four o'clock next morning [sic] ... When the mild gentleman was told that the story going the rounds was that Sir Halliday himself had put the prisoner under lock and key his incredulous smile was a sight to see.[162]

The interpreter appears to have been the kind of person who, when pressed harder, resisted (and in this case, lied) harder. It is interesting, also, to note how readily the porter gave away the whereabouts of Macartney to the *Morning Leader*. Probably, after the failure of the repeated performance of the interpreter to impress the reporters, the Legation felt that it was time to divert all enquiries to the English secretary.

From the Legation, the *Morning Leader* headed straight for the Midland Hotel, which was part of the St Pancras Railway Station complex owned by the Midland Railway Company.[163] Meanwhile, the *Daily Telegraph* and reporters from other organizations who had visited the Legation earlier and had wasted some time trying to locate the English secretary, also arrived. The time must have been around 8.30 p.m. or 9 p.m., after Macartney had returned from his interview at the Foreign Office,

160. Sun Yatsen, *Kidnapped in London*, p. 87.
161. *Morning Leader*, 23 October 1896, p. 5, col. 1.
162. *Morning Leader*, 23 October 1896, p. 5, col. 1.
163. Greater London Council Records, Photograph Division, 70/10317, St Pancras Midland Grand Hotel, *circa* 1890s.

which began at 7 p.m.[164] 'Sir Halliday at first seemed incredulous that any story relating to an arrest or detention at the Chinese Legation could have obtained circulation. On being shown a cutting from the evening paper containing the report he read it very carefully',[165] 'with an occasional twitching of the muscles of his face, which indicated increasing seriousness. When he reached the end of the story he looked up, and quietly said, "There is such a man at the Embassy"'.[166]

Some of the details of this impromptu press conference will be dealt with in the next chapter. Suffice it to say here that by the time the journalists had finished with Macartney and proceeded to their next target — 8, Gray's Inn Place — they found the building 'closed up, and no response was made when the bell was rung'.[167] Some were more persistent than others. The *Morning Leader*, for example, rang every doorbell in the neighbourhood; 'but no one connected with the buildings appears to have any knowledge of a Chinese gentleman. Indeed, the doorkeeper at the private entrance to Gray's Inn Place, which is a little further down Holborn, declared without reserve that no person answering the description given had ever to his knowledge lived there'.[168]

Obviously, this group of journalists arrived just a little too late. The *Star*, for example, had beaten them, and had managed to interview the landlady earlier. '[Miss] Pollard has been warned by Scotland Yard officials not to give any information whatever regarding her Chinese lodger. All she would admit to a *Star* man was that the gentleman had lived there, and that she had been in a state of intense anxiety since his mysterious disappearance nearly a fortnight ago'. The *Star* even managed to inspect the place: 'At present his rooms are under lock and key, and the key is in the possession of Scotland Yard authorities but one wonders that the door is not further guarded for the Embassy had possession of all the prisoner's keys, including that of the street door —

---

164. FO 17/1718, pp. 33–5, Sanderson to Salisbury, 22 October 1896.
165. *Daily Telegraph*, 23 October 1896, p. 7, col. 6.
166. *Morning Leader*, 23 October 1896, p. 5, col. 2.
167. *Daily Telegraph*, 23 October 1896, p. 7, col. 6.
168. *Morning Leader*, 23 October 1896, p. 5, col. 3. The description here of the persistence of the *Morning Leader* is not intended as a reflection on the *Daily Telegraph*. The latter had interviewed Cantlie earlier whereas the former had not. See note 169.

which, by the way, is open all day for the convenience of those having offices there'.[169]

But getting to one's destination early is not always an advantage, at least not before one has done one's homework thoroughly. The *Westminster Gazette*, for example, read about the reference to Gray's Inn Road,[170] and somehow appears to have learnt that the street number involved was 8, subsequently went to the wrong place, and then complained in its columns: 'A statement which has been published that Sun was at the time of the arrest living at 8 Gray's Inn Road is incorrect. The premises in question are used as a coffee place, and lodgers are not catered for there'.[171] Such was the excitement and eagerness of the press.

Reuters even wired Washington, requesting their men there to enquire at the Chinese Legation if previously a telegram had been sent by the minister to his counterpart in London concerning Sun Yatsen's departure from America for England.[172]

The Central News was not idle either. Having threatened the interpreter, on an earlier occasion, with 10,000 men pulling the place down about his ears, the Central News appears to have paid the Legation another visit. Late at night, but not too late for it to be printed in the *Morning*, the Central News released the following information: 'The officials of the Legation, finding concealment no longer possible, now admit that Sun Yatsen is a prisoner within the Legation building'.[173] It seems that Macartney, after his encounter with reporters at the Midland Hotel, had hurried back to the Legation to see what had been happening and told his colleagues that they had to change their approach.

The next day, Friday, 23 October 1896, the London papers were full of startling headlines: 'Kidnapped?' (*Daily Chronicle*),

---

169. *Star*, 23 October 1896, p. 2, col. 7. Here again, the success of the *Star* in obtaining information in this quarter is no reflection on, say, the *Morning Leader*, which the *Star* quoted extensively because the *Star* had not been to either the Chinese Legation or the Midland Hotel.

170. As foreshadowed in a footnote in this chapter, the *Globe*'s reference to Sun Yatsen having lived 'in the neighbourhood of Gray's Inn Road' was bound to cause some confusion.

171. *Westminster Gazette*, 23 October 1896, p. 7, col. 2.

172. The answer, almost to be anticipated, was that the Chinese Legation in Washington had 'no information to impart'. (Reuters' telegram, Washington, 23 October 1896, in *Daily Chronicle*, 24 October 1896, p. 5, col. 6.)

173. *Morning*, 23 October 1896, p. 1, col. 3. The *Morning* is not to be confused with the *Morning Advertiser*, the *Morning Leader*, or the *Morning Post*.

'A Chinaman Kidnapped in London' (*Daily Graphic*), 'Caught in London' (*Daily Mail*), 'Alleged Kidnapping at the Chinese Legation' (*Daily News*), 'Extraordinary Action of the Chinese Embassy' (*Daily Telegraph*), 'Sensational Story from Portland Place' (*Morning Leader*) ... and one can go on reproducing similar headlines from nearly all the London newspapers. Those papers that had dispatched their journalists to the scenes proudly reported their findings. Those that had not either copied the news from another paper,[174] or relied heavily on news agencies such as the Central News for their information.[175]

But those papers that had been slow on the previous day became very active this day. 'At 7 o'clock this morning', wrote the *Echo*,

Portland Place presented a quiet and deserted appearance to the usual passer-by. Posted opposite the Chinese Legation, however, standing idly on the pavement, were two detectives from Scotland Yard, who hardly looked as though they had kept a midnight vigil. Two other detectives were strolling about the immediate neighbourhood, and it was apparent that Sun Yat Yen [*sic*] could not be removed from the Legation unobserved. About the Chinese headquarters there was nothing to indicate any unusual occurrence; the blinds and window-shutters were drawn, and the doors seemed heavily barred against intruders.[176]

Undeterred by this formidable-looking building, the *Echo* tapped on the door with a walking-stick, a door that had no brightening brass knocker or bell to ornament it. 'Receiving no reply', continued the *Echo*,

I again tapped with my walking stick. The door was then opened by a

---

174. The *Star* (23 October 1896, p. 2, cols. 2–7), for example, liberally used the story written up by the *Morning Leader*. Later, the *St James's Gazette* (24 October 1896, p. 9, cols. 1–2) and the *Echo* (24 October 1896, p. 3, col. 5), among others, were to use the findings of the *Daily News*. In most such cases, the source was given.

175. See, for example, the *Daily Chronicle* (23 October 1896, p. 5, col. 5) and the *Daily Graphic* (23 October 1896, p. 7, col. 4). *The Times* (23 October 1896, p. 3, col. 6), on the other hand, appears to have relied on the Press Association for information. Indeed, this issue of *The Times* shows an extraordinary lack of interest in the case, reproducing the story of the *Globe*, albeit in full, and adding: 'The Press Association, having made inquiries last night, confirms the statement published by the *Globe* in all its important details'. Having allowed the *Globe* to have the scoop, the coolness of *The Times* is not surprising.'

176. *Echo*, 23 October 1896, p. 3, col. 1. See, also, *Westminster Gazette*, 23 October 1896, p. 7, col. 2.

gentleman, whose olive skin and long slit-like eyes at once betrayed the Chinaman. 'Can I see Sir Halliday Macartney?' was my first question. The Chinaman, who, by the way, wore one of those long flowing robes, with ample sleeves, thick-soled boots of a dirty-white colour, with a glossy pigtail reaching almost to the boots, shook his head, indicating either a negative or that he did not understand. Assuming it to mean the latter, I again mentioned the name of Sir Halliday. This time it acted like a charm, 'Sir Halliday Macartney not here', was the reply, the Chinaman scarcely moving a muscle of his mobile face. 'I wish to ask something concerning the prisoner you have here', I next ventured, but the imperturbable and implacable doorkeeper stood holding the door and never replying. I repeated the question again and again, and all I could get from him was a stolid shake of his oily and well-groomed head. He either did not or would not understand, or could not or would not afford the smallest tittle of information. It was of no use.[177]

Given the sort of attitude adopted by the Legation, it is not surprising that one of the onlookers loudly asked why they should 'allow such an outrage as this upon the person in the heart of fashionable London and at the end of this glorious nineteenth century?' — a question that 'drew a responsive concurrence from the others'.[178] One wonders if it was the same crowd that began throwing missiles at the Chinese servants who emerged from the Legation. One of them, the chief cook, was hit by a dead cat.[179]

As the morning wore on, more and more journalists arrived, until the 'building was literally besieged by newspapermen. Some of them stood in the extensive portico at the main entrance, others chatted with the detectives who were watching the Legation, while a few, more privileged, or with more self-confidence, went inside the premises and made themselves quite at home. Care, however, was taken that they did not find their way upstairs, where Sun Yatsen sat in his carefully guarded room wondering if his head would be cut off after the homely but effectual fashion of his native land'.[180] At 10 a.m., the Press Association released the following news: 'Sun Yatsen is still a captive at the Chinese Embassy. It is said that he is kindly treated and well cared for, but he is not allowed to leave his apartment, a bed-sitting room, which is guarded by Chinese officials night and

177. *Echo*, 23 October 1896, p. 3, cols. 1–2.
178. *Echo*, 23 October 1896, p. 3, cols. 1–2.
179. *Echo*, 23 October 1896, p. 3, col. 2.
180. *Daily Telegraph*, 23 October 1896, p. 7, col. 7.

day. Two detectives from Scotland Yard are still patrolling outside the Embassy under the direction of Inspector Jarvis, but they
can do nothing at present but await events'.[181] Shortly after 10
a.m., Macartney himself arrived,[182] which was described as 'earlier than usual'.[183] He 'declined to answer any questions concerning the imprisoned Chinaman',[184] but went straight to 'the room
of the Chinese Minister, who was ill in bed, and had a long
consultation with him'.[185]

The disappointment of the journalists, who had been waiting
for quite some time for Macartney to come on duty, can be
imagined. Some began to leave, to pursue their enquiries elsewhere. No. 8, Gray's Inn Place, was a favourite spot. But Miss
Pollard, 'on being interviewed by a reporter this morning', wrote
one paper, 'had been warned by the Scotland Yard officials not
to give any information whatever regarding her Chinese lodger or
his friends'.[186] The *Morning*, among others, went to East London, but 'the reply of a representative of the Glen Line Company
to a question as to whether a passage had been booked by the
Chinese Legation for the captive was in the following guarded
terms:– "We must decline to say anything on the subject"'.[187]
The Press Association proceeded to interview 'a well-known barrister [who] expressed the opinion ... that as soon as the British
Government are assured that the prisoner is a British subject
they will demand his immediate release'.[188]

The Central News interviewed a Mr Cavendish, who was one
of the authorities at Bow Street on the law of extradition. This
lawyer said he could cite no case at all parallel to that of Sun
Yatsen.[189] In fact, the Central News had another and more

---

181. *St James's Gazette*, 23 October 1896, p. 9, col. 1.
182. *Pall Mall Gazette*, 23 October 1896, p. 7, col. 2.
183. *Daily Telegraph*, 24 October 1896, p. 7, col. 7. This is corroborated by
FO 17/1718, pp. 116–19, Cole's statement at the Treasury, 2 November 1896,
para. 3: 'Macartney's usual hours were from 10.30 or 11 a.m. till 7 p.m.'
184. *Pall Mall Gazette*, 23 October 1896, p. 7, col. 2.
185. *Daily Telegraph*, 23 October 1896, p. 7, col. 7.
186. *Westminster Gazette*, 23 October 1896, p. 7, col. 2.
187. *Morning*, 24 October 1896, p. 6, col. 2.
188. *Echo*, 23 October 1896, p. 3, col. 3. Sun Yatsen, in his message to
Cantlie, claimed to have been born in Hong Kong and therefore to be a British
subject (FO 17/1718, pp. 22–3, Sun Yatsen to Cantlie, 19 October 1896). This
enabled Cantlie to tell the Central News: 'Sun Yatsen is a British subject, having
been born in Hong Kong'. (*Daily Chronicle*, 23 October 1896, p. 5, col. 5.)
189. *Daily Chronicle*, 24 October 1896, p. 5, col. 6.

exciting story to offer. Under the catching headline of 'Bold Scheme of Recapture', the *Daily Chronicle* wrote,

The Central News has ascertained that Sun's friends had arranged a bold scheme to bring about his rescue had they not been definitely assured by the Foreign Office and Scotland Yard that no harm whatever should come to him. It was to be effected by means of breaking the window of the room in which he was imprisoned and descending from the roof of No. 51, the house adjoining, which is the residence of Viscount Powerscourt. His friends had succeeded in informing him of the plan they intended to pursue, and although information which was subsequently obtained pointed to the fact that Sun Yatsen was being kept closely watched, a promise of inside assistance in opening the window satisfied his friends of the feasibility of the plan. Indeed, so far matured was the scheme that a cab was held in waiting at the corner of Weymouth Street to convey the prisoner to the home of a friend.[190]

So much for the journalists who had left Portland Place by mid-morning.

Those that arrived after them naturally found a slightly different situation. 'The scene outside the Chinese Embassy when I arrived was not inspiring', the *Sun*'s so-called *special kidnapping-investigator* telegraphed from Portland Place.

About a dozen people, including a couple of detectives and a butcher-boy, stood gazing at the dingy mansion from the safe points on the opposite side of the broad street. They were not going to be kidnapped if they knew it ... I crossed the street, and rang the bell, and in a few moments the door was opened by the chief warder. He was not a Chinaman, but an ordinary English domestic, and in response to my

---

190. *Daily Chronicle*, 24 October 1896, p. 5, col. 6. See, also, the *Evening News*, 24 October 1896, p. 2, col. 5, and the *Overland Mail*, 30 October 1896, p. 45, col. 2. In my reconstruction of the events of 20 October 1896, I mentioned that the rescue was Cole's idea and that Scotland Yard dissuaded Cantlie from it. Cantlie referred to this episode in the signed statement, dated 23 October 1896, which he gave to the Central News: 'At one time in this singular affair it was put in my power to effect a rescue. We were seriously inclined to do this on being constantly met at the Legation with the direct lie that Sun was not there. Considering, however, the slur cast upon the laws of this country by the Chinese, we thought, and were advised, that it would be more in keeping with the dignity of British law that justice should be effected through the ordinary channels'. (*Evening News*, 23 October 1896, p. 3, col. 2.) As for the business of a cab being held in waiting at the corner of Weymouth Street, Cantlie later explained that it was a mistake on the part of the journalists to regard the cab which he had hired earlier for the use of his private detective as having been intended for a rescue attempt (Sun Yatsen, *Kidnapped in London*, p. 81).

query whether Sir Halliday was within he answered that he was, but that it was uncertain whether he would see me ... [Later] the butler returned with the announcement that Sir Halliday Macartney was too busy to see anyone.[191]

Other journalists reported the same experience: 'Inquirers who applied to see Sir Halliday were politely informed that he was engaged'.[192]

Getting to the Legation before or after Macartney began his day's work appears to have made little difference to many newspapers, one of which had its revenge by printing the following subsequently: 'Yesterday's rumours were appalling. It was said that Sir Halliday Macartney was being followed about by a mob, exclaiming *"Civis Romanus est"*',[193] when he stepped into the street. The rumours may or may not have been true, but their publication can only have served to facilitate their circulation and highlight the sensation.

The *Daily Telegraph*, on the other hand, appears to have been singularly skilful in handling the affair. Instead of pressing for an interview when Macartney was obviously too involved to see anybody or leaving abruptly when rebuffed, the *Daily Telegraph* simply waited for the right moment to act while observing all the while what was going on in the Legation.

Sir Halliday Macartney, immediately on his arrival at the Legation, went to the room of the Chinese Minister ... and had a long consultation with him. Shortly before noon a despatch was received from the Foreign Office ... As a result of this, a long telegram was despatched to the Chinese Government at Peking. While awaiting the reply, further communications passed between the Legation and the Foreign Office, and a consultation took place in the Minister's room. Afterwards, Sir Halliday Macartney was seen by our representative, and while he refused to make any statement as to whether the Foreign Office was insisting on the

191. *Sun*, 23 October 1896, p. 2, col. 7.
192. *Westminster Gazette*, 23 October 1896, p. 7, col. 2.
193. *Pall Mall Gazette*, 24 October 1896, p. 2, col. 2. *Pax Romana, Pax Britannica*. As mentioned, Sun Yatsen claimed to have been born in Hong Kong and therefore to be a British subject; hence the alleged exclamation '*Civis Romanus est*'. Having publicized the rumours, the newspaper then skilfully added, 'We have the highest authority for asserting that these rumours were not true. In fact, it is rather hard to get at anything particularly veracious at all'. But it is quite obvious that the damage had been done.

release of Sun Yatsen, he added a few interesting particulars to the statement he had made on the previous evening ...[194]

Later, in fact shortly after noon, the Press Association also managed to obtain access to him.[195] After these extended interviews, it is not surprising that the only observation the *Daily Chronicle* could extract from Macartney was : 'I don't think that such a point as here concerned has ever arisen before'.[196] The newspaper regretted that Macartney 'did not discuss the subject one way or the other, but simply mentioned it, and hurried away to attend to pressing business'.[197]

The pressing business to which Macartney hurried away to attend was at the Foreign Office, where he arrived at 1.30 p.m.[198] At exactly the same time, the *Westminster Gazette* reported that there was 'quite a small crowd collected on either side of the road outside the Legation; newsboys, crying, "'Orrible scenes inside the Legation", solicited custom from the passers-by ... but Sir Halliday Macartney, as our representative was informed on inquiring at the Legation, had left. Consequently, it was added, no information could be furnished to members of the Press, as while there were other officials connected with the Legation who could speak English, Sir Halliday was the only person who could make any statement on the matter'.[199] However, the *Daily News* had its own way of getting round this particular obstacle.

An English footman opened the door, and my inquiry was for Mr Tseng [Zeng Guangquan[200]], secretary to the Legation, and son of the famous

194. *Daily Telegraph*, 24 October 1896, p. 7, col. 7. Some details of this interview will be dealt with in Chapter 2.

195. *Daily Graphic*, 24 October 1896, p. 13, col. 2. It was said that Macartney had been 'pressed by a Press Association reporter' to give the interview (*Westminster Gazette*, 23 October 1896, p. 7, col. 2). Probably, Macartney succumbed to the pressure because he knew that the Press Association was a major source of information for *The Times*. Indeed, *The Times* faithfully transcribed the interview into a statement by Macartney (*The Times*, 24 October 1896, p. 6, col. 2).

196. *Daily Chronicle*, 24 October 1896, p. 5, col. 4.

197. *Daily Chronicle*, 24 October 1896, p. 5, col. 4.

198. FO 17/1718, pp. 69-76, Sanderson's record of his interview with Macartney, 23 October 1896, para. 1. The significance of this lengthy interview will be examined in Chapter 2.

199. *Westminster Gazette*, 23 October 1896, p. 7, col. 2.

200. The *Foreign Office List 1896* (p. 337) has the following entry for the Chinese Legation: 'Secretary: Kingeast-Tseng'. I am grateful to Mr Joseph Ford, CMG, OBE, formerly British chargé d'affaires in Beijing, and later director of the Research Department of the Foreign and Commonwealth Office in London,

Marquis. He and I came to be well acquainted the time Li Hungchang [Li Hongzhang] entertained his English entertainers. The footman was disposed to be abrupt.

'Mr Tseng is not here.'

'My business admits of no delay. Where is he?'

'In China.'

'Then be good enough to take my card to his representative.'

'Mr Tang?'

'Yes.'

A minute later I had passed down the spacious hall and was shown into a reception room on the left. A Chinaman, with lank, black, shining hair, left the apartment as I entered it. Mr Tang [Deng Tingkeng] was standing in the middle of the room ...[201]

There followed a fascinating interview, in which the interpreter alleged in graphic detail that Sun Yatsen had gone to the Legation of his own free will. Another paper, the *Evening News*, somehow also managed to have a lengthy conversation with the interpreter.[202] The records of both interviews will be scrutinized in Chapter 3. It suffices here to point out that his allegations, like his strenuous denials of Sun Yatsen's imprisonment in the Legation as late as the day before, only served to incense the British public even further.[203]

V The Hero

Macartney arrived at the Foreign Office at 1.30 p.m. on Friday, 23 October 1896. The permanent under-secretary of state recorded:

I asked him whether he was aware that a formal Note from Lord Salisbury had been delivered to the Chinese Legation last night ... if the

(200. *continued*)
for informing me that Kingeast was the Anglicized form of Jingyi, which in turn was the *hao* of Zeng Guangquan, who was the adopted son of Marquis Zeng Jize. For details, see Jin Liang (ed.), *Jinshi renwu zhi* (Taipei, 1955), pp. 140–1.

201. *Daily News*, 24 October 1896, p. 5, col. 4. The subsequent interview was quoted extensively by the *Echo*, 24 October 1896, p. 3, col. 6.

202. *Evening News*, 24 October 1896, p. 2, cols. 6–7.

203. The *Sun* (23 October 1896, p. 2, col. 7), for example, accused 'the Chinese officials at the Embassy' of not having 'even an elementary regard for the truth'. The Treasury solicitor also wrote, '... we have a specimen of his [the interpreter's] veracity in what occurred when Dr Manson called at the Legation on the 18 October'. (FO 17/1718, pp. 113–16, Cuffe to Home Office, 12 November 1896, para. 13.)

Minister did not comply with the demand, we should be justified in requesting his immediate recall and in withdrawing the diplomatic privilege from any British subjects on the staff of the Legation who were concerned in the matter. I added that the story was in all the newspapers, that I had been in consultation with the Under Secretary of State for the Home Department this morning, that it was felt strongly that the detention could not be allowed to continue, and that I was expecting telegraphic instructions from Lord Salisbury to send up to the Legation a demand for immediate compliance with his Note of yesterday.

Sir Halliday begged that I would at all events wait till 4 o'clock, by which time he hoped to be able to send me a Note intimating the Minister's consent to the man's release.[204]

Back to Portland Place Macartney went; then he returned to Whitehall, a little before 4 p.m.[205] 'At all events', wrote the *Daily Chronicle*, 'the next time I saw Sir Halliday Macartney he was wending his way from Whitehall to the Foreign Office. No doubt he was calling to inform Sir Thomas Sanderson that Sun Yatsen would be given up'.[206] The newspaper was indeed correct. Consequently, Sanderson added the following to his record: 'I arranged that a Queen's Home Messenger should attend at the Legation at half past four with an Inspector of the Police and one of the man's friends able to identify him, and should report his release'.[207]

'The Chinese Legation was the centre of much excitement and activity between four and five o'clock. Little groups of people were to be seen around the door and on the opposite pavement, whilst two or three enterprising photographers had their instruments directed towards the windows. It had become known that Sun Yat Yen [sic] was to be liberated, and all were eager to catch a glimpse of him. About half past four, Detective Inspector Jarvis of Scotland Yard, and an elderly gentleman from the Foreign Office, made their appearance, and were ushered into a private room'.[208]

---

204. FO 17/1718, pp. 69–76, Sanderson's record of his interview with Macartney, 23 October 1896.

205. FO 17/1718, pp. 69–76, Sanderson's record of his interview with Macartney, 23 October 1896.

206. *Daily Chronicle*, 24 October 1896, p. 5, col. 4.

207. FO 17/1718, pp. 69–76, Sanderson's record of his interview with Macartney, 23 October 1896.

208. *Echo*, 24 October 1896, p. 3, col. 5.

'After a little time Sir Halliday Macartney came out of his office, which is at the back of the Legation, and went to Inspector Jarvis and his companions. Then they all entered Sir Halliday's office, and he was given the Foreign Office letter, which he read with the remark, "Yes: very well"'.[209] At this juncture a reporter, one of many who roamed about the Legation 'in the most free and easy fashion wherever they could obtain admittance', entered the room by accident and was ignominiously expelled.[210] Immediately outside this room in the rear part of the Legation, a little knot of men had formed around Dr Cantlie, who had come to witness Sun Yatsen's release,[211] and who could hardly hide the 'pleased expression' on his face.[212] He was in constant request, regaling 'his hearers with amusing accounts of the ingenious means by which communication with the prisoner was established and his release brought about'.[213] 'A plain straight forward death', he was saying, 'hanging or poisoning, or anything like that; but to be taken back and tortured — pah!'[214]

All this time, the other reporters who were waiting in the front part of the Legation, and the crowd without that had been gathering in increasing numbers,[215] were confidently predicting that Sun Yatsen would walk through the front door into Portland Place.[216] The drama of it was, however, to be hidden; 'but then', reflected a reporter afterwards, 'half the strength of the picture lay in that'.[217]

After Chief Inspector Jarvis and Sir Halliday Macartney had agreed upon the best way to cope with the multitude of people, word was sent upstairs for Sun Yatsen, who latterly had been able to hear at least the echoes of friendly voices and consequently to hold himself up with more courage.[218]

---

209. *Daily Chronicle*, 24 October 1896, p. 5, col. 4.
210. *Westminster Gazette*, 24 October 1896, p. 5, col. 1. As it turned out, the private deliberations inside Macartney's office were related partly to the problem of getting Sun Yatsen out of the Legation without having to negotiate the enormous crowd, which was estimated as close to a thousand people (*Daily Mail*, 24 October 1896, p. 5, col. 4).
211. *Sun*, 24 October 1896, p. 3, col. 1.
212. *Globe*, 24 October 1896, p. 4, col. 4.
213. *Westminster Gazette*, 24 October 1896, p. 4, col. 1.
214. *Sun*, 24 October 1896, p. 3, col. 1.
215. *Echo*, 24 October 1896, p. 3, col. 1.
216. *Globe*, 24 October 1896, p. 4, col. 4.
217. *Daily Chronicle*, 24 October 1896, p. 5, col. 4.
218. *Daily Chronicle*, 24 October 1896, p. 5, col. 4.

A few privileged journalists happened to be at the rear part of the Legation when the release took place. 'The prisoner came down behind his attendants, gingerly enough', observed one reporter.[219] 'He came downstairs blithely enough', wrote another, 'a smile on his face, and an expression of immense relief in his dark eyes. He is a man of thirty or thirty-five, rather under what we should call average size, and very sparely built. He wore European dress — a light covert coat and a darkish suit — and while his Oriental origin was apparent enough, he might have been taken either for a Chinaman or a Japanese. He looked a man of real intelligence, and presently, when he met Dr Cantlie, he showed that he speaks English very well'.[220] 'He looked little the worse for his confinement', commented another witness, 'perhaps because he is naturally of the too-hard-student type of man. He is of small build, and his features are of a delicate caste. However, his is an extremely pleasant face, and his eyes are singularly bright'.[221] 'As a representative of the Chinese Minister, I deliver up this man, but without prejudice to any of the diplomatic rights and privileges belonging to this Legation', said Macartney.[222] Jarvis accepted him upon Cantlie's positive identification. Then the visitors left by the back door that opened into Weymouth Street. 'At about 5 o'clock last evening', recorded another reporter, 'a low-sized, young-looking Chinaman, seeming pale and rather ill, but with a jubilant expression in his bright almond eyes, stepped out of the bit of Chinese territory which is covered by the Embassy'.[223]

Directly it was known that Sun Yatsen had left the building, there was a stampede towards him.[224] Those that were in the front portion of the Legation rushed into Portland Place; and those that had been in Portland Place rushed along Weymouth Street. 'About a thousand persons were gathered and they gazed curiously at the hero of the great generation of the day'.[225] He was immediately the centre of a group of enquirers, while an

219. *Daily Mail*, 24 October 1896, p. 5, col. 4.
220. *Daily Chronicle*, 24 October 1896, p. 5, col. 4.
221. *Morning Leader*, 24 October 1896, p. 7, col. 2.
222. FO 17/1718, p. 79, Jarvis' report, 24 October 1896.
223. *Sun*, 24 October 1896, p. 3, col. 1.
224. *Globe*, 24 October 1896, p. 4, col. 4.
225. *Sun*, 24 October 1896, p. 3, col. 1.

artist pulled out his book and proceeded to make a sketch.[226]
There was some delay in getting a cab, and the crowd had a good
view of him.[227] All the newspapermen present were anxious to
talk to him, and even more they wanted him to talk to them.[228]
He was 'not disinclined to be talkative, but before he had time to
exchange many words with those around him he was ushered into
a cab',[229] and driven away.

· Through Reuters, news of the imprisonment and subsequent
release of Sun Yatsen was transmitted instantly by telegraph to
the rest of the world. In America, the *New York Times*;[230] in
Australia, the *Age*,[231] the *Brisbane Courier*,[232] and the *Sydney
Morning Herald*;[233] in Hong Kong, the *China Mail*;[234] in Shanghai, the *Wanguo gongbao* and the *Shiwubao*;[235] in Singapore, the
Straits Times and the *Lebao*;[236] in Japan, the *Kobe yushin
nippo*,[237] the *Osaka asahi shinbun*,[238] and the *Kokka gakkai
zasshi*,[239] just to name a few, all carried the sensational story.

226. *Morning*, 24 October 1896, p. 6, col. 1.
227. *Westminster Gazette*, 24 October 1896, p. 5, col. 1.
228. *Globe*, 24 October 1896, p. 4, col. 4.
229. *Morning*, 24 October 1896, p. 6, col. 1.
230. *New York Times* (New York), 23 October 1896, p. 5, col. 1.; and 24
October 1896, p. 5, cols. 1–2.
231. *Age* (Melbourne), 24 October 1896, p. 7, col. 5; and 26 October 1896, p.
5, col. 4.
232. *Brisbane Courier* (Brisbane), 24 October 1896, p. 5, col. 3; and 26
October 1896, p. 6, col. 2.
233. *Sydney Morning Herald* (Sydney), 24 October 1896, p. 9, col. 4; 26
October 1896, p. 5, col. 3; and 28 October 1896, p. 6, col. 7.
234. *China Mail* (Hong Kong), 26 October 1896, p. 3, col. 5, and p. 2, cols.
6–7; and 31 October 1896, p. 3, col. 2. I am grateful to Mr Kung Chi Keung
(Gong Zhiqiang) for sending me negatives of these columns initially; and to Mr
A.I. Diamond of the Public Records Office in Hong Kong, and Mr Malcolm
Quinn and Mr Sze King Keung (Shi Jingqiang) of the University of Hong Kong,
for helping me to acquire a microfilm copy of the *China Mail* for the months
October–December 1896, when I passed through Hong Kong in May 1984.
235. *Wanguo gongbao* (Shanghai), November 1896, Vol. 8, No. 94, p. 31b;
and *Shiwubao* (Shanghai), 5 November 1896, Vol. 10, p. 20b. I wish to thank the
academic vice-president of Zhongshan University in Guangzhou, Professor Hu
Shouwei, for kind permission to read these Chinese newspapers.
236. *Straits Times* (Singapore), 24 October 1896; and *Lebao* (Singapore), 27
October 1896. I am indebted to Dr Lee Laito (Li Litu) of the National University
of Singapore for having searched for, and sent me photocopies of, the relevant
parts of these two newspapers.
237. *Kobe yushin nippo* (Kobe), 1 November 1896.
238. *Osaka asahi shinbun* (Osaka), 1 November 1896.
239. *Kokka gakkai zasshi* (Tokyo), 15 February 1897, Vol. II, No. 120, pp.
182–93; and 14 April 1897, Vol. II, No. 122, pp. 373–87.

Then there were those newspapers designed for the overseas market, such as the *London and China Express*[240] and the *Overland Mail*,[241] which, though slower in getting to their readers, contained far more details. And of course there was *The Times*,[242] to which major institutions of the world and many individuals would have subscribed. On arrival at their destinations, these papers not only circulated among the local communities but were also liberally transcribed[243] or translated[244] by the local newspapers. In Japan, at least one newspaper digested all these reports and wrote out a long story of its own. This story, in turn, was translated into Chinese and published in Shanghai in a two-part series.[245]

Small wonder that Sun Yatsen was hailed by a London newspaper as 'the hero of the great generation of the day'.[246]

---

240. *London and China Express* (a weekly), 23 October 1896, p. 896, col. 2, to p. 896, col. 2; and 30 October 1896, p. 916, col. 1, to p. 919, col. 1.

241. *Overland Mail*, 23 October 1896, p. 19, col. 1; and 30 October 1896, p. 44, col. 2, to p. 46, col. 2.

242. *The Times*, 23 October 1896, p. 3, col. 6; 24 October 1896, p. 6, cols. 1–3, and p. 9, cols. 1–3; 26 October 1896, p. 8, col. 4; and 30 October 1896, p. 6, col. 6.

243. See, for example, *China Mail* (Hong Kong), 26 November 1896, p. 5, cols. 4–6; 27 November 1896, p. 5, col. 3; 1 December 1896, p. 5, col. 5; 2 December 1896, p. 3, cols. 5–6; and 24 December 1896, p. 3, col. 2.

244. See, for example, *Shiwubao* (Shanghai), 15 December 1896, Vol. 14, pp. 13a–14b; 25 December 1896, Vol. 15, pp. 12a–13b; 13 January 1897, Vol. 17, pp. 15a–16a; and 3 March 1897, Vol. 19, pp. 14b–15a. I am indebted to Mr Sang Bing of Zhongshan University for drawing my attention to some of these references, which I subsequently consulted with kind permission of the University authorities. Mr Chen Yongsheng and Mr He Yuefu, also of the same University, helped me copy out these items.

245. *Shiwubao* (Shanghai), 23 March 1897, Vol. 21, pp. 22b–24b; and 22 May 1897, Vol. 27, pp. 23b–25a. The Japanese paper was referred to as the *Kokka gakkai zasshi*, but no date was given; see note 239 for details.

246. *Sun*, 24 October 1896, p. 3, col. 1. The sensational story appears to have had its own way of penetrating the overseas Chinese communities. When Sun Yatsen arrived at Vancouver in July 1897, for example, the private detective who had been following him 'conducted discreet inquiries in the Chinese quarter and it was elicited that the circumstances of his arrest in London were well known' (Chinese Legation Archives, Slater to Chinese minister, 11–24 July 1897, in Luo Jialun, *Shiliao*, p. 174). An ordinary overseas Chinese might not have subscribed to a newspaper printed in the English language, but if the *Lebao* of Singapore is any guide, the community newspapers in the Chinese language also printed Reuters' telegrams. I am grateful to Dr Lee Laito for having sent me a photocopy of the relevant column in the *Lebao* of 27 October 1896. Historians have claimed, often enough, that the kidnapping in London made Sun Yatsen world-famous, but have provided little detail as to how this came about (see, for example, Shang

Zhang Taiyan, upon hearing the news of Sun Yatsen's kidnapping on account of his subversive activities against the Manchu regime, said in Shanghai, 'I am proud of him'.[247] Zhang Taiyan was later to become Sun Yatsen's right-hand man, for a time at least, in his capacity as editor of the *Minbao* in Tokyo.[248]

Slater, on the other hand, did not wish to be left out. He claimed in a London newspaper to be 'the greatest detective of the age',[249] apparently on the strength of having been hired briefly by Dr Cantlie to watch the Chinese Legation at the time when the hero was kept behind bars.[250] There is no sign that this claim was ever relayed to other parts of the world.

(246. *continued*)
Mingxuan, *Sun Zhongshan*, p. 44; and Schiffrin, *Origins*, p. 138). It is hoped that the above narrative has substantiated their claim.

247. Tang Zhijun (comp.), *Zhang Taiyan nianpu changbian* (Beijing, China Press, 1979, 2 vols.), Vol. 1, p. 39. I missed Professor Tang Zhijun by a month when I was in Tokyo in September 1983, and by one day when I was in Shanghai in May 1984. Eventually, I met him in Guangzhou during the Sun Yatsen conference in November 1984, when I was rewarded with, among other things, this reference.

248. Tang Zhijun (comp.), *Zhang Taiyan nianpu changbian*, Vol. 1, p. 223ff.

249. Slater's advertisement in *The Times*, 13 January 1897, p. 1, col. 3. See note 250.

250. Slater's extravagant claim was not repeated at any time during Sun Yatsen's stay in London. Dr Lance Eccles and I have, between us, checked every single issue of *The Times* from 1 September 1896 to 30 July 1897 (from roughly a month before to a month after Sun Yatsen's sojourn in London), since I stumbled on Slater's unusual advertisement of 13 January 1897. Slater had been mentioned in many official documents, but they were confidential. To the best of my knowledge, the only place in which he was referred to publicly was in Sun Yatsen, *Kidnapped in London*, pp. 75–6 and 83. Is it possible that this booklet was published shortly before 13 January 1897, thus inspiring Slater to claim to be the greatest detective of the age? Why Slater subsequently abandoned this claim, although he continued to advertise in *The Times*, remains an interesting question.

2 Sensation Breeds Sensation

'He came of his own accord ...'
Macartney[1]

I The Rebuke

The whole of London was on the boil. As if the sensation was not great enough, Macartney made two moves which heightened it still further. After his visitors had left, and after he had reported Sun Yatsen's release formally to the Foreign Office,[2] he went home and immediately put pen to paper. The result was a lengthy article, which appeared in *The Times* the next day, Saturday, 24 October 1896, under the pseudonym of 'A Correspondent', and entitled 'From the Chinese Point of View'.[3] This issue of *The Times* also contained, in its leading article, some very unfavourable remarks about Macartney, whereupon he lost no time in writing to the editor. His letter was printed in the next issue of *The Times*, on Monday, 26 October 1896.[4] Judging from the reaction of the *Speaker*,[5] Macartney's two pieces of work must have infuriated many. However, the daily papers appear to have declined to add any more in their editorials to what they had already expressed on 23 and 24 October 1896. But because the *Speaker* was a weekly, whose next issue was not due until 31 October 1896, this journal felt that it had not had its say on the matter and that it was, therefore, in a much better position to respond to the 'spectacle of Sir Halliday Macartney fussing and fuming in *The Times*'.[6]

'Sir Halliday Macartney is an official in the service of the Chinese Government', began the *Speaker*. 'That fact seems to

---

1. *Daily Telegraph*, 24 October 1896, p. 7, col. 7.
2. *Echo*, 24 October 1896, p. 3, col. 5. Chief Inspector Jarvis also went there to report the same (*Echo*, 24 October 1896, p.3, col. 5).
3. *The Times*, 24 October 1896, p. 6, cols. 2–3.
4. *The Times*, 26 October 1896, p. 8, col. 4. The letter was dated 24 October 1896.
5. *Speaker*, 31 October 1896, p. 463, col. 1, to p. 464, col. 1.
6. *Speaker*, 31 October 1896, p. 463, col. 1, to p. 464, col. 1.

have deprived him of any sense of humour he might otherwise have had, which, we imagine, would in no circumstances have been conspicuous. The Secretary of the Chinese Legation has struck an attitude of injured innocence in *The Times*. He is like Woods Pasha, when that undiscerning personage stands up for the Turkish Government in an English newspaper. What in a true Oriental would seem natural and characteristic, in the sham Oriental is merely ridiculous'.[7]

Harsh words indeed. What had Macartney said in *The Times* that could have led to such severe criticism?

In his article,[8] Macartney began by describing in some detail the so-called Canton plot[9] in an attempt to show that Sun Yatsen was no ordinary conspirator, and that his ultimate goal was to overthrow the Manchu dynasty, 'as the Taiping rebellion very nearly did between thirty and forty years ago'. The failure of the plot resulted in Sun Yatsen's flight from China, closely shadowed by agents of the Chinese government. On Saturday, 10 October 1896, he left his lodgings in Gray's Inn Place 'unobserved, and in the course of the morning, called at the Chinese Legation in Portland Place ... No one in the Legation had the slightest suspicion during the visit that he was the notorious Sun Wen[10] ... On Sunday, the 11 inst., Sun returned, of his own accord, to the Legation, spent the morning there, and stayed to dinner. By this time suspicion had grown into certainty, and it was decided to detain Sun pending instructions from Peking [Beijing]'. The article concluded:

---

7. *Speaker*, 31 October 1896, p. 463, col. 1, to p. 464, col. 1. In December 1895, the grand vizier of Turkey, Said Pasha, sensed that he was about to be thrown into gaol by his sovereign. He took refuge in the British Embassy at Constantinople. The irate Turkish sovereign demanded his release. Woods Pasha argued the case for the Turkish government in an English newspaper. (See *Pall Mall Gazette*, 24 October 1896, p. 3, col. 1.)

8. *The Times*, 24 October 1896, p. 6, cols. 2–3.

9. The article referred to the date of the plot as September 1894. The correct date should have been 26 October 1895 (see Schiffrin, *Origins*, p. 61).

10. Sun Yatsen was given the name (*ming*) 'Dixiang' when he was a baby, then the name 'Wen' and the *hao* 'Rixin' when he was a child. In 1886, he changed his *hao* to 'Yixian (Yatsen)'. While in Japan in 1897, he adopted the alias of 'Zhongshan'. (See *Sun Zhongshan nianpu* (Beijing, China Press, 1980), p. 2.) In Manchu government records, he was invariably referred to as Sun Wen; in mainland China today and among overseas Chinese communities he is known as Sun Zhongshan; historians in the West (and increasingly those in Taiwan as well) have continued to call him Sun Yatsen.

the Chinese view of their rights under the circumstances is that, as they used neither force nor fraud within the territory of the Queen to get this Chinese subject into their possession, they were justified in International Law in detaining him when he went of his own accord into the Legation. Had he gone, in the same way, on board a Chinese man-of-war in the Thames, there would probably be no question of the right of the commander to sail away with him. The right of foreign Legations to give shelter to fugitive political leaders of the countries to which they are accredited has long been well recognised, and our [*my italics*] Ambassador at Constantinople acted in accordance with the principle a very few months ago, when his extraterritorial privileges sheltered a Turkish statesman from his Sovereign. If inviolability of this kind can extend to a native of the country to which the Ambassador is accredited it might be thought that *a fortiori* it extends to a subject of the country which the Ambassador represents, even though, in the place of being a fallen statesman ... he is a *criminal* [*my italics*]'.[11]

Macartney's letter to the editor of *The Times*, written on Saturday, 24 October 1896, and published on Monday, 26 October 1896, complained that the paper took it for granted that Sun Yatsen's statement was correct and that his was wrong. 'I do not know why you make this assumption', he continued, 'for you undoubtedly do so when you say the case is as if the Turkish Ambassador has inveigled some of the members of the Armenian colony of London into the Embassy with a view to making them a present to His Majesty the Sultan'.[12]

The *Speaker's* reaction to Macartney's letter to *The Times* was: 'To the obvious suggestion that Sun Yatsen would never have walked into the Chinese Embassy of his own accord, had he known the real identity of his entertainers, Sir Halliday vouchsafes no reply'.[13] As for the article, the *Speaker* did not point out the contradiction between Macartney's reference to Sun Yatsen as a *criminal* and the graphic description of the latter's political offence. Perhaps the paper considered that its affirmation of Sun Yatsen's status as a political refugee was a sufficient rebuttal. But

---

11. *The Times*, 24 October 1896, p. 6, cols. 2–3. The essence of this article is no different from the interview which Macartney had given to the Press Association and which was turned into a statement by *The Times* and published on the same day as Macartney's article (see Section IV of this chapter). Fear of being misquoted might have been partly responsible for Macartney's decision to put pen to paper himself.

12. *The Times*, 26 October 1896, p. 8, col. 4.

13. *Speaker*, 31 October 1896, p. 463, col. 1.

probably it was Macartney's use of the term *our Ambassador at Constantinople*, which left little doubt as to the true identity of the author of the article, that had prompted the *Speaker* to label Macartney as a *sham Oriental*, adding, 'Sir Halliday Macartney is in the pitiable position of an Englishman who is forced by his official obligations to palliate in London what would be the ordinary course of justice at Canton'.[14]

How had Macartney put himself into this pitiable position? It might be useful here to give some brief details about Macartney's career up to this point.

II *Macartney's Background*

Macartney came from the same family branch as the famous Lord Macartney who had been the first British envoy to the Court of Beijing in 1792.[15] He was born on 24 May 1833 in Scotland. At the age of 15, he went to Liverpool as a junior clerk in a mercantile firm.[16] In 1852, he matriculated at Edinburgh University to read for a medical degree.[17] He interrupted his studies in 1855, in an impulsive burst of patriotism, to join the medical staff of the Anglo-Turkish Contingent that was to serve in the Crimean War.[18] He took the opportunity to study the Turkish language and soon qualified as an interpreter.[19] After the war he resumed his medical studies at Edinburgh, graduating in 1858.[20] He joined the 99th Regiment as assistant-surgeon and left for India in the same year, where the great Mutiny had just drawn to a close.[21]

At the end of 1859, he sailed with the regiment to China,[22] where he participated in the storming of the Taku (Dagu) forts in the summer of 1860,[23] and the subsequent march on Beijing.[24] Afterwards, the regiment was posted to Guangzhou where by

14. *Speaker*, 31 October 1896, p. 463, col. 1.
15. Boulger, *Macartney*, pp. 1 and 6–7.
16. Boulger, *Macartney*, p. 7.
17. Boulger, *Macartney*, p. 8.
18. Boulger, *Macartney*, pp. 9–12.
19. Boulger, *Macartney*, p. 20.
20. Boulger, *Macartney*, p. 21.
21. Boulger, *Macartney*, p. 23.
22. Boulger, *Macartney*, p. 23.
23. Boulger, *Macartney*, pp. 29–30.
24. Boulger, *Macartney*, pp. 31–3.

chance he witnessed a trial at which the judge tried to extract information from the defendant by torture. Losing all control over himself, he 'rushed up to the table at which the mandarin was sitting, raised the saucer of indian ink and brought it down with a crash on the table smashing it and splattering its contents over the astonished judge and his secretaries'.[25] It was also at Guangzhou that he began to learn the Chinese language,[26] and by the time his regiment was dispatched to Shanghai to engage the Taipings in 1862,[27] he was able 'to hold some intercourse with the Chinese merchants and officials'.[28] In the battlefield around Shanghai, he won himself the reputation of being far more fond of 'the fighting part of it ... than the healing'.[29]

Consequently, he was invited by the Chinese authorities, Li Hongzhang among them, to join the Chinese service. He was offered the position of military secretary to the Ever-Victorious Army.[30] Thus, in October 1862, he resigned from the British Army.[31] On 22 September 1862, the commander of the Ever-Victorious Army, Frederick Ward, died in action.[32] He was succeeded by Henry Burgevine.[33] However, Burgevine soon fell out with the Chinese authorities. At Songjiang, 'Burgevine — fearing arrest by the Chinese authorities — ordered his men to stand watch atop the city walls on the pretext that the rebels were near', writes a modern scholar. 'Soon, however, he went to Shanghai under Western protection and then to Peking to plead his case'.[34] How Burgevine's fears were sufficiently allayed for him to go to Shanghai has never been explained. In fact, the situation was far more serious than is generally understood.

---

25. Boulger, *Macartney*, p. 36. British protests resulted in the arrest of the mandarin, who was then 'put in a large wooden room attached to the wall of the Shamseen [Shamian] Garden, and in such a position that the people could see through the open window this high mandarin, guarded by a British sentry, in his degradation'. (Boulger, *Macartney*, p. 37.)

26. Boulger, *Macartney*, p. 57.

27. Boulger, *Macartney*, pp. 49–53.

28. Boulger, *Macartney*, p. 57.

29. Boulger, *Macartney*, p. 49.

30. Boulger, *Macartney*, p. 58. See, also, Richard J. Smith, *Mercenaries and Mandarins: The Ever-Victorious Army in Nineteenth Century China* (New York, KTO Press, 1978) (hereafter cited as *Ever-Victorious Army*).

31. Boulger, *Macartney*, p. 60.

32. Smith, *Ever-Victorious Army*, p. 79.

33. Smith, *Ever-Victorious Army*, pp. 108–10.

34. Smith, *Ever-Victorious Army*, p. 113.

Burgevine had collected a fleet of some thirty boats and was about to go over to the Taipings with his army. Li Hongzhang was greatly worried and sent Macartney to reason with Burgevine. Macartney went alone, and skilfully changed the mind of the would-be turncoat.[35] It was probably on the basis of this achievement that Li Hongzhang wanted to put Macartney in command of the Army.[36] But the British general, Charles Staveley, preferred Charles Gordon. Staveley prevailed.[37]

Soon Gordon quarrelled bitterly with the commander of a Chinese army in the area. The ill-feeling ran so high that the two armies lined up ready to do battle. Again, Li Hongzhang dispatched Macartney to the scene. After several days of difficult negotiations, the differences were patched up.[38] Thus, Macartney increasingly gained the confidence of Li Hongzhang, and gradually became his right-hand man, helping him control the supply and purchase of arms and ammunition for the corps and 'seeing that he was not swindled'.[39] He also suggested to him, and took full responsibility for, the establishment and administration of an arsenal at Songjiang,[40] which was later moved to Suzhou,[41] and finally to Nanjing.[42] It was at Suzhou that he married a Chinese lady. His ambition then was to make China his home and eventually to acquire 'the position and influence that Verbiest, Schaal, and other Catholic missionaries had possessed'.[43]

However, his life changed course again in 1875, when, on 5 January, 'two 68-pounder cast iron shell guns which had been made at the Nanking [Nanjing] Arsenal and were mounted in the North and South Forts at Taku [Dagu] burst simultaneously,

---

35. Beijing Palace Museum Records, Waiwubu 871, Macartney to Zhang Deyi, *circa* January 1905. Zhang Deyi was the Chinese minister in London. See notes 36–8.

36. Boulger, *Macartney*, p. 67. Boulger did not explain the reasons for Li Hongzhang's intention to appoint Macartney as commander.

37. Boulger, *Macartney*, p. 67.

38. Beijing Palace Museum Records, Waiwubu 871, Macartney to Zhang Deyi, *circa* January 1905. Although the document was addressed to the Chinese minister in London, it was intended for scrutiny by the authorities in Beijing, Li Hongzhang among them. Thus, it is unlikely that Macartney would have exaggerated his achievements.

39. Boulger, *Macartney*, p. 75.

40. Boulger, *Macartney*, pp. 78–9.

41. Boulger, *Macartney*, p. 123.

42. Boulger, *Macartney*, p. 148.

43. Boulger, *Macartney*, p. 140.

killing five men and seriously wounding thirteen others'.[44] Macartney admitted his responsibility, but refused to 'petition the Throne for punishment' in the orthodox Chinese fashion as demanded by Li Hongzhang, preferring to 'put it in the form of a despatch'.[45] He was dismissed.[46] But before the end of the year, he was appointed English secretary and interpreter to the first permanent Chinese Mission to London.[47] On 1 December 1876, the steamer with Macartney, his family, and the rest of the Mission on board left Shanghai for Europe,[48] reaching Southampton and then London on 21 January 1877.[49] The minister was Guo Songtao.[50]

The Mission had barely settled down in London, at 49, Portland Place, when an incident of some significance occurred. A Chinese servant of the Legation was window-shopping in Oxford Street when his pigtail was pulled by a mischievous boy. A brawl ensued. Guo Songtao 'ordered the immediate decapitation of the delinquent [the servant, not the boy] in the back kitchen'[51] for having undermined the reputation of his Mission. With great difficulty, Macartney managed to convince Guo Songtao that such a proceeding was not covered by diplomatic privileges and, if anything, would only serve to 'put a speedy end to the existence of the Chinese Legation itself'.[52] Consequently, Guo Songtao ordered that the culprit be shipped back to China to be executed there, 'but during the voyage Macartney succeeded in making milder counsels prevail and a free pardon was conveyed by cable'.[53]

44. Li Hongzhang to Macartney, 7 July 1875, in Boulger, *Macartney*, p. 239.

45. An entry in Macartney's diary, 26 May 1875, in Boulger, *Macartney*, p. 235.

46. Boulger, *Macartney*, p. 235. His successor was his future superior in London, the Chinese minister Gong Zhaoyuan. See Li Enhan, 'Qingmo Jinling jiqiju de chuangjian yu fazhan', p. 296. I am grateful to Professor Li Enhan for sending me a photocopy of his article, which gives a good history of the Nanjing Arsenal.

47. Boulger, *Macartney*, pp. 244-5.

48. Boulger, *Macartney*, pp. 266-7.

49. Boulger, *Macartney*, p. 282; and Guo Songtao, *Riji*, Vol. 3, p. 87. See note 50.

50. For a chronology of his life, see Guo Tingyi, *Guo Songtao*.

51. Boulger, *Macartney*, pp. ix-x.

52. Boulger, *Macartney*, p. 286.

53. Boulger, *Macartney*, p. x. This is corroborated by Guo Tingyi, *Guo Songtao*, Vol. 2, p. 694, which indicates that the date of the incident was 1

On 30 July 1880, Macartney arrived at St Petersburg in the company of Marquis Zeng Jize in a difficult but ultimately successful attempt to regain the territories which Russia had occupied in north-west China.[54] One important result of this episode for him was that he 'got into closer touch with the [British] Foreign Office'[55] which always took an active interest in what the Russians did. This connection proved particularly valuable during the negotiations which paralleled the Sino-French War of 1884. Lord Granville was anxious for a reconciliation, 'and Macartney approached him with a cautious suggestion' about a possible way out of the debacle.[56] Lord Granville agreed to mediate.[57] Meanwhile, Macartney carried on informal discussions with, oddly enough, a correspondent of a leading newspaper in Paris.[58] Private and official negotiations ended in peace in March 1885.[59] He had 'devoted himself assiduously to improving his knowledge of French' since he embarked on a diplomatic career.[60] This did him great service not only in his negotiations in Paris, but also in a private capacity, because it was in the French capital that he met Mademoiselle Jeanne du Sautoy, whom he married on 12 August 1884,[61] his Chinese wife having died in 1878.[62] She was to be 'a graceful and influential partner in [his] official work as well as the life and soul of his domestic circle'.[63] Soon, she was to bear him

---

(53. *continued*)
November 1877. Guo Songtao's diary (*Riji*, Vol. 3, pp. 324–6), however, makes no reference to the incident. Given that his avowed aim of writing these diaries was to keep the Court of Beijing informed of Western affairs of state (see Guo Tingyi, *Guo Songtao*, Vol. 2, p. 666), it is not surprising that the punishment of a servant was not considered worthy of an entry.

54. Boulger, *Macartney*, pp. 342–56. See, also, I. C. Y. Hsu, *The Ili Crisis*; and Li Enhan, *Zeng Jize de waijiao* (Taipei, 1966).

55. Boulger, *Macartney*, p. 361.

56. Boulger, *Macartney*, p. 381. Lord Granville was the British foreign secretary.

57. Boulger, *Macartney*, p. 382.

58. Boulger, *Macartney*, pp. 371–87. The name of the newspaper was not disclosed.

59. Boulger, *Macartney*, pp. 387 and 393.

60. Boulger, *Macartney*, p. 20.

61. Boulger, *Macartney*, p. 394.

62. She had borne him four children, the eldest of whom, George Macartney, was later to become British consul-general in Chinese Turkestan (Boulger, *Macartney*, pp. 141–4). His second wife also bore him four children. See notes 63 and 64.

63. Boulger, *Macartney*, p. 394.

four children in rapid succession.[64] On 10 August 1885, he was knighted.[65]

Thus in October 1896 and at the age of 63, Sir Halliday had had a successful career. He had a happy and young family, and he was established in British society. Would he lightly risk offending the British Foreign Office, to which he owed his knighthood and on which he was so heavily dependent for the smooth performance of his duties? Would he submit his young family to the harsh public gaze which was bound to accompany a scandal as great as the kidnapping of Sun Yatsen in the middle of London? Would he want to negate all the achievements of his life by incurring the general condemnation which the kidnapping would inevitably arouse? The arguments against getting himself involved in such a saga were so strong that it is inconceivable that Macartney should have had anything to do with it. Yet he had. Therefore, it is of some significance to find out the circumstances and the extent of his involvement in this extraordinary affair.

III The Detention

As mentioned, Sun Yatsen arrived at Liverpool from New York on 30 September 1896. No sooner had he landed than he was shadowed by a private detective.[66] Who, among the Chinese Legation staff, hired the detective?

For this, we need to go back to 18 July 1896, when the Chinese minister in Washington, Yang Ru, wrote to his counterpart in London, enclosing a description of Sun Yatsen's appearance and transmitting Beijing's command that extradition from England should be explored.[67] The minister in London, Gong Zhaoyuan, replied on 8 August 1896 that extradition would be attempted should Sun Yatsen set foot in England; otherwise he would be

---

64. Boulger, *Macartney*, pp. 440–1.

65. Boulger, *Macartney*, p. 394. He was promoted to Knight Commander in the Order of St Michael and St George, having been granted a Companionship of that Order in 1881 by the Queen on the recommendation of Lord Granville (Boulger, *Macartney*, p. 361).

66. Slater to Macartney, 6 October 1896, in Luo Jialun, *Shiliao*, p. 114.

67. Chinese Legation Archives, Yang Ru to Gong Zhaoyuan, 18 July 1896, in Wang Chonghui, 'Zongli Lundun mengnan shiliao', in *Zhonghua minguo kaiguo wushinian wenxian: Xing Zhong Hui, xia* (Taipei, 1964, 2 vols.), p. 188 (hereafter cited as 'Shiliao').

placed under close surveillance.[68] On 25 September 1896 Yang Ru cabled London with the accurate intelligence that Sun Yatsen had left New York for Liverpool on board the SS *Majestic* of the White Star Line on Wednesday, 23 September 1896.[69] The French interpreter of the Legation, Wu Zonglian, recalled that the minister immediately sent Macartney to the Foreign Office.[70] His recollection is corroborated by the Foreign Office records.[71]

The response of the Foreign Office to extradition being negative,[72] 'the Minister's nephew, Gong Xinzhan', continued the French interpreter, 'hired a private detective to lie in wait in Liverpool'.[73] Luo Jialun and Harold Schiffrin, on the other hand, are inclined to believe that it was Macartney who had employed the detective, on the grounds that the detective's reports were addressed to Macartney.[74] A primary source that has become available recently confirms that Macartney was the man responsible.[75] But there is nothing illegal about the hiring of detectives. It is odd, though, that the French interpreter should have asserted that it was the minister's nephew, and not Macartney, who had hired the detective — a point which will be dealt with in Chapter 3.

Three days after Sun Yatsen's arrival in London, on Saturday, 3 October 1896, Macartney received a telegram from Slater the detective, which read: 'Party removed from Haxell's Hotel to 8, Gray's Inn Place, Holborn'.[76] Thereupon, Macartney replied, 'Thanks for telegram. Has the Party seen any of his countrymen?

---

68. Chinese Legation Archives, Gong Zhaoyuan to Yang Ru, 8 August 1896, in Wang Chonghui, 'Shiliao', pp. 190–1.

69. Chinese Legation Archives, Yang Ru to Gong Zhaoyuan [cypher], 23 September 1896, in Luo Jialun, *Shiliao*, pp. 16–17.

70. Wu Zonglian, *Biji, juan* 2, p. 39b. This particular section of the memoirs was written in 1899 (see p. 40b). I am grateful to Mr Wu Deduo of the Shanghai Academy of Social Sciences for having allowed me to photocopy his own rare and fragile copy of the memoirs.

71. The event was recorded subsequently in FO 17/1718, pp. 54–8, Sanderson's record of an interview with Macartney, 22 October 1896.

72. The reason for the refusal of extradition was that no such treaty existed between Great Britain and China.

73. Wu Zonglian, *Biji, juan* 2, pp. 39b–40a. The translation is mine.

74. Luo Jialun, *Shiliao*, p. 117. Schiffrin, *Origins*, p. 105, n. 25.

75. Beijing Palace Museum Records, Waiwubu 870, Legation financial report, London, 22 April 1897.

76. Chinese Legation Archives, Slater to Macartney (telegram), 3 October 1896, in Luo Jialun, *Shiliao*, p. 112.

Would it be possible to get a Kodack [*sic*] of him?'[77] Again, these instructions can hardly be described as anything out of the ordinary. The question of the photograph, however, does highlight one factor: the minister in Washington, while enclosing a description of Sun Yatsen's appearance, had not enclosed a copy of Sun Yatsen's photograph in his correspondence with the minister in London.

Then, in his article in *The Times*[78] and in his letter to the editor,[79] Macartney claimed that Sun Yatsen had visited the Legation on Saturday, 10 October 1896. This is a controversial point which will be scrutinized in Chapter 3. Even if the claim were true — and there is no conclusive evidence to suggest that it was — it appears that Sun Yatsen had come and gone freely, and there is no question of misconduct on the part of the English secretary, at least up to this point. The French interpreter, Wu Zonglian, went further in his memoirs and asserted that the visitor made an appointment to return the next day. Thereupon, the already suspicious English interpreter, Deng Tingkeng, reported the matter to the minister's nephew; the nephew told the minister; and the minister consulted his two secretaries, Macartney and Wang Xigeng, both of whom agreed that the visitor could be arrested should he pay another visit to the Legation.[80] This is a serious allegation which warrants some consideration. The minister's action may have been related to, but not entirely dependent on, the claim that Sun Yatsen had visited the Legation earlier, because information about the fugitive's movements could have been obtained in other ways.[81] If the minister did consult Macartney on this day, the crucial question is: did Macartney respond in the manner asserted by the French interpreter?

The French interpreter's memoirs do not offer any assistance in answering this question. They simply go on to say that Sun

77. Chinese Legation Archives, Macartney to Slater (telegram), 3 October 1896, in Luo Jialun, *Shiliao*, p. 112.

78. *The Times*, 24 October 1896, p. 6, cols. 2–3.

79. *The Times*, 26 October 1896, p. 8, col. 4.

80. Wu Zonglian, *Biji*, *juan* 2, p. 40a. This source gives the name of the Chinese secretary as Wang Pengjiu, which is repeated in nearly all the secondary sources. In fact, the man was known officially as Wang Xigeng (Beijing Palace Museum Records, Waiwubu 870, Legation financial report, London, 22 April 1897).

81. For a detailed analysis of this aspect, see Chapter 3.

Yatsen returned the next day as had been expected (as a result of the alleged previous visit to the Legation), that he was served a meal, was given a guided tour of the first floor of the Legation building, then spent quite some time chatting away in Li Shengzhong's room on the second floor, at which point Macartney arrived at the Legation and ushered Sun Yatsen to a room on the third floor; the room had been cleared beforehand and Sun Yatsen was subsequently locked inside.[82] On the surface, this narrative is a logical development of what has been described in the memoir of the previous day: a room had been cleared, Sun Yatsen returned, and Macartney arrived to lock him up. But why did the Legation staff have to wait for Macartney to come and order the turning of the key?[83]

In fact, the Legation staff did not begin looking for a room to detain Sun Yatsen until 11 a.m. on Sunday, 11 October 1896.[84] If everything had been decided on Saturday, 10 October 1896, as the author of the memoirs would have liked his readers to believe, such a step would probably have been taken on the same day so as to ensure that everything was fully prepared; and in any case not leaving things as late as 11 a.m. on the following day. In addition, Macartney did not go to the Legation on that Sunday as a matter of course, as the memoirs indicate. He was fetched from his home, on this day of rest, at 10 a.m.[85]

All this suggests that the Legation made a hasty decision to act on the morning of Sunday, 11 October 1896. It seems that the Legation had found out only the day before that Sun Yatsen intended to go to France fairly shortly, which appears to have prompted this decision.[86]

Macartney was fetched from his home at 10 a.m., and the

----

82. Wu Zonglian, *Biji*, *juan* 2, p. 40a. Li Shengzhong was an attaché in the Legation (Beijing Palace Museum Records, Waiwubu 870, Legation financial report, London, 22 April 1897).

83. FO 17/1718, pp. 116–19, Cole's statement at the Treasury, 2 November 1896, para. 6.

84. FO 17/1718, pp. 116–19, Cole's statement at the Treasury, 2 November 1896, para. 5. Cole may be described as a disinterested party. With good reason, the Treasury solicitor commented, 'I believe Cole. He impressed me most favourably, and, indeed, it is difficult to see that he can have any object in saying anything that is untrue'. (FO 17/1718, pp. 113–16, Cuffe to Home Office, 12 November 1896, para. 19.)

85. FO 17/1718, pp. 116–19, Cole's statement at the Treasury, 2 November 1896, para. 5.

86. See Chapter 3, Section II.

search for a room to detain Sun Yatsen did not begin until 11
a.m. What happened during this hour?[87]

With this, we return to the alleged consultation between the
minister and his two secretaries on Saturday, 10 October 1896. If
such a meeting had taken place at all,[88] it is inconceivable that, given
his background, Macartney would have agreed to the *arrest* of Sun
Yatsen as asserted in the memoirs. Inveigling the fugitive into the
Legation, and smuggling him out of the country to be dealt with in
China, would both have been in breach of British criminal law.
Detaining him in the Legation *might* have been argued in terms
of international law under the guise of extraterritoriality against
interference by the British police, but on this point the Legation
was already on very shaky ground. As events were to prove, such
detention would not have been tolerated for a moment by the
British government once news leaked out. In any case, the detention could not go on for ever, even if the secret were successfully
guarded. One option was secret execution in the back kitchen, a
move against which Macartney had remonstrated most vehement-
ly twenty years before, on the grounds that such an action would
put a speedy end to the Legation itself. The alternative was to
smuggle the fugitive out of England, in direct contravention of
British criminal law. Whichever way he looked at it,[89] Macartney
could see that the arrest of Sun Yatsen might very well turn out
to be 'a transaction manifestly doomed to failure, and the success
of which would have been ruinous to all engaged in it'.[90] Thus, if
there had been a conference between the minister and his two
secretaries on Saturday, 10 October 1896, and if the question of
arresting Sun Yatsen had been put to Macartney, it is probable

---

87. Macartney lived at 3, Harley Place. As explained in Chapter 1, the Place
no longer exists. But it is important to find out its exact location, so as to estimate
the amount of time it would have taken the butler of the Legation, who was 'sent
specially to find him about 10 o'clock' (FO 17/1718, pp. 116–19, Cole's statement
at the Treasury, 2 November 1896, para. 2), to return with his man. Thanks to the
help of the authorities of the Greater London Record Office and a map printed in
1864 (Map 143 J.St.M. 1864), I have been able to pinpoint the site and thereby
cover the distance between the Legation and Macartney's residence. I have come
to the conclusion that the short distance and the urgency of the matter would have
meant that Macartney was inside the Legation within a few minutes.

88. The indications are that a meeting probably did take place, but not in the
manner described in the memoirs. See later in this chapter and also Chapter 3.

89. For some details about Macartney's knowledge of the law, see the next
section.

90. *The Times*, 24 October 1896, p. 9, cols. 2–3.

that the English secretary would have opposed the idea in the strongest language possible.

If such a meeting did not take place on Saturday, 10 October 1896,[91] it is quite possible that it did on Sunday, 11 October 1896, between 10 a.m. and 11 a.m., a meeting which the French interpreter omitted in his memoirs. The duration of the consultation is an indication of the tenacity with which Macartney argued his case. He failed. Furthermore, he agreed to the arrest of Sun Yatsen. What happened?

Macartney lost where he had prevailed twenty years before. Had his position within the Legation weakened during that time? On the contrary, his influence had increased greatly, especially during the previous ten years. Indeed, it is not an exaggeration to say that Macartney was at the climax of his power at the Legation in 1896. As his biographer put it, the minister and his two immediate predecessors neither knew much English nor were they 'remarkable for any exceptional diplomatic capacity, so that all the work and all the responsibility fell upon Sir Halliday Macartney'.[92] If the words of a biographer have to be taken with a pinch of salt when it comes to praising his hero,[93] then what about those of the interpreter, Deng Tingkeng: 'The Minister is only a figure. Macartney knows everything'?[94] What about the views of the ministers concerned? Gong Zhaoyuan's immediate predecessor, Xue Fucheng,[95] for example, sent a secret memorial to the throne upon the expiry of his term of office in London in 1894. In it, he listed all the major diplomatic incidents in the previous twenty years or so which involved negotiations on the

---

91. As foreshadowed, such a meeting probably did take place, but not in the manner described in the memoirs. See later in this chapter and also Chapter 3.

92. Boulger, *Macartney*, p. 471.

93. As mentioned, Boulger alleged that Gong Zhaoyuan did not know English (Boulger, *Macartney*, p. 471). According to the British minister in Beijing who met Gong Zhaoyuan before the latter went to London to take up his position, 'He understands English fairly well, but he is unwilling to speak it'. (FO 17/1158, O'Conor to Foreign Office, Dispatch 294, 31 December 1893.) However, Boulger's allegation may have been caused by a lack of intimate knowledge of the minister rather than a deliberate attempt to exaggerate the importance of his hero.

94. FO 17/1718, pp. 119–20, Sun Yatsen's statement at the Treasury, 4 November 1896, para. 13.

95. The first six Chinese ministers in London were, successively, Guo Songtao, Zeng Jize, Liu Ruifen, Xue Fucheng, Gong Zhaoyuan, and Luo Fenglu. See Qian Shifu, *Qingji xinshe zhiguan nianbiao* (Beijing, China Press, 1977), pp. 16–23, for details.

part of the minister in London, detailing in each case the almost indispensable service rendered by Macartney. He concluded by saying that Macartney was loyal, hard-working, quick to grasp the real issues in complicated situations, and was therefore of immense value to China's diplomatic service.[96]

Gong Zhaoyuan must have shared this view wholeheartedly even before he took up his appointment in London, as may be glimpsed from the following facts. Macartney's contract was renewable each time there was a change of ministers.[97] When Gong Zhaoyuan received his commission, he quickly declared that he wished to keep Macartney.[98] The decision meant a fair amount of financial loss to him personally, and must have been arrived at with some difficulty. The monthly salary of a minister was fixed according to the rank he had reached in the Chinese civil service at the time of his appointment. The first minister, Guo Songtao, had been governor of the province of Guangdong[99] and therefore his monthly salary was fixed at 1,200 taels of silver.[100] Gong Zhaoyuan was one rank lower, having been provincial treasurer of Sichuan; and his was originally fixed at 1,000 taels.[101] A recent increase took it up to 1,080 taels.[102] Macartney's monthly salary, that of a second secretary, had been fixed at 400 taels.[103] However, he had asked to be paid the equivalent in English currency, £100 sterling; and his request had been granted.[104] The gradual depreciation of the Chinese currency, greatly aggravated by the Sino-Japanese War of 1894-5, meant that more Chinese taels had to be found to pay Macartney's monthly salary of £100 sterling. In 1895, for example, £100 was worth more than 666

96. Xue Fucheng to Emperor, 26 April 1894, in Xue Fucheng, *Yongan quanji xubian* (Shanghai, 1897), *juan* 2, pp. 16a-b.

97. Boulger, *Macartney*, p. 473.

98. FO 17/1158, O'Conor to Foreign Office, Dispatch 294, 31 December 1893.

99. Guo Tingyi, *Guo Songtao*, Vol. 1, pp. 265 and 408. His proper title was 'Acting Governor', but he acted in that capacity for almost three years.

100. Guo Tingyi, *Guo Songtao*, Vol. 2, p. 536.

101. Beijing Palace Museum Records, Waiwubu 870, Legation financial report, London, 30 May 1896.

102. Beijing Palace Museum Records, Waiwubu 870, Legation financial report, London, 30 May 1896.

103. Beijing Palace Museum Records, Waiwubu 870, Legation financial report, London, *circa* March 1887.

104. Beijing Palace Museum Records, Waiwubu 870, Legation financial report, London, 30 May 1896.

taels. Beijing had refused to foot the extra bill and had decreed that any minister who wished to keep Macartney had to do so by meeting the additional expenses out of his own salary. Gong Zhaoyuan knew this beforehand, but still wanted Macartney to stay on in the Legation, thus effectively reducing his own monthly salary in 1895 to about 814 taels.[105] If pay is any indication of the importance of office, Table 1 shows where Macartney stood in the Legation in 1895.

Table 1 Selected Payroll in the Chinese Legation, London, 26 January 1895 to 21 January 1896[106]

Name	Position	Annual Pay (taels)
Gong Zhaoyuan	Minister	1,080
Macartney	Second secretary	666
Song Yuren	Second secretary	360
Zong Guanquan	Third secretary	270
Wu Zonglian	French interpreter	180
Geng Xinzhan	Attaché	160
Zhu Shouci	Attaché	140
Pan Chenglie	Attaché	140
Li Shengzhong	Attaché	120
Deng Tingkeng	Student interpreter	60
Xie Bangqing	Guard	40

The loss of 266 taels of silver might not have meant a great deal to, say, the first minister, who had a reputation for not caring much about private financial gain.[107] But Gong Zhaoyuan appears to have had very different priorities. As mentioned, he was the provincial treasurer of Sichuan when he was appointed minister to London. When the announcement was made, an Australian who was in Sichuan at the time observed that Gong

---

105. Beijing Palace Museum Records, Waiwubu 870, Legation financial report, London, 30 May 1896.

106. Beijing Palace Museum Records, Waiwubu 870, Legation financial report, London, 30 May 1896.

107. Guo Tingyi, *Guo Songtao*, Vol. 1, p. 260, and Vol. 2, pp. 555–6, the latter pages quoting the *North China Herald*, 16 November 1876, p. 481.

Zhaoyuan's chagrin was intense, because the new posting meant the vacation of 'the most coveted post in the empire, a post where the opportunities of personal enrichment are simply illimitable', while the overseas position carried with it only a 'fixed salary'.[108] A Chinese commentator also wrote that Gong Zhaoyuan, having received many bribes himself, had planned to bribe his way into a governorship. However, the eunuch to whom the bribe had been promised waited in vain for the present to arrive, and in his annoyance recommended to the Empress Dowager that Gong Zhaoyuan be posted to London.[109]

In view of these reports, it is fair to say that however greedy Gong Zhaoyuan may have been, he was at least shrewd enough to recognize the importance of Macartney's service and hence decided to renew Macartney's contract even at the price of foregoing almost a third of his already greatly reduced income. The logic was plain: if anything should go seriously wrong during his incumbency in London, his entire career could be ruined. He had worked with Macartney before, when both were under Li Hongzhang in the 1860s and 1870s,[110] and regarded him as an 'old and personal friend for whom he had much esteem'.[111] He would also have been briefed about Macartney's performance in London for the previous twenty years or so, the honorific titles Beijing had bestowed on him,[112] and the fact that successive ministers had continued to employ him partly at their own expense. Thus, it is all the more remarkable that in the case of Sun Yatsen's arrest, Gong Zhaoyuan appears to have rejected the advice of the man on whom he had relied to steer him safely through his three years

108. G.E. Morrison, *An Australian in China* (London, H. Cox, 1902), p. 73.

109. *Zhongguo jinshi mingren xiaoshi* (1927), p. 102. The eunuch involved was alleged to have been the influential Li Lianying.

110. It was said that Gong Zhaoyuan was related to Li Hongzhang by marriage (*Zhongguo jinshi mingren xiaoshi*, p. 102). Macartney's career under Li Hongzhang has been noted earlier in this chapter. It has also been mentioned that Gong Zhaoyuan took over control of the Nanjing Arsenal after Macartney had been dismissed by Li Hongzhang in 1875. Indeed, Macartney's initial appointment to the Mission to London late in 1875 was officially announced through Gong Zhaoyuan in his capacity as the new director of the Nanjing Arsenal (Guo Tingyi, *Guo Songtao*, Vol. 2, pp. 556-7).

111. FO 17/1158, O'Conor to Foreign Office, Dispatch 294, 31 December 1893.

112. These included the so-called button of a second-class official in a hierarchy of nine and a precious star (*baoxing*). In addition, he was rewarded with the privilege of handing down these special honours to his descendants for three

of office in London. He must have had very strong reasons for doing so.

One such reason may have been the irresistible temptation to try to advance his career by capturing one of the men most wanted by his government. The goal is consistent with that of his decision to employ Macartney to begin with: self-preservation, or better still, advancement. By October 1896, he was rapidly coming to the end of his commission[113] and had only an undistinguished record, to say the least, to show his master on his return. His time in London had been bedevilled by ill-health. One of the most outstanding features of his financial reports, when compared with those of his predecessors, was his medical bills, which had to be paid by his government: £298. 10s. 6d. in 1895, and £570. 10s. 8d. in 1896, in stark contrast to the £14. 10s. 0d. of 1886.[114] Probably because of his ill-health, and inability or unwillingness to face the British public, he appears to have done absolutely nothing to promote the cause of his country during the Sino-Japanese War of 1894–5. His mentor, Li Hongzhang, was publicly disgraced because of China's defeat. His younger brother, Gong Zhaoyu, who had been charged with the defence of Port Arthur, fled before the Japanese on 21 November 1894.[115] Obviously he was considerably distressed by the news of his brother's fate as printed in *The Times*.[116] He must also have worried greatly about his own future position. The arrival of Sun Yatsen in London in 1896 was, therefore, a godsend to him. He saw in the capture of the fugitive prospects for improving his fortunes; or his last chance to make his mark in history, should

(112. *continued*)
generations. See Beijing Palace Museum Records, Waiwubu 536, Gong Zhaoyuan to Emperor, *circa* July 1897.

113. His duties officially ended on 22 April 1897. See Beijing Palace Museum Records, Waiwubu 870, Legation financial report, London, 22 April 1897.

114. Beijing Palace Museum Records, Waiwubu 870, Legation financial reports, London, 30 May 1896, 3 April 1897, and *circa* March 1887 respectively.

115. Li Hongzhang to Emperor, 27 November 1894, in Li Hongzhang, *Li Wenzhong gong wenshu: zougao, juan* 79, p. 36.

116. *The Times*, 19 December 1894, p. 5, col. 1, and 29 December 1894, p. 5, col. 6. Western reports gave Gong Zhaoyu's name as Kung Chou Shuan. He was arrested and sent to Beijing for trial. On 18 February 1895, execution was considered (Veritable Records of the Qing period, Guangxu 20th year, *juan* 354, p. 12a). However, there are no records of the sentence actually being imposed and the likelihood is that sufficient money subsequently changed hands for his life to have been spared.

his health continue to worsen. Indeed, he died within two months of his return to China in 1897.[117] Even if Macartney had warned him against the risks involved, therefore, he might have been sufficiently excited about the prospects of reward to have dismissed the warnings or regarded the risks as worth taking. Only a drastic deterioration in his health could have prevented him from taking any action; and it very nearly did. On 27 August 1896, barely a month before Sun Yatsen's arrival in London, he suffered a stroke. 'The paralysis is evident in the muscles of the right cheek, the right side of the tongue, and the right arm', reported the doctor. 'His mind seems to be quite clear and he gets impatient at not being able to make himself understood'.[118] His condition improved markedly the next day, so much so that the doctor said he was no longer as apprehensive as he had been the day before of the minister sinking rapidly. 'On the contrary the probability is that there may be some slight improvement in the paralytic symptoms'.[119] Where would his thoughts have been wandering when he lay in bed with his mind quite clear? What did he have to show his government when he went home? Was he going to report that, say, in the year 1896, up to the time of his stroke, he had signed four dispatches to the British Foreign Office?[120] What about his pathetic incompetence in defending his country against the 'judaic demand'[121] by the Indo-China Steam Navigation Company for compensation for the sinking by the Japanese of the ship *Kowshing* which had been chartered by the Chinese government to convey troops to Korea?[122] The dispute was still unsettled when the stroke came. In the dire financial straits of the Court at Beijing, would he be made a scapegoat? What about the enormous medical expenses which he was incurring and which he would have to ask his government to pay?

---

117. Wu Zonglian, *Biji, juan* 2, Preface.
118. FO 17/1286, pp. 232–3, Medical report, 28 August 1896.
119. FO 17/1286, pp. 232–3, Medical report, 28 August 1896.
120. FO 17/1286, pp. 202–3, 210–12, 224 and 226, Gong Zhaoyuan to Salisbury, 18 March 1896, 12 June 1896, 16 July 1896, and 6 August 1896.
121. FO 17/1286, p. 213, Salisbury's minute on an FO memorandum on the case of the *Kowshing* [*Gaosheng*], 27 April 1896. See note 122.
122. FO 17/1286, pp. 213–20, FO memorandum on the case of the *Kowshing*, 17 April 1896. Properly romanized nowadays, the name of the ship would be spelt *Gaosheng*.

Then came a cypher from Washington on 25 September 1896, announcing Sun Yatsen's imminent arrival in England.[123] Here at last, it seemed, was his big chance to write a page of Chinese history. His French interpreter, Wu Zonglian, captured the spirit of subsequent developments when he entitled his relevant memoir thus: 'An Account of How Minister Gong Zhaoyuan Seized the Wanted Cantonese Sun Wen by Stratagem and How He Subsequently Released Him'.[124]

Another reason why Gong Zhaoyuan might have decided to reject Macartney's wise counsel could have been his refusal to believe that any government would not behave in the same way as the Chinese government, when dealing with political offenders. Political asylum as an esteemed principle was unheard of in traditional China; and harbouring a political refugee was considered an unfriendly act towards the offender's country of origin. It sounds incredible that the minister should appear to have been so ignorant of Western values and principles. But his attitudes, as reflected in Macartney's interview at the Foreign Office on 22 October 1896, leave little doubt that this was so. It will be recalled that during the interview, despite great pressure being exerted on him by the permanent under-secretary of state, Sir Thomas Sanderson, to release Sun Yatsen immediately, Macartney said that the minister would have to telegraph for instructions from Beijing. Under further pressure, Macartney's response was confined to saying that 'he was sure the Minister would telegraph at once, that evening'. Even when the Honourable Francis Bertie, assistant under-secretary of state, who was also present at the interview, threatened to take 'very serious steps', Macartney was still unable to offer anything better than the statement 'that he would inform the Chinese Minister at once of what had passed, and that he was sure he would be anxious to give a prompt reply to Lord Salisbury's communication'.[125] Sanderson got the mes-

123. Chinese Legation Archives, Yang Ru to Gong Zhaoyuan (cypher), 25 September 1896 (received), in Wang Chonghui, 'Shiliao', p. 191.

124. Wu Zonglian, *Biji, juan* 2, p. 39b.

125. FO 17/1718, pp. 54–61, Sanderson's record of his interview with Macartney, 22 October 1896. When Gong Zhaoyuan was appointed minister to London, the British minister in Beijing reported, 'I understand he was very popular with foreigners at the various ports where he held the position of *taotai*, and he has the reputation of being a *bon vivant*'. (FO 17/1158, O'Conor to Foreign Office,

sage. Swiftly he dispatched the diplomatic Note, already signed by Salisbury. This Note was delivered at the Chinese Legation that same evening, at 9.50 p.m.[126] What the Chinese minister did was simply to ask his son to take the Note to Macartney at the Midland Hotel.[127] Macartney, for his part, felt unable to urge the minister to telegraph Beijing that evening, as he had so solemnly promised the Foreign Office. Instead, he went from Whitehall straight back to his hotel, bypassing the Legation. His explanation was that, in view of the minister's health, he had thought it better to leave the matter to the next morning.[128] Not surprisingly, even after the minister had let it be known that he would release his prisoner, it was still reported that 'Mr Jarvis had authority from the Home Office to use full force, and had six men, fully armed, ready to demand the surrender of Sun Yatsen. Luckily, the Chinese authorities gave way'.[129] This report may very well be untrue, but it certainly highlights the journalists' impression of the minister's intransigence.

Yet another reason for the minister's obstinacy could have been his apparent failure to understand Western popular opinion and the way in which it operated, both being alien to traditional China. Small wonder that some reports made the following observation: 'The Chinese officials of the Legation were evidently much astonished at the stir made by the capture of Sun Yatsen, and made no effort to conceal their chagrin at having to surrender their prisoner. They insisted that the man was a dangerous criminal, and that he ought to have been sent [back] to China to answer for his misdeeds'.[130] Another commented, '. . . it is well

---

(125. *continued*)
Dispatch 294, 31 December 1893.) It seems that Gong Zhaoyuan's popularity with foreigners in the treaty ports had not gone beyond having had a good time with them.

126. FO 17/1718, pp. 24–5, Salisbury to Gong Zhaoyuan [draft], 22 October 1896, para. 2.

127. FO 17/1718, pp. 69–76, Sanderson's record of his interview with Macartney, 23 October 1896, para. 2.

128. FO 17/1718, pp. 69–76, Sanderson's record of his interview with Macartney, 23 October 1896, para. 1.

129. *Daily Chronicle*, 24 October 1896, p. 5, col. 6. See, also, *Evening News*, 24 October 1896, p. 2, col. 5, and *Star*, 24 October 1896, p. 3, col. 2.

130. *Overland Mail*, 30 October 1896, p. 45, col. 2. See, also, *Daily Telegraph*, 24 October 1896, p. 8, col. 1, and *Morning Advertiser*, 24 October 1896, p. 6, col. 1.

to remember that Dr Sen's [sic] arrest was probably the work of very ignorant persons who were not aware of the serious offence they were committing'.[131] Yet another asked, 'If these are the manners of the Chinese Legation in London, what kind of official life is that of Pekin [sic]?'[132]

If the first minister had listened to Macartney, why, twenty years later, should the fifth minister have behaved differently? One would think that later generations would have learnt more about the West. The secret lies in the fact that the first minister was subsequently impeached for having been too susceptible to Western influence; and the journals of his travels, which he kept and published with a view to informing his countrymen of civilizations other than the Chinese, were banned by his government even when he was still in office in London.[133] It is not suggested that the fifth minister shared the sympathies but learnt the lesson of the first. Indeed, he had very different priorities in life, having been described as a *bon vivant*.[134]

In all probability, therefore, the minister ordered his English secretary to do as he was told. It seems that Macartney resisted the order for about an hour, from roughly 10 a.m. to 11 a.m., during which time protracted arguments must have taken place. In the end, Macartney gave in. There may have been two possible explanations.

The minister could have endeavoured to sweeten the pill by assuring Macartney that Sun Yatsen was going to walk[135] into the Legation of his own free will; in which case there would be no question of abduction on the part of the Legation and consequently no breach of British criminal law. Once Sun Yatsen was safely inside the premises, then international law would apply and it could be argued that it was a case of the Chinese authorities arresting a Chinese subject on Chinese territory. The minister and his Chinese colleagues might not have been familiar with

131. *Speaker*, 31 October 1896, p. 452, col. 1.
132. *Evening News*, 24 October 1896, p. 2, col. 3.
133. Guo Tingyi, *Guo Songtao*, Vol. 2, pp. 712–13.
134. FO 17/1158, O'Conor to Foreign Office, Dispatch 294, 31 December 1893.
135. The timing of Sun Yatsen's arrival at the Legation will be examined in Chapter 3.

British customs and conventions, but this amount of international law and diplomatic privilege they appear to have known.[136]

Alternatively, the minister could have threatened Macartney with dismissal for refusing to obey orders. Of course, Macartney could resign. But what would be his chances of getting another job at the age of 63? Indeed, what kind of job could he apply for, given his background?[137] What sort of reference could he expect from the Legation? Would anybody believe the reasons for his resignation?[138] What about the pension which he had been hoping to get from the Chinese government upon his retirement?[139] One must not forget that Macartney had four children by his first wife and another four by his second wife, the latter four still very young. What about their maintenance, their education? What about his own standard of living, a standard expected of a Knight Commander of St Michael and St George in the Victorian era? There are no statistics about his monthly expenditure, although we do know that his monthly income was £100 sterling.[140] To accommodate himself, his wife, his young children, and an appropriate number of servants, he would have needed a fairly large Victorian house. Then he chose to live in Harley Place, which was an expensive area. The rent alone,

---

136. Thus, it was subsequently reported as follows: 'The question of international law which the Chinese Minister is said to be determined to fight out with the British Government is a very delicate one ... the only law in force [in a foreign Legation being] that of the country represented by the Minister'. *Daily News*, 23 October 1896, p. 7, col. 2. See, also, *Echo*, 23 October 1896, p. 3, col. 1; *Morning Leader*, 23 October 1896, p. 5, col. 3; and other newspapers which appear to have obtained their information from the Central News.

137. Macartney had studied medicine at Edinburgh University; but not having practised for over thirty years, it would have been very difficult for him to start at the age of 63. See the previous section of this chapter for an outline of his early career.

138. Given the general disbelief Dr Cantlie was to encounter when he tried to tell his story about Sun Yatsen's kidnapping, as described in Section II of the previous chapter, Macartney might have expected the same reaction if he were to say there had been a plot to kidnap the fugitive, and that he was sacked for having refused to be involved in it.

139. When he eventually retired in 1905 at the age of 72, he successfully requested a pension of £50 sterling per Chinese calendar month, which was half his current salary. The Chinese calendar had a leap-year month once every four years. In real terms, therefore, Macartney's Gregorian monthly salary and then pension were more than £100 and £50 respectively. See Beijing Palace Museum Records, Waiwubu 871, Zhang Deyi to Emperor, 23 June 1905.

140. Beijing Palace Museum Records, Waiwubu 870, Legation financial report, London, 30 May 1896.

therefore, would have taken up a sizeable portion of his income.[141] He had to balance savings against his reputation when he considered using his diplomatic privileges to avoid paying parochial rates. It appears that he decided in favour of savings, and had to put up with newspaper reports such as the following: 'This distinguished official some years ago successfully claimed by virtue of his status to be exempt from paying parochial rates. In consequence of this we believe that the Foreign Office decided in future not to receive British subjects when accredited as diplomatic officers by foreign powers'.[142]

In considering the case of Sun Yatsen, Macartney also had to balance the living given him by the Legation against his own reputation and the risks involved. He appears to have decided in favour of his living. His subsequent defence was: 'What I did was in execution of the orders of the government I serve'.[143]

After the minister had obtained the promised co-operation from his English secretary, his nephew Gong Xinzhang ordered the English servants in the Legation to begin clearing a room on the top (fourth) floor, at about 11 a.m. This room was then found to be unsuitable,[144] and a room on the third floor, that of the French interpreter Wu Zonglian, was cleared.[145] At about 11.45 a.m., Macartney summoned the porter George Cole, ordered him to guard a man for a few days and to bring directly to him any papers the man might give him.[146] By about 12 noon, Macartney was alone with Sun Yatsen in the room on the third

---

141. No. 49, Portland Place, which housed the Chinese Legation, was no doubt a much bigger building than Macartney's residence at 3, Harley Place. But the rent for the former should offer some guide to that of the latter. Initially the Legation paid £107 sterling per Gregorian month, which was later reduced to £100 with a seven-year lease. (Beijing Palace Museum Records, Waiwubu 870, Legation financial report, London, *circa* March 1887.)

142. *British Review*, 31 October 1896, p. 89, col. 2.

143. Boulger, *Macartney*, p. 467; see, also, pp. 475–6.

144. FO 17/1718, pp. 116–19, Cole's statement at the Treasury, 2 November 1896, para. 5.

145. FO 17/1718, pp. 116–19, Cole's statement at the Treasury, 2 November 1896, para. 6. Cole said it was a Mr Liou's room. Deng Tingkeng later said M. Liou was the French interpreter (*Evening News*, 24 October 1896, p. 2, col. 7). In the Suzhou dialect, 'Wu' is pronounced 'Ng'. Perhaps 'Liou' was chosen to avoid the pronunciation difficulties 'Ng' would pose for Westerners. Or perhaps, since the Mandarin pronunciation of 'Wu' sounds just like the French *où* (where), Frenchmen found it funny.

146. FO 17/1718, pp. 116–19, Cole's statement at the Treasury, 2 November 1896, para. 6.

floor. Macartney told the fugitive that his proposal for reform which he had sent to the Zongli Yamen some time ago was a good piece of work, that the Zongli Yamen now wanted him, and that he had to wait for a reply in eighteen hours.[147] He did not say a word about Sun Yatsen's subsequent plot to overthrow the government at Guangzhou. Why?

Macartney's approach must be seen in the context of the cyphers that subsequently went between the Legation and Beijing. On the day of Sun Yatsen's detention, the minister cabled to the effect that he had the fugitive under lock and key, and that he was considering transporting him back to China.[148] Beijing replied immediately that he had better consult a lawyer before taking such a step, in case it backfired.[149] Very probably, this reply was what Macartney had been hoping for, or even expecting. With twenty years of experience in the diplomatic world and about fifteen years in the public service in China before that, he must have had a shrewd suspicion that the high mandarins in Beijing might be anxious to lay their hands on Sun Yatsen, but could not be anywhere near as desperate as the minister in London. So soon after China's disastrous defeat in the Sino-Japanese War, Beijing could do without an international incident in the middle of London, especially one which was potentially so offensive to the British. The reluctance to let go the prey is evident in the absence of an instruction for his instant release. But the order to consult a lawyer leaves no doubt that Beijing wanted to be on the safe side. As mentioned, an earlier request for extradition had been turned down by the British Foreign Office. Any other means of transporting him back to China would be illegal. The minister did not need to ask a lawyer; Macartney could tell him that much. This may explain why Macartney pretended to Sun Yatsen that he did not know the latter was a political refugee by ignoring his subversive activities but concentrating on his proposal for reform; why he pretended

---

147. FO 17/1718, pp. 119-20, Sun Yatsen's statement at the Treasury, 4 November 1896, para. 10.

148. Gong Zhaoyuan to Zongli Yamen (cypher), 11 October 1896, in Luo Jialun, *Shiliao*, p. 26. This cypher will be analysed further in Chapter 3, Section III, Part ii. Zongli is commonly spelt Tsungli in all Western documents, but to conform with the *pinyin* system, it is spelt Zongli throughout this text.

149. Zongli Yamen to Gong Zhaoyuan (cypher), 12 October 1896, in Luo Jialun, *Shiliao*, p. 44.

that Beijing now wanted him for his talents as a reformer; and why he so confidently predicted that a reply would be received within eighteen hours, when Sun Yatsen would know what to do. Everything went as he seems to have expected: a reply was received within eighteen hours; the order to consult a lawyer ought to have left the minister with no choice but to release the man, whereupon Macartney could say that the reformer's talents were no longer required and disclaim any suggestion that a political refugee had been detained. What he underestimated, apparently, was the determination of a dying man to leave his mark on history. The minister, it seems, refused to obey orders from Beijing, and wanted Macartney to find a ship for the fugitive. It looks as though Macartney then began to employ delaying tactics, almost as a bid to wear down the minister's nerves. The turning-point came on Wednesday, 14 October 1896, when it was discovered that the captive 'was endeavouring to communicate with the outer world'.[150] So far, all the notes which Sun Yatsen had given to the English servants had been faithfully handed to Macartney.[151] The attempt to bypass the Legation staff opened up possibilities, the consequences of which Macartney could not face. He immediately telegraped his friend, a Mr Macgregor of the Glen Line, to call on him that evening.[152]

The interview appears to have taken place as scheduled; because, at the end of the day, the minister cabled Beijing that negotiations were under way to charter a ship for about £7,000 sterling. It was a very crafty cable. It began by alleging that Sun Yatsen had told Deng Tingkeng about his determination to overthrow the government. The obvious aim of this allegation was to make anybody in Beijing think twice about again instructing him to release the prisoner. Then it claimed that Sun Yatsen was known to Westerners as a rebel, implying, according to mandarin logic, that the British had no sympathy for him. It went on to say that the Foreign Office had refused extradition, and hence negotiations had been started to charter a ship to transport him back

150. FO 17/1718, pp. 113–16, Cuffe to Home Office, 12 November 1896, para. 24.
151. FO 17/1718, pp. 116–19, Cole's statement at the Treasury, 2 November 1896, paras. 12, 13, and 16.
152. FO 17/1718, pp. 113–16, Cuffe to Home Office, 12 November 1896, para. 24. FO 17/1718, pp. 119–20, Sun Yatsen's statement at the Treasury, 4 November 1896, para. 21.

to China. The price would be about £7,000 sterling. The alternative was to release him and continue to have him shadowed.[153] Beijing was somewhat taken aback, and did not reply for almost two days. The minister kept up the pressure. He cabled again on Friday, 16 October 1896, saying that if the rebel were to be released, it would have to be done quickly so as to cover the tracks.[154] After he had sent this cable, a reply reached him, approving the expenditure of £7,000 sterling.[155] Apparently, nobody in Beijing wanted to take the responsibility for releasing someone who still vowed to overthrow the government.[156] On about Tuesday, 20 October 1896, the Chinese servants noticed that the Legation was being watched by the British police.[157] The minister was not moved. He had the two English servants given a sovereign each, promising to reward them well 'when this is all over'.[158] In the end, he had to send another cable to Beijing on Friday, 23 October 1896,[159] after Sun Yatsen was released.[160] The cable is a masterpiece of mandarin deceit. It began by alleging that on the *third* day of the detention, Sun Yatsen's fellow gangsters started patrolling outside the Legation day and night and following members of the staff whenever they went out, so that the prisoner could not be smuggled out even in a box. Here, the minister accused the six British detectives of being gangsters[161] and tried to exaggerate his difficulties by advancing

---

153. Chinese Legation Archives, Gong Zhaoyuan to Zongli Yamen (cypher), 14 October 1896, in Luo Jialun, *Shiliao*, p. 26.

154. Beijing Palace Museum Records, Gong Zhaoyuan to Zongli Yamen (cypher), 16 October 1896, in Luo Jialun, *Shiliao*, pp. 54–5.

155. Beijing Palace Museum Records, Zongli Yamen to Gong Zhaoyuan (cypher), 16 October 1896, in Luo Jialun, *Shiliao*, p. 54.

156. This shows that, although the authorities in Beijing were anxious to avoid offending the British, they apparently wanted Sun Yatsen so badly that they were prepared to take such a risk.

157. FO 17/1718, pp. 116–19, Cole's statement at the Treasury, 2 November 1896, para. 20.

158. FO 17/1718, pp. 116–19, Cole's statement at the Treasury, 2 November 1896, para. 23.

159. Beijing Palace Museum Records, Gong Zhaoyuan to Zongli Yamen (cypher), 23 October 1896, in Luo Jialun, *Shiliao*, p. 62. I shall use this version for analysis, a version which is different from the draft in the Legation, as Luo Jialun found out (pp. 62–3). See note 160.

160. Chinese Legation Archives, Gong Zhaoyuan to Zongli Yamen (draft cypher), 23 October 1896, in Luo Jialun, *Shiliao*, p. 63.

161. Only the police, and not the lone agent employed by Cantlie after midnight on Sunday, 18 October, or Slater on Monday, 19 October 1896, had the instruction or the manpower to follow individual members of the Legation.

the date of police surveillance from 20 to 13 October 1896, in an obvious attempt to forestall the charge of not having taken action earlier. In so doing, however, he contradicted his cable of 16 October 1896, in which he had boasted that to date nobody outside knew about the detention.[162] This contradiction, in turn, he tried to resolve by claiming that he had discovered the surveillance only afterwards. Under the circumstances, he continued, the ship had been cancelled; and to avoid complications, he had initiated negotiations with the Foreign Office in order to secure a guarantee that the governor of Hong Kong would watch Sun Yatsen closely should the latter return there, whereupon the Foreign Office had asked him to put his request in writing so that it might be acted upon. In view of what has been unearthed in Chapter 1, Section III, this was all a pack of lies. He ended by saying that he had no choice but to release the prisoner, leaving it vague as to whether or not he had already done so,[163] so as to allow himself room for further defence if necessary.

To return to the events of Wednesday, 14 October 1896, the fact that Macartney could have telegraphed McGregor of the firm McGregor, Gow, and Company[164] to call on him at such short notice, and the fact that McGregor appears to have responded positively, may be seen as an indication of the intimacy between the two friends. Apart from the obvious need for co-operation, it is even possible that Macartney might have hoped that his friend would do something to help him out of an impossible situation, such as releasing Sun Yatsen by some means somewhere on the way; for the execution in China was bound to be widely publicized as a deterrent to would-be rebels, with serious repercussions for Macartney himself and the Legation. The risky business of getting Sun Yatsen from the Legation to the ship, however, remained potential dynamite. He quickly sent his family away to Scotland.[165] He locked up his house and told his neighbours that he and his family were going to take a six-month

---

162. Beijing Palace Museum Records, Gong Zhaoyuan to Zongli Yamen (cypher), 16 October 1896, in Luo Jialun, *Shiliao*, pp. 54–5.

163. This is Luo Jialun's interpretation, with which I agree; see Luo Jialun, *Shiliao*, p. 64. The minister had already released Sun Yatsen by this time.

164. As mentioned in a footnote in Chapter 1, Section III, the registered name of the firm that owned the Glen Line was McGregor, Gow, and Company.

165. *Morning Leader*, 23 October 1896, p. 5, col. 1.

holiday in the country.[166] He himself took refuge in the Midland Railway Hotel,[167] whence he could take the next train to Scotland as well, if need be. In the end, it was not the window or any other means but George Cole (to whom Macartney had chosen to entrust the task of guarding the prisoner) who was the avenue through which Sun Yatsen's appeal for help finally reached Dr Cantlie.

IV The Defence

On 22 October 1896, Macartney was summoned to the Foreign Office. He arrived there a little before 7 p.m. and was interviewed by Sir Thomas Sanderson and some of his senior colleagues.[168] From that point onwards, he was on the defensive. His defence concentrated on four major issues. First, Sun Yatsen went to the Legation of his own free will. This case he made out both to the Foreign Office and to the press later that same evening. Second, 'nobody has any jurisdiction within the walls of the Chinese Legation except the Chinese Minister. The Legation, according to International Law, is Chinese territory ... It is really the case of a Chinese subject arrested and detained by the competent authority'.[169] This view he offered to the press, but not to the Foreign Office, which had made it quite clear right from the beginning that 'the detention of the man was an abuse of diplomatic privilege'.[170] Third, Sun Yatsen had not been ill-treated during the detention. On this point he was adamant, whether he was in Whitehall or confronted by journalists. Fourth, he had never contemplated smuggling the fugitive out of England and back to China to stand trial. He was extremely lucky not to have been questioned by the Foreign Office on this point,[171] even after he had made this statement to the press.

Let us examine these four issues one by one.

---

166. Sun Yatsen, *Kidnapped in London*, p. 64.

167. *Daily Telegraph*, 23 October 1896, p. 7, col. 6.

168. FO 17/1718, pp. 54–61, Sanderson's record of his interview with Macartney, 22 October 1896, para. 2.

169. Macartney's words as reported in the *Daily Telegraph*, 23 October 1896, p. 7, col. 6.

170. FO 17/1718, pp. 54–61, Sanderson's record of his interview with Macartney, 22 October 1896, para. 3.

171. See notes 172 and 173 for the references.

First, the claim that Sun Yatsen walked into the Legation of his own accord.

Inseparable from this claim was yet another claim, that Sun Yatsen had visited the Legation previously. Macartney told the Foreign Office during his first interview there, on 22 October 1896, that the fugitive had called at the Legation on 'Friday the 9th instant'.[172] During the second interview, on 23 October 1896, Macartney described 'the events which had led to the man's detention. He said that Sun had called at the Legation but that no one had any *suspicion* [*my italics*] at the moment that he was the man who was being watched at their desire. Sun had, however, spoken to a Cantonese in the Legation of the instability of the Chinese government. This, and the fact that some sheets of a Chinese translation which was being prepared for Sir Halliday were missing after his visit, had given rise to *suspicion* [*my italics*], and on his calling again he had been detained'.[173] Upon comparing the record of these two interviews, Professor Harold Schiffrin has asked, 'And if Sun did steal documents from the Legation, why did Macartney wait until his second interview at the Foreign Office before making this accusation, which would have strengthened his case for holding Sun?'[174] The reference in this question to Macartney's strengthening his case is slightly off the mark. Macartney was trying to explain how Sun Yatsen allegedly had aroused *suspicion*, and was not attempting to strengthen his case for having detained the political refugee. Nor did Sir Thomas Sanderson appear to have listened to Macartney's explanation in the wrong spirit, for Sanderson began the relevant paragraph of his record of the second interview with Macartney thus: 'He then described to me the events which had led to the man's detention'.[175]

In other words, Macartney was merely elaborating on the allegation that Sun Yatsen had visited the Legation previously, although he did not repeat the date of Friday, 9 October 1896. When writing to *The Times* subsequently, however, Macartney

172. FO 17/1718, pp. 54–61, Sanderson's record of his interview with Macartney, 22 October 1896, para. 4.

173. FO 17/1718, pp. 72–6, Sanderson's record of his interview with Macartney, 23 October 1896, para. 9.

174. Schiffrin, *Origins*, p. 109.

175. FO 17/1718, pp. 72–6, Sanderson's record of his interview with Macartney, 23 October 1896, para. 9.

stated that Sun Yatsen went to the Legation 'the first time on Saturday, the 10th, the second on Sunday, the 11th'.[176] Professor Schiffrin thinks that the attribution of two different dates to the alleged first visit 'of course is no small inconsistency'.[177] Schiffrin also mentions, without comment, an inference from the inconsistency that Macartney 'had no personal knowledge of Sun's first visit but merely repeated what others had told him'.[178] The inference was made by the Treasury solicitor, Mr H. Cuffe, who took the view that, 'having regard to the fact that the detention occurred on a Sunday, which would make it easy for any one having personal knowledge of the visits to remember the days',[179] Macartney's inconsistency about the date of the alleged first visit might be taken as an indication that he had not been involved in it.[180]

The object of reviving this inference here is to suggest that, given the reconstruction and assessment of events so far, I am inclined to think that the inference should be taken more seriously. I also think that due attention should be paid to the Treasury solicitor's suggestion that Macartney's informant on each occasion could very well have been the unveracious English interpreter, Deng Tingkeng.[181]

Schiffrin refers to a certain 'interview' given by Macartney and published in *The Times* on 24 October 1896, in which Macartney was quoted as saying that he had personally met Sun Yatsen on the first visit 'and became suspicious as a result of their conversation'.[182] Schiffrin then asks, 'But if he himself had received Sun upon the first visit, why did he not mention it at the Foreign Office or in his letter to the paper?'[183] Before Schiffrin, the Treasury solicitor had examined the same report and looked at it from a completely different angle: 'It seems to me very

---

176. *The Times*, 26 October 1896, p. 8, col. 4, publishing Macartney's letter dated 24 October 1896.
177. Schiffrin, *Origins*, p. 108.
178. Schiffrin, *Origins*, p. 109.
179. FO 17/1718, pp. 113–16, Cuffe to Home Office, 12 November 1896, para. 13.
180. FO 17/1718, pp. 113–16, Cuffe to Home Office, 12 November 1896, para. 13.
181. FO 17/1718, pp. 113–16, Cuffe to Home Office, 12 November 1896, para. 13.
182. Schiffrin, *Origins*, p. 108.
183. Schiffrin, *Origins*, p. 108.

extraordinary, if it be correct, that when Sir Halliday was telling his story to the Foreign Office, and was, under his own hand, writing the story to *The Times*, he should not have said a word about having himself seen Sun on his first visit'.[184] The Treasury solicitor was inclined, therefore, 'to doubt the accuracy of this report'.[185]

Upon checking the relevant column of *The Times*,[186] it is found that the interview was not printed as such, but under the heading 'Sir Halliday Macartney has made the following statement'.[187] Comparing this version with those printed in other London newspapers, it transpires that *The Times* had doctored the interview in such a way as to retain only Macartney's answers, which were then turned into a 'statement'. It was an interview after all, and was conducted by a representative of the Press Association in the early afternoon of 23 October 1896. The reporter asked, 'Was he recognised at the Legation?' Macartney answered,

No, nobody here knew him by sight. He came voluntarily, and got into conversation with a native of the same province who is on our staff, and who introduced him to me under the name he had given. We chatted together for a while, and some remarks made by the visitor led me afterwards to suspect that he might be the person we were having watched, but by this time he had left the Legation. I communicated with our private detective, and then learned that he had somehow lost sight of the suspect during his visit to us at Portland Place. Next day, however, our visitor returned. We then detained him, and he is still under detention.[188]

The clarity with which the question was asked and the answer given, which characterized the entire interview, makes it difficult to accept that the reporter put words into Macartney's mouth.[189]

---

184. FO 17/1718, pp. 113–16, Cuffe to Home Office, 12 November 1896, para. 13.

185. FO 17/1718, pp. 113–16, Cuffe to Home Office, 12 November 1896, para. 13.

186. *The Times*, 24 October 1896, p. 6, col. 2.

187. *The Times*, 24 October 1896, p. 6, col. 2.

188. *Daily Graphic*, 24 October 1896, p. 13, col. 3.

189. The doctored version as printed in *The Times* (24 October 1896, p. 6, col. 2), in which Macartney's answers were forcibly strung together into a statement and consequently did not read at all well, would have been regarded by most people as suspect. If the Treasury solicitor had looked at only this version, it is not surprising that he should have been inclined to doubt its accuracy (FO 17/1718, pp. 113–16, Cuffe to Home Office, 12 November 1896, para. 13).

Was Macartney telling the truth? With this, we have to consider the circumstances under which Macartney was interviewed. The place was in the Chinese Legation, the time was shortly after noon on 23 October 1896, when the Legation was literally besieged by reporters; when Macartney was under tremendous pressure to release the man but the minister still refused to oblige; when Macartney was expecting a stormy time at the Foreign Office where he was to go later at 1.30 p.m.; and after Macartney had been hounded since the previous evening by journalists,[190] who showed disbelief one after the other when he told them that Sun Yatsen had twice visited the Legation.[191] Is it possible that, in his desperation to convince his listeners, he invented the story of *his* meeting with Sun Yatsen in an attempt to give some credibility to his talk about the visits?[192] We do know that the same answer contains at least one untruth: Macartney did not communicate with the private detective before Sunday, 11 October 1896, as he claimed; in fact, he saw the detective only on Monday, 12 October 1896.[193]

Macartney's untruth about the timing of his communication with the private detective, and the probable untruth about his having received Sun Yatsen on an alleged first visit, affect the credibility of his defence that Sun Yatsen had not been inveigled into the Legation. They do not solve the problem as to whether Sun Yatsen had been inveigled into the Legation or whether he had gone there of his own free will. This problem will be examined in Chapter 3. At this stage, it can only be said that the ineffectiveness of Macartney's defence lends weight to the speculation that Sun Yatsen had been inveigled into the Legation and left Macartney at the mercy of newspaper editors at the time, and of historians later.

---

190. For details about this sequence of events, see Chapter 1.

191. See, for example, the *Sun* (23 October 1896, p. 2, col. 7), which wrote, '. . . it is exceedingly improbable that he [Sun Yatsen] played the part of the fly with such amazing simplicity, and walked of his own accord into the spider's web in Portland-place'.

192. Macartney could have been in real fear of being suspected of having had a part in the alleged inveiglement of Sun Yatsen into the Legation, in which case he could have been accused of having breached British criminal law.

193. Compare Chinese Legation Archives, Slater to Macartney, 12 October 1896, in Luo Jialun, *Shiliao*, p. 115-16. For more details about the sequence of events, see Chapter 1, Section I.

Macartney's second defence was the right of the Chinese minister to arrest Sun Yatsen within the premises of the Legation.

As mentioned, Macartney never argued his case with the Foreign Office. He was not allowed to, even if he had dared. Right from the beginning, Sir Thomas Sanderson told him that 'the detention of the man was an abuse of diplomatic privilege'.[194] Macartney would have had to be exceedingly foolish to contradict the permanent under-secretary of state. Why he should then have gone on to argue his case with the press is intriguing. Perhaps he felt obliged, in his capacity as English secretary to the Legation, to do so. Perhaps he considered it fatal for the Legation to admit guilt publicly. In fact, Macartney's argument was not as absurd as it may appear today. Most London newspapers agreed at the time that the question of international law was a delicate one. For example, the *Globe* wrote, '. . . the important point that is raised by this curious incident is the uncertainty which exists as to the actual powers and status of a foreign Embassy'.[195] The *Evening Standard* shared this view: 'The technical questions raised by the arrest of a Chinaman by the Chinese Legation are numerous and difficult, and the legal points involved have been in some aspect or another, the subject of international controversies, at different times, for more than a couple of centuries'.[196] Even some of the law journals were at a loss to express a definite opinion. The *Law Times* wrote, 'The detention of the Chinaman at the Chinese Legation raises a question of great importance as to the privileges of the Ambassadors'.[197] It then traced the law of extraterritoriality as it had developed, but made no comment about the current case. Similarly, the *Law Journal Notes of Cases* stated, 'The proceedings of the officials of the Chinese Legation with respect to their Cantonese compatriot on his version amount to kidnapping and on their own to false imprisonment. But the whole transaction opens up the question as to what really are the privileges and

---

194. FO 17/1718, pp. 54–61, Sanderson's record of his interview with Macartney, 22 October 1896, para. 3.
195. *Globe*, 24 October 1896, p. 4, col. 2.
196. *Evening Standard*, 24 October 1896, p. 4, cols. 4–5.
197. *Law Times*, Vol. 101, 1896, p. 599. I am grateful to Mr Keith Eddey, himself a lawyer, for this reference. See note 198.

immunities of a foreign Ambassador in England'.[198] It then also discussed the history of the law since 1708, when an Act of Parliament, entitled 'An Act for preserving the Privileges of Ambassadors and other publick Ministers of Foreign Princes and States', was passed,[199] but this journal likewise paid no further attention to the case of Sun Yatsen. Presumably both journals agreed that the Chinese minister was covered by this Act.

The difficulty lay in the fact 'that there is no case on record at all analogous to the one under consideration. Phillimore, Calvo, Marteus, Hall, Wheaton — in fact, all the standard text-book writers may be searched in vain for anything like a precedent to the difficulty just at an end. It has never been denied that a foreign Minister has jurisdiction over all those persons composing his suite ... in the recent difficulty the person detained was simply a countryman of the Minister, and for the imprisonment or punishment of such, in the circumstances claimed by the Ambassador, there is no previous instance to serve as a guide'.[200] Thereupon, one of the papers made a public appeal, '. . . were it not for Sun Yatsen's personal convenience we should like to have had a final authoritative definition as to the limitation of the inviolability. Otherwise, the question may arise, at some period of crisis, in a more acute and unpleasant form'.[201] Subsequently, the case of Sun Yatsen was made a precedent in international law.[202] But that was for the guidance of later generations. In Macartney's time, at least, there was no such precedent, and Macartney's defence should be given the benefit of the doubt. Indeed, he might even be given credit for his knowledge of the law.[203] But in the midst of the sensation, the public was simply

---

198. *Law Journal Notes of Cases*, Vol. 31, 1896, p. 582. Again, I wish to thank Mr Keith Eddey for this reference.

199. I am indebted to Mr David Clune of the Parliamentary Library of New South Wales in Australia for a photocopy of this Act.

200. *Pall Mall Gazette*, 24 October 1896, p. 3, col. 1.

201. *Daily Telegraph*, 24 October 1896, p. 6, col. 7.

202. Schiffrin, *Origins*, pp. 113-14, n. 51, quoting Oppenheim's *International Law*, Vol. 1, p. 796. See, also, Gerald E. Bunker, 'The Kidnapping of Sun Yatsen in London, 1896', Seminar paper, Harvard University, 1963, in which he has come to the same conclusion.

203. Further evidence of Macartney's knowledge of the law may be found in the interview he gave to journalists in the Midland Hotel late in the evening of 22 October 1896. The reporter asked, 'Then, of course, there is no foundation for the statement that an attempt has been made to serve a writ of *Habeas Corpus*, or

not prepared to accept such cold-blooded arguments, and Macartney fell victim to his own defence.

Macartney himself was quick to realize this particular weakness in his own position, especially in view of the fact that Britain has a long and romantic tradition of giving asylum to political refugees. When he was first confronted by journalists late in the evening of 22 October 1896 in his refuge in the Midland Hotel, his answer to the question of what charge had been preferred against the prisoner was short and simple. He said, 'It is a charge of treason, for having attempted to get up a rebellion in the province of Canton [sic]'.[204] Apparently he thought it over during the night and added another charge the next day, when he was interviewed for a second time by the same reporter shortly before noon. Describing the alleged first visit by Sun Yatsen, he said, '... and he was left alone in a room in which there were certain papers. Something then occurred — I admit we have only circumstantial evidence as to the incident — which led us to conclude that he was the man whose description had been sent to us. The question then for us was: Should we not be justified in detaining an individual whom we believed to be dangerous?'[205] Here, Macartney was adding a criminal offence to Sun Yatsen's already known political offence. The reporter was quick to take him to task: 'But why, if he had a definite charge to prefer against him, did you not call in a policeman and give him into custody?' This question really put Macartney in deep water, the implication being that the Legation took the law into its own hands. Macart-

---

(203. *continued*)
some process of that kind, on the Chinese Minister?' Macartney replied, 'Oh! no; that is absurd, because any act of that kind is expressly forbidden by a statute passed in the reign of Queen Anne'. (*Daily Telegraph*, 23 October 1896, p. 7, col. 6.) By Queen Anne's statute Macartney was referring to the Act of Parliament passed in 1708, mentioned above. As described in Chapter 1, Section III, the writ of habeas corpus for which Scotland Yard had arranged for Dr Cantlie and Dr Manson to apply was not granted by Judge R. S. Wright. Instead, their affidavits were used to summon Macartney to the Foreign Office. Judge Wright's action, in turn, became a precedent in international law. The *English and Empire Digest* (Vol. 16, case 2731), for example, cites the case, entitled 'Re Sun Yatsen [1896]', as authority for the view that a writ of habeas corpus cannot be issued to a foreign Legation. I am grateful to Mr Keith Eddey of Oxford for this reference, and to Mr David Clune of the Parliamentary Library of New South Wales in Australia for having furnished me with a photocopy of the case.
204. *Daily Telegraph*, 23 October 1896, p. 7, col. 6.
205. *Daily Telegraph*, 24 October 1896, p. 7, col. 7.

ney's response to this question dragged him into even deeper water: 'What would have been the use? China has no extradition treaty with England'.[206]

Another mistake had been made, and it had to be repaired.

Within an hour, he was interviewed again, this time by a representative of the Press Association, shortly after noon on 23 October 1896, as mentioned in the analysis of Macartney's first defence. In this interview, he dropped the charge about Sun Yatsen having been a thief. Instead, he said, 'We chatted together for a while, and some remarks made by the visitor led me afterwards to suspect that he might be the person we were having watched'.[207] This alleged conversation in the alleged first visit has been dealt with before. It remains to be said that the ineffectiveness of Macartney's second defence lends more weight to the speculation that Sun Yatsen had not gone to the Legation on Sunday, 11 October 1896, of his own free will, and was going to subject Macartney to more severe criticism by the press, as we shall see in the next section.

Macartney's third defence was that Sun Yatsen had not been ill-treated during the detention.

Physically speaking, Sun Yatsen's treatment while in detention may be examined under five headings: food, clothing, entertainment, the degree of his freedom, and whether he had been subjected to torture. Mentally speaking, there is of course no question that he was under a great deal of stress.

In terms of food, Macartney told one reporter that Sun Yatsen ate very well,[208] and another that the fugitive had plenty of good food.[209] Macartney did not specify how well Sun Yatsen ate. But 'other officials' of the Legation said that he 'was supplied with an abundance of food suitable to his condition — boiled mutton, rice, and the like, prepared by the Chinese cook of the Legation'.[210] This account is corroborated by what appears to have been a record of what Sun Yatsen subsequently told one of his close associates: 'He was well treated at the Legation, each

206. *Daily Telegraph*, 24 October 1896, p. 7, col. 7.
207. *Daily Graphic*, 24 October 1896, p. 13, col. 2.
208. *Daily Telegraph*, 24 October 1896, p. 7, col. 7.
209. *Daily Graphic*, 24 October 1896, p. 13, col. 2.
210. *Morning Leader*, 24 October 1896, p. 7, cols. 3-4.

meal consisting of four courses of Hunanese dishes'.[211] Shortly after his release, Sun Yatsen said, 'I was given food when I asked for it, I mostly had bread and milk'.[212] This version is, in turn, corroborated by the English interpreter, Deng Tingkeng: 'The prisoner had been, and is, amply supplied with food, of which, it is said, he partakes freely. He is very partial to tea, raw eggs mixed with milk, boiled eggs, and various Chinese dishes'.[213] George Cole, the impromptu warder, also said that Sun Yatsen had 'a Chinese dinner about 6 o'clock' on the first day of his confinement;[214] but afterwards changed to bread and milk. 'He had it when he asked for it. He asked me for it when I was on duty. He had about four meals of bread and milk a day, sometimes he would have two raw eggs with it. We had orders to give him everything he asked for, so far as food was concerned'.[215]

Thus, all accounts agree that Sun Yatsen could have had as much good food as he liked. The fact that he changed his diet to one of bread, milk, and eggs may not be put down to ill-treatment strictly within the terms of foodstuffs. But why did he change his diet? Apparently, this had something to do with a visit from the English interpreter, Deng Tingkeng. The interpreter threatened to smuggle the prisoner back to China for execution, and if that should fail, to kill him in the Legation.[216] These threats seem to have frightened the fugitive into taking much simpler staples, such as raw eggs, milk, and bread, which would have been difficult to tamper with without detection. Sun Yatsen himself was a medical practitioner.

There is no evidence to suggest that Macartney was ever aware

---

211. Chen Shaobai, *Xing Zhong Hui geming shiyao* (Nanjing, 1935), as reprinted in Luo Jialun, *Shiliao*, p. 181. Chen Shaobai was among the first whom Sun Yatsen saw after leaving England and going to Japan. In fact, Sun Yatsen stayed with Chen Shaobai on his arrival at Yokohama (p. 184).

212. *Daily Telegraph*, 24 October 1896, p. 8, col. 1.

213. *Evening News*, 24 October 1896, p. 2, col. 7.

214. FO 17/1718, pp. 116–19, Cole's statement at the Treasury, 2 November 1896, para. 6.

215. FO 17/1718, pp. 116–19, Cole's statement at the Treasury, 2 November 1896, para. 6.

216. FO 17/1718, pp. 119–20, Sun Yatsen's statement at the Treasury, 4 November 1896, para. 13. These threats were made in an attempt to extract a statement from the prisoner. This episode will be scrutinized in more detail later on in this section and in Chapter 3.

of these threats having been made. Indeed, there were other incidents about which Macartney had been kept in the dark, as we shall see later. For the purpose of the present analysis, however, it suffices here to say that Macartney's claim, albeit made in good faith, that the prisoner ate 'very well', was bound to create much cynicism when contradicted by Sun Yatsen's story of having survived on a meagre diet.[217]

As regards clothing, Sun Yatsen said, 'During all this time, I had never taken off my clothes'.[218] But again, this was his own decision, and not something which had been forced upon him by members of the Chinese Legation. On the other hand, if bedding may be regarded as clothing, one might mention that the English housekeeper went with fresh 'bedclothes'[219] to make his bed for him on the first night of his confinement. Two days later, on Tuesday, 13 October 1896, Macartney asked Cole about the man under his care:

'How is the man going on? Is he giving you any trouble?'
'No; he complains of being cold at night.'
'Has he not got enough bedclothes? Get him a Chinese blanket.'
'He has one, and an English one also.'
'He will be all right. If he says anything more of being cold go to the housekeeper and get him some more clothes.'[220]

In addition, the English servant went into Sun Yatsen's room each morning to light a fire for him.[221] In the end, the baskets of coal turned out to be a convenient means of helping the prisoner to have messages smuggled in and out of the Legation.[222]

---

217. Even when Sun Yatsen was still behind bars, but news of his lean diet had already got out, the *Evening News* commented, '. . . it is highly desirable that friendly negotiations should be opened on the subject of his commissariat, as at present he is said to be starving himself from fear of being poisoned. Could not some one intercede with Sir Halliday Macartney for Sun to be treated as a first-class misdemeanant, and have his meals sent in from outside? Who will be the intercessor? Will Kruger oblige?' (*Evening News*, 23 October 1896, p. 2, col. 4).

218. Sun Yatsen, *Kidnapped in London*, p. 59.

219. FO 17/1718, pp. 116–19, Cole's statement at the Treasury, 2 November 1896, para. 20.

220. FO 17/1718, pp. 116–19, Cole's statement at the Treasury, 2 November 1896, para. 16.

221. Compare FO 17/1718, pp. 116–19, Cole's statement at the Treasury, 2 November 1896, paras. 12 and 21.

222. Sun Yatsen, *Kidnapped in London*, pp. 58 and 94; and *Star*, 24 October 1896, p. 3, col. 2.

Entertainment, according to Macartney, consisted of 'books to read'.[223] The English interpreter elaborated on this: 'For his amusement he is supplied with papers and English novels, which he devours greedily'.[224] Here again, one might expect that such a statement would have been greeted with cynicism.[225]

The degree of Sun Yatsen's freedom, or lack of it, involved more than his obvious confinement to a room on the third floor of the Legation building. As mentioned, Macartney had instructed Cole to bring him direct all papers that the prisoner might give to Cole for transmission to the outside world. Indeed, Cole was so faithful to his orders that he even climbed over to the next house to pick up a note which Sun Yatsen had thrown out of his window, and took it directly to Macartney:

'How did he manage to throw it?'
'He had his window opened for a little fresh air, and must have put [his] hands through the bars and jerked it over.'
'You will see that the window is fastened down, and search him and see that he has no writing materials, and for the future let him have no more papers.'[226]

Thereupon the window was nailed down.[227] Sun Yatsen claimed that Macartney had initially asked him to send for his luggage, whereupon some ink and paper were produced.[228] This claim was supported independently by Cole, who said that Macartney had

---

223. *Daily Graphic*, 24 October 1896, p. 13, col. 3.
224. *Evening News*, 24 October 1896, p. 2, col. 7.
225. The *Daily Mail* (24 October 1896, p. 4, col. 4) wrote, 'It may be that he fared sumptuously every day, and that he greedily devoured English novels ... A noted humorist insisted that
        For ways that are dark
        And tricks that are vain,
        The heathen Chinee is peculiar.'
The humorist was Francis Bret Harte (1836–1902). The full text of his verse may be found in Richard Gray (ed.), *American Verse of the Nineteenth Century* (London, Dent & Totowa; New Jersey, Rowman & Littlefield, 1973), pp. 183–4. I am grateful to my colleague, Mr Grahame Harrison, for his help in identifying the humorist.
226. FO 17/1718, pp. 116–19, Cole's statement at the Treasury, 2 November 1896, para. 21.
227. FO 17/1718, pp. 116–19, Cole's statement at the Treasury, 2 November 1896, para. 21.
228. FO 17/1718, pp. 119–20, Sun Yatsen's statement at the Treasury, 4 November 1896, para. 6.

'looked out of the room and called for pen and ink and writing paper'.[229] Sun Yatsen wrote to Dr Manson, 'I am in the Chinese Legation. Please send my baggage'.[230] With the words, 'I must ask the Minister before I can send this letter',[231] Macartney left the prisoner. The letter was, of course, never delivered to Dr Manson.

Sun Yatsen also said, 'The only occasions on which I saw Sir Halliday Macartney were when I arrived and when I left'.[232] There is no evidence to contradict this, or to suggest that Macartney went anywhere near the room subsequently.[233] The confinement officially began at about noon on Sunday, 11 October 1896, when Macartney said to Cole, 'Turn that key, and see that that man does not escape'.[234] Macartney went downstairs, and then home, presumably to have lunch with his family. Cole was left to guard the door, alone. An hour later, 'they sent a Chinaman to keep me company and I remained on duty till 6 in the evening'.[235] That day was Sunday: there is no reason to suppose that Macartney stayed on or returned to the Legation to partake in the decision to send a Chinese servant to keep Cole company. Nor is there evidence to show that he knew then or subsequently that the Chinese guard had a sword. 'He would not ordinarily carry a sword', said Cole.[236] Nor is there information to suggest that Macartney was told that in the evening on the same Sunday, in his absence, the English interpreter had seen to it that an

---

229. FO 17/1718, pp. 116–19, Cole's statement at the Treasury, 2 November 1896, para. 10.

230. FO 17/1718, pp. 119–20, Sun Yatsen's statement at the Treasury, 4 November 1896, para. 10.

231. FO 17/1718, pp. 119–20, Sun Yatsen's statement at the Treasury, 4 November 1896, para. 10.

232. FO 17/1718, pp. 119–20, Sun Yatsen's statement at the Treasury, 4 November 1896, para. 19.

233. Macartney's office was situated on the ground floor at the back of the Legation (*Daily Chronicle*, 24 October 1896, p. 5, col. 4). The second, third, and fourth floors were the residential areas of the Chinese staff. Macartney would not have gone anywhere near the third floor, where Sun Yatsen was kept, in the normal course of events.

234. FO 17/1718, pp. 116–19, Cole's statement at the Treasury, 2 November 1896, para. 6.

235. FO 17/1718, pp. 116–19, Cole's statement at the Treasury, 2 November 1896, para. 6.

236. FO 17/1718, pp. 116–19, Cole's statement at the Treasury, 2 November 1896, para. 21.

additional lock was put on the prison door.[237] These details are not important in themselves, except to show that a few more things had been done behind Macartney's back.

One other incident deserves some consideration. On about Tuesday, 20 October 1896, the Chinese servants noticed that the Legation was being watched by detectives. 'Policeman stopee outside, I think', said one of them.[238] Schiffrin commented, 'Up to the last, *Macartney* [*my italics*] tried to keep his staff in line, and on the 22nd gave Cole and the other English servant a sovereign each with a promise of a better reward when "all this is over"'.[239] The source used, upon checking, is Cole's statement, which distinctly named the *Minister* as the man in question.[240] This is a minor error on the part of the historian, which would not have mattered normally. But in the context of the present analysis, it goes to show that because Macartney appears to have been in charge of the operation, it is easy to attribute to him an action which he had not taken, indeed yet another action which might have been taken without his knowledge.

On the subject of torture, Macartney was quite incensed that suggestions of the kind should have been made: 'I have seen some statement of that sort in the newspapers; but of course it is preposterous, as nothing in the nature of torture or undue pressure would be thought of by any member of the Legation, and certainly not by myself'.[241] In view of the incident, mentioned in the summary of Macartney's early career, in which he lost control over himself when he saw a Chinese mandarin trying to extract information by torture, one may assume that in the present case he never dreamt of using coercive methods himself. Some jour-

237. FO 17/1718, pp. 116–19, Cole's statement at the Treasury, 2 November 1896, para. 10.

238. FO 17/1718, pp. 116–19, Cole's statement at the Treasury, 2 November 1896, para. 22.

239. Schiffrin, *Origins*, p. 122.

240. FO 17/1718, pp. 116–19, Cole's statement at the Treasury, 22 November 1896, para. 23. The full text of this paragraph reads: 'On Thursday the 22nd Mr Tang [Deng Tingkeng] the English interpreter came to me and said "The Minister has told me to give you a sovereign, and one to Henry, and promises he will well reward you when this is all over." He then gave me a five pound note to get change, telling [me] to take my sovereign, and Henry's and to hand the change to a Mr Pung, the Paymaster of the Legation'. Checking this with the Beijing Palace Museum Records, Waiwubu 870, Legation financial report, London, 3 April 1897, I can confirm that the paymaster was Pan Chenglie.

241. *Daily Graphic*, 24 October 1896, p. 13, col. 3.

nalists, however, were not so convinced that other members of the Legation shared Macartney's sentiments: '. . . the realistic descriptions by travellers of Chinese administration, the gentle coercion of witnesses in the courts by smashing their ankles, the slicing of criminals to death . . .' were shadows that had haunted one paper.[242] '[It] is extremely unlikely that the neighbours will be shocked by the tortured shrieks of the imprisoned Sen [sic]. The Chinese Legation may be trusted to proceed in the matter with some regard for Western prejudices', wrote another.[243] Macartney was very familiar with these prejudices: he himself was deeply imbued with them. He also had an intimate knowledge of Chinese practices in the nineteenth century. Is it possible that Macartney had taken steps to warn his colleagues in the Legation that he would not tolerate coercion of any kind being used on the prisoner? Ultimately, Sun Yatsen did leave the Legation unscathed; he told the Treasury solicitor, 'Apart from the confinement, I cannot complain of the treatment I received'.[244]

Still on the subject of torture, a representative of the Press Association asked Macartney, 'Has he made any statement?' 'No, he has not made any statement, and he has not even been questioned, and I do not know that he will be catechised', replied Macartney.[245]

'Has he confessed?' asked the *Echo*. 'Yes', replied Deng Ting-keng promptly, 'he has made a full confession, and his statements have been taken down in writing'.[246]

Deng Tingkeng's version is corroborated by those of Sun Yatsen[247] and George Cole.[248] The Chinese text of the confession is appended to the memoirs of the French interpreter of the

---

242. *Speaker*, 31 October 1896, p. 463, col. 1, to p. 464, col. 1.

243. *Globe*, 23 October 1896, p. 5, col. 3, quoting the *Daily Graphic* of the same day.

244. FO 17/1718, pp. 119–20, Sun Yatsen's statement at the Treasury, 4 November 1896, para. 41.

245. *Daily Graphic*, 24 October 1896, p. 13, col. 3.

246. *Echo*, 24 October 1896, p. 3, col. 6. See, also, *Daily News*, 24 October 1896, p. 5, cols. 4–5.

247. FO 17/1718, pp. 119–20, Sun Yatsen's statement at the Treasury, 4 November 1896, para. 13.

248. FO 17/1718, pp. 116–19, Cole's statement at the Treasury, 2 November 1896, para. 26.

Legation.[249] Three attempts had been made to obtain the confession, one in the small hours of the fifth day of his imprisonment,[250] when Macartney would have been sound asleep. With good reason, the Treasury solicitor speculated, 'Except on the hypothesis that Sir Halliday Macartney had been kept in ignorance of what was happening, he would hardly have said that Sun had not made any statement in the Legation, which, I think, is almost certainly untrue'.[251]

Macartney's fourth and final defence highlights the degree to which he was kept in the dark.

'There is a rumour, Sir Halliday, that the Chinese officials made an attempt to remove what I suppose I may call your prisoner from the Legation, and get him aboard a ship', said a reporter, who was among the first to have located Macartney in his refuge in the Midland Hotel late in the evening of 22 October 1896. 'That is entirely baseless. There has been no attempt to get him out of the Legation whatever', said Macartney.[252] The same diplomatic reporter asked the same question the next day, 'You will admit that the question involved is a knotty one. Have you any intention of solving it, or rather of cutting the knot by smuggling the man out of the country?' Macartney became rather desperate. 'None. There never was any such idea'.[253] By this time, other journalists had gone off to East London to interview representatives of the Glen Line, who replied, 'We must decline to say anything on the subject'.[254]

The reporters got to know about the Glen Line through Dr Cantlie.[255] The doctor was informed about it by Sun Yatsen.[256] Sun Yatsen, in turn, was told about it by Deng Tingkeng when that interpreter was trying to extract the confession from his prisoner.[257] As for the interpreter, he might have learnt about it from Macartney, or, more likely, from the minister, who had cabled

249. Wu Zonglian, *Biji*, *juan* 2, pp. 37a–39b. See Chapter 3 for more details.
250. Sun Yatsen, *Kidnapped in London*, pp. 44–53.
251. FO 17/1718, pp. 113–16, Cuffe to Home Office, 12 November 1896, para. 13.
252. *Daily Telegraph*, 23 October 1896, p. 7, col. 6.
253. *Daily Telegraph*, 24 October 1896, p. 7, col. 7.
254. *Morning*, 24 October 1896, p. 6, col. 2.
255. *Evening News*, 23 October 1896, p. 3, col. 1.
256. FO 17/1718, p. 30, Sun Yatsen to Cantlie [18 October 1896].
257. FO 17/1718, pp. 119–20, Sun Yatsen's statement at the Treasury, 4 November 1896, para. 13.

Beijing about his intention of having Sun Yatsen smuggled back to China on the very first day of the detention.[258] On 14 October 1896, he cabled again to report that negotiations were under way to charter a ship for a fee of £7,000.[259] On 21 October 1896, Chief Inspector Jarvis of Scotland Yard interviewed McGregor and was told that the firm had been approached by the Chinese Legation for a passage to China.[260] McGregor did not specify who had conducted the negotiations on behalf of the Chinese Legation. In any case, Jarvis' report about this interview was dated 23 October 1896, and presumably did not reach the Foreign Office either before 1.30 p.m., when Macartney was summoned there for the second time, or before 4 p.m. on the same day, when he went there to convey the Chinese minister's consent to release Sun Yatsen.[261] Even if Jarvis' report had reached the Foreign Office by 6 p.m., when Macartney went there to say that Sun Yatsen had been released,[262] the officials probably did not take as much interest in it as they might otherwise have done.

Macartney was extremely lucky. If he had been confronted with the question of the Glen Line by the Foreign Office, what could he have said? An admission would have meant pleading guilty to an accusation of illegal trafficking in human beings, and a denial such as the one he had offered to the press would have amounted to perjury. A subsequent inquiry, ordered by the Home Office and conducted by the Treasury solicitor, found that Macartney was the man who had contacted the Glen Line.[263] But by that time, the British government appears to have been reluctant to pursue the subject any further.[264]

---

258. Chinese Legation Archives, Gong Zhaoyuan to Zongli Yamen [cypher], London, 11 October 1896, in Wang Chonghui, 'Shiliao', p. 191.

259. Chinese Legation Archives, Gong Zhaoyuan to Zongli Yamen [cypher], London, 14 October 1896, in Wang Chonghui, 'Shiliao', pp. 191–2.

260. FO 17/1718, p. 94, Jarvis' report, 23 October 1896.

261. FO 17/1718, pp. 69–76, Sanderson's record of interviews with Macartney, 23 October 1896, para. 14.

262. *Echo*, 24 October 1896, p. 3, col. 5.

263. FO 17/1718, pp. 113–16, Cuffe to Home Office, 12 November 1896, paras. 23–4.

264. This is not surprising, in view of the fact that even before the official inquiry started with George Cole giving evidence at the Treasury on 2 November 1896, Lord Salisbury had complied with the wishes of the Chinese minister to the effect that Her Majesty's government would do all that was 'legally in their power to prevent any British territory being used for preparing conspiracies against the

V The Victim

In the last two sections, we have seen how Macartney changed his role from being apparently the sole opponent of the minister's plot to becoming its chief, though reluctant, defendant. The fact that he seems to have been kept in the dark over several important issues did not help him either. Not surprisingly, his arguments lacked conviction, his statements were often inconsistent, and more than once he was obliged to tell lies in order to get out of some exceedingly embarrassing situations. Consequently, his vigorous defence of the Legation's position attracted severe criticism from the press.

Commenting on Macartney's first defence, the *Sun* wrote, 'Sir Halliday Macartney denies that the man was kidnapped. But perhaps this is one of those diplomatic denials which may prove to be only an ingenious play upon words. We will only say that it is inconceivable that Sun Yatsen should have gone of his own free will and accord into the Embassy, there to surrender the liberty which he has evidently been at some pains to preserve'.[265] This newspaper was not alone in expressing such an opinion.[266] Then, there were those papers which took it for granted that Sun Yatsen had been inveigled into the Chinese Legation.[267] Some even suggested that Sun Yatsen should sue Macartney for illegal arrest[268] and seek compensation.[269] Only one paper thought initially that, since there was a direct conflict of testimony between the two parties, both, being equally interested, were 'equally to be disbelieved';[270] then decided to believe Macartney's version, 'both because it is corroborated by the independent evidence of several witnesses, and because there are obvious reasons for a

---

(264. *continued*)
Chinese government or its officers'. (Chinese Legation Archives, Salisbury to Gong Zhaoyuan, 31 October 1896, in Luo Jialun, *Shiliao*, pp. 107–9.) See, also, FO 17/1286, p. 239, Gong Zhaoyuan to Salisbury, 26 October 1896; and pp. 240–1, Salisbury to Gong Zhaoyuan [draft], 31 October 1896. This is a subject which will be looked at more closely in Chapter 4.

265. *Sun*, 23 October 1896, p. 2, col. 3.

266. *Standard*, as quoted by the *London and China Express*, 23 October 1896, p. 896, col. 2.

267. *Daily Telegraph*, 24 October 1896, p. 6, col. 6; *Illustrated London News*, 31 October 1896, p. 556; and *The Times*, 24 October 1896, p. 9, cols. 2–3.

268. *St James's Gazette*, 24 October 1896, p. 4, col. 2.

269. *Sun*, 24 October 1896, p. 3, col. 2.

270. *Evening News*, 23 October 1896, p. 2, col. 3.

prisoner suffering under such a gross injustice as Sun's enforced captivity making the most of his case'.[271] It would be fascinating to know who those independent witnesses were; but unfortunately the paper did not name them, and posterity has to remain tantalized.

Macartney's reaction to all these comments, favourable or otherwise, was to reiterate his position in *The Times*: 'Now, I repeat what I have said before — that in this case there was no inveiglement. The statement of Sun Yatsen — or, to call him by his real name, Sun Wen, — that he was caught in the street and hustled into the Legation by two sturdy Chinamen is utterly false'.[272] This drew an angry response from the *Speaker*: 'To the obvious suggestion that Sun Yatsen would never have walked into the Chinese Embassy of his own accord, had he known the real identity of his entertainers, Sir Halliday vouchsafes no reply'.[273]

If Macartney had been in the same position as the *Speaker*, very probably he would have made the same comment. But a very different set of circumstances applied when he considered this question initially. The minister wanted to *arrest* Sun Yatsen. Macartney's primary concern then was to oppose the arrest. When that opposition failed, his next priority was obviously the protection of himself and his family, which included safeguarding the secret by every means possible, persuading his family as gently as possible to take shelter in Scotland for the winter, and finding himself a refuge where he could get away from London as quickly as possible if need be — hence the Midland Railway Hotel.

The present assessment of the degree to which Macartney had fallen victim to his own inadequate defence has wider objectives than simply one of attempting to put the record straight. It is also

271. *Evening News*, 24 October 1896, p. 2, col. 3.

272. Macartney's letter to the editor of *The Times*, dated 24 October 1896 and printed in the next issue of that paper on Monday, 26 October 1896, p. 8, col. 4.

273. *Speaker*, 31 October 1896, p. 463, col. 1. Macartney did not respond to this scathing attack. Perhaps he could not. Forty-three years later, in 1939, the biography of Dr Cantlie, entitled *Sir James Cantlie* and written by his son Neil Cantlie in collaboration with George Seaver, was published. Macartney's son, D. Halliday Macartney, wrote to a newspaper to protest about the unfavourable references to his father penned by a reviewer, but was still unable to do any more than to restate his father's position as previously put to *The Times* on 24 October 1896 (Cantlie Family Papers, p. 352, newspaper cutting, n.d.).

intended to show that the great majority of the inquisitive journalists of the time believed, or were inclined to believe, that Sun
Yatsen had been inveigled into the Legation. This is a point
which will be dealt with in more detail in Chapter 3.

As regards Macartney's defence of the extraterritorial right of
the minister to arrest the fugitive, the *Daily Mail* wrote,

Yet, to carry to their logical conclusion the methods and the arguments
of the Chinese Embassy, he [Sun Yatsen] should never have come out
alive, for the contention is that so far as the law is concerned, poor Mr
S. Y. Sen [*sic*] was, while in the headquarters of the Legation, just as
much in China as though he were in Pekin [Beijing]. The house is a
piece of Chinese territory which happens, geographically, to be situated
in London; and inasmuch as the heads of those of Mr Sen's [*sic*] fellow
conspirators who were captured have long since parted company with
their bodies, the delay in the execution of this latest capture — always
according to the arguments of the Chinese Legation — was unaccount-
able. 'Something lingering, with boiling oil in it' should have been Mr
Sen's fate; but nevertheless, so far as can be ascertained, Sir Halliday
Macartney did not even go so far as to order the oil.[274]

Having successfully stopped the exercise of the Qing Code in
the Legation twenty years previously to forestall the use of coercive methods, Macartney probably did not know whether to
laugh or cry when he read the above passage. Indeed, this piece
of work by the *Daily Mail* highlights the ignorance, not of
Macartney but of the minister, about international law and Western sentiments, which again has some bearing on the question as
to whether or not Sun Yatsen had been inveigled into the Legation. It is important to remember that Macartney's defence of the
extraterritorial rights of the Legation was *ex post facto*, and it
would be illogical to use such an *ex post facto* defence to prove
that Macartney had set out to do what he was subsequently
accused of doing.

The Treasury solicitor made the following evaluation of
Macartney's third defence: '. . . except for the absence of prison
clothes and the fact that he was furnished with good food, the
conditions of imprisonment seem to have been complete. A window barred and nailed down; the door locked and guarded (one
man on guard having a sword); all letters and documents con-

---

274. *Daily Mail*, 24 October 1896, p. 5, col. 4.

fiscated; and all communication with the outer world stopped. If Sir Halliday is prepared to say that, in view of these facts, Sun was not treated like a prisoner, I can only say the meaning of language is different to him from what it is to most people'.[275] Therefore, the solicitor was inclined to doubt the accuracy of the report in which Macartney was alleged to have said that Sun Yatsen had not been treated like a prisoner.[276]

The report in question was printed in *The Times* on 24 October 1896.[277] As mentioned before, a comparison between this and other newspapers has revealed that *The Times* had turned what was originally an interview between a representative of the Press Association and Macartney into a statement, in which the questions had been omitted.[278] Without the questions, the answers were in many ways out of context. The context in which Macartney gave his answer was that of nineteenth-century Chinese methods of justice. Therefore, when Macartney replied that Sun Yatsen had not been treated like a prisoner, he could only have meant that Sun Yatsen had not been treated like a prisoner in China. The problem is really not one of Macartney having been misquoted, but one of his answers having been quoted out of context.[279] At least the Treasury solicitor was sharp enough to query the accuracy of the newspaper report, and he gave his reason for doing so.[280] It is unfortunate, therefore, that a modern historian, Professor Wu Xiangxiang, should have mistakenly interpreted that reason as being a condemnation of Macartney.[281] Even more unfortunate is the fact that Professor Wu Xiangxiang should then use this supposed condemnation as evidence to sup-

---

275. FO 17/1718, pp. 113–16, Cuffe to Home Office, 12 November 1896, para. 13.

276. FO 17/1718, pp. 113–16, Cuffe to Home Office, 12 November 1896, para. 13. Schiffrin (*Origins*, p. 109) probably misread Cuffe's report when he believed that the solicitor thought otherwise.

277. FO 17/1718, pp. 113–16, Cuffe to Home Office, 23 November 1896, para. 13. See *The Times*, 24 October 1896, p. 6, col. 2.

278. Compare *The Times* (24 October 1896, p. 6, col. 2) with the *Daily Graphic* (24 October 1896, p. 13, col. 2).

279. Compare *The Times* (24 October 1896, p. 6, col. 2) with the *Daily Graphic* (24 October 1896, p. 13, col. 2).

280. FO 17/1718, pp. 113–16, Cuffe to Home Office, 12 November 1896, para. 13. His reason has been quoted at length earlier in the text: '. . . except for the absence of prison clothes . . . language is different to him from what it is to most people'.

281. Wu Xiangxiang, *Sun Yixian zhuan*, Vol. 1, p. 1789.

port his claim that Macartney had planned and conducted the kidnapping of Sun Yatsen.[282]

So far as Macartney's fourth and final defence is concerned, Professor Wu Xiangxiang is right in reading the Treasury solicitor's report to mean that Macartney had negotiated with the Glen Line for a passage to take Sun Yatsen back to China.[283] But again, to use the solicitor's findings as the basis for accusing Macartney of having been the arch conspirator who had initiated and conducted the kidnapping of the fugitive,[284] leaves much to be desired in terms of logic.

Macartney's biographer lamented that because of the kidnapping, Macartney's 'long and most honourable career in China's service will never be fully known or adequately appreciated'.[285] History has shown that the biographer has been correct in his prediction.

---

282. Wu Xiangxiang, *Sun Yixian zhuan*, Vol. 1, p. 1789.
283. Wu Xiangxiang, *Sun Yixian zhuan*, Vol. 1, p. 1789.
284. Wu Xiangxiang, *Sun Yixian zhuan*, Vol. 1, p. 1789.
285. Boulger, *Macartney*, p. 469.

3 The Creation of an Heroic Image

Mr Sun told me that he already knew the place was the Legation. But he assumed a different name and went there every day to spread the word of revolution.

Chen Shaobai[1]

I The Intention

It is alleged that, after Sun Yatsen had left London, he said that he had not been kidnapped at all, but that he had walked fearlessly into the Legation himself. The first person to commit such a report to writing was Luo Jialun, in his now authoritative book in which he evaluated all the evidence available to him in relation to the kidnapping. The first edition appeared in 1930.[2] Luo Jialun had not heard the story directly from Sun Yatsen, but indirectly from two of Sun Yatsen's close associates who had survived him. They were Hu Hanmin and Dai Jitao. On 20 July 1930, Hu Hanmin said, 'Whether [Sun Yatsen] went into the Legation voluntarily, or he was forced into it, is an open question; because, one day, he told us that he went into it of his own accord'.[3] On 2 September 1930, Dai Jitao told Luo Jialun the same story.[4] Hard on the heels of these two pieces of oral history, Luo Jialun wrote, 'Given the courageous character of Sun Yatsen, it is quite possible that he went into the Legation to propagate his beliefs, to collect his followers and to reconnoitre the land; because, such an action is to be expected of a revolutionary leader, and is evidence of his fearless spirit. In addition, because the episode later became an international incident, and the focus of press attention in both Europe and America, it is possible that he claimed to have been kidnapped in

---

1. Chen Shaobai, *Xing Zhong Hui geming shiyao* (Nanjing, 1935), reprinted in Chai Degeng *et al*. (eds.), *Xinhai geming* (Shanghai, 1957; second edition, Shanghai, People's Press, 1981, 8 vols.), Vol. 1, p. 35 (hereafter cited as *Xing Zhong Hui*, in *Xinhai geming*). The translation is mine.

2. Luo Jialun, *Shiliao*, preface dated 1 August 1930. Compare preface to the second edition, dated 10 October 1935.

3. Luo Jialun, *Shiliao*, p. 42. The translation is mine.

4. Luo Jialun, *Shiliao*, p. 42.

order to expose the wickedness and ignorance of the Manchu Court, and to gain sympathy for the revolutionary movement in China'.[5]

Luo Jialun has put the cart before the horse. Sun Yatsen wrote numerous messages for help during his detention in the Legation. The two that have survived, because they successfully reached Dr James Cantlie, read as follows:

I was kidnapped into the Chinese Legation on Sunday & shall be smuggled out from England to China for death. Pray rescue me quick?[6]

A ship is already charter by the C.L. [Glen Line] for the service to take me to China and I shall be locked up all the way without communication to any body. O! Woe to me![7]

These messages give the distinct impression that the overriding concern of the writer was to escape death. They were written long before the press knew anything about his fate. To use the subsequent sensation retrospectively to argue that the great revolutionary leader had foreseen this and therefore twisted the story, only shows the intensity of the heroic image which had developed up to Luo Jialun's time. As for the intention of converting to his revolutionary cause those who were after his head, such a suggestion may be seen as an attempt to show that the great leader possessed unusual courage. When personal adoration reaches a certain point, logic turns upside down. With regard to the business of reconnoitring the Legation, what was the purpose of it? To attack the Legation single-handedly and then hold it to ransom? If Luo Jialun had hoped to use his arguments to promote the image of Sun Yatsen, he might have hesitated had he read some of the leading articles on the incident. Commenting on the Legation's version that Sun Yatsen had walked into the Legation of his own free will, the *Sun*, for example, wrote, 'If this view is right, we shall have to credit a conspirator who had fled from Chinese soil to the United States, and knew that he carried his life in his hands, with an abnormal degree of simplicity. "He came to spy on us" is one of the explanations

5. Luo Jialun, *Shiliao*, p. 43. The translation is mine.
6. Photographic reproduction of Sun Yatsen's message, in Luo Jialun, *Shiliao*, p. iii.
7. Photographic reproduction of Sun Yatsen's message, in Luo Jialun, *Shiliao*, p. iv.

suggested by the officials. That is, on the face of it, an absurdity'.[8] Certainly, Luo Jialun would not have liked the *Guofu* to be 'credited with an abnormal degree of simplicity'.

On the other hand, Luo Jialun made it clear that he was only speculating. He did not say that Sun Yatsen had definitely walked into the Legation. However, he did provide evidence of a different kind in favour of his speculation. This evidence will be examined in the next section of this chapter.

In the spring of 1935, Chen Shaobai's book on the Xing Zhong Hui was published posthumously. It contained some important information about the kidnapping, which reinforced Luo Jialun's speculation. Consequently, Luo produced a second edition of his own book, incorporating this information.[9] Chen Shaobai had written:

Do we know how Mr Sun was detained by the Legation? According to his *Kidnapped in London*, he met Deng Tingkeng in the street, who was an attaché in the Legation. Deng Tingkeng claimed to be a fellow native of Xiangshan, and took Mr Sun home to socialize. His home was none other than the Legation. Subsequently, they met a few more times, but on the last occasion, he was forced upstairs and detained in a room.

The truth is, in fact, otherwise. Mr Sun told me that he already knew that the place was the Legation. But he assumed a different name and went there every day to spread the word of revolution. Afterwards, people in the Legation became suspicious, because news of the uprising in Guangzhou was still prevalent. It was thought that the visitor was perhaps Sun Yatsen himself. Deng Tingkeng had come from the same district as [Sun Yatsen], and succeeded in confirming the suspicion. Thus, Mr Sun was detained.[10]

Chen Shaobai and Sun Yatsen were two of the original 'Four Bandits', so called because, as very young men in Hong Kong, they met regularly to voice their discontent with the Manchu government.[11] From the beginning, Chen Shaobai was a staunch supporter of Sun Yatsen. He joined Sun Yatsen in the uprising at Guangzhou in 1895, and fled with him to Japan when it failed. He is one of the very few who have written systematically about

---

8. *Sun*, 23 October 1896, as quoted in the *London and China Express*, 23 October 1896, p. 896, col. 2.

9. Luo Jialun, *Shiliao*, p. 43.

10. Quoted in Luo Jialun, *Shiliao*, p. 43. The translation is mine.

11. Feng Ziyou, *Geming yishi* (Beijing, 1981, reprint, 6 vols.), Vol. 1, pp. 8–9.

the revolutionary activities in China at the turn of the century, in the form of memoirs. Thus, his work carries with it great authority. But, like all memoirs, I think they should be used with care. In the passage quoted above, the first paragraph is certainly wrong. *Kidnapped in London* does not contain any reference whatsoever to Sun Yatsen having met Deng Tingkeng prior to the day of the incident, let alone going home with him several times beforehand. The second paragraph, however, deserves serious consideration. If it were true that Sun Yatsen had told Chen Shaobai orally about his having walked into the Legation, the earliest he could have done so would have been in August 1897, on his arrival in Japan from London.[12] In terms of timing, this would have been at least eight years before Hu Hanmin might have heard anything about it, because Hu Hanmin did not get to know Sun Yatsen until 1905;[13] and at least fifteen years before Dai Jitao, who met Sun Yatsen for the first time in 1912.[14] Thus, among the three pieces of oral history, that by Chen Shaobai might be regarded as the most authoritative. Small wonder that Luo Jialun quickly produced a second edition of his book in order to quote Chen Shaobai at length.

Another historian, Harold Schiffrin, has also written what has been regarded as an authoritative account of the kidnapping. It is interesting to note how he treats Chen Shaobai's evidence:

... Chen Shaobai, probably the first close friend he saw upon his return to the East, relates how Sun *boasted* [*my italics*] of having visited the Legation daily. Later, in a more *modest* [*my italics*] vein, he told both Hu Hanmin and Tai Chitao that he entered the Legation of his own accord.[15] His friends admired the daring and the revolutionary fervour which had propelled Sun squarely into the enemy stronghold. They also understood the need for lying in order to blacken the Manchu regime and win the support of world opinion.

That the truth would have to be modified in order to achieve this end was something Sun intuitively grasped when he told his story to the British.[16]

12. *Sun Zhongshan nianpu*, p. 36.
13. Hu Hanmin, 'Hu Hanmin zizhuan', *Jindaishi ziliao*, No. 2, 1981, p. 13. I am grateful to Professor Jin Chongji for this information.
14. I am grateful to Professor Jin Chongji for this information.
15. Schiffrin, *Origins*, pp. 112–13, quoting Luo Jialun, *Shiliao*, p. 42.
16. Schiffrin, *Origins*, pp. 112–13.

In a footnote, Schiffrin writes, '... this is further corroborated by another of Sun's old comrades, [Deng] Muhan, in a memorandum [about the kidnapping] submitted to the Kuomintang Archives'.[17] Of course, Deng Muhan also got to know Sun Yatsen much later than 1897.[18] Like Luo Jialun, therefore, Schiffrin believes these pieces of oral history, and believes that Sun Yatsen twisted the story 'in order to blacken the Manchu regime'. But unlike Luo, he attaches more importance to the later pieces of oral history than to the earliest, obviously because he believes the earliest piece contains certain elements of boasting. He was probably not impressed by Chen Shaobai's version that Sun Yatsen went to the Legation to preach revolution, either. Perhaps this explains why he completely ignores Luo Jialun's speculation about Sun Yatsen's possible intention of visiting the Legation, which is similar to Chen Shaobai's version. Instead, Schiffrin attributes Sun Yatsen's motives to 'audacity and love of adventure'.[19]

The question of intention arises only because it is assumed that Sun Yatsen went to the Legation of his own free will. But is such an assumption valid? Schiffrin does not seem to like the boasting elements in Chen Shaobai's version. But was it Sun Yatsen or Chen Shaobai who was boasting?

A clue may be found in one of the appendices in *Kidnapped in London*. Having described in some detail Sun Yatsen's abortive *coup* in Guangzhou in 1895, in which 'forty or fifty of his supposed accomplices were executed, and a reward was offered for his arrest', the appendix continues, 'The story goes that this indomitable patriot immediately set to work converting the Chinese at the Washington Embassy to the cause of reform, and that afterwards he tried to do the same in London'.[20] Who could have written this article? *Kidnapped in London* attributed it to the *China Mail* of Hong Kong, dated 3 December 1896.[21] I have checked this newspaper. There is no such report on that date. Repeated searching yielded a similar, but not identical, article in

---

17. Schiffrin, *Origins*, p. 113, n. 49.
18. I am indebted to Professor Jin Chongji for this information.
19. Schiffrin, *Origins*, pp. 111-12.
20. Sun Yatsen, *Kidnapped in London*, p. 119.
21. Sun Yatsen, *Kidnapped in London*, p. 113.

the issue of 26 November 1896.[22] To begin with, the appendix bears the title 'The Supposed Chinese Revolutionist',[23] while the newspaper has 'The Reformation of China'[24] for a title. In addition, the appendix refers to Sun Yatsen having been a medical student in 'Dr Kerr's School in Tientsin',[25] which is obviously wrong; while the newspaper describes him as having been a medical student in 'Dr Kerr's School in Canton',[26] which shows intimate knowledge of Sun Yatsen's early career.[27] Most importantly, the newspaper begins by saying that the article is a transcription from the *Kobe Chronicle*,[28] a reference which is absent in the appendix. Who in Japan at this time was in a position to write such an article?

After the failure of the uprising in Guangzhou in 1895, Sun Yatsen fled to Japan with two of his closest associates, Chen Shaobai and Zheng Shiliang.[29] Soon, Sun Yatsen went on to Hawaii; Zheng Shiliang went back to Hong Kong; but Chen Shaobai stayed on in Japan,[30] and was still there when Sun Yatsen returned in August 1897.[31]

The *Kobe Chronicle* was an English newspaper. Chen Shaobai was the first student to have enrolled in the Canton Christian College started by the Revd A.P. Happer in 1888,[32] where he received a good grounding in the English language. Later, he joined Sun Yatsen at the medical college in Hong Kong,[33] where the medium of teaching was English. In terms of language ability,

22. *China Mail*, 26 November 1896, p. 2, cols. 5–7. An explanation for this phenomenon will be attempted in Chapter 4, Section IV.

23. Sun Yatsen, *Kidnapped in London*, p. 113.

24. *China Mail*, 26 November 1896, p. 2, col. 5.

25. Sun Yatsen, *Kidnapped in London*, p. 115.

26. *China Mail*, 26 November 1896, p. 2, col. 5.

27. Most reports in 1896 referred to Sun Yatsen as having studied medicine in Hong Kong, but not Canton previously.

28. *China Mail*, 26 November 1896, p. 2, col. 5.

29. Schiffrin, *Origins*, p. 98.

30. Schiffrin, *Origins*, p. 102.

31. Schiffrin, *Origins*, p. 141; and Chen Shaobai, *Xing Zhong Hui*, in *Xinhai geming*, Vol. 1, pp. 38–42.

32. Boorman and Howard (eds.), *Biographical Dictionary of Republican China*, Vol. 1, p. 230, col. 1.

33. Boorman and Howard (eds.), *Biographical Dictionary of Republican China*, Vol. 1, p. 230, col. 1

therefore, Chen Shaobai was well qualified to have written such an article for the *Kobe Chronicle*.

The article, as reproduced in the *China Mail*, begins thus: 'Sun Yatsen, who has recently been in trouble in London through the Chinese Minister attempting to kidnap him for execution as a rebel, is not unlikely to become a prominent character in history'.[34] It goes on, '. . . he is a remarkable man, with most enlightened views on the undoubtedly miserable state of China's millions . . . Dr Sun was the only man who combined a complete grasp of the situation with a reckless bravery of the kind which alone can make a national regeneration'.[35] This praise is in line with Chen Shaobai's well-known admiration for his leader.

'He is of average height, thin and wiry, with a keenness of expression and frankness of feature seldom seen in Chinese. An unassuming manner and an earnestness of speech, combined with a quick perception and resolute judgement, go to impress one with the conviction that he is in every way an exceptional type of his race. Beneath his calm exterior is hidden a personality that cannot but be a great influence for good in China sooner or later, if the Fates are fair'.[36] Who else in Japan at this time could have written about Sun Yatsen with such admiration?

In addition to admiration for Sun Yatsen, the article was also full of praise for Dr Cantlie; and the combination of the two again turns my thoughts to Chen Shaobai.

. . . and it is due to Dr Cantlie, Sun's friend and teacher in Hong Kong, that one of the best men China has ever produced was rescued by British justice from the toils of treacherous mandarindom. All who knew Dr Cantlie — and he is well known in many parts of the world — agree that a more upright, honourable and devoted benefactor of humanity has never breathed. Dr Sun is in good hands, and under the protection of such a man as Dr Cantlie there can be little doubt that he will pursue his chosen career with single-hearted enthusiasm and most scrupulous straightforwardness of methods, until at last the good work of humanising the miserable condition of the Chinese Empire is brought to a satisfactory state of perfection.[37]

---

34. *China Mail*, 26 November 1896, p. 2, col. 5.
35. *China Mail*, 26 November 1896, p. 2, col. 5.
36. *China Mail*, 26 November 1896, p. 2, col. 5. If this was written by Chen Shaobai, as I suspect it was, it is likely that the original article had to be polished before it was printed.
37. *China Mail*, 26 November 1896, p. 2, cols. 6–7.

Who else in Japan at this time could have had such intimate knowledge about Dr Cantlie and Sun Yatsen, and the friendship between the two? When Sun Yatsen was a second-year medical student under Dr Cantlie, he introduced Chen Shaobai to Dr Cantlie and arranged for him to study under the doctor as well.[38]

Referring to the uprising in Guangzhou in October 1895, the writer commented,

No doubt, much of the support accorded to the scheme was promoted by *ulterior motives* [*my italics*], for there are more of that sort than of any other in China. The rebellion was almost precipitated in March, when funds were supplied from Honolulu, Singapore, Australia, and elsewhere; but men of the right sort were still wanting, and arms had not been obtained in great quantity, and *wiser counsels* [*my italics*] prevailed. It would have been better perhaps if wiser counsels had prevailed in October ... His allies, never very confident in *pacific methods* [*my italics*], planned a bold *coup d'etat*, which might have had a momentary success, but made no provision for what would happen in the next few moments.[39]

How does this passage compare with what Chen Shaobai recalled subsequently? 'The next day, Yang Quyun suddenly asked Sun Yatsen if he might have the Presidency, a position which would be returned to Sun Yatsen after the successful seizure of Guangzhou. Mr Sun was very hurt to realize that the struggle for power had begun even before the uprising, and called me and Zheng Shiliang to a secret meeting. Zheng Shiliang said, "This cannot be done. I shall go and kill him. I must kill him." ... In the evening of the same day, Mr Sun voluntarily handed over the title of President to Yang Quyun'.[40] On a separate occasion, Chen Shaobai recalled that, initially, after Sun Yatsen and Yang Quyun had become friends, the two were one day involved in a fierce argument, with Yang Quyun insisting on a rebellion to establish a republic, while Sun Yatsen preferred more *pacific methods*. Yang Quyun was so annoyed that he seized Sun Yatsen's pigtail and was about to beat him when Chen Shaobai separated them.[41]

38. Chen Shaobai, *Xing Zhong Hui*, in *Xinhai geming*, Vol. 1, p. 25.
39. *China Mail*, 26 November 1896, p. 2, col. 6.
40. Chen Shaobai, *Xing Zhong Hui*, in *Xinhai geming*, Vol. 1, pp. 30–1. The translation is mine.
41. Liu Chengyu, 'Xian Zongli jiuzhilu', *Guoshiguan guankan*, Vol. 1, December 1947, pp. 48–9. I am grateful to Professor Lin Zengping for this reference.

If Chen Shaobai was the writer of the article in the *Kobe Chronicle*, as seems very likely, his object appears to have been twofold: to create an heroic image of Sun Yatsen and to attack his former allies. It is not surprising, therefore, that the other faction should have been goaded by it. Two days after the *China Mail* reprinted the article from the *Kobe Chronicle*, a letter was addressed to the editor of the *China Mail*: 'Sir, — In order to remove a false impression created by the recent arrest and detention of Dr Sun Yat Sin [Sun Yatsen] by the Chinese Legation in London, allow me to inform you that the leader of the reformers is Yeong Kuwan [Yang Quyun], a progressive man of sterling worth and unblemished reputation, a thorough patriot and reformer. He is styled Lord Protector of the Commonwealth. Dr Sun Yat Sin [*sic*] is only one of the chief organisers of the reform movement ... P.S. — At present excuse the absence of name and address. Hong Kong, 28 November 1896'.[42] Of all the leaders known to have been involved secretly with the uprising in Guangzhou, Xie Zuantai was the only one who managed to stay on in Hong Kong at this time,[43] because he had been well covered. He was a staunch supporter of Yang Quyun. He was born and educated in Sydney, Australia. At the age of 16, he went to Hong Kong with his mother, and continued his education there at Queen's College.[44] His proficiency in the English language would have been sufficient for him to have written the letter to the editor of the *China Mail*. Indeed, he had had various articles published in the English newspapers in Hong Kong even before 1896.[45] Subsequently, he also wrote a book entitled *The Chinese Republic: Secret History of the Revolution*, which first appeared in serial form in the *South China Morning Post*.[46]

It would be interesting to know if the writer attached his name to the article he contributed to the *Kobe Chronicle*. So far,

---

42. *China Mail*, 30 November 1896, p. 3, col. 2.
43. Feng Ziyou, *Geming yishi*, Vol. 2, pp. 22–3.
44. Tse Tsan Tai, *The Chinese Republic: Secret History of the Revolution* (Hong Kong, 1924), p. 6, col. 2 – p. 7, col. 1 (hereafter cited as *The Chinese Republic*).
45. Tse Tsan Tai, *The Chinese Republic*, p. 8, col. 2.
46. Tse Tsan Tai, *The Chinese Republic*, Note.

however, I have been unable to locate the 1896 issues.[47] Even if I do, I suspect that under the circumstances he would have remained anonymous, just like his counterpart in Hong Kong; or, worse still, he would have used a pseudonym which may prove misleading.

The bitter rivalry between the two factions puts Sun Yatsen's kidnapping in a different light. While Sun Yatsen had fled east, first to Japan, then to Hawaii, America, and finally England,[48] Yang Quyun fled west, first to Saigon, then to Singapore, Madras, Colombo, and finally South Africa;[49] leaving what appears to have been Chen Shaobai and Xie Zuantai to carry on a war of words between Japan and Hong Kong. Recent research shows that, contrary to common belief, Yang Quyun's faction had been much stronger than that of Sun Yatsen.[50] This alone would have prompted Chen Shaobai to try to strengthen Sun Yatsen's faction by whatever means possible. If he did write the article for the *Kobe Chronicle*, it seems that he went to extraordinary lengths to create an heroic image of his leader, fabricating the story that Sun Yatsen had walked fearlessly into the Chinese Legation first in Washington and then in London,[51]

47. At the suggestion of Mr Toshihiko Kobayashi, I first tried the Meiji Shinbun Zasshi Bunko of Tokyo University. But my friend, Professor Hiroshi Watanabe, replied on 18 February 1985 that the Bunko holds only the weekly *Kobe Chronicle* from 1897. Then I tried the National Diet Library. Its director for interlibrary services, Mr Azusa Tanaka, replied on 8 March 1985 that his issues date from 1 December 1904 only. Mr Tanaka's further search shows that neither the British Library nor the Library of Congress has the issues I want. The British Library confirmed on 22 April 1985 that its holdings begin only on 21 March 1900. At Mr Tanaka's suggestion, I also wrote to the Yokohama Archives of History, which was given the task of conducting 'the location research of publications in Western languages in the pre-war period', in 1983. However, Miss Hisaka Ito of that institution replied on 24 April 1985 that extensive searches so far had yielded no results. I am grateful to all the scholars who have helped me in this matter.

48. Schiffrin, *Origins*, pp. 98–104.

49. Tse Tsan Tai, *The Chinese Republic*, p. 10, col. 1.

50. Yuan Honglin, 'Xing Zhong Hui shiqi de Sun Yang liangpai guanxi', in *Jinian Xinhai geming qishi zhounian qingnian xueshu taolunhui lunwen xuan* (Beijing, China Press, 1983, 2 vols.), Vol. 1, pp. 1–22.

51. There is absolutely no evidence to support the claim about the Legation in Washington. As for the Legation in London, a telegram from Sun Yatsen, immediately upon his release, to Chen Shaobai might have reached Japan for the latter to write such a story. But it is inconceivable that he would have telegraphed Japan to say that he had ventured into the Legation at a time when he was

at a time when Sun Yatsen himself was busy telling the British that he had been kidnapped. Thus, if Sun Yatsen had actually been kidnapped in London, it would not have been a matter of Sun Yatsen subsequently telling Chen Shaobai an untruth in Japan in 1897, but of Chen Shaobai retrospectively suggesting to Sun Yatsen that he had not been kidnapped. Whatever the truth may have been, it appears that Sun Yatsen did choose to tell his new faithfuls, Hu Hanmin, Dai Jitao, and Deng Muhan, the heroic version of his adventure, albeit never publicly. I think that Hu Hanmin took it in the right spirit when he said that the question of kidnapping was an open one.[52] Indeed, until it can be proved beyond doubt that Sun Yatsen entered the Legation in London of his own accord, attempts at speculation over an alleged intention to do so are unnecessary. Such speculation can even be misleading, as in the case of Luo Jialun, who claimed that going into the Legation to preach revolution was to be expected of a revolutionary leader,[53] because this is tantamount to conjuring up a possible intention to suggest that such an action may have taken place. The same may be said about Schiffrin's assertion that Sun Yatsen had 'modified' the truth 'in order to blacken the Manchu regime and win the support of world opinion',[54] given the fact that such an intention was also put forward in a similar context, originally by Luo Jialun in the 1930s.[55]

One must remember that it was not Sun Yatsen, but the person writing to the *Kobe Chronicle* in November 1896,[56] who was the

---

(51. *continued*)
constantly pursued by reporters eager to have his story about the kidnapping. On the other hand, a letter to this effect would have reached Japan too late for the article in the *Kobe Chronicle*. The London newspapers carrying the story reached Hong Kong late in November 1896, and were reprinted in the *China Mail* on 26 November 1896, the same day that the article in the *Kobe Chronicle* was reprinted in the same newspaper. Such was the speed of steamships at the time. When Sun Yatsen finally settled down to write about his ordeal to a friend in Hong Kong, he said that he had been kidnapped (Sun Yatsen to Qu Fengzhi, November 1896, in *Sun Zhongshan quanji*, Vol. 1, pp. 45–6). See note 56.

52. Luo Jialun, *Shiliao*, p. 42.
53. Luo Jialun, *Shiliao*, p. 42.
54. Schiffrin, *Origins*, p. 113.
55. Luo Jialun, *Shiliao*, p. 43.
56. Reuters' telegraph about the kidnapping first appeared in Japanese newspapers on 1 November 1896. See, for example, the *Kobe yushin nippo*, the *Osaka asahi shinbun* and the *Osaka mainichi shinbun* of the same date.

first we know of to suggest that Sun Yatsen had not been kidnapped.

II A Previous Visit

Apart from oral history, Luo Jialun and Schiffrin also used archival material. Luo's greatest *coup* was his discovery, in the Chinese central government archives, of materials pertinent to the kidnapping. He also consulted copies of the papers of the Chinese Legation in London, as well as the memoirs of one member of the Legation staff and the diary of another.[57] Schiffrin's contribution lies mainly in his meticulous use of the British Foreign Office records[58] in the light of Luo Jialun's findings.[59]

The Treasury solicitor, Mr H. Cuffe, using the same Foreign Office records, believed that Sun Yatsen had been kidnapped.[60] Schiffrin has argued, 'Had Cuffe been able to investigate the Legation evidence and examine the pertinent Chinese documentary material, he would undoubtedly have formed a different opinion of Sun's behaviour on October 10 and 11, and might have discovered what actually took place'.[61] All the Chinese material, to which Schiffrin has referred, may be found in Luo Jialun's book. Thus, it is not so much the British records, but the Chinese material, which has enabled Schiffrin to conclude that Sun Yatsen had visited the Legation previously, on Saturday, 10 October 1896, and was detained on his return on Sunday, 11 October 1896. But the same Chinese material allowed Luo Jialun to write only that '. . . it is quite possible that he went into the Legation . . . it is possible that he claimed to have been kidnapped . . .'[62] An assessment of the Chinese material in question is clearly necessary.

First and foremost, Schiffrin has referred to Luo Jialun's use of the memoirs of the French interpreter, Wu Zonglian, to prove his

57. Luo Jialun, *Shiliao*, pp. 1–42.

58. FO 17/1718, Chinese Revolutionaries in British Dominions: Sun Yatsen, Kang Youwei, etc.

59. Schiffrin, *Origins*, pp. 102–25.

60. FO 17/1718, pp. 113–16, Cuffe to Home Office, 12 November 1896, para. 5.

61. Schiffrin, *Origins*, p. 112.

62. Luo Jialun, *Shiliao*, pp. 42–3.

point.[63] Some unsatisfactory aspects of these memoirs have been
noted in Chapter 2, Section III. For example, the memoirs allege
that it was the minister's nephew, and not Sir Halliday
Macartney, who initially employed Slater to shadow Sun
Yatsen.[64] I have found documentary evidence in the Palace
Museum Archives in Beijing that Macartney was indeed the man
responsible.[65] Subsequently, Macartney appears to have shown
his distaste for the saga by dissociating himself from the
transaction after Sun Yatsen's release.[66] It is possible that the
minister's nephew was then dispatched to renew the employment
of the detective. Chinese society attaches a great deal of
importance to harmony. Macartney's apparent dissociation from
the affair symbolized discord within the Legation, which, were it
to be known publicly, was not going to help the career of
anybody who had been involved in the affair. This reason alone
could have prompted the writer of the memoirs to cover up the
apparent disharmony, by saying that the minister's nephew was
the man who had employed the detective right from the
beginning. Alternatively, his memory could have been faulty.

The memoirs continue, 'The detective reported that Sun
Wen,[67] having had his pigtail cut and having changed to
European dress, landed at Liverpool on 30 September 1896,
proceeded to London by train on the same day and found
accommodation in a hotel, accompanied by two Europeans'.[68]
The detective's report itself made no reference to Sun Yatsen
having travelled in the company of two Europeans.[69] Very
probably, the writer of the memoirs confused the report by the
detective with the one by the Chinese consul-general in San
Francisco, which had been enclosed in a letter from the Chinese
minister in Washington to the Chinese minister in London,[70] and
which the writer appears to have read. The consul-general's

63. Schiffrin, *Origins*, p. 112, quoting Luo Jialun, *Shiliao*, pp. 31–2.
64. Wu Zonglian, *Biji, juan* 2, p. 39b.
65. Beijing Palace Museum Records, Waiwubu 870, Legation financial report,
London, 22 April 1897.
66. Luo Jialun, *Shiliao*, p. 117.
67. As mentioned early in Chapter 2, Section I, Sun Wen was one of Sun
Yatsen's many names.
68. Wu Zonglian, *Biji, juan* 2, p. 40a. The translation is mine.
69. Slater to Macartney, 1 October 1896, in Luo Jialun, *Shiliao*, pp. 110–11.
70. Yang Ru to Gong Zhaoyuan, 18 July 1896, in Luo Jialun, *Shiliao*, pp.
8–9.

report did mention that Sun Yatsen had landed in San Francisco, with his pigtail cut, dressed in European clothes, and in the company of two Europeans.[71]

Then comes this assertion in the memoirs: 'On 10 October 1896, Sun Wen passed the Legation's door. He met a student by the name of Song Zhitian'.[72] I can confirm that there was such a student in the Legation.[73] As for the probability of Sun Yatsen passing the Legation on this day, Dr Cantlie testified subsequently that Sun Yatsen had called at his house,[74] which was around the corner from the Legation. Sun Yatsen himself said that he went to Regent's Park,[75] which was still further to the north-north-west. Thus, Sun Yatsen might very well have called at the Cantlies either on his way to the Park or on his return from it, and in so doing, passed the Chinese Legation. As for his meeting someone from the Legation, this is also likely, as the Legation staff seem to have been in the habit of taking walks in the vicinity.[76] However, as the memoirs have shown instances of confusing people and events, the identity of the person and the manner in which he met Sun Yatsen remain to be seen.

But the memoirs go on to allege that Sun Yatsen asked the student 'if there were Cantonese among the Legation staff'.[77] This allegation assumes that Sun Yatsen *knew* that he was standing outside the Legation and that he was talking to someone from the Legation. There is no evidence to suggest that the Legation staff, at this stage, were in a position to make such an assumption. The sketches of the Legation drawn in October 1896 show that the building did not have a plate fixed on one of its walls to announce its identity,[78] as such institutions invariably do nowadays. Nor did the national flag fly on the flag-pole.[79] One

---

71. Feng Yongheng to Yang Ru (1896), in Luo Jialun, *Shiliao*, p. 10.
72. Wu Zonglian, *Biji, juan* 2, p. 40a. The translation is mine.
73. Beijing Palace Museum Records, Waiwubu 870, Legation financial report, London, 22 April 1897.
74. FO 17/1718, pp. 121–2, Cantlie's statement at the Treasury, 4 November 1896, para. 5.
75. FO 17/1718, pp. 119–20, Sun Yatsen's statement at the Treasury, 4 November 1896, para. 7.
76. See, for example, Boulger, *Macartney*, pp. 284–5.
77. Wu Zonglian, *Biji, juan* 2, p. 40a. The translation is mine.
78. *Morning Leader*, 24 October 1896, p. 7, cols. 1–2; *Westminster Gazette*, 24 October 1896, p. 5, col. 1; and *Evening News*, 24 October 1896, p. 2, col. 4.
79. See note 78.

reporter actually wrote that the yellow flag was not floating over the roof as it had done during Li Hongzhang's visit to London earlier in the year.[80] Otherwise, Sun Yatsen would have been queried immediately about these obvious features by the reporters who surrounded him after his release, when he told them that he did not know that the building into which he had been pushed on 11 October 1896 was the Legation.[81]

The memoirs go on, 'The answer being positive, he asked to be introduced, whereupon he was ushered into the Legation'.[82] This is tantamount to saying that Sun Yatsen, having wanted to escape the notice of the Chinese authorities abroad by having his pigtail cut, growing a moustache and changing to European dress while he was in Japan so that he looked more like a Westernized Japanese,[83] now went straight into the arms of the Chinese authorities to expose not only his Chinese, but also his Cantonese, identity by asking to speak to a Cantonese. Being convinced that Sun Yatsen did venture into the Legation on Saturday, 10 October 1896, Schiffrin has explained, 'He apparently thought that he had shaken off his pursuers. Moreover he assumed that the Chinese would not dare harm him on British soil. Aside from being tempted by the thrill of infiltrating the Legation and haranguing any fellow Cantonese who were available, he simply may have been lonely for Chinese companionship'.[84] To begin with, there is no evidence to suggest that Sun Yatsen thought he had shaken off his pursuers.[85] Second, if Sun Yatsen assumed that the Chinese authorities would not dare harm him on British soil in particular, and I suppose on foreign soil in general, why did he go to the trouble and expense of undergoing 'a change of appearance'?[86] Third,

---

80. *Daily News*, 24 October 1896, p. 5, col. 4.

81. See, for example, *Daily Chronicle*, 24 October 1896, p. 5, col. 5. His exact words were, '. . . I did not know where I was'.

82. Wu Zonglian, *Biji*, *juan* 2, p. 40a. The translation is mine.

83. Schiffrin, *Origins*, p. 101. (See, also, Cantlie and Jones, *Sun Yat-sen*, pp. 47–8.)

84. Schiffrin, *Origins*, p. 107; see, also, pp. 111–12, in which Schiffrin has used a similar argument, referring to Sun Yatsen's 'audacity and love of adventure'.

85. On the contrary, Sun Yatsen subsequently testified, 'I had reason to suppose that my movements were being watched, because I know the Chinese government is always watching me'. (FO 17/1718, pp. 119–20, Sun Yatsen's statement at the Treasury, 4 November 1896, para. 3.)

86. Schiffrin, *Origins*, p. 101.

searching for thrills may be typical of adventurers, but certainly
indiscreet of revolutionary leaders of whom, Schiffrin agrees, Sun
Yatsen was one. Fourth, haranguing fellow Cantonese in the
Legation would have exposed his own Cantonese identity and
endangered his own life. Fifth, Chinese companionship need not
necessarily be the same as Cantonese companionship to a
Cantonese, given the different dialects and customs in China.

The allegation goes further: having been ushered into the
Legation, Sun Yatsen was met by Deng Tingkeng. He was
described as being exceptionally pleased to meet a fellow
Cantonese while abroad, introducing himself as Chen Zaizhi.
'Then he produced a gold watch to see the time, whereupon
Deng Tingkeng asked to see it. On it was engraved the word
SUN. At once Deng Tingkeng realized the true identity of the
visitor, but managed to hide his excitement'.[87] This business of
the watch was described by Luo Jialun as highly imaginative,[88]
but has been used by Schiffrin without comment.[89] For my part, I
have unearthed the original version as told by Deng Tingkeng
himself. It is contained in an exclusive interview with the *Evening
News*.[90] But in another exclusive interview, with the *Daily News*,
he appears to have made no reference to the tell-tale watch.
Instead, he said, 'He came here of his own accord. That was on
Saturday, the 10th. He sat in that seat' — pointing to one of a
row of plain oak chairs placed against the wall.[91] Be it a tell-tale
watch or a plain oak chair, it is likely that Deng Tingkeng
mentioned them in an attempt to convince his listeners that the
fugitive *had been* there on Saturday, 10 October 1896.
Apparently, the *Evening News* was so impressed by the story of
the watch that it changed its stand. Only the day before, this
paper had proclaimed that since both Sun Yatsen and the
Legation were interested parties, neither was to be believed.[92]
After its exclusive interview with Deng Tingkeng, it declared that
it preferred to believe the Legation, referring to the independent
evidence of several *unspecified* witnesses.[93] Here, it may be

87. Wu Zonglian, *Biji*, *juan* 2, p. 40a. The translation is mine.
88. Luo Jialun, *Shiliao*, p. 42.
89. Schiffrin, *Origins*, p. 112.
90. *Evening News*, 24 October 1896, p. 2, col. 6.
91. *Daily News*, 24 October 1896, p. 5, col. 5.
92. *Evening News*, 23 October 1896, p. 2, col. 4.
93. *Evening News*, 24 October 1896, p. 2, col. 6.

recalled that during Sun Yatsen's detention, even Dr Manson, an old China hand of twenty-two years' experience, was so impressed with Deng Tingkeng's denials that he began to suspect his former student had pulled a trick on him.[94] It is not clear whether Deng Tingkeng subsequently told the writer of the memoirs only about the watch, or the oak chair as well. What is clear, however, is that the writer faithfully recorded the story about the watch, which, in view of the circumstances in which it had originally been told, must be used with care.

The memoirs go on to allege that Sun Yatsen proposed to return to the Legation the next day in order to go with Deng Tingkeng to the docks area to visit the Cantonese merchants there.[95] This gives the impression that Sun Yatsen already knew that the Chinese community was in East London, but simply wanted some company to go there. It is unlikely that a conspirator would have asked a Chinese official to introduce him to the Chinese community so that he might begin his subversive activities in it. Deng Tingkeng's original story was different. He alleged that Sun Yatsen went to the Legation to enquire about the Chinese community, was told that they were in East London, and then expressed a desire to go and meet them with Deng Tingkeng.[96] Even this story is suspect. Why could Sun Yatsen not have found out about the Chinese in London from Dr Cantlie? Indeed, any Londoner could have told him about, and even directed him to, the docks area. It would have been different if he did not speak a word of English, in which case the stalwart revolutionary leader might have deemed it worth risking his life to acquire such information from the Legation. Even then, he might have hesitated about asking a Legation official to go with him. Deng Tingkeng's story should be considered in the context of the numerous reports by agitated Chinese officials both in China and abroad, about Sun Yatsen having continued to strive to recruit followers and purchase arms in preparation for another uprising.[97] The Legation publicly alleged that he 'had not given up his treasonable ideas, as he was strongly suspected of

94. Sun Yatsen, *Kidnapped in London*, p. 72.
95. Wu Zonglian, *Biji, juan* 2, p. 40a.
96. *Daily News*, 24 October 1896, p. 5, col. 5; and *Evening News*, 24 October 1896, p. 2, col. 6.
97. Luo Jialun, *Shiliao*, pp. 1-16.

negotiating for the purchase of arms for the use of rebellious Chinamen'.[98] It was probably in this spirit that Deng Tingkeng told his story, to convince the reporters that the determined conspirator had braved the Legation in order to obtain information about his future recruiting-ground. The writer of the memoirs appears to have had a different perspective, and greatly toned down this supposed bravery.

The memoirs continue, 'Deng Tingkeng gleefully agreed. After Sun was gone, Deng lost no time in reporting the matter to the Minister's nephew, who in turn told the Minister. The Minister consulted his two Secretaries, Macartney and Wang Xigeng, both of whom agreed that the visitor could be arrested'.[99] The claim that Macartney agreed to the arrest has been scrutinized in Chapter 2, Section III, with the conclusion that it was highly implausible. Here, I may add that, in his separate interviews with the two reporters mentioned above, Deng Tingkeng did not even mention that Macartney had been consulted.[100] Therefore, the claim was made in the memoirs, probably in another attempt to give the impression of unity and harmony within the Legation. The next passage of the memoirs describes what happened the following day, which will be dealt with in Section III of this chapter.

In addition to using Luo Jialun's research on the memoirs of the French interpreter of the Legation, Schiffrin has also used Luo's research on the diary of the naval attaché of the Legation to prove that Sun Yatsen visited the Legation on Saturday, 10 October 1896. He thinks that the essentials of the memoirs are corroborated by the diary,[101] a view originally expressed by Luo Jialun.[102] What Schiffrin has overlooked is Luo's additional opinion, which was that the diary seems to have been written retrospectively, at least two or three days afterwards.[103] This 'additional' opinion has been arrived at independently by Mr J.F.

---

98. *Morning*, 24 October 1896, p. 1, col. 4; *Morning Leader*, 24 October 1896, p. 7, col. 1; and *Daily Chronicle*, 24 October 1896, p. 5, col. 6.

99. Wu Zonglian, *Biji, juan* 2, p. 40a. The translation is mine.

100. *Daily News*, 24 October 1896, p. 5, col. 5; and *Evening News*, 24 October 1896, p. 2, col. 6.

101. Schiffrin, *Origins*, p. 112, quoting Luo Jialun, *Shiliao*, pp. 32–3.

102. Luo Jialun, *Shiliao*, p. 34.

103. Luo Jialun, *Shiliao*, p. 34.

Ford, who has done extensive research on the diary.[104] Hence, it is clear that the naval attaché merely wrote down what he learnt subsequently, rather than recording judiciously as first-hand knowledge what happened day by day.

Thus, the two pieces of evidence — the memoirs and the diary — on which Schiffrin has relied so heavily and yet so indirectly (by quoting Luo Jialun's work, as Schiffrin appears not to have used the originals himself) for his conclusion that Sun Yatsen visited the Legation on Saturday, 10 October 1896, turn out to be very shaky indeed. Only the claim that Sun Yatsen passed the Legation on this day, and in so doing met someone from the Legation, seems to have been corroborated to some degree by Cantlie's statement and to a lesser extent by Sun Yatsen's, as mentioned earlier in this section. Even this claim is challenged by two other groups of evidence, and corroborated by one other piece.

First, the challengers. The detective reported that, on this day, Sun Yatsen went to 'the Houses of Parliament where he remained for over two hours and on leaving he proceeded by foot to the Strand looking in the shop windows etc. returning to 8 Gray's Inn Place and was not again seen'.[105] If this version is true, then Sun Yatsen could not have gone to Regent's Park from about 11 a.m. to about 4 p.m. as he himself said.[106] Slater's other reports generally gave the exact time of his subject's coming and going. The report about Saturday is exceptionally vague in this regard, and should be considered together with the report about Sunday, in which Slater vowed that Sun Yatsen 'was not seen to leave, no doubt owing to the *inclement state of the weather* [*my italics*]'.[107] This is atrocious. I have checked the weather report for this day. How could Slater have described 'a mere trace of rain'[108] as inclement? I have suggested before that Macartney

---

104. Among his publications is one entitled 'An Account of England 1895–1896, by Fung Ling, Naval Attaché at the Imperial Chinese Legation in London', China Society Occasional Papers, No. 22 (London, 1983).

105. Chinese Legation Archives, Slater to Macartney, 12 October 1896, in Luo Jialun, *Shiliao*, p. 115.

106. FO 17/1718, pp. 119–20, Sun Yatsen's statement at the Treasury, 4 November 1896, para. 7.

107. Chinese Legation Archives, Slater to Macartney, 12 October 1896, in Luo Jialun, *Shiliao*, p. 115.

108. *The Times*, 12 October 1896, p. 6, col. 2.

went to Slater's office on Monday, 12 October 1896,[109] demanding to know the whereabouts of the man Slater was supposed to have been following. If Slater had lost his subject, or worse still, had not done his job on either Saturday or Sunday, it is quite possible that under the circumstances he concocted the reports about both days in a feeble attempt to satisfy an angry customer. In this case, Slater's version offers no challenge at all.[110]

Then Deng Tingkeng told reporters on two separate occasions that Sun Yatsen had turned up at the Legation on Saturday, 10 October 1896,[111] but on both occasions made no reference to Sun Yatsen having been ushered into the Legation by the student as claimed in the memoirs. This might be interpreted as evidence that would compromise the claim in the memoirs. On the other hand, it must be remembered that the interviews were given some time on 23 October 1896 (after the Legation had admitted very late the previous night that Sun Yatsen was a detainee and before he was released at about 5 p.m. that day), when the Legation was fiercely defending the position that Sun Yatsen had walked voluntarily into the Legation on Sunday, 11 October 1896; more than that, he had visited the Legation previously, on Saturday, 10 October 1896![112] In the circumstances, if Deng Tingkeng had alluded in the interviews to the meeting in the street, as Wu Zonglian in his memoirs subsequently did, the Legation could easily have been accused of having lured Sun Yatsen into the Legation on the Saturday in addition to forcing him into it on the Sunday. Thus, Deng Tingkeng's omission of the meeting in the street does not necessarily mean that it did not happen. So much for the challengers.

Now let us look at the corroborating evidence. On Saturday, 10 October 1896, the Chinese minister in London sent a coded cable to his counterpart in Washington to the effect that Sun

<hr/>

109. See Chapter 1, Section I.
110. For my own convenience, I have tabulated the available reports prepared by Slater during the entire period of Sun Yatsen's sojourn in London, and have found that all the Sunday reports are invariably vague or offer no news whatsoever. This phenomenon may suggest that Slater had a habit of not working on Sundays, a habit which does not seem to have been altered even by the extraordinary events of Sunday, 11 October 1896.
111. *Evening News*, 24 October 1896, p. 2, col. 6; and *Daily News*, 24 October 1896, p. 5, col. 5.
112. *Evening News*, 24 October 1896, p. 2, col. 6; and *Daily News*, 24 October 1896, p. 5, col. 5.

Yatsen was about to go to France.[113] It was a simple message of the day, with no mention of any visit, and certainly no embellishment such as a tell-tale watch or a row of plain oak chairs to which Deng Tingkeng subsequently alluded. But it does suggest that on this day, someone from the Legation might have spoken to Sun Yatsen somewhere and obtained this information from him. Where could this have happened? There is evidence to indicate, but no reliable evidence to contradict, the claim made in the memoirs that it was outside the Legation. Who could have met him? Was it the student as alleged in the memoirs, or could it have been Deng Tingkeng himself? This question is inextricably linked with another: was Sun Yatsen met by accident or by design? If by design, then there was not much point in sending someone who could not speak Cantonese. Indeed, sending a Mandarin speaker would arouse immediate suspicion of an official connection. Therefore, it seems that the meeting in the street took place by accident.

It is obvious that the Legation was anxious to identify the stranger who suddenly appeared in Portland Place on 1 October 1896[114] and whose appearance fitted the description given by the minister in Washington.[115] On 3 October 1896, Macartney telegraphed Slater to take a photograph of his subject.[116] Why was this instruction not issued right at the beginning? Does this mean that Sun Yatsen had aroused sufficient suspicion to warrant such a telegram? A photograph taken by the detective would confirm whether his subject was the same as the stranger. It is probably with the same object in mind that the telegram contained this question: 'Has the party *seen* [*my italics*] any of his countrymen?',[117] assuming that some Legation staff were aware of having been seen by the stranger. As for Sun Yatsen, Dr Cantlie testified:

---

113. Chinese Legation Archives, Gong Zhaoyuan to Yang Ru (cypher), 10 October 1896, in Luo Jialin, *Shiliao*, pp. 25–6.

114. FO 17/1718, pp. 121–2, Cantlie's statement at the Treasury, 4 November 1896, para. 2.

115. Chinese Legation Archives, Yang Ru to Gong Zhaoyuan, 18 July 1896, in Luo Jialun, *Shiliao*, pp. 8–10.

116. Chinese Legation Archives, Macartney to Slater (telegram), 3 October 1896, in Luo Jialun, *Shiliao*, p. 112.

117. Chinese Legation Archives, Macartney to Slater (telegram), 3 October 1896, in Luo Jialun, *Shiliao*, p. 112.

On the 4th October we were talking about the Chinese Legation — I think it was the 4th — and I said, 'Well, I suppose you are not going to the Chinese Legation', and he laughed, and said, 'I don't think so.' Then my wife said, 'you had better not go there; they will ship you off to China, and you will lose your head.' He said, 'Oh, no, I won't go there.'[118]

How did the conversation begin? Did it begin, at luncheon, with a 'reference to the Chinese Legation's close proximity' to where the Cantlies were living, as alleged by Dr Cantlie's son, Neil?[119] Standing on the east side of Portland Place and using a 35mm lens, I have been able to take a photograph that includes part of the Legation building on the extreme left, and part of Dr Cantlie's former residence on the extreme right, with the corner house in the middle of the picture. It took me only a minute or so to reach one from the other on foot. Is it possible that Sun Yatsen had already *seen* some of his compatriots in the vicinity and asked about them, and that Dr Cantlie replied that they were probably members of the Chinese Legation which was just around the corner? If this were the case, it would seem that both Sun Yatsen and the Legation staff began to make enquiries about the other party at about the same time.

It is not known if Sun Yatsen's conversation with Dr Cantlie about the Chinese Legation was cut short by Mrs Cantlie's stern warning. In any case, he appears to have made further enquiries with Dr Manson, as his testimony to the Treasury solicitor shows:

I had a conversation with Dr Manson about going to the Chinese Legation. I asked him if it would be wise for me to go there. He said, 'No'. I think the first question I asked was, 'Who is the Chinese Minister here?' and then I asked him, 'Do you think it is a wise thing for me to see anyone there?' and Dr Manson said, 'No'.[120]

One must remember that Sun Yatsen offered this information in the course of the official inquiry conducted by the Treasury solicitor, probably in the form of questions and answers; and then the answers were subsequently put together as a statement. This

---

118. FO 17/1718, pp. 121–2, Cantlie's statement at the Treasury, 4 November 1896, para. 4.
119. Cantlie and Seaver, *Sir James Cantlie*, p. 101.
120. FO 17/1718, pp. 119–20, Sun Yatsen's statement at the Treasury, 4 November 1896, para. 5.

indicates that the solicitor, in view of the Legation's allegation
that Sun Yatsen had gone of his own free will, wanted to find out
if the fugitive had intended to do so. Subsequently,[121] Dr Manson
also stated:

Sun came to me two or three days after his arrival in this country, and
dined with me two or three days afterwards. He told me what he had
been doing in Canton, and how he was engaged in a political affair
there, and how his companions had come to grief. I congratulated him
on getting away, and told him he had better stop that sort of thing. He
spoke about going to the Chinese Legation here, and I told him it was
not advisable. He said he would take my advice and not go.[122]

As far as intentions went, therefore, the solicitor concluded that
'something of the kind was on his mind'.[123] But, in the light of all
the other evidence he managed to put together, he still believed
that Sun Yatsen had been introduced into the Legation in the
manner claimed by the victim.[124] Schiffrin regards Sun Yatsen's
conversation with Dr Manson as evidence that 'Sun was weighing
the notion'.[125] Wu Xiangxiang thinks otherwise. He points out
that Dr Manson does not seem to have been at all amused by Sun
Yatsen's story of the uprising and of his narrow escape, and
suggests that the embarrassed Sun Yatsen tried to enliven the
atmosphere by referring to Dr Cantlie's jovial remark about
going to the Chinese Legation, thus effecting a change of
subject.[126]

Sun Yatsen's enquiries about the Legation seem to have stopped with Dr Manson, who, like Mrs Cantlie, warned him strongly
not to go to the Legation. The Legation's enquiries about the
stranger also seem to have stopped with Slater, who replied on 6
October 1896 that his subject had not been seen to meet any of
his countrymen, and that a photograph would have to wait for

---

121. FO 17/1718, pp. 113–16, Cuffe to Home Office, 12 November 1896,
para. 4, in which Cuffe wrote, 'These statements were taken in the order in which
I have placed them'. Manson's statement was put behind that of Sun Yatsen.
122. FO 17/1718, p. 122, Manson's statement at the Treasury, 4 November
1896, para. 2.
123. FO 17/1718, pp. 113–16, Cuffe to Home Office, 12 November 1896,
para. 9.
124. FO 17/1718, pp. 113–16, Cuffe to Home Office, 12 November 1896,
para. 5.
125. Schiffrin, Origins, pp. 106–7.
126. Wu Xiangxiang, Sun Yixian zhuan, Vol. 1, p. 153.

more propitious weather.[127] If this were the case, it would strengthen my earlier suggestion that Sun Yatsen had been met by someone (assuming that such a meeting did take place) in the street by accident rather than by design, on Saturday, 10 October 1896. But the information which seems to have been acquired in this way about the stranger's imminent departure for France, appears not only to have rekindled great interest within the Legation but also to have generated a sense of urgency. What looks like a hasty decision for immediate action was taken the next day. The result of that action has been narrated. Macartney was summoned to the Legation on this day of rest. Sun Yatsen was detained. With this, let us look at three additional groups of evidence, produced after the mission was accomplished.

On Sunday, 11 October 1896, the minister sent a coded cable to Beijing, saying that Sun Yatsen had turned up at the Legation on that day and was thereupon detained, but making absolutely no reference to the alleged visit on the previous day.[128] Nor was such a reference ever made in all the ensuing cables, one of which was quite long (133 words) and reiterated that Sun Yatsen had entered the Legation voluntarily.[129] Does all this mean that the alleged previous visit had not taken place at all? Subsequently, after Sun Yatsen had been released on 23 October 1896, the minister appears to have prepared a full report for Beijing. It was dated 4 November 1896. It cannot be found either in the Palace Museum Archives in Beijing or in the Legation Archives, but was transcribed in Wu Zonglian's memoirs.[130] There is doubt as to whether it was ever dispatched. It contains an allegation about the previous visit, as do the memoirs. So far, none of the *official* Chinese documents I have looked at contains such an allegation. Nor do any of the British records. George Cole, the porter, testified that there were ten or twelve Chinese servants. He knew

---

127. Chinese Legation Archives, Slater to Macartney, 6 October 1896, in Luo Jialun, *Shiliao*, p. 114.

128. Beijing Palace Museum Records, Gong Zhaoyuan to Zongli Yamen (cypher), 11 October 1896, in *Zhonghua minguo kaiguo wushinian wenxian: Xing Zhong Hui, shang* (Taipei, 1964), pp. 191–2 (hereafter cited as *Zhonghua minguo*). See *Zhonghua minguo* for the other cyphers.

129. Beijing Palace Museum Records, Gong Zhaoyuan to Zongli Yamen (cypher), 14 October 1896, in *Zhonghua minguo*, pp. 191–2.

130. Wu Zonglian, *Biji, juan* 2, pp. 37b–39b. See, also, Luo Jialun, *Shiliao*, pp. 73–6.

them; they could all speak sufficient English for him to understand them.[131] Among the numerous things they said to him, such as, 'Very funny, which way this man come Chinese Legation',[132] 'he likee to buy too many guns and swords',[133] 'Chinese Emperor very cross with him, and Chinese Emperor quick takee head away',[134] 'Policeman stopee outside, I think',[135] and 'Minister no longer keep this man now before he go. Chinese Emperor no wantee now',[136] Cole vowed that he 'never heard that Sun had been to the Legation before the 11th October'.[137] Security, or the lack of it, at the Legation was such that the servants not only knew but openly talked about sending Sun Yatsen back to China for execution.[138] But however talkative they were, they do not seem to have talked about the supposed previous visit.

Finally, Dr Manson testified, 'I asked him [Sun Yatsen, shortly after his release from the Legation] if he had ever been in the Legation before the Sunday. I put this question very straightly to him twice, and he denied it distinctly. I have known Sun for many years and have found him trustworthy'.[139]

In sum, it is probable that Sun Yatsen had passed the Legation on 10 October 1896, had spoken with someone from the Legation in a chance encounter in the street, and had indicated the possibility of another visit to the area on the next day. However, there is no independent evidence to support the Legation's claim that Sun Yatsen had been inside the Legation building on this day,

---

131. FO 17/1718, pp. 116–19, Cole's statement at the Treasury, 2 November 1896, para. 3.

132. FO 17/1718, pp. 116–19, Cole's statement at the Treasury, 2 November 1896, para. 7.

133. FO 17/1718, pp. 116–19, Cole's statement at the Treasury, 2 November 1896, para. 14.

134. FO 17/1718, pp. 116–19, Cole's statement at the Treasury, 2 November 1896, para. 14.

135. FO 17/1718, pp. 116–19, Cole's statement at the Treasury, 2 November 1896, para. 22.

136. FO 17/1718, pp. 116–19, Cole's statement at the Treasury, 2 November 1896, para. 24.

137. FO 17/1718, pp. 116–19, Cole's statement at the Treasury, 2 November 1896, para. 28.

138. FO 17/1718, pp. 116–19, Cole's statement at the Treasury, 2 November 1896, para. 14.

139. FO 17/1718, p. 122, Manson's statement at the Treasury, 4 November 1896, paras. 6–7.

or had made an appointment to 'return to the Legation' the next day.

III Between the Street and the Cell

i. Between the Street and the Hall

Both Sun Yatsen and, ultimately, the Legation, agreed that Sun Yatsen entered the building on Sunday, 11 October 1896. However, they disagreed about the circumstances under which his entry took place.

None of the Legation evidence, official or private, gave any detail about Sun Yatsen's arrival. The pertinent cyphers from the minister simply said that Sun Yatsen turned up at the Legation.[140] The minister's supposed dispatch of 4 November 1896 only alleged that Sun Yatsen *returned* the next day.[141] In his interview with the *Daily News*, Deng Tingkeng merely said, 'Next day he came punctually';[142] and to the *Evening News* he claimed, 'Punctually at eleven o'clock the next morning the visitor made his reappearance'.[143] When asked by the *Daily Telegraph*, 'Can you say on what business he called at the Legation?', Macartney replied, 'I cannot tell you that'.[144] In his memoirs, the French interpreter recalled, 'On 11 October 1896, before noon, Sun came unsuspiciously as appointed'.[145] In his so-called diary, the naval attaché retrospectively entered that Sun Yatsen kept his appointment.[146] Thus, the official documents (that is, the coded cables) simply alleged that Sun Yatsen came, and the unofficial records (that is, the memoirs and the diary) claimed that he returned on that day.

Sun Yatsen, on the other hand, gave graphic descriptions of the way in which he had been introduced into the Legation. The first details emerged on 19 October 1896 on a visiting card which he had had smuggled out of the Legation.[147] A second account

---

140. Beijing Palace Museum Records, Gong Zhaoyuan to Zongli Yamen (cypher), 11 and 14 October 1896, in *Zhonghua minguo*, pp. 191–2.
141. See Luo Jialun, *Shiliao*, pp. 73–6. Wu Zonglian, *Biji, juan* 2, pp. 37a–37b.
142. *Daily News*, 24 October 1896, p. 5, col. 5.
143. *Evening News*, 24 October 1896, p. 2, col. 6.
144. *Daily Telegraph*, 23 October 1896, p. 7, col. 6.
145. Wu Zonglian, *Biji, juan* 2, p. 40a.
146. Fengling, *Jinzhi, juan* 2, p. 9b.
147. FO 17/1718, pp. 22–3, Sun Yatsen to Cantlie (19 October 1896).

was made available during an impromptu news conference[148] he gave in the Shades public house immediately after his release on 23 October 1896.[149] A third account may be found in the police files in Scotland Yard,[150] where he made a statement after the impromptu news conference. A fourth account was obtained by reporters after Sun Yatsen had had dinner, at Dr Cantlie's place.[151] A fifth account was acquired by the Treasury solicitor, who interrogated Sun Yatsen while conducting an official inquiry.[152] The sixth account was prepared in *Kidnapped in London*.[153] The details vary a bit, but the main theme of his kidnapping and detention remain substantially the same.

The first account is too brief for the purpose of this study.[154] The second account is in some ways more informative than the fifth (and the longest), because the reporters not only bombarded Sun Yatsen with questions as the solicitor apparently did later, but some of the reporters recorded the questions as well. In addition, the impromptu news conference was closer to the event, and did not allow Sun Yatsen as much time to give considered answers. Finally, it was engineered by the reporters, and not called by the victim. Hence, I have decided to use it here as the basis for analysis; supplemented, of course, by details from the other accounts.

It seems that the Press Association asked the first question, 'It has been stated that you went to the Chinese Embassy of your accord — is that so?'[155] Sun Yatsen answered, 'That is not true. I met a Chinaman in the street, and he took me in'.[156] Here, he was probably referring to Deng Tingkeng luring him into the

---

148. See Chapter 4, Section II, for details.

149. See, in particular, *Daily Chronicle*, 24 October 1896, p. 5, cols. 4–5; and *Daily Telegraph*, 24 October 1896, p. 7, col. 7 – p. 8, col. 1.

150. A copy of this may be found in the Foreign Office records; see FO 17/1718, pp. 80–3, Sun Yatsen's statement at Scotland Yard, 23 October 1896.

151. See, in particular, *Daily News*, 24 October 1896, p. 5, cols. 3–4.

152. FO 17/1718, pp. 119–20, Sun Yatsen's statement at the Treasury, 4 November 1896.

153. Sun Yatsen, *Kidnapped in London*, pp. 32–5.

154. It simply said, 'I was pulled into the Chinese Legation by two Chinamen outside the street [*sic*] near the doorway on Sunday 11th Oct. Before I got in they each held a hand on my side urging me to go in to have a talk. When I got in they locked the front door'. (FO 17/1718, pp. 22–3, Sun Yatsen to Cantlie, 19 October 1896.)

155. *Daily Telegraph*, 24 October 1896, p. 7, col. 7.

156. *Daily Telegraph*, 24 October 1896, p. 7, col. 7.

Legation, and not the two able-bodied men who, he claimed, more or less took him physically into the Legation. He continued, 'I was walking alone in a part of the town which I now know as Portland Place. I had no knowledge that I was in the street in which the Chinese Legation is situated, nor had I ever been to the Legation'.[157] He might not have been to the Legation previously, but it is difficult to believe that he did not know Portland Place. Subsequently, he told the Treasury solicitor, 'I took a bus to Oxford Circus, and walked through Portland Place. This was my usual route [to the Cantlie's]'.[158] This, I think, is nearer the truth. As for his disclaiming any knowledge that he was in the street in which the Chinese Legation was situated, this is again incredible in the light of his conversations with Dr Cantlie and then Dr Manson, which have been quoted and assessed in the previous section. I can imagine that the solicitor initially exhibited the same sort of disbelief when he questioned Sun Yatsen on this point, which is evident in the answers recorded, 'I did not ask where the Legation was. I did not know where it was. I did not know where it was until I was taken in there. I did not ask either Dr Cantlie or Dr Manson where it was'.[159] But the solicitor subsequently allowed himself to be persuaded;[160] probably because he seems to have remembered, incorrectly, that Dr Manson subsequently testified to the same effect.[161] In fact, it was Dr Cantlie who said so.[162] This is not an insignificant point, considering that the solicitor might have made a distinction between Dr Cantlie, who had been thoroughly preoccupied with Sun Yatsen, and Dr Manson, who had not been involved to the same extent.[163] In the end, the solicitor argued that, as a matter of probability, if Sun Yatsen had known that the house was the

157. *Daily Chronicle*, 24 October 1896, p. 5, col. 4.
158. FO 17/1718, pp. 119–20, Sun Yatsen's statement at the Treasury, 4 November 1896, para. 8.
159. FO 17/1718, pp. 119–20, Sun Yatsen's statement at the Treasury, 4 November 1896, para. 5.
160. FO 17/1718, pp. 113–16, Cuffe to Home Office, 12 November 1896, para. 16.
161. FO 17/1718, pp. 113–16, Cuffe to Home Office, 12 November 1896, para. 9. I have checked Dr Manson's testimony. He did not testify to this effect. See FO 17/1718, p. 122, Manson's statement at the Treasury, 4 November 1896.
162. FO 17/1718, pp. 121–2, Cantlie's statement at the Treasury, 4 November 1896, para. 4.
163. See Chapter 1 for details.

Chinese Legation, he would not have entered it.[164] I shall deal with this particular aspect later in this paragraph. I should like to point out here that Sun Yatsen first visited Dr Cantlie at 46, Devonshire Street, from Haxell's Hotel on 1 October 1896.[165] Thereafter, he visited him 'nearly every day', according to himself,[166] as well as Dr Cantlie,[167] from 8, Gray's Inn Place. When asked to name the specific dates of these visits, Dr Cantlie was able to pinpoint at least five.[168] The map on p. *xx* shows the location of the various places of relevance, and demonstrates the very high probability that each time Sun Yatsen went to see the Cantlies he would have passed the front door of the Legation both on the outward and return journeys. Thus, it is likely that he walked past the building at least ten times before the fateful Sunday of 11 October 1896. As mentioned before, the building does not seem to have had a plate to announce its identity, nor to have flown the national flag in ordinary times; and therefore the staff was not in a position to assume that any stranger to the place would have recognized it to be the Chinese Legation.[169] From Sun Yatsen's point of view, the perspective is slightly different. Had he not, even once, while passing the Legation (which he did at least ten times), spotted any Chinese entering or leaving that building? If he had not, then he might indeed not have suspected that the house was the Legation. But his claim that he did not even know that the Legation was in Portland Place, as made in the impromptu news conference, remains suspect. It is possible that Sun Yatsen, in view of the nature of what appears to have been the very first question[170] that hit him so soon after his ordeal, was over-anxious to convince the world that he had been kidnapped.

---

164. FO 17/1718, pp. 113–16, Cuffe to Home Office, 12 November 1896, para. 16.

165. See the very beginning of Chapter 1, Section I.

166. FO 17/1718, pp. 119–20, Sun Yatsen's statement at the Treasury, 4 November 1896, para. 5.

167. FO 17/1718, pp. 121–2, Cantlie's statement at the Treasury, 4 November 1896, para. 5.

168. FO 17/1718, pp. 121–2, Cantlie's statement at the Treasury, 4 November 1896, para. 5.

169. See previous section.

170. As mentioned, the question was: 'It has been stated that you went to the Chinese Embassy of your own accord — is that so?' (*Daily Telegraph*, 24 October 1896, p. 7, col. 7).

I have noted that he no longer made such a claim when he was interrogated by the Treasury solicitor twelve days later.

The news conference continued. 'You were simply out for an afternoon walk?', asked the *Daily Chronicle*. 'Just that', replied Sun Yatsen.[171] Here, he might have expressed himself badly, or might have said something that he did not really mean, or might have told the truth. Another journalist, who did not report word for word, subsequently alleged that Sun Yatsen was 'on his way to Dr Cantlie's'.[172] Sun Yatsen himself later told the solicitor, 'I intended to go to Dr Cantlie's'.[173] *Kidnapped in London* spelt out his intention further, 'to go to church with the doctor and his family'.[174] The last version has since been taken for granted in a lot of writings. I have checked Mrs Cantlie's diary. The entry for Saturday, 10 October 1896, begins as follows: 'The boys and Nannie went down to Mother's [at Barnes]. Hamish took Mr Carlill down to Hind Head until *Monday* [*my italics*]. Miss Master called & after she left I went down to Barnes'.[175] The entry for Sunday, 11 October 1896, reads, 'Mother & I went to Roehampton to church. We all dined with Ken & Jeannie. Mother & I went over to the cemetery [where Mrs Cantlie's father was buried]. The boys & Nannie went home but I stayed till tomorrow [*sic*]'.[176] I have discussed these entries with Dr Cantlie's grandson. Apparently, going to Barnes in those days was not simply a matter of packing and leaving. The old lady at Barnes had to be given plenty of notice, if only to get enough provisions to feed an additional three adults (usually Dr and Mrs Cantlie and Nannie) and the three boys (Keith, born 1886, Colin, born 1888, and Neil, born 1892). Thus, it is unlikely that the Cantlies would have made an appointment to go to Barnes, and at the same time made an appointment with Sun Yatsen to go to church (St Martin-in-the-Fields)[177] on the Sunday. In addition, my study of events in the previous section suggests that Sun Yatsen had

---

171. *Daily Chronicle*, 24 October 1896, p. 5, col. 4.
172. *Globe*, 24 October 1896, p. 4, col. 4.
173. FO 17/1718, pp. 119–20, Sun Yatsen's statement at the Treasury, 4 November 1896, para. 8.
174. Sun Yatsen, *Kidnapped in London*, p. 33.
175. Mrs Cantlie's diary, 10 October 1896.
176. Mrs Cantlie's diary, 11 October 1896.
177. The Cantlies' church was St Martin-in-the Fields (Mrs Cantlie's diary, 20 September 1896).

called at 46, Devonshire Street, on the Saturday, after Dr Cantlie
had gone. Whether Mrs Cantlie was still there is not clear. If she
had gone as well, then the servants,[178] I should expect, would
have told him what had happened. If she was still there, it would
have been up to her to say something. But did she? Her diary
shows that she had a great deal of compassion for the fugitive
after he had been detained in the Legation and faced the possibility of a cruel death. But before that, references to him were
rather indifferent. The entry made in Honolulu on 27 February
1896 reads: 'Sun Yat Sen (Hamish's old student in Hong Kong)
and the [*sic*] Conspirator of Canton, saw us in the road & took us
out'.[179] I can imagine that, like Dr Manson, she could have told
Sun Yatsen to 'stop that sort of thing',[180] if she had the opportunity to do so. What could have worried her, too, was that her
husband might jeopardize his chances of getting a knighthood by
continuing to be so close to a wanted man, having him in the
house practically every day 'from 10 o'clock in the morning till 6
o'clock at night'.[181] On the basis of his enormous contribution to
the medical and other aspects of life during his long stay in Hong
Kong until earlier in the year,[182] tradition within the Cantlie
family has it that Dr Cantlie was being considered for a knighthood at the time. This tradition goes on to say that his
subsequent and open involvement with Sun Yatsen, particularly
his relentless efforts to rescue him, made the British government
hesitate to add insult to injury by awarding Dr Cantlie a knighthood in the wake of such a saga.[183]

Suppose that on 10 October 1896 Sun Yatsen did call at the
Cantlies, and suppose that Mrs Cantlie was still there and did not
say anything about the family being away the next day, could their
absence on Sunday have been her way of hinting to Sun Yatsen

---

178. Mrs Cantlie's diary, Cash account 1896. An entry in this account dated
29 September 1896 shows that apart from Nannie, there were three other servants: Bessie, Bella, and Giles.

179. Mrs Cantlie's diary, 27 February 1896.

180. FO 17/1718, p. 122, Manson's statement at the Treasury, 4 November
1896, para. 2. Apparently he spent most of the time in Dr Cantlie's study,
reading. See Sun Yatsen, *Kidnapped in London*, p. 31.

181. FO 17/1718, pp. 121–2, Cantlie's statement at the Treasury, 4 November
1896, para. 5.

182. Mrs Cantlie's diary, 8 February 1896.

183. He was eventually knighted in 1909 (Cantlie and Seaver, *Sir James
Cantlie*, p. 147).

that he was getting too close? If this was the case, it would also appear less improbable that Sun Yatsen was indeed on his way to the Cantlies, when he was lured into the Legation. I must emphasize, however, that this is speculation. The evidence available so far does not enable me to say with certainty that this was the case.

The news conference went on. 'As I was walking along, a Chinaman came up and asked me whether I was a Chinaman or a Japanese. I was in the dress which I am wearing now — European dress — and he was wearing the Chinese dress'.[184] On the question 'Are you Japanese or Chinese?', the Treasury solicitor ruled, 'I can hardly give credit to Sun for such ingenuity as to have invented this statement in order to support an untrue story ... He does look exactly like a Japanese, and I think any person meeting him for the first time would hesitate as to his nationality'.[185] Sun Yatsen continued, 'I answered that I was a Chinaman, and then, as the fashion of Chinamen is, he asked, "Which province do you come from?"'[186] It is intriguing that, having undergone a complete change of appearance which made him look like a Westernized Japanese, he should have revealed his true identity so readily, especially in view of the fact that he probably knew the Chinese in that area were members of the Legation. Possibly, the reporters were somewhat taken aback by this; because one of them asked rather anxiously, 'You informed him which province of China you came from?' 'Yes, I told him Canton'.[187] If the conversation did go like this, I can only say that Sun Yatsen could have been more on his guard.

'I was born in Hong Kong', he continued, 'but in speaking to a Chinaman about where you belong to, Hong Kong is regarded as being included in Canton'.[188] I shall deal with this claim about his birthplace in the next section. '"Then", remarked the stranger, "you are a countryman of my own", meaning that he also came from the province of Canton. We walked along together a short way, chatting like this, when a second Chinaman joined us'.[189] At this point, a reporter again interjected, 'Did you know him —

---

184. *Daily Chronicle*, 24 October 1896, p. 5, col. 5.
185. FO 17/1718, pp. 113–16, Cuffe to Home Office, 12 November 1896, para. 11.
186. *Daily Chronicle*, 24 October 1896, p. 5, col. 5.
187. *Daily Chronicle*, 24 October 1896, p. 5, col. 5.
188. *Daily Chronicle*, 24 October 1896, p. 5, col. 5.
189. *Daily Chronicle*, 24 October 1896, p. 5, col. 5.

had you seen him before?' 'Oh, no; but the first Chinaman introduced him saying he likewise was a countryman. I shook hands with the new Chinaman, but I observed he was not from the province of Canton because his dialect of Chinese was not the same as mine and I found it difficult to understand him. Both of them said there were many Chinese in London and that some day they would take me to visit some of those whom they know'.[190] This reference to the Chinese community in London, when considered in the light of the Legation's intelligence about Sun Yatsen having continued to endeavour to recruit followers, reads very much like a bait. Later he told the solicitor that it was he who started the subject by asking, 'Are there any Chinese in London?',[191] which is still consistent with the version here, but would have confirmed the suspicion of the Legation about the true identity of the stranger, given the Legation's state of mind.

'Well, what happened next?'
'A third Chinaman joined us and he was introduced to me. Soon after I noticed that the first Chinaman had gone away and I wondered what had become of him so hurriedly. I forgot to mention that when we exchanged names — which again is a part of Chinese fashion — he had told me that his name was Tang [Deng]. Later I knew him as Mr Tang [Deng] of the Chinese Legation, because, as I shall tell you, I saw him in the Legation. Meantime with the second and third Chinaman I was always talking and moving along the pavement, and they asked me would I not come with them.'
'Did you go?'
'The next minute — before I had time to speak — I was pushed on to the steps of a door which we had come opposite. The door opened or was opened by them, and I was shoved inside, and it was shut behind me.'[192]

When interrogated by the solicitor, Sun Yatsen went into more detail:

We were standing inside the porch when Tang [Deng] left us, and left me with the two Chinamen, and when these two men asked me to go in for a talk I began to look for Tang [Deng]. They said, 'Oh, let us go in', and began to pull me in, but there was no real violence used; it was done

---

190. *Daily Chronicle*, 24 October 1896, p. 5, col. 5.
191. FO 17/1718, pp. 119-20, Sun Yatsen's statement at the Treasury, 4 November 1896, para. 8.
192. *Daily Chronicle*, 24 October 1896, p. 5, col. 5.

in a friendly manner. When they were half pulling me in I looked upon them as friends. When I got in I heard the door locked.[193]

The solicitor observed, 'It appears to me that if Sun had desired to invent a story and to dwell on the kidnapping as an important feature of it, he would have alleged that actual force was used, and would not have admitted the half consent which he, in effect, does admit. I cannot see that, except on the hypothesis that he wants to make out a strong case against the Legation, there would be any object in saying anything untrue on this point. The real complaint on which he dwells and which he emphasises is the detention, and the manner in which he was treated while in the Legation'.[194]

On the basis of this observation, the solicitor felt that there was no real conflict between Sir Halliday Macartney's denial of inveiglement and Sun Yatsen's description of the manner in which he had been introduced into the Legation, because, 'taking Sun's account as the correct one, it is possible that it might be contended that he was not on that occasion *inveigled* into the Legation. He does not himself suggest, nor as I read his various statements, do I understand him ever to have committed himself to the proposition that he was actually forced into the Legation. He puts it rather that he was induced to get into a friendly conversation with countrymen of his own, and that, following that conversation, he was half persuaded, half led, but, as he says himself, without any actual exercise of force, into the hall. In a sense, he did go in of his own accord, but so far as he did this, it was because he believed he was with friends, and, as he states, in entire ignorance of the character of the house which he was entering'.[195]

This argument does not alter the fact that whatever means, friendly or otherwise, had been adopted, the sole object was to get the fugitive inside the walls of the Legation. And, if Sun Yatsen's version is correct, it was an operation which was well thought out and very well conducted: no arguments, and certain-

---

193. FO 17/1718, pp. 119–20, Sun Yatsen's statement at the Treasury, 4 November 1896, para. 8.

194. FO 17/1718, pp. 113–16, Cuffe to Home Office, 12 November 1896, para. 17.

195. FO 17/1718, pp. 113–16, Cuffe to Home Office, 12 November 1896, para. 15.

ly no scuffles. But how reliable was Sun Yatsen's version? I note that the question, 'Are you Japanese or Chinese?' was regarded by the solicitor as something which Sun Yatsen could not have invented.[196] I may add that his Japanese appearance had proved convincing on at least two previous occasions. When the Cantlies were in Hawaii on their way back to England from Hong Kong, they were stopped in the street by him. They completely failed to recognize him, and their Japanese nurse began addressing him in Japanese.[197] Then they went to a shop, and the shopkeeper began talking to him in Japanese as well.[198] As for the way in which he had been introduced into the Legation, the solicitor thought that he had no object in saying anything untrue.[199] Luo Jialun, who did not read Sun Yatsen's statement at the Treasury, and Schiffrin, who did, both believe that he had an object, which was to blacken the Manchu regime. Their views have been dealt with in the previous section. I only wish to add here that, if he did have such an object in mind, he would probably have insisted that violence had been used. The solicitor also observed that when he interrogated him, 'his manner was not in any way indicative of a desire to conceal the truth or to exaggerate his injuries'.[200] The solicitor was an experienced lawyer who had been asked by his government to conduct an official inquiry. His judgement, at least in this regard, deserves attention. Furthermore, Dr Cantlie, who stated that the subject of going to the Legation had emerged in the course of a conversation with Sun Yatsen, testified at the same time that he did not think Sun Yatsen 'knew where the Chinese Legation was'.[201]

I am still somewhat uneasy about Sun Yatsen's claim that he did not know the real identity of the house which was the Legation. Only on the assumption that, during his passing and re-passing the house, he had not actually seen any Chinese in

196. FO 17/1718, pp. 113–16, Cuffe to Home Office, 12 November 1896, para. 11.
197. Cantlie and Jones, *Sun Yat-sen*, p. 48.
198. Cantlie and Jones, *Sun Yat-sen*, p. 48.
199. FO 17/1718, pp. 113–16, Cuffe to Home Office, 12 November 1896, para. 17.
200. FO 17/1718, pp. 113–16, Cuffe to Home Office, 12 November 1896, para. 17.
201. FO 17/1718, pp. 121–2, Cantlie's statement at the Treasury, 4 November 1896, para. 4.

Chinese dress (or, worse still, official dress) leaving or entering the building and hence arousing his suspicion, may such a claim stand. If he had known, or suspected, the nature of the establishment, but still allowed himself to be lured into it, the question becomes one of how quickly it happened, how alert he was at the time, what mood he was in, how much he was on his guard, and so on. Absolute certainty on this point will probably never be reached. But having assessed the evidence of both the Legation and Sun Yatsen, I am inclined to think that Sun Yatsen's version as presented here seems more plausible.

Finally, let us look at the evidence of a third party, George Cole, the porter, on whom the Treasury solicitor passed the following judgement: 'I believe Cole. He impressed me most favourably and, indeed, it is difficult to see that he can have any object in saying anything that is untrue'.[202] Cole testified to the solicitor that he had overheard Chinese servants in the Legation say, 'Very funny which way this man come Chinese Legation'.[203] The solicitor said he did not pretend he could interpret exactly the meaning of this, but should certainly infer that it meant that Sun Yatsen had not been an ordinary visitor who had come in in the usual way.[204] Cole also testified that he heard Deng Tingkeng say, 'I very clever; I knowledge; I getee inside'.[205] Cole recalled having heard this at the end of his interview with the solicitor, just as he was going to leave. The solicitor commented that both from Cole's manner and from the way in which it came out, 'I am quite satisfied that he did hear, or honestly believes he heard Tang [Deng] say this'. If Deng Tingkeng had said this, the solicitor continued, 'it seems to me practically conclusive as showing that either force or trickery, more probably the latter,

---

202. FO 17/1718, pp. 113–16, Cuffe to Home Office, 12 November 1896, para. 19. The solicitor's comment was based on a very long interview with Cole. Such a comment would have carried even more weight if the solicitor had furnished more information about the background career and character of Cole.
203. FO 17/1718, pp. 116–19, Cole's statement at the Treasury, 2 November 1896, para. 7.
204. FO 17/1718, pp. 113–16, Cuffe to Home Office, 12 November 1896, para. 21.
205. FO 17/1718, pp. 116–19, Cole's statement at the Treasury, 2 November 1896, para. 29. The full paragraph reads: 'Tang said one day, "I very clever; I knowledge; I getee inside." Tang could speak English well, but sometimes, and when excited, would go into broken English'. It is not clear to whom he said this, probably to one of the English servants.

was used to get Sun inside the walls of the Legation'.[206] I may
reiterate here that the French interpreter of the Legation gave
the following title to that part of his memoirs dealing with this
particular incident: 'An Account of How Minister Gong Captured the Cantonese Rebel Sun Wen by *Stratagem* [*my italics*]
and How He Subsequently Released Him'.[207] The interpreter
elaborated on this in his preface, 'Having failed in his plot in
Guangdong, the rebel Sun Wen fled overseas and spent quite
some time in America. Minister Gong, following secret instructions from Beijing, lost no time in setting up a trap to capture
and detain him as soon as he set foot in London'.[208] As to how he
was in a position to plan such an operation, Schiffrin is quite right
in pointing out that Slater could not have supplied the necessary
information.[209] I submit that Sun Yatsen's passing and re-passing
of the Legation at least ten times might not have enabled him to
suspect what was inside, but appears to have enabled those inside
to know his routine fairly well.[210]

ii. Between the Hall and the Cell

Sun Yatsen said in the impromptu news conference that after
he had entered the Legation, the door was locked behind him.
'More Chinamen there now were, but I did not know where I was
or what all this meant. I looked for Mr [Deng], who spoke to me
in the street. He was not to be seen, and I was forced up a
staircase: that is to say, two big men took me up. I am small, as
you see, and I could not in any case make resistance against
powerful Chinamen'.[211]

'What happened after you had been taken upstairs?'
'I think they put me into a room. They locked the door, and though I

---

    206. FO 17/1718, pp. 113–16, Cuffe to Home Office, 12 November 1896,
para. 21.
    207. Wu Zonglian, *Biji, juan* 2, p. 39a. The translation is mine.
    208. Wu Zonglian, *Biji, juan* 2, preface. The translation is mine.
    209. Schiffrin, *Origins*, p. 111.
    210. The Treasury solicitor was the first to point out this possibility, although
he does not seem to have done the same kind of field-work that I have done. In
addition, he wrongly assumed that the Legation had obtained information about
Sun Yatsen's routine mainly from Slater. (FO 17/1718, pp. 113–16, Cuffe to
Home Office, 12 November 1896, para. 9.)
    211. *Daily Chronicle*, 24 October 1896, p. 5, col. 5.

asked again for Mr [Deng] I did not see him. Instead, a European gentleman entered ...'[212]

His interrogation by the Treasury solicitor produced more details: 'Then the men began to force me to go upstairs. Their tones changed directly I got inside the house; their friendly manner was changed. I then came to the conclusion that I was entrapped. They said, "Go upstairs", not in a friendly manner. I said, "What is the matter?" They said, "Never mind; go upstairs." This was about 11 o'clock'.[213]

I went into a room. I think it was on the second storey, and stopped there a short time. When I got into that room there were one or two Chinamen there. I did not hear their names; they did not say anything to me. I was there only a very short time. Then I was asked to go upstairs another storey. I was taken there by the same men as brought me in, and there were *several other people, some going in front and some being behind me* [*my italics*]. After I got into this other room I was left alone. An Englishman (Sir H. Macartney) came into the room with me. We two were alone.[214]

The French interpreter of the Legation, however, painted a rather different picture in his memoirs.

On 11 October 1896, some time before noon, Sun Yatsen arrived as expected, unsuspectingly. [He was entertained to] a meal, after which Deng Tingkeng invited him upstairs, where, on the first floor, they toured the minister's reception room and the chancellery. Then they went to the second floor to Mr *Li Shengzhong's* [*my italics*] room where they sat and chatted for quite a while. When Sir Halliday Macartney arrived, [Deng Tingkeng] said to Sun Yatsen 'Would you like to go one floor higher to visit my room?' Sun Yatsen replied, 'With pleasure.' He followed Deng Tingkeng upstairs, with Sir Halliday leading the way. When the room, which had been cleared out beforehand, was reached, Sir Halliday entered it and invited Sun Yatsen to follow him. [Deng Tingkeng] pointed to the room and said, 'That is my room, please go in first.' Sun Yatsen went in, hesitantly, whereupon Sir Halliday closed the door.[215]

---

212. *Daily Chronicle*, 24 October 1896, p. 5, col. 5.

213. FO 17/1718, pp. 119–20, Sun Yatsen's statement at the Treasury, 4 November 1896, para. 8.

214. FO 17/1718, pp. 119–20, Sun Yatsen's statement at the Treasury, 4 November 1896, para. 8.

215. Wu Zonglian, *Biji, juan* 2, p. 40a. The translation is mine.

There are fundamental differences between this version and that of Sun Yatsen. To begin with, the memoirs insisted that Deng Tingkeng was present throughout, while Sun Yatsen maintained that Deng Tingkeng left him at the front porch of the Legation. Second, the alleged lunch and tour of the Legation building were both absent in Sun Yatsen's version. This business of Macartney arriving, as if naturally, has been proved incorrect in Chapter 2, Section III: he had been *fetched* specially from the comfort of his home on this Sunday morning. The alleged luring of Sun Yatsen, who was already *inside* the Legation, into a particular room by Deng Tingkeng, was the only episode in the memoirs in which a sense of stratagem might be detected. What is so special about that? In addition, what did Deng Tingkeng himself say? To the *Daily News*, he said:

Next day he came punctually, and I told him, 'It is too early. Can you take breakfast with me before going there [East London]?' He said, 'Yes', and then he breakfasted with me in my office with another gentleman. When breakfast was finished I took him upstairs to look at the Chinese Saloon and the English Saloon, and then I took him back to my office. He is there now. That is all.[216]

This account and the one quoted before suggest a firm official line, insisting that Sun Yatsen went to the Legation of his own accord. To the *Evening News*, Deng Tingkeng gave a story which was basically similar in so far as the breakfast in his office and the tour of the Legation were concerned, but provided more details about what happened thereafter:

'Perhaps you would like to see my bed-room', placidly remarked Mr Tang [Deng].
'I should very much indeed', replied Sun, who seemed very desirous of perambulating the entire premises.
Together they ascended a storey higher and Mr Tang [Deng] ushered him into a room occupied by M. Liou, the French Interpreter attached to the Legation, and quickly turned the key upon him.[217]

Unlike the French interpreter, Deng Tingkeng here denied by omission any part played by Macartney, to the extent of assuming sole responsibility for having locked up Sun Yatsen, albeit in his

---

216. *Daily News*, 24 October 1896, p. 5, col. 5.
217. *Evening News*, 24 October 1896, p. 2, col. 7.

own bedroom in one version and in that of the French interpreter in another. But like the French interpreter, he highlighted the sense of stratagem, as if he had been *alone* with Sun Yatsen most of the time until he cleverly locked him up. According to George Cole, however, there had been quite a *procession* up the stairs:

He [Macartney] then told me to keep close behind him and follow him. We went a floor higher, and in Mr Lee's [Li Shengzhong's] room they stopped at the door. Sir Halliday asked Mr Kung [Gong Xinzhan, the Minister's nephew], 'What is the gentleman's name?' Mr Kung [Gong] turned round and said, I think, 'Lou Wen Sun', and with that Sir Halliday went into Mr Lee's [Li's] room. I stayed outside. Sir Halliday came out again, and *five or six* [*my italics*] Chinese followed behind him, and they all went a floor higher. I followed as close as I could behind the Chinamen. They all went upstairs. Sir Halliday came to Mr Liou's [Wu Zonglian's] room and said to a gentleman who was a stranger to me at the time — a Chinaman in English clothes, whom I afterwards knew as Sun — 'This is the room', or words to that effect, and they both went into the room. Sir Halliday, and the Chinaman I did not know. I waited outside, as also did all the other Chinamen. In the meantime other Chinamen had gathered, and the passage was full of them.[218]

Cole's statement substantially corroborates Sun Yatsen's statement, and contradicts the essential points made by Wu Zonglian[219] in his memoirs and by Deng Tingkeng in his interviews, which, increasingly, read like fairy tales.

Why were such fairy tales necessary? I have pointed out, in Chapter 2, the probability of Macartney objecting to the arrest of Sun Yatsen if the question had been put to him. To obtain his co-operation, therefore, it is likely that the fairy tales were invented initially to convince him, and later the world, that Sun Yatsen entered the Legation of his own accord. It is even possible that the very friendly method which was apparently used to get Sun Yatsen into the Legation was staged partly for Macartney's benefit. If violence had been used, resulting in cuts and bruises, it would have been difficult to persuade Macartney that the fugitive had come of his own free will. The two strong men

---

218. FO 17/1718, pp. 116–19, Cole's statement at the Treasury, 2 November 1896, para. 6.
219. The only point on which both Wu Zonglian and Cole agreed was the sojourn in Li Shengzhong's room on the first floor. Sun Yatsen also referred to such a sojourn but, of course, was unable to name the occupant of that room.

remaining on both sides of Sun Yatsen even after he had entered the Legation were probably intended as a deterrent to any attempt on his part to disrupt the peace.

Sun Yatsen recalled that once he was inside the room alone with Macartney, the first thing that Macartney said was: 'Here is China for you'. The second thing he said was: 'Is your name Sun Wen?' Sun Yatsen replied, 'My name is Sun'. Macartney continued, 'We had a telegram from the Chinese Minister in Washington to say that Sun Wen was coming over by the *Majestic*'. Then he told the fugitive to wait till the Legation had received a telegraphic reply from Beijing, which would take eighteen hours.[220]

Coming from Sun Yatsen, an account of a conversation between himself and Macartney is not surprising. What is surprising is that the French interpreter should have provided very similar details in his memoirs.[221] This may suggest that, after Macartney had agreed to the detention of Sun Yatsen, he was briefed by the minister and his confidants about the immediate actions which would have to be taken, including what questions to ask the fugitive. His question: 'Is your name Sun Wen?'[222] is reminiscent of Deng Tingkeng's question in the street: 'Are you Japanese or Chinese?',[223] and of Macartney's own question directed earlier to the minister's nephew: 'What is the gentleman's name?'[224] It also foreshadowed a subsequent remark attributed to Deng Tingkeng while he was interrogating the captive: 'Now surely your name is Sun Wen'.[225] Small wonder that the solicitor should have made this observation: 'I doubt whether they were then certain that he was the man for whom they were seeking, although they had a

---

220. FO 17/1718, pp. 119–20, Sun Yatsen's statement at the Treasury, 4 November 1896, paras. 8–10. The rest of the conversation will be dealt with in the next section of this chapter.

221. Wu Zonglian, *Biji*, *juan* 2, p. 40a.

222. FO 17/1718, pp. 119–20, Sun Yatsen's statement at the Treasury, 4 November 1896, para. 8.

223. FO 17/1718, pp. 119–20, Sun Yatsen's statement at the Treasury, 4 November 1896, para. 8.

224. FO 17/1718, pp. 116–19, Cole's statement at the Treasury, 2 November 1896, para. 6.

225. FO 17/1718, pp. 119–20, Sun Yatsen's statement at the Treasury, 4 November 1896, para. 13. Compare this with Wu Zonglian, *Biji*, *juan* 2, p. 38a.

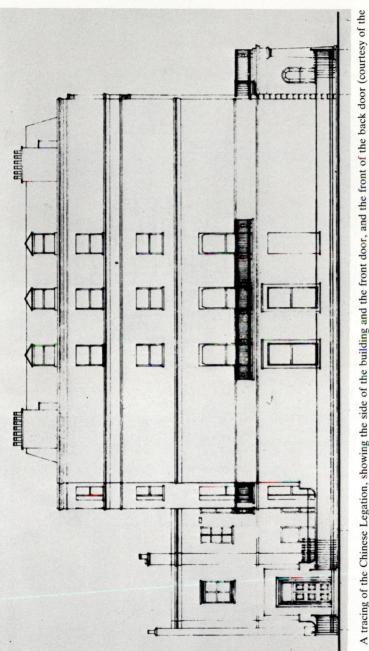

1 A tracing of the Chinese Legation, showing the side of the building and the front door, and the front of the back door (courtesy of the Chinese Embassy in London)

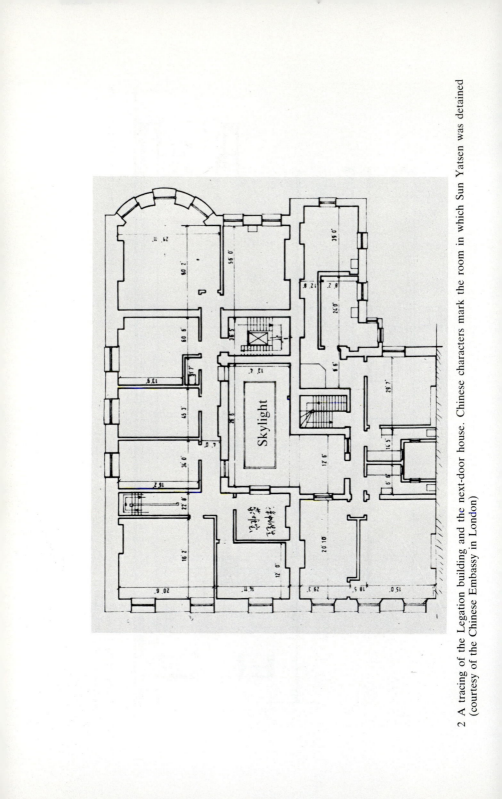

2 A tracing of the Legation building and the next-door house. Chinese characters mark the room in which Sun Yatsen was detained (courtesy of the Chinese Embassy in London)

Photo Taber, San Francisco.

3 Sun Yatsen, 1896 (courtesy of the *Illustrated London News*)

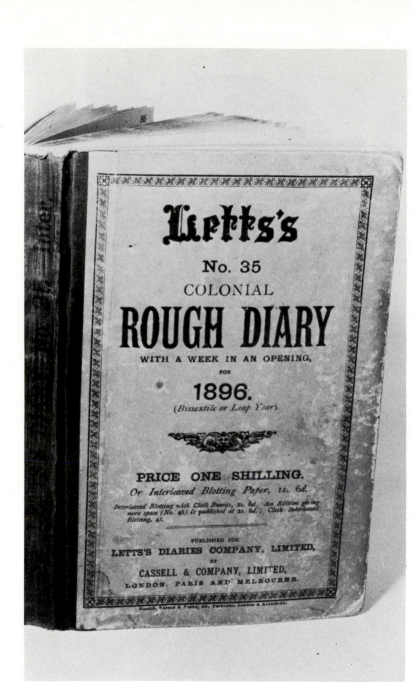

4 Mrs Cantlie's diary for 1896, external view (courtesy of Dr J. Cantlie)

15 THURSDAY [289-77]

Very rainy weather still. Mrs Lea is much
better at present.

Miss Pollard came & I gave her 10/° for
trimming two hats.
Began fires in drawing room.

Called on Mrs Godlee.
Sent back my Marriage Settlement to Mr Cubross.

16 FRIDAY [290-76]   9 Pinning Lane. EC.

Very wet all day Could not go out.

Had a pleasant note from Mr Cubross also
letter from the other lawyer Mr Holmes.
He has sent the Contract to Mrs Bray's
Solicitor & all questions seem answered
satisfactorily.

17 SATURDAY [291-75]

Had my hair cut & Shampooed
Jessie Bloxam & Daisy Bridgwater
in the morning.
Mrs Thorne & her daughter called. Also
Drury. Hamish took the boys to the Natural History
Museum. Turned out very wet. Pat & Cox

18 Sunday—20 aft Trin [292-74]   St. Luke, Evan.

What a day of hopes &
Hamish went first thing to see
Ackroyd. There Mr Hughes
Chinese. But got no satisfaction about doing something for
Sun Yat Sen. Met us at church where Mr Pitts preached
a lovely sermon on the late Archbishops Benson. Saw

5 A page from Mrs Cantlie's diary showing her entry for Saturday, 17 October
1896 (courtesy of Dr J. Cantlie)

6 Fengling, naval attaché of the Chinese Legation, wearing a sword similar to those worn by the Chinese warders guarding Sun Yatsen (courtesy of Mr J. F. Ford, CMG, OBE)

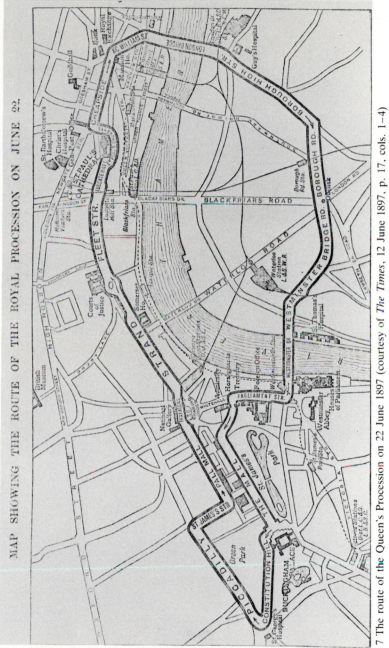

MAP SHOWING THE ROUTE OF THE ROYAL PROCESSION ON JUNE 22.

7 The route of the Queen's Procession on 22 June 1897 (courtesy of *The Times*, 12 June 1897, p. 17, cols. 1–4)

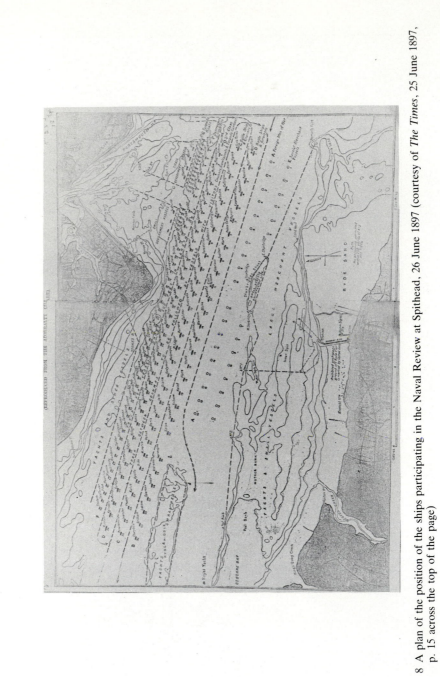

8 A plan of the position of the ships participating in the Naval Review at Spithead, 26 June 1897 (courtesy of *The Times*, 25 June 1897, p. 15 across the top of the page)

shrewd suspicion that he was Sun Yat Sen'.[226] In this sense, the Legation had made a daring decision to get a stranger inside the building, a stranger of whose identity they were not absolutely certain. As suggested towards the end of the previous section, it is possible that news of Sun Yatsen's imminent departure for France might have prompted swift action on this Sunday. Indeed, so swift that the butler was sent at about 10 a.m.[227] to fetch Macartney. The assumption might have been that, should the suspect pass the Legation again, but then prove to be a Japanese, Macartney could be sent home without difficulty. But if he were the wanted man, then no time must be lost in securing Macartney's services. Furthermore, the uncertainty about the stranger's identity probably explains why, according to Sun Yatsen, Deng Tingkeng walked on past the Legation, leaving the two other men to do the crucial work. He was the official interpreter of the Legation and had to avoid subsequent identification by the stranger, if he turned out *not* to be the wanted man, as having been present at the act of inveiglement.

Macartney told Sun Yatsen to wait for a telegraphic reply from Beijing.[228] Subsequently, a cypher was dispatched to Beijing. Did Macartney play any part in formulating it, given that he appears to have taken command of the operation? In this regard, it may be useful to consider this cypher in the light of subsequent cyphers pertinent to the saga. Luo Jialun found that the texts of nearly all the cyphers that reached Beijing were somewhat different from the drafts that were kept in the Legation.[229] The differences in the first cypher are particularly interesting. The Legation draft has the sentence: 'It will not be easy to smuggle [him back] to Guangdong', while the Beijing version reads: 'It will not be easy to convey [him back] to Guangdong'. The Legation draft also has the sentence: 'Do not let Minister Dou know', while the Beijing version reads: 'Do not let the British Minister know'.[230] The British minister was known in official Chinese

---

226. FO 17/1718, pp. 113–16, Cuffe to Home Office, 12 November 1896, para. 9.

227. FO 17/1718, pp. 116–19, Cole's statement at the Treasury, 2 November 1896, para. 5.

228. FO 17/1718, pp. 119–20, Sun Yatsen's statement at the Treasury, 4 November 1896, para. 10.

229. Luo Jialun, *Shiliao*, pp. 26, 52–3, 54–5, and 62–3.

230. Luo Jialun, *Shiliao*, p. 26. The translation is mine.

circles as Dou-na-le.[231] As extremely few Chinese officials could speak English at the time, his original English name, Sir Claud MacDonald, was practically unknown. An Englishman, however, would have found the term 'Minister Dou' awkward and would have wanted to change it to 'the British Minister'.[232] He would also have thought it discreet to change 'smuggle' to 'convey'. Therefore, I am inclined to think that Macartney was responsible for making these changes. True, the word 'smuggle' might not have mattered in a cypher. But cyphers, and the breaking of them, had had a long history in Europe.[233] Macartney had twenty years of experience in the diplomatic world. Even when he was negotiating on behalf of the Chinese government, either in St Petersburg or in Paris, he had kept in close touch with the British Foreign Office, which subsequently recommended him for a knighthood in 1885.[234] It is difficult to believe that he had never heard of the cracking of codes. In addition, Anglo-Chinese relations were going through a sensitive period, with the British strongly suspecting that Li Hongzhang had signed a secret treaty with Russia during his visit there earlier in the year. Macartney's own suspicion, and therefore displeasure, was so great that when Li Hongzhang was in London after his visit to Russia, Macartney refused to go and see his former mentor.[235] Under the circumstances, it is not impossible that Macartney suspected that the British Foreign Office *might* take a keen interest in cyphers emanating from the Chinese Legation. I think he would have preferred to be cautious even in cyphers.

In this same cypher of 11 October 1896, it was alleged that Sun Yatsen had come to the Legation of his own accord.[236] Both Luo Jialun and Schiffrin have used this cypher in an attempt to prove that Sun Yatsen did indeed enter the building of his own free will.

---

231. Luo Jialun, *Shiliao*, p. 26.
232. Luo Jialun speculated that the change might have been caused by the absence of the character 'dou' in the telegraph manual (Luo Jialun, *Shiliao*, p. 26). Until such a manual is found, I reserve my judgement.
233. See C.H. Carter, *The Western European Powers, 1500–1700* (London, Hodder & Stoughton, 1971), Chapter 6. I am grateful to my colleague, Mr G.B. Harrison, for this reference.
234. See Chapter 2, Section II.
235. Boulger, *Macartney*, pp. 464–5.
236. Chinese Legation Archives and Beijing Palace Museum Records, Gong Zhaoyuan to Zongli Yamen, 11 October 1896, in Luo Jialun, *Shiliao*, p. 26.

If the Legation had inveigled him from the street, they have argued, there would have been no reason for the minister to hide such an achievement from Beijing.[237] Their argument overlooks the very likely role which Macartney seems to have played in the cypher. It is even possible that the cypher was prepared in the expectation that Macartney might look at it, either to be on the safe side or to make Macartney feel that he was really in charge of the whole affair. If this were the case, as it appears to have been, it is not surprising that the cypher made no reference to the 'Capturing of the Wanted Cantonese Sun Wen by Stratagem',[238] however much the minister might have wanted to show off his achievement to his government. In addition, the cypher did not allege that Sun Yatsen had visited the Legation previously — a feature which has not attracted the attention of either Luo Jialun, or Schiffrin, who has tried so hard to prove that Sun Yatsen had.[239] The first *public* reference to a previous visit was made by Macartney on 22 October 1896 at the Foreign Office. On that occasion, he pinpointed the date of the alleged previous visit as being 'Friday the 9th instant'.[240] He did not correct this date when he called at the Foreign Office again on 23 October 1896.[241] But writing to *The Times* on 24 October 1896, he claimed that the visit took place on 'Saturday, the 10th'.[242] The Treasury solicitor inferred from these three statements that Macartney was in each case repeating what he had been told, and was not speaking from his own knowledge.[243] I am inclined to agree with the solicitor. But when was Macartney told about the alleged previous visit?

The cypher in question suggests that it might *not* have been Sunday, 11 October 1896, or before, because the cypher made no reference to such a visit. The earliest subsequent date could have been Monday, 12 October 1896, when George Cole took to

---

237. Luo Jialun, *Shiliao*, p. 41; and Schiffrin, *Origins*, p. 112.
238. Wu Zonglian, *Biji*, *juan* 2, p. 39b.
239. Schiffrin, *Origins*, p. 112. Compare Luo Jialun, *Shiliao*, p. 41.
240. FO 17/1718, pp. 54–8, Sanderson's record of his interview with Macartney, 22 October 1896, para. 4.
241. FO 17/1718, pp. 69–76, Sanderson's record of his interview with Macartney, 23 October 1896, para. 9.
242. *The Times*, 26 October 1896, p. 8, col. 4. The letter was dated 24 October 1896.
243. FO 17/1718, pp. 113–16, Cuffe to Home Office, 12 November 1896, para. 13.

Macartney a note which had been given him by Sun Yatsen and which was addressed to Dr Cantlie.[244] This note no longer exists. If it were similar to the one he had written for Macartney's transmission to Dr Manson the day before, in which he said, 'Am confined in the Chinese Legation',[245] Macartney would not have been worried. But if it were similar to the note which eventually reached Dr Cantlie, and in which he said, 'I was kidnapped into the Chinese Legation',[246] then Macartney would have had every reason to begin questioning his Chinese colleagues. It looks as though the notes which Sun Yatsen gave to Cole to be taken out of the Legation, before he had won over the porter, did not cause any concern on the part of Macartney. But the note which he threw out of the window, and which was recovered by Cole and taken to Macartney, on Wednesday, 14 October 1896,[247] seems to have caused a bit of a stir. It sent Deng Tingkeng running to the captive, threatening him with death, and extracting a statement from him[248] in which he *confessed* not only to having entered the Legation voluntarily but to having done so by appointment as the result of a visit on the previous day.[249] This is the first private reference to a previous visit — private, because there is no sign of the document becoming official subsequently;[250] unlike the record of Macartney's interviews at the Foreign Office, which has remained in the official files.[251] I am inclined to interpret this episode as having been started by Sun Yatsen's complaining about kidnapping in his note. This greatly alarmed Macartney, who began to question fiercely the English interpreter, Deng Tingkeng, and warned him of the dire consequences if Sun Yat-

---

244. FO 17/1718, pp. 116–19, Cole's statement at the Treasury, 2 November 1896, paras. 12–13.

245. FO 17/1718, pp. 119–20, Sun Yatsen's statement at the Treasury, 4 November 1896, para. 10.

246. FO 17/1718, p. 30, Sun Yatsen to Dr Cantlie (18 October 1896).

247. FO 17/1718, pp. 116–19, Cole's statement at the Treasury, 2 November 1896, paras. 12 and 16. FO 17/1718, pp. 119–20, Sun Yatsen's statement at the Treasury, 4 November 1896, para. 13.

248. FO 17/1718, pp. 119–20, Sun Yatsen's statement at the Treasury, 4 November 1896, para. 13.

249. Chinese version of Sun Yatsen's confession, in Wu Zonglian, *Biji, juan* 2, pp. 37a–39b. The original was in English, and cannot be found.

250. Wu Zonglian, *Biji, juan* 2, pp. 37a–39b.

251. FO 17/1718, pp. 54–8, and 69–76, Sanderson's records of interviews with Macartney, 22 and 23 October 1896.

sen's version were true. To allay Macartney's fears, and perhaps having exhausted all other means of convincing Macartney that the fugitive had indeed come voluntarily, Deng Tingkeng probably invented the previous visit to give his story more credibility. To strengthen his hand, therefore, it is conceivable that he went under the cover of darkness[252] to begin coaxing the prisoner to 'write to Macartney to pray for mercy',[253] to say that he had visited the Legation previously on Saturday, 10 October 1896, and had made an appointment to return the next day, whereupon he was detained.[254] Sun Yatsen said that the confession was dictated to him by Deng Tingkeng.[255] An attempt to pinpoint the date of the confession will be made in the next section.

It is not clear what Macartney's immediate reaction was when he was shown the confession. If his revulsion at the sight of a Chinese magistrate extracting information by torture is any guide,[256] he would have been disgusted. He subsequently denied, along with his other transparent denials, any knowledge of the interrogation of Sun Yatsen.[257] Deng Tingkeng, on the other hand, had no qualms about announcing to the British public that the prisoner had confessed.[258] He knew very well that a confession of this kind would be accepted by a Chinese magistrate as valid evidence. Little did he realize that the British had a different legal system, and had different sympathies. The *Daily News* described this part of the interview with Deng Tingkeng as follows:

Yet there was one question I could not refrain from putting.
'Has he confessed?'
'Yes', was the reply; 'he has made a full confession, and his statements have been taken down in writing.' And now there was a further inquiry that required to be made. Travellers have reported horrible stories of the way in which confessions are sometimes wrung from culprits in the interior of China; and some ominous rumours were

---

252. Sun Yatsen, *Kidnapped in London*, p. 50.
253. FO 17/1718, pp. 119–20, Sun Yatsen's statement at the Treasury, 4 November 1896, para. 13.
254. Chinese version of Sun Yatsen's confession, in Wu Zonglian, *Biji, juan* 2, p. 38a.
255. FO 17/1718, pp. 119–20, Sun Yatsen's statement at the Treasury, 4 November 1896, para. 13.
256. Boulger, *Macartney*, p. 36.
257. *Daily Telegraph*, 24 October 1896, p. 7, col. 7.
258. *Daily News*, 24 October 1896, p. 5, col. 5.

afloat. Yet one naturally shrank from putting a most disagreeable question to so gentle and courteous a gentleman. So the circuitous language of diplomacy had to be resorted to.
'May I ask whether the confession was obtained without difficulty?'
'Yes; without any difficulty at all', was the prompt answer.[259]

Macartney must have wished that he had had a better informed co-conspirator than Deng Tingkeng! At least two Chinese professors have suggested that it was Macartney who, with a view to covering himself in the event of an attack by the British government, had instructed Deng Tingkeng to make Sun Yatsen confess his voluntary entry into the Legation.[260] I doubt it.

IV Perseverance

About midday on Sunday, 11 October 1896, when Sun Yatsen was alone with Macartney, he was persuaded to try to have his luggage taken to the Legation. He seems to have remained fairly alert despite the shock, for he replied that his luggage was at a friend's place and that he would have to write for it. But he attempted to be too clever when he began by writing, 'Am confined in the Chinese Legation', to which Macartney naturally objected. He started again, 'I am in the Chinese Legation. Please send my baggage'. Macartney was not foolish either; 'I must ask the Minister before I can send this letter', he said, and left him.[261] Sun Yatsen looked at the only window in the room. It faced the interior of the building, overlooking the skylight (see Plate 2). There was no chance of communicating with anybody in the street. In addition, the window was 'barred with four or five iron bars running vertically'.[262] He noticed, too, that the door

---

259. *Daily News*, 24 October 1896, p. 5, col. 5.

260. Luo Jialun, *Shiliao*, pp. 48–9; and Wu Xiangxiang, *Sun Yixian zhuan*, Vol. 1, p. 158.

261. FO 17/1718, pp. 119–20, Sun Yatsen's statement at the Treasury, 4 November 1896, para. 10. In this section I shall use mainly the statements made at the British Treasury, and some information which may be found only in *Kidnapped in London*. The latter was written much later, and will be assessed in Chapter 4, Section III.

262. FO 17/1718, pp. 119–20, Sun Yatsen's statement at the Treasury, 4 November 1896, para. 10. See, also, FO 17/1718, pp. 116–19, Cole's statement at the Treasury, 2 November 1896, para. 6.

was guarded all the while outside.[263] In the evening, he heard some noises outside his door, and realized that an additional lock was being installed.[264] He failed to sleep that night, but simply lay down with his clothes on.[265]

On Monday, 12 October 1896, at about 7.45 a.m., Cole went into Sun Yatsen's room to light a fire for him.

'Will you take a note to a friend for me?'
'I must not do it.'
'Do do it, to save a fellow creature's life.'
'It is more than my place is worth.'
'Do do it, for God's sake, I beg and pray of you to do it.'[266]

With that, Sun Yatsen slipped a piece of newspaper into Cole's hand, saying, 'If you cannot take it outside, throw it from the window'.[267] This is rather revealing of Sun Yatsen's character. He did not know Cole. He made no attempt to get to know him, to cultivate his friendship, and to win him over. What made him think that he could simply ask his warder to leak the news of his captivity? Not surprisingly, Cole acted according to his instructions,[268] took the note to Macartney,[269] and then told Sun Yatsen that he had 'flung it out of the window'.[270]

On Tuesday, 12 October 1896, at about 8 a.m., Cole came on duty, relieving the footman, Henry Mulliner, who had watched the prisoner together with a Chinese servant during the night. Sun Yatsen called Cole in to make his fire, and gave him another piece of paper, saying, 'Try and take this yourself; if you cannot take it throw it out of the window; but if you take it and I get a free man I will well reward you'.[271] This is more business-like,

---

263. FO 17/1718, pp. 119–20, Sun Yatsen's statement at the Treasury, 4 November 1896, para. 10; and Cole's statement, para. 10.
264. Sun Yatsen, *Kidnapped in London*, p. 40.
265. Sun Yatsen, *Kidnapped in London*, p. 43.
266. FO 17/1718, pp. 116–19, Cole's statement at the Treasury, 2 November 1896, para. 12.
267. FO 17/1718, pp. 116–19, Cole's statement at the Treasury, 2 November 1896, para. 12.
268. FO 17/1718, pp. 116–19, Cole's statement at the Treasury, 2 November 1896, para. 6.
269. FO 17/1718, pp. 116–19, Cole's statement at the Treasury, 2 November 1896, para. 13.
270. FO 17/1718, pp. 116–19, Cole's statement at the Treasury, 2 November 1896, para. 14.
271. FO 17/1718, pp. 116–19, Cole's statement at the Treasury, 2 November 1896, para. 16.

but did he really think that a mere promise of an unspecified reward would move his warder? Cole replied, 'I will try, but I do not think I can manage it'. With that, Cole took this note, together with the one which Sun Yatsen had given to the footman, to Macartney.[272] Sun Yatsen also asked to see Macartney, whose response was, 'Tell him I will not go'.[273]

On Wednesday, 14 October 1896, he asked successfully to have the window opened to have some fresh air, then put his hands through the bars and jerked a note out over the skylight on to the roof of the next house (see Plate 2). This was spotted by a Chinese servant, whereupon Cole climbed over and retrieved it.[274] Sun Yatsen saw Cole do this, and asked him to give it back to him through the window, which was still open. 'I must not do it', said Cole. 'For God's sake give it to me', pleaded the desperate prisoner. 'I cannot, Sir, I am very sorry', replied the warder.[275] The available sources show that this was the only occasion on which a note from Sun Yatsen left the Legation through a window. But it cost him dearly. 'You will see that the window is fastened down, and search him and see that he has no writing materials, and for the future let him have no more paper', ordered Macartney.[276] Then Macartney telegraphed Mr McGregor of the Glen Line, requesting an interview that evening.[277] Meanwhile, Sun Yatsen persevered. The next time he saw Cole on the same day, he gave him another message to take out of the Legation.[278] It is not clear where he found paper to write on after he had been searched. Cole took the note to Macartney. Evening came, and Mr McGregor of the Glen Line seems to have been able to call on Macartney at short notice, because, by the end of

---

272. FO 17/1718, pp. 116-19, Cole's statement at the Treasury, 2 November 1896, para. 16.
273. FO 17/1718, pp. 116-19, Cole's statement at the Treasury, 2 November 1896, para. 16.
274. FO 17/1718, pp. 116-19, Cole's statement at the Treasury, 2 November 1896, para. 12.
275. FO 17/1718, pp. 116-19, Cole's statement at the Treasury, 2 November 1896, para. 16.
276. FO 17/1718, pp. 116-19, Cole's statement at the Treasury, 2 November 1896, para. 12.
277. FO 17/1718, pp. 113-16, Cuffe to Home Office, 12 November 1896, para. 24.
278. FO 17/1718, pp. 116-19, Cole's statement at the Treasury, 2 November 1896, para. 16.

the day, the minister was in a position to cable Beijing that a passage for about £7,000 sterling was being negotiated.[279]

On Thursday, 15 October 1896, Sun Yatsen gave Cole yet another note.[280] This is a conspicuous feature of his character: when he had decided to achieve a certain goal, he would simply keep at it regardless. Cole took the note to the minister's nephew, who, in turn, told him to take it to Macartney.[281] It seems that it was on this day, too, that Deng Tingkeng went to see Sun Yatsen and told him that all his messages had been intercepted, because the next day Sun Yatsen accused Cole of having betrayed him. It also seems that on this occasion, Deng Tingkeng said to him, 'We are going to gag you (motioning with his hand) and tie you up, put you in a bag, and take you to a steamer which we have already chartered . . . we will keep you on board the same as we keep you here — have several guards on you, and lock you up in a room, and we will not let you speak to anybody on board. If we cannot smuggle you out, we will kill you here'.[282] According to *Kidnapped in London*, Sun Yatsen responded by pointing out that it had been a similar incident that had led to the Sino-Japanese War; and that his people in Guangdong would revenge themselves on the interpreter and his family for treating him in the manner threatened.[283] If this were true,[284] and there is no reason to doubt it,[285] Sun Yatsen must be given credit for having remained calm even under such enormous pressure. The account ended by saying that Deng Tingkeng 'then changed his tone, desisted from his arrogant utterances, and remarked that all he was doing was by the direction of the Legation, and that he was merely warning me in a friendly way of my plight'.[286] The same account stated that he returned at mid-

---

279. Beijing Palace Museum Records, Gong Zhaoyuan to Zongli Yamen (cypher), 14 October 1896, in Luo Jialun, *Shiliao*, pp. 52–3.

280. FO 17/1718, pp. 116–19, Cole's statement at the Treasury, 2 November 1896, para. 16.

281. FO 17/1718, pp. 116–19, Cole's statement at the Treasury, 2 November 1896, para. 16.

282. FO 17/1718, pp. 119–20, Sun Yatsen's statement at the Treasury, 4 November 1896, para. 13.

283. Sun Yatsen, *Kidnapped in London*, pp. 48–9.

284. As far as I know, this is the only account that contains such a story.

285. I do not know of any account that contradicts this story.

286. Sun Yatsen, *Kidnapped in London*, p. 49.

night, offering to release the prisoner secretly one day in the small hours.[287]

On Friday, 16 October 1896, Sun Yatsen denounced Cole: 'You have been betraying me. You told me that you had thrown my letters out of the window, but Mr Tang [Deng] tells me that you have been giving them to Sir Halliday all the time'.[288] The startled porter hurriedly left the room and said to the Chinese servant on duty with him, 'Mr Tang [Deng] is very bad; he has told the prisoner that I have been taking his papers to Sir Halliday, and perhaps by-and-bye [sic] he may get cross and try to kill me. If he has more papers for me I will take them out'.[289] Cole recalled that Sun Yatsen seemed rather sulky all day, but still asked him to give his word to take the papers out. Cole declined.[290] It is not clear from Cole's account whether he was given any more paper that day. But *Kidnapped in London*, in a way,[291] said he was; and that the note was taken to Macartney, who consequently 'scolded him [Deng Tingkeng] very much for telling me how they intended to dispose of me'.[292] Deng Tingkeng, in turn, told Sun Yatsen, probably the next day (see next paragraph), that the note 'had spoiled all his plans for rescuing' him.[293]

Saturday, 17 October 1896, appears to have been the day on which Sun Yatsen succumbed to Deng Tingkeng's threats and coaxing, and made a statement.[294] Sun Yatsen himself could not remember which day he did it when interrogated by the Treasury solicitor, but gave graphic details of the circumstances and the contents. He said he was asked to write to the minister to pray for mercy; but to write in English and to address the letter to Macartney. He was told to deny any connection with the plot at

---

287. Sun Yatsen, *Kidnapped in London*, pp. 50–1.

288. FO 17/1718, pp. 119–20, Cole's statement at the Treasury, 2 November 1896, para. 17.

289. FO 17/1718, pp. 119–20, Cole's statement at the Treasury, 2 November 1896, para. 17.

290. FO 17/1718, pp. 119–20, Cole's statement at the Treasury, 2 November 1896, para. 18.

291. Sun Yatsen, *Kidnapped in London*, p. 51, refers to Thursday, 15 October 1896, which, I think, is inaccurate. See Chapter 4, Section III.

292. Sun Yatsen, *Kidnapped in London*, p. 51.

293. Sun Yatsen, *Kidnapped in London*, p. 51.

294. FO 17/1718, pp. 116–19, Cole's statement at the Treasury, 2 November 1896, para. 26.

Guangzhou; to say that he had been to the Chinese Legation in America in an attempt to see the minister and explain himself; but that the minister there would not listen to him, so he had come to London to pray to this minister. He said he wrote all that because 'I thought it was the only way in which I could get out. I thought they were going to send me back to China. I never thought I should get out again'.[295] At least he was astute enough not to put all his eggs in one basket. He continued to work on Cole; and adopted, at last, some kind of tactic. According to Cole, he told him on this day that he might be compared with the leader of the Socialist party in London.[296] Later, he denied to the Treasury solicitor that he had made such a comparison; instead, he said that he had compared his position to that of the Armenians, and that if his letter could reach his friends, the British government would intervene.[297] Cole promised to think about it.

On Sunday, 18 October 1896, Sun Yatsen changed his tactics again. He offered Cole £20 to take a note to Dr Cantlie. Cole accepted the offer, took the note out, and returned with Dr Cantlie's visiting card, on which Dr Manson had signed his name. Sun Yatsen gave him the £20 and said he would give him more.[298] In a way, he also hoped that Dr Cantlie might reward the messenger, because he inserted the following in his message: 'Please take care of the Messenger for me at present; he is very poor and will lose his work by doing [sic] for me'.[299] It is not clear whether Cantlie gave him anything; probably he did, because Dr Manson said that the kitchen-hand of the Legation, 'seeing that Cole was making something out of it, ... wanted to do the same'.[300] Sun Yatsen said he was happier after he received Cantlie's visiting card, but was still suspicious because he did not quite remember Dr Manson's signature and Cole could have got

---

295. FO 17/1718, pp. 119–20, Sun Yatsen's statement at the Treasury, 4 November 1896, paras. 13 and 20.

296. FO 17/1718, pp. 119–20, Cole's statement at the Treasury, 2 November 1896, para. 19.

297. FO 17/1718, pp. 119–20, Sun Yatsen's statement at the Treasury, 4 November 1896, para. 16.

298. FO 17/1718, pp. 116–19, Cole's statement at the Treasury, 2 November 1896, paras. 31 and 21.

299. FO 17/1718, p. 30, Sun Yatsen to Cantlie (18 October 1896).

300. FO 17/1718, p. 122, Manson's statement at the Treasury, 4 November 1896, para. 5.

one of Cantlie's cards indirectly.[301] Therefore, he asked the already nervous porter to take a second note to Dr Cantlie on the same day, requesting the doctor to write something to him.[302] While Cole's memory of the first message was quite accurate, his description of the second is somewhat off the mark and probably reflects more truthfully his recollection of Sun Yatsen's state of mind than the written message itself. Cole recalled: 'I know it was similar to the previous one begging and praying them to act quickly as he was sure things were drawing to a close. I think there was on it "What are you doing? Where is the hitch? I claim to be an English subject. Was born in Hong Kong. What does Salisbury think?"'[303] Dr Cantlie sent him some words on a small sheet of paper.[304]

Sun Yatsen waited for another five anxious days, while his British friends did their best to mobilize the British government, before he was finally set free at 5 p.m. on Friday, 23 October 1896. 'I did not know I was to be released until I was called downstairs', he recalled.[305]

V The Debtor

On Saturday, 17 October 1896, when Cole was still wondering whether he should take a note from Sun Yatsen to Dr Cantlie, his superior, Mrs Howe, the housekeeper, wrote an unsigned letter and seems to have delivered it personally to 46, Devonshire Street, at 11.30 p.m.[306] She had seen Sun Yatsen only once, on the first day of the detention, when she took some bedclothes to him and made his bed. They did not speak to each other then, and it is not clear what kind of impression she formed of him. But subsequently Cole told her how Sun Yatsen had continued to beg and pray him to take messages out for him, and she had

301. FO 17/1718, pp. 119–20, Sun Yatsen's statement at the Treasury, 4 November 1896, para. 17.

302. FO 17/1718, pp. 119–20, Sun Yatsen's statement at the Treasury, 4 November 1896, para. 17. See note 303.

303. FO 17/1718, pp. 116–19, Cole's statement at the Treasury, 2 November 1896, para. 21.

304. FO 17/1718, pp. 119–20, Sun Yatsen's statement at the Treasury, 4 November 1896, para 17.

305. FO 17/1718, pp. 119–20, Sun Yatsen's statement at the Treasury, 4 November 1896, para. 18.

306. See Chapter 1, Section I.

encouraged him to do so. Cole still hesitated, and said that he would go and talk to her again when he finished work on Friday, 16 October 1896; but he did not; nor did he do so the next day, whereupon the housekeeper took action independently. It seems that she did so entirely out of pity for the prisoner.

It also seems that Sun Yatsen had promised Cole a vast amount of money as a reward, in addition to the £20 which he had given him. On 31 December 1896, the Treasury solicitor wrote to Sir Thomas Sanderson, 'Sun Yatsen called here today and as he will probably write to you I send you a memorandum of what passed when he was here'. Here is the full text of the memorandum:

Sun called

Produced a claim by Cole for £500 alleged to have been promised by Sun to him for communicating his position to his friends. £20 paid on account.

Sun told me he had promised £1,000, and did not wish to dispute the claim, but wanted to know if anything was being done about the Legation.

I said this was a matter on which I could give him no information and that on such a matter his course was to write to the Foreign Office.[307]

Here is a typical example of Sun Yatsen's extravagant language when he promised Cole £1,000. It is intriguing, however, that Cole should have claimed only half of that amount two months later. Even before Sun Yatsen's release, Dr Cantlie had appealed to the public for donations to reward his informants (Mrs Howe and George Cole).[308] As pointed out by Schiffrin, some money may have been raised in this way;[309] but there is no evidence to show that Mrs Howe ever got any money. Schiffrin also quotes Chen Shaobai to the effect that Sun Yatsen 'made a number of public addresses after his release and collected several hundred pounds which he turned over to the porter'.[310] I have

---

307. FO 17/1718, pp. 151–2, Cuffe to Sanderson (with enclosure), 31 December 1896.

308. Cantlie's signed statement, which he gave to the Central News for dissemination. See *Morning Leader*, 24 October 1896, p. 7, col. 4; and *Evening News*, 24 October 1896, p. 3, col. 2.

309. Schiffrin, *Origins*, p. 177, n. 66.

310. Schiffrin, *Origins*, p. 177, n. 66, quoting Chen Shaobai, *Xing Zhong Hui geming shiyao*, p. 18.

been able to identify two occasions when he made such addresses, and a third when he possibly did. On 30 October 1896, 'Hamish & Dr Sun who is still here went to the Students Club Dinner C.C. [Charing Cross] Hospital. Hamish is the Chairman. It was a record dinner, 222 old & new students & they gave Hamish a great welcome'.[311] There was no reference to Sun Yatsen making a speech or collecting donations; but both were quite possible under the circumstances. On 14 November 1896, 'Hamish & Sun Yatsen were guests of the Savage Club at dinner. Had a delightful evening'.[312] A newspaper report gave more details: 'Dr Sun Yat Sen was a guest at the Savage Club dinner on 14th Nov., and in response to an urgent demand gave an account of some of his recent experiences at the Chinese Embassy in Portland Place. In very halting English, Dr Sun told the story of his escape ... Dr Cantlie supplemented Dr Sun's story, and caused some amusement by his account of the incredulity of Scotland Yard ...'[313] Here is a definite record of Sun Yatsen having made a public address; but still no reference to the collection of donations, although such a possibility seems remote. On 16 January 1896, Mrs Cantlie wrote, 'Dr Sun is to lecture at Oxford the end of the month so he brought his written MS to show Hamish. It is very good'.[314]

On 11 March 1897, Mrs Cantlie wrote, 'The lecture on "Things Chinese" at St Martin's Town Hall came off tonight for the benefit of Charing Cross Hospital. Dr Sun read an article on the Government of China & Hamish talked about different things'.[315] If Sun Yatsen could help raise funds for the Hospital, it is possible that he had settled his debt with Cole by this time.[316]

---

311. Mrs Cantlie's diary, 30 October 1896.
312. Mrs Cantlie's diary, 14 November 1896.
313. *China Mail*, 24 December 1896, p. 3, col. 2.
314. Mrs Cantlie's diary, 16 January 1897.
315. Mrs Cantlie's diary, 11 March 1897.
316. There was also the possible revenue from the sale of *Kidnapped in London*, which will be considered in Chapter 4, Section III.

4 The Origins of the Heroic Image

With regard to the reason of his arrest, he said he was told it was for sending a memorial for reform in China.

Evening Standard[1]

I Self-help

After Sun Yatsen was released from the Chinese Legation late in the afternoon of 23 October 1896, he was driven away in a cab heading for Scotland Yard. Some journalists, however, could not wait to interview him. One actually climbed on to the cab uninvited, sat beside the driver, and stopped it outside the Shades public house.[2] Immediately, Sun Yatsen was surrounded by a dozen journalists, and he 'was hustled from the pavement into the back premises of the hostelry'.[3] There, he gave the first news conference of his life, detailing his kidnapping and detention by the Chinese Legation. What brought the news conference to an abrupt end was this question from one of the reporters: 'Is there anything to be said about this revolutionary business in which the Legation alleges you to be implicated?'[4] Sun Yatsen replied, 'Ah! that is a long story, and this is not the time to discuss it'.[5] Obviously he did not want to answer the question. Why?

There are several possible explanations. Perhaps he was too tired to go on to another subject; but would a devoted revolutionary have thrown away so easily such an excellent opportunity to give world-wide publicity to his cause? Judging from the reaction of Dr Cantlie, who was also present, it seems that Sun Yatsen was quite embarrassed by the question, because Dr Cantlie immediately called out, 'Time, gentlemen!', and carried him off to Scotland Yard.[6] This raises the question of his image

---

1. *Evening Standard*, 24 October 1896, p. 2, col. 3.
2. Sun Yatsen, *Kidnapped in London*, p. 100. See, also, Chinese Legation Archives, Slater's report, 23–8 October 1896, in Luo Jialun, *Shiliao*, p. 118.
3. Sun Yatsen, *Kidnapped in London*, p. 100.
4. *Daily Chronicle*, 24 October 1896, p. 5, col. 5.
5. *Daily Chronicle*, 24 October 1896, p. 5, col. 5.
6. Sun Yatsen, *Kidnapped in London*, p. 101.

of himself and what he thought could have been in the minds of others at this juncture in his life.

The available sources show that at this time, he probably had only two devoted admirers and followers: Zheng Shiliang, who had threatened to kill Sun Yatsen's rival in 1895,[7] and Chen Shaobai, who seems to have been responsible for creating the legend that Sun Yatsen had walked fearlessly into the Legation.[8] Even before rivalry had developed between the two factions, Xie Zuantai had this to say in his diary of 5 May 1895: 'Sun proposes things that are subject to condemnation — he thinks he is able to do anything — no obstructions — "all paper!"' Again, on 23 June 1895, he wrote: 'I believe Sun wishes every one to listen to him. This is impossible, as, so far, his experience shows that it would be risky to rely solely on him'.[9] If these criticisms are regarded as being as extreme as the praise lavished upon him by what appears to have been his own party faithful,[10] what about those of foreign observers in the Far East? After the failure of the plot in Guangzhou, and commenting on rumours that Sun Yatsen had been the leader, a foreign correspondent in Guangzhou wrote: 'Those who know him are not surprised that the scheme so deeply planned has turned out such a ridiculous fiasco. His qualifications for leadership are not attested by his wisdom in making good his escape twenty hours before the arrival of his comrades, but it will be a happy deliverance to his followers and friends if the uncertain tenure by which he hereafter holds his head will prevent his return to his old haunts'.[11]

By 'comrades', the correspondent meant the four hundred or so coolies who eventually reached Guangzhou from Hong Kong by steamer on the morning of 28 October 1895. They were supposed to have arrived on the morning of 26 October 1895; but in the small hours of that day, Yang Quyun telegraphed that the 'goods' could not arrive on schedule; and later, on the same day, government troops began to seize all suspects in hiding.[12] Thus, it was not fair to accuse Sun Yatsen of having fled twenty hours

---

7. See Chapter 3, Section I.
8. See Chapter 3, Section I.
9. Tse Tsan Tai, *The Chinese Republic*, p. 4.
10. See Chapter 3, Section I.
11. *China Mail*, 2 November 1895, p. 4, col. 5.
12. Schiffrin, *Origins*, pp. 85–6.

before the coolies arrived.[13] But that is beside the point. What is relevant in the context of the present analysis is that such widely publicized accusations were very damaging to the image of Sun Yatsen as a leader, at least in the eyes of foreigners and of those Chinese who could read English, whose support Sun Yatsen had been trying hard to secure. Foreigners did not have much faith in the ability of any Chinese national to change China anyway; and the failure of the plot simply confirmed such prejudice. One commentator wrote, '... the fiasco now known as the late Revolution at Canton [Guangzhou] may perhaps provide food for reflection for thinking Europeans ... I am inclined to agree with the enlightened writer in the London *Times* that there is no hope for China now within the influence of her own rotten system: help must come from outside, through the honest administration of an upright foreign power'.[14]

To the educated Chinese élite of the time, Sun Yatsen was no longer a harmless medical practitioner, but a wanted man whose company was to be avoided. To the secret societies and disaffected elements, on which he had depended as the main source of manpower, he had proved a failure. It may not be an exaggeration to say that his image, if he had had any, was in ruins. His kidnapping in London gave him unexpected and favourable publicity, which, as we have seen, he did not exploit to create an heroic image for himself at the first opportunity. At this stage, he seems to have been content with that of a victim of Oriental despotism.

He was given a second chance in the evening. After he had made a statement at Scotland Yard and after he had had dinner with the Cantlies, reporters who were absent from the Shades public house interviewed him at 46, Devonshire Street. He began with a touch of melodrama by producing 'half a newspaper page, across which, in a bold hand, the following words were written in ink:- "This will inform the public that, I Sun, was kidnapped by the Chinese Legation ..." He said that he wrote it during his detention'.[15] According to another report, he had concealed the

---

13. Indeed, according to Sun Yatsen himself, he was still in Guangzhou three days after the government had taken action. See Sun Yatsen, 'Jianguo fanglue zhiyi', in *Sun Zhongshan quanji*, Vol. 1, p. 194.
14. *China Mail*, 2 November 1895, p. 4, col. 3.
15. *Daily News*, 24 October 1896, p. 5, col. 3.

half page in his sock but had folded it in such a way as to enable it to float in the air once he threw it out of the window.[16] Clearly, his thoughts had not gone beyond dwelling on the sensation of the saga. Then he told the story of his kidnapping, in the course of which he referred to the threat of the Legation to kill him and embalm his body in order for it to be sent back to China for execution. '"Execute a dead body?" I exclaimed. "Oh, yes", was the reply. "In China, punishment is extended to the dead"'.[17] It seems that Sun Yatsen was just as surprised by this reaction as the reporter had been by his story, and that he was still not consciously using the occasion to blacken the Manchu regime.

In the course of his narrative, he introduced some interesting details which were absent in the first news conference, as well as in the statement he had made at Scotland Yard. For example, he alleged that he had been arrested by the Legation 'for sending a memorial for reform in China'.[18] Possibly, after a relaxing dinner with the Cantlies, when 'the air was yet aromatic with the mingled suggestion of pineapple, port, and cigars',[19] he had had time to reflect on a suitable response to 'this revolutionary business',[20] about which the reporters might ask again. And he appears to have decided to forestall the question by portraying himself as a peaceful reformer rather than as a violent revolutionary.[21] He seems to have had some degree of success; because, towards the end of the interview, he was asked, instead, 'Are you a member of the White Lily Society?'[22] He replied, 'Oh, no; that is quite a different body. Our movement is a new one, and is confined to educated Chinamen, most of whom live out of China'.[23] For the

---

16. *Evening Standard*, 24 October 1896, p. 2, col. 3.

17. *Daily News*, 24 October 1896, p. 5, col. 4.

18. *Evening Standard*, 24 October 1896, p. 2, col. 3. See, also, *Daily News*, 24 October 1896, p. 5, col. 4.

19. *Daily News*, 24 October 1896, p. 5, col. 3.

20. *Daily Chronicle*, 24 October 1896, p. 5, col. 5.

21. At the Sun Yatsen conference in Beijing in March 1985, there was a fierce debate as to whether the Sun Yatsen of 1895–6 was a reformer or a revolutionary. This debate has tempted me to explore the question in Chapter 5.

22. The White Lily was a secret society which was active mainly in North China. The journalist asked the question about the White Lily apparently because as soon as news of Sun Yatsen's detention was made public, a special correspondent of the Central News alleged that Sun Yatsen was a member, asserting that the White Lily was the most malignant of all Chinese secret societies (*Globe*, 23 October 1896, p. 5, col. 2).

23. *Daily News*, 24 October 1896, p. 5, col. 3.

first time, he gave publicity to the enlightened nature of his movement, but again he had to be prodded to do so, and then did not pursue the subject any further. He had thrown away another excellent opportunity.

Sun Yatsen's performance during these two news conferences shows that there was no deliberate attempt either to condemn Manchu rule or to propagate his own cause, further weakening the arguments of Luo Jialun and Schiffrin that he had twisted the story about his kidnapping for these purposes.[24] It also throws doubt on Schiffrin's observation that Sun Yatsen 'was endowed with radar-like sensitivity in adjusting to his targets'.[25] Nor was there any sign of his using the publicity to create an heroic image for himself. Rather, as with the case of the contributor to the *Kobe Chronicle* starting the legend of a fearless Sun Yatsen preaching revolution in the Legation, the origins of his heroic image lie in the efforts (deliberate or otherwise) of others, as we shall see in the rest of this chapter.

II The Help of the British Press

What Sun Yatsen failed to do, upon his release, in terms of blackening the Manchu regime and creating an image of himself as a champion of enlightenment in China, some of the British press had been hard at work doing, albeit unwittingly. The very first report, which broke the news of his kidnapping and detention by the Legation, described him as 'a prominent Chinese gentleman' and 'a medical man well known in Hong Kong'.[26] It also gave some details about the plot at Guangzhou the year before, saying that the immediate object was to seize the viceroy, but that the ultimate goal 'was no less than to depose the Manchu or Tartar dynasty' on the grounds that China had been 'distinctly going to the bad under that rule', and that no improvement in the

---

24. See Chapter 3, Section I.
25. Schiffrin, *Origins*, p. 144. Schiffrin made this remark when he analysed Sun Yatsen's discussion (in writing) with Miyazaki about China's future in general and Pan-Asianism in particular. But as a general observation. Schiffrin has applied this in spirit to his treatment of Sun Yatsen's adventures in London, which, as we have seen, is not the case. I shall attempt to deal, on a very limited scale, with Sun Yatsen's early involvement with Japanese Pan-Asianists in Chapter 6.
26. *Globe*, 23 October 1896, p. 5, col. 2, reprinting its report of the previous evening.

affairs of the nation could be expected until the dynasty was removed.[27]

In response to this description of the plot, an old China hand of the Central News offered his expertise: 'There is nothing remarkable in the conspiracy itself. Canton Province [sic] is the hotbed of sedition ... The people of the south are, moreover, born pirates, and kidnapping ... is a profession and almost a fine art. The fact that one of the kidnappers should be kidnapped in London is only a grim instance of Chinese humour ... Both Canton and Hunan [sic] are honey-combed with secret societies, and here flourishes the Chinese form of Nihilism locally known as the *Kolao Wai* [sic], or Society of the White Lily ...'[28] It is a pity that the British public had to be guided by an expert who called the city of 'Canton' a province, who confused the While Lily of North China with the 'Kolao' of central China, and who did not realize that the secret societies in South China were generally called Triads, all of which were quite separate organizations. And it was probably this misinformation that subsequently led a reporter to ask Sun Yatsen if he was a member of the White Lily, thus giving him a chance to put the record straight.[29]

Even before he was offered this chance, Dr Cantlie seems to have jumped to his defence by giving a signed statement to the same news agency (that is, the Central News), in which he stated, 'I knew Sun in Hong Kong intimately. He studied medicine in the college there during the year 1887 until he qualified. He was a brilliant student, and started practice in Macao, a Portuguese settlement some 30 miles from Hong Kong. He was, owing to the success attending him on his practice there, induced by his friends to go to Canton. I then lost sight of him for one month, but eventually he called upon me in Hong Kong, and said he had got into trouble with the Chinese Government'.[30] This signed statement produced favourable reactions in most London newspapers. Among them, the 'extremely popular'[31] *Daily Telegraph*, which had an enormous circulation of some 241,000 copies daily,[32] was

27. *Globe*, 23 October 1896, p. 5, col. 2.
28. *Globe*, 23 October 1896, p. 5, col. 2.
29. See Section I of this chapter.
30. *Evening Standard*, 23 October 1896, p. 5, col. 2.
31. *Sell's Dictionary of the World's Press* (London, 1897), p. 350.
32. *Sell's Dictionary of the World's Press*, p. 350.

the most complimentary to the fugitive. It commented, 'Within a very short time of Sun Yatsen's arrival at Canton — a month only according to Dr Cantlie — he began to conspire, as brilliant, educated Orientals invariably do when they return from the light of civilization to the stupid barbarism of their own countries'.[33]

Indeed, the British press played a far more important role in building up an image for Sun Yatsen than he could ever have expected. Besides the high praise for his attainments in Western education and his courage in using such an education to try to change China, the press also portrayed him as an attractive and presentable gentleman. As soon as the reporters got their first glimpse of him upon his release, they were all favourably impressed. One wrote, 'He is of small build and his features are of a delicate cast. However, his is an extremely pleasant face, and his eyes are singularly bright'.[34] Another commented, 'Sun Yatsen is about the mildest looking member of the race which is childlike and bland that [it] is possible to imagine ... and his black eyes twinkled good humouredly as he received the congratulations of one and all upon his escape'.[35] Yet another went even further, casting doubt on the suggestion that such a delicate person could ever have been embroiled in violence: 'In his light overcoat and suit of West-end cut, and underneath a distinctly Western black soft felt hat, Sun Yatsen did not look the Oriental conspirator the Chinese Embassy picture him'.[36]

The reporters were equally impressed when they had a chance to talk to him during the two news conferences later the same evening. At the Shades public house, one wrote, 'Sun Yatsen is a slow talker of very good English'.[37] Some letters, in Sun Yatsen's own hand, written between 1908 and 1910, have been con-

33. *Daily Telegraph*, 24 October 1896, p. 6, col. 6. Sun Yatsen went from Macau to practise in Guangzhou [Canton] in the spring of 1893, and his plot was exposed in October 1895. Meanwhile, he visited Hong Kong regularly, which probably explains why Dr Cantlie said that he lost sight of him for one month. But the newspaper seems to have misunderstood Dr Cantlie to mean that Sun Yatsen began plotting against the Manchu government within a month of setting up his practice in Guangzhou.

34. *Morning Leader*, 24 October 1896, p. 7, col. 2. See, also, *Star*, 24 October 1896, p. 3, col. 1.

35. *Westminster Gazette*, 24 October 1896, p. 5, col. 1.

36. *Daily Mail*, 24 October 1896, p. 5, col. 4.

37. *Daily Mail*, 24 October 1896, p. 5, col. 4.

sulted.[38] They are full of grammatical errors. Assuming that his English had not deteriorated since 1896, as he had been living abroad all this time, I do not think that he spoke 'very good English'.[39] I suggest that this remark by the reporter should be seen in the light of the fact that extremely few Chinese at this time spoke any English; and that the Chinese community in London consisted mainly of sailors, who might have had a little pidgin. However, the British public was not in a position to qualify the reporter's comment, and might have readily accepted that Sun Yatsen did indeed speak very good English. Far more important than the mere question of his proficiency in the language is the fact that the British journalists appear to have felt that they could relate to him. Time and again they stressed his 'English' outlook. This is how one of them began his report on the second news conference at 46, Devonshire Street: 'The door opened, and there entered a young Chinaman of small stature, with a handsome smiling face, and dressed as *Englishmen [my italics]* dress'.[40] At a time when most Britons associated civilization with anything British, and barbarism with most things Chinese,[41] Sun Yatsen's English appearance seems to have worked to his advantage.

As if words were insufficient to give full justice to this Anglicized Oriental gentleman, at least four newspapers published portraits of him in his English clothes.[42] And as if portraits were still not enough, at least two ballads about him appeared in print.[43] One of these two ballads was entitled 'The Anglo-Chinee'.[44] Even heads of state might not have been given the same attention by the press, however much they would have wanted it.

---

38. Some of these may be found among the Boothe Papers in the Hoover Institution at Stanford. Others are in the British Library in London (Ref. BL Add 39168/138–141).

39. *Daily Mail*, 24 October 1896, p. 5, col. 5.

40. *Daily News*, 24 October 1896, p. 5, col. 3. See, also, *Echo*, 24 October 1896, p. 3, col. 5; and *St James's Gazette*, 24 October 1896, p. 9, cols. 1–2.

41. See, for example, *Daily Telegraph*, 24 October 1896, p. 6, col. 6.

42. *Daily Graphic*, 24 October 1896, p. 13; *Graphic*, 31 October 1896; *Black and White*, 31 October 1896, p. 550; and *Illustrated London News*, 31 October 1896, Vol. 109, No. 3002, p. 556.

43. *Daily Chronicle*, 24 October 1896, p. 5, col. 6; and *Sun*, 24 October 1896, p. 3, col. 2.

44. *Daily Chronicle*, 24 October 1896, p. 5, col. 6.

This enormous interest in him on the part of the press may be attributed to several factors. First, the British were obviously proud that they had had a 'civilizing' effect on the rest of the world, albeit in the person of a lone Oriental. Second, his claim to have been born in Hong Kong and thus to be a British citizen[45] aroused a feeling of *Civis Romanus sum*.[46] The rumour that he had been tortured,[47] or at least handcuffed,[48] during his detention must have heightened such a feeling still further. Third, kidnapping 'on British soil', as one newspaper put it, 'seems so monstrous a solecism that we cannot believe it has happened'.[49] Worse still, it had happened in the middle of London:

> Well, bli'me, this is cheek
> Fer ter come an' gow and sneak
> A feller wot's a-walkin' in the streets o' London tahn.[50]

These factors may be identified as expressions of British nationalism, from which Sun Yatsen appears to have benefited indirectly.

This is not to deny that the concern for Sun Yatsen's safety was genuine. 'It may transpire that Sun Yatsen is not a British citizen', wrote one paper, 'But ... he is a human being, and here in England a human being, even though he be a Chinaman, has certain inalienable rights'.[51] Another paper elaborated on these rights: '... except in conformity with the Extradition Law, every foreigner who sets his foot on English soil, and who observes the temporary allegiance which he owes to the English Crown, is entitled to the same freedom from arrest and imprisonment which an English subject enjoys'.[52] The second half of the verse in the ballad quoted in the previous paragraph reads:

> Whether that sime feller be
> Jest a yeller-mug Chinee
> Or a mighty ryal pussonage a-wearin' of a crahn.[53]

---

45. FO 17/1718, pp. 22–3, Sun Yatsen to Cantlie (19 October 1896).
46. *Sun*, 23 October 1896, p. 2, col. 3.
47. *Daily Graphic*, 24 October 1896, p. 13, col. 3.
48. *Overland Mail*, 30 October 1896, p. 45, col. 2.
49. *Evening News*, 23 October 1896, p. 2, col. 4.
50. *Sun*, 24 October 1896, p. 3, col. 2.
51. *Sun*, 23 October 1896, p. 2, col. 3.
52. FO 17/1718, p. 84, newspaper cutting: *Standard*, 24 October 1896.
53. *Sun*, 24 October 1896, p. 3, col. 2.

The reporting of Lord Salisbury's demand for Sun Yatsen's release, and the speed with which it was met, revealed another facet of the British nationalistic response. The *Globe*, which was the first paper to break the news of his kidnapping, commented in its editorial, 'The promptness with which Lord Salisbury has compelled the liberation of Sun Yatsen will meet with the warmest approval throughout the British Empire ... Not less praiseworthy than the Premier's quickness of action is the *contemptuous* [*my italics*] character imparted to the order for release. A Foreign Office official, accompanied by a single detective, sufficed for the delivery of the mandate, and its *peremptoriness* [*my italics*] may be judged from the speed with which it was obeyed'.[54] Indeed, nearly all the London papers referred to Salisbury's Note as 'peremptory', and overwhelmingly congratulated him for his decisiveness of action.[55] The same ballad, part of which has been quoted above, and the title of which was, indeed, 'Awkins Champions the Heathen Chinee', finished with the following verses:

It's a hinsult, so it is,
    This 'ere 'ole an' corner biz,
An' Mr Bloomin' Chin 'ad better mind 'is p's and q's,
Ow 'e thought 'isself so smawt
But by gum, 'e 'ad ter pawt
With 'is keptive w'en Lord Sawlsberry 'ad trotted aht 'is views

An' I 'ope as Sun Yat Sun
'Fore 'is little kyse is done,
Will git some cawmpinsyshun jest for bein messed abaht;
An' if 'e 'as a shot,
If 'e gets 'is oof or not,
E'll 'ev 'Awkins an' the Nyshun et 'is back withaht a daht.

'Awkins.[56]

---

54. *Globe*, 24 October 1896, p. 4, cols. 2-3.

55. See, for example, *Black and White*, 31 October 1896, p. 550, col. 2; *Daily Chronicle*, 24 October 1896, p. 4, col. 6; *Daily News*, 24 October 1896, p. 5, col. 3; *Daily Mail*, 24 October 1896, p. 4, col. 4; *Daily Telegraph*, 24 October 1896, p. 6, col. 6; *Echo*, 24 October 1896, p. 2, col. 2; *Morning Advertiser*, 24 October 1896, p. 4, cols. 4-5; *Morning Leader*, 24 October 1896, p. 6, col. 3; *Morning Post*, 24 October 1896, p. 4, cols. 5-6; *Pall Mall Gazette*, 24 October 1896, p. 2, col. 2; *Speaker*, 31 October 1896, p. 452, col. 1; and *The Times*, 24 October 1896, p. 9, cols. 2-3.

56. *Sun*, 24 October 1896, p. 3, col. 2.

People today may not approve of the jingoism of the late Victorian era, but Sun Yatsen was deeply touched. 'He has had nearly a fortnight during which to admire the quickness and despatch with which the Chinese Legation carries out arrests that, owing to our prejudice in favour of legal forms, sometimes here take an unconscionable time; but we have no doubt that Chinese celerity only won from him an unwilling admiration, whereas English promptitude is now the theme of his enthusiastic praise'.[57]

Some of the criticisms of the British press were even aggressive. That mighty newspaper, *The Times*, described the Chinese minister's action as 'ludicrous',[58] and accused him of having 'claimed a right which is not recognised by any *civilised* [*my italics*] country'.[59] Demands for his recall,[60] or at least an apology[61] and compensation,[62] were voiced loudly. The *Globe* also remarked, 'No *civilised* [*my italics*] Power would have advanced such an extravagant claim, much less have endeavoured to give it stealthy effect'.[63] Another commented, 'If these are the manners of the Chinese Legation in London, what kind of official life is that of Pekin?'[64] These systematic attacks on the Manchu regime were more than Sun Yatsen could ever have hoped for, and certainly more effective than those he launched later.[65] But that is by the way. In the context of the present exploration into the origins of Sun Yatsen's heroic image, these attacks were instrumental in at least arousing sympathy for 'the timid Sun [having been] mewed up by the gentle Tang [Deng Tingkeng]',[66] for no other reason than having been 'civilised' and, in turn, having tried to 'civilise' his own government.

Some of these attacks became rather excessive, and were extended to the Chinese people as a whole. At least three

---

57. *Evening News*, 24 October 1896, p. 2, col. 2.
58. *The Times*, 24 October 1896, p. 9, col. 2.
59. *The Times*, 24 October 1896, p. 3.
60. *Daily Chronicle*, 24 October 1896, p. 4, col. 6.
61. *Pall Mall Gazette*, 24 October 1896, p. 2, col. 2.
62. *Daily Chronicle*, 24 October 1896, p. 4, col. 6.
63. *Globe*, 24 October 1896, p. 4, cols. 2–3.
64. *Evening News*, 24 October 1896, p. 2, cols. 2–3.
65. See Chapter 5, Sections II and III.
66. *Sun*, 24 October 1896, p. 1, col. 4.

newspapers[67] quoted part of the first verse of a poem, which reads:

> Which I wish to remark, —
> And my language is plain,
> That for ways that are dark,
> And for tricks that are vain,
> The heathen Chinee is peculiar, —
> Which the same I would rise to explain.[68]

The *Sun* continued, 'There is no doubt about it. The story of Sun Yatsen ... is as brilliant a specimen of the ways and tricks of the Aborigines of the Celestial Empire as has been discussed since Bret Harte sang of the Oriental card-player'.[69] Such a remark is certainly racist by today's standards. Whether or not Sun Yatsen took the same view is an open question. He himself lamented the backwardness of his own people in his writings;[70] and, after all, it was the backwardness of both the system and the people which he had been endeavouring to banish from China. Indeed, the intensity of the dislike for such backwardness, as expressed in the poem and the related press comments, might well have aroused further sympathy for his cause, and contributed to his image as a hero who had been persecuted for trying to do something about it.

Even those who might not normally read editorials would probably have looked at them on account of the magnitude of the scandal which had 'afforded pleasurable excitement to hundreds of thousands of newspaper readers in the dull season'.[71]

Thus, the sensation, national pride, and humanitarianism all seem to have contributed to the enormous interest of the British press in Sun Yatsen, unwittingly building up for him an heroic image which would not have come about but for the eleven days he had spent as the guest of the Chinese minister in London.

In this regard, Schiffrin's view merits reconsideration. Alluding to the period after Sun Yatsen's release from detention, he

---

67. *Daily Mail*, 24 October 1896, p. 6, col. 6; *Evening News*, 23 October 1896, p. 2, col. 4; and *Sun*, 23 October 1896, p. 2, col. 7.
68. This poem was written by Bret Harte (1836–1902). The full text is to be found in Gray (ed.), *American Verse of the Nineteenth Century*.
69. *Sun*, 23 October 1896, p. 2, col. 7.
70. See Chapter 5, Sections II and III.
71. *Evening News*, 24 October 1896, p. 2, col. 2.

writes, 'But this was no time for retirement into the shadows. Sun discovered that he was famous and seized the opportunity to rebuke his enemies and glorify the anti-Manchu cause'.[72] Schiffrin uses the following information to support his view:

The next day the reporters clamoured for interviews and found Sun not disinclined to talk of his incarceration. The journalists were favourably impressed and one wrote of his 'comely features' and his 'diminutive stature'. Though tired, he told in an 'unfaltering voice' how he had been 'decoyed' into the Legation, and it was observed that he spoke English 'remarkably well' but 'with a definite foreign accent'.[73]

The recorded interviews, as published in the newspapers and analysed thus far, do not exactly give the impression that Sun Yatsen deliberately set out 'to rebuke his enemies or to glorify the anti-Manchu cause'.[74] As mentioned earlier in this section, he was prodded along by reporters much of the time, and I still think that if one were to look for the origins of his heroic image, they lie more in the unintentional efforts of others than in deliberate attempts (if any) of his own. Indeed, there were occasions when he could have been more co-operative with the journalists, one of whom remarked, 'In reply to further questions, Sun admitted that he was the man wanted by the Legation, but he would not state on what mission he had come to England, or what his future movements would be, now that he had regained his liberty'.[75]

Consistent with his view that Sun Yatsen twisted the story of the kidnapping in order to blacken the Manchu regime,[76] and on the assumption that Sun Yatsen 'was endowed with radar-like sensitivity in adjusting to his targets',[77] Schiffrin has accused him of 'petty deceit, ... subterfuge, ... conspicuous church attendance, and all ... other devices necessary to prove [his] Christian respectability'.[78] In this book, I have attempted to show that Sun Yatsen did not twist the story, and that he was not as sensitive as

---

72. Schiffrin, *Origins*, p. 125.
73. Schiffrin, *Origins*, p. 125.
74. Schiffrin, *Origins*, p. 125.
75. *Evening Standard*, 24 October 1896, p. 2, col. 3.
76. Schiffrin, *Origins*, p. 113.
77. Schiffrin, *Origins*, p. 144.
78. Schiffrin, *Origins*, p. 145.

radar to his targets. Therefore, I am not prepared to accuse him of deceit or subterfuge.

As for the church attendance, I doubt whether that was planned or intended to attract attention. Schiffrin bases his assertion on one single event, about which he writes, 'In London, Sun did his best to live up to this new image. He attended church under the watchful eyes of the press',[79] and gives the *Globe* as his source of information.[80] In fact, the newspaper merely stated that 'Sun Yatsen, who is a Christian, attended Divine Service at St Martin's Church yesterday [Sunday, 25 October 1896] morning'.[81] Indeed, this statement must be read in the context of the entire report, which began with the words: 'Dr Cantlie stated last night . . .'[82] Thus, it appears that Dr Cantlie had been the *Globe*'s informant, in which case the assertion that Sun Yatsen tried to live up to his new image by attending 'church under the watchful eyes of the press'[83] cannot stand. Rather, it was Dr Cantlie who attempted to influence the press.[84] In addition, we must remember that Sun Yatsen was staying with the Cantlies at this time, and if the Cantlies decided to go to church that Sunday, ordinary courtesy would have dictated that Sun Yatsen go with them. Mrs Cantlie's diary of Sunday, 25 October 1896, contained this entry: 'Hamish & I took Sun Yatsen to St Martin's-in-the-Fields.[85] He is a Christian so it was a thanksgiving service *to us* [*my italics*]'.[86] This entry has a distinctly private overtone to it. There is no evidence that Sun Yatsen's attendance with the Cantlies attracted public attention. There is no reference to him, for example, in the sermon delivered by the vicar, the Revd

---

79. Schiffrin, *Origins*, p. 127.
80. Schiffrin, *Origins*, p. 128, n. 100.
81. *Globe*, 26 October 1896, p. 7, col. 2.
82. *Globe*, 26 October 1896, p. 7, col. 2.
83. Schiffrin, *Origins*, p. 127.
84. This is something which will be dealt with more fully in Section IV of this chapter.
85. I am told by the authorities of that church that the correct way to refer to it is either St Martin's Church or St Martin-in-the-Fields; here, Mrs Cantlie combined the two.
86. Mrs Cantlie's diary, 25 October 1896.

Kitto[87] (whom the Cantlies appear to have known quite well),[88] as summarized in the *St Martin-in-the-Fields Monthly Messenger*.[89]

In the final analysis, it does not matter by what means the news of Sun Yatsen being a Christian and going to church got into the press. What is important is that the report, like so many others of its kind, must have helped in the creation of an heroic image of Sun Yatsen by making a favourable impression on the British public of the Victorian era.

III The Help of Dr James Cantlie

Dr Cantlie was no doubt the man who first released the news that the prisoner in Portland Place was 'an intelligent and educated man of 30. He possesses a medical diploma'.[90] And when the old China hand of the Central News alleged that Sun Yatsen was himself a pirate and kidnapper, belonging to a secret society by the name of the White Lily, Dr Cantlie, as mentioned in Section II of this chapter, handed a signed statement to the Central News for dissemination among the newspapers. In this statement, he gave a glowing report about his former student. If the reaction of the press is any guide, it seems that Dr Cantlie's voice drowned that of the old China hand almost completely.[91]

Dr Cantlie came to his rescue again during the impromptu news conference at the Shades public house, when he was obviously embarrassed by the question about his revolutionary activities the year before. As mentioned, Dr Cantlie shouted, 'Time, gentlemen', and hustled him away from the press gathering.[92] During the second news conference he took great

87. For a short biography of the Revd Kitto, see the obituary in *St Martin-in-the-Fields Monthly Messenger*, No. 158, May 1903, pp. 9–13.

88. See Mrs Cantlie's diary, 20 July and 20 September 1896; and 2 October 1896, on which day, 'The Rev. Mr & Mrs & Miss Kitto called & stayed admiring our curios a long time'.

89. I am grateful to the authorities of the church for giving me access to their records, the most relevant parts being the October and November issues of their *Monthly Messenger* in 1896 (Nos. 82 and 83 respectively).

90. *Sun*, 23 October 1896, p. 2, col. 7.

91. See Section II of this chapter.

92. See Section I of this chapter.

care to protect his former student. Sun Yatsen began, 'On Sunday morning, at eleven o'clock, I met a Chinaman in the streets, and he asked me whether I was Japanese or Chinese'. At this point, Dr Cantlie interjected, 'It was in or near Portland-place? but he did not know where he was because he is almost a stranger in London'.[93] It is clear what Dr Cantlie was driving at, in view of the Legation's allegation that the fugitive had entered the building voluntarily, and his own counter-claim that he had been kidnapped. The image of an honest man was at stake. When he said, 'I would take nothing but bread and milk [for fear of being poisoned]', Dr Cantlie again interjected, 'And he has lost a couple of stone in a fortnight'.[94] Obviously, the doctor was aiming at getting maximum sympathy from the pressmen.

After the flurry of the interviews, a public letter appeared in all the major newspapers in London on Monday, 26 October 1896:

Sir, — Will you kindly express through your columns my keen appreciation of the action of the British Government in effecting my release from the Chinese Legation? I have also to thank the Press generally for their timely help and sympathy. If anything were needed to convince me of the generous public spirit which pervades Great Britain, and the love of justice which distinguishes its people, the recent acts of the last few days have conclusively done so.

Knowing and feeling more keenly than ever what a constitutional Government and an enlightened people mean, I am prompted still more actively to pursue the cause of advancement, education, and civilisation in my own well-beloved but oppressed country.

Yours faithfully,
Sun Yatsen.
46 Devonshire-street,
Portland-place, W.[95]

The writer of the letter signed himself Sun Yatsen; but in view of Sun Yatsen's proficiency (or lack of it) in the English language as assessed in Section II of this chapter, this letter is probably too sophisticated to have come from him. Since he was staying with Dr Cantlie at this time, perhaps the doctor was responsible, and even initiated the idea.

---

93. *Daily News*, 24 October 1896, p. 5, col. 3.
94. *Evening Standard*, 24 October 1896, p. 2, col. 3.
95. See, for example, *The Times*, 26 October 1896, p. 8, col. 4; and *Globe*, 24 October 1896, p. 7, col. 2.

It has always been assumed that Sun Yatsen wrote the booklet *Kidnapped in London*. But there is strong evidence to the contrary. The liveliness of style, the refinement of language, the fluency of expression, and the touch of Scottish humour here and there are all more typical of Cantlie's writings,[96] than of Sun Yatsen's English manuscripts.[97] In addition, Dr Cantlie was just as qualified as Sun Yatsen, if not more so, to write such an account. He was present at all the interviews with reporters when the story of the kidnapping was told, but Sun Yatsen was not there when he made those relentless efforts to rescue him.

But speculation cannot replace historical evidence. In this regard, Mrs Cantlie's diary provides some crucial evidence. Her diary strikes me as something strictly private, so much so that I doubt if even her husband saw it.[98] On Wednesday, 18 November 1896, she recorded that her mother had given Sun Yatsen £50 that day. The next day, she wrote, 'Hamish is helping Dr Sun to write the history of his life'. On Monday, 21 December 1896, she wrote, 'Hamish has just written the history of Sun Yatsen & sent it to the printers'.[99] The book was clearly written with speed. Dr Cantlie might have set out to help Sun Yatsen write, but it seems that he ended up by writing it all himself. The three entries in Mrs Cantlie's diary, when taken together, indicate that it might very well have been Mrs Cantlie's mother, Mrs Barclay-Brown, who suggested that the poverty-stricken exile might be helped by publishing an autobiography while public interest in him was still alive. Mrs Barclay-Brown, who was the wife of a wealthy ship-builder and repairer on the Clyde in Glasgow, would have had

---

96. Dr Cantlie had such a distinctive style that when I read the book, *Sun Yat-sen*, which he wrote in collaboration with Sheridan Jones, I could easily tell which parts might be attributed to him. See, also, the typescript of his public lecture, given in London, about Hong Kong (Wellcome Institute Library, Western MS 1488).

97. Some of these are preserved among the Boothe Papers in the Hoover Institution at Stanford; others are in the British Library (BL Add. 39168/138–141).

98. See, for example, Mrs Cantlie's diary. On 27 July 1896, she wrote, 'Hamish went to Carlisle with the Harts to British Medical Association. As usual I feel very lost without him'. On 4 August 1896, she wrote, 'Hamish went to London as he cannot be down here [at their holiday home] all the time which is very sad for me'. And on 8 August 1896, she wrote, 'But oh! it was nice to have Hamish. I do not enjoy being away from him at all'.

99. Mrs Cantlie's diary, 21 December 1896.

the kind of business acumen that neither Dr Cantlie nor Sun Yatsen appears to have had.[100]

I checked with the printer of *Kidnapped in London*, J. W. Arrowsmith of Bristol,[101] to see if the manuscript was indeed in Dr Cantlie's hand; and to establish if the printer did receive the manuscript on the day mentioned by Mrs Cantlie, or shortly after. Unfortunately, the firm has no records of the coming and going of manuscripts; and in this particular case, it is believed that the manuscript was returned to the author.[102] On Wednesday, 20 January 1897, Mrs Cantlie again wrote, 'Hamish's book on Sun Yatsen comes out tomorrow'.[103] The next day she wrote, 'The book on Sun Yatsen came out to-day, numerous good critiques on it'.[104] I checked *The Times* of 21 January 1897 and, sure enough, *Kidnapped in London* was listed under 'PUBLICATIONS TODAY'.[105] Then a full review appeared on 29 January 1897, under 'BOOKS OF THE WEEK'.[106]

Other major British newspapers also carried, on 21 January 1897, notices of the publication of the booklet. They included the *Daily Chronicle*,[107] the *Daily News*,[108] the *Daily Telegraph*,[109] the *Morning Leader*,[110] the *Scotsman*,[111] the *Standard*,[112] and the *Sun*.[113] These notices were followed by book reviews, which I shall deal with later.

---

100. I am grateful to Dr Audrey Cantlie, the granddaughter of Dr James Cantlie, for having shared with me some of her family history. See also Cantlie and Seaver, *Sir James Cantlie*, p. 21; and Stewart, *Quality of Mercy*, p. 26.

101. My first letter was returned to me unopened, with the words 'gone away' scribbled on the envelope. I wrote to Dr Janet Hunter of the London School of Economics for help. She found out the new address and forwarded a copy of my letter to the firm.

102. V. Arrowsmith-Brown to Wong, 11 December 1984. I was told, further, that 'J. W. Arrowsmith had a reputation of being willing to start new authors, and it is possible the *Kidnapped* book came through a connection with one of them'.

103. Mrs Cantlie's diary, 20 January 1897.

104. Mrs Cantlie's diary, 21 January 1897.

105. *The Times*, 21 January 1897, p. 12, col. 2.

106. *The Times*, 29 January 1897.

107. See p. 3, col. 7.

108. See p. 6, col. 3.

109. See p. 7, col. 4.

110. See p. 6, col.

111. See Books Received column.

112. See p. 3, col. 2.

113. See p. 1, col. 7.

With the information provided by Mrs Cantlie's diary and by the newspapers, I sought advice from Dr Cantlie's descendants. After some consultation within the family, it was agreed that some information hitherto confined to members of the family might be made public. Apparently, Dr Cantlie's eldest son, Sir Keith Cantlie, had told his children that Dr Cantlie had written the book. Sir Keith, in turn, had heard it from Dr Cantlie himself.[114] Dr Cantlie's fourth and youngest son, Mr Kenneth Cantlie, whom I interviewed subsequently for the fifth time, confirmed the story.

Conversely, I wondered if it would have been physically possible for Sun Yatsen, given his lack of proficiency in English, to have written the booklet after his release on the evening of 23 October 1896, in time for it to be published on 21 January 1897. The Preface of the booklet contains the following: 'I must beg the indulgence of all readers for my shortcomings in English composition, and confess that had it not been for the help rendered by a good friend, who *transcribed* [*my italics*] my thoughts, I could never have ventured to appear as the Author of an English book'. In the light of the above evidence, I am inclined to interpret this quotation to mean that the 'good friend' *wrote* the booklet for him. My interpretation of the English usage in this quotation is confirmed by a book reviewer of the time, who described Sun Yatsen as 'the titular author of the little book', pointing out that his thoughts had been transcribed by a good friend.[115] At this time, the only good friends he had in London were Dr Cantlie and Dr Manson, and there is nothing to suggest that Dr Manson was ever involved with Sun Yatsen to this extent. The detectives shadowing Sun Yatsen reported that he stayed with the Cantlies until 2 November 1896, when he resumed residence at 8, Gray's Inn Place.[116] This should have given Dr Cantlie sufficient time to jot down whatever information he wanted from Sun Yatsen to be transcribed on paper.

In addition, I have pointed out in Chapter 3, Section I, that an appendix in the booklet, attributed to the *China Mail* of 3 De-

---

114. I am grateful to Dr Audrey Cantlie, a lecturer in Anthropology at the School of Oriental and African Studies, University of London, and the daughter of Sir Keith Cantlie, for agreeing to tell me about this.

115. *Morning Leader*, 28 January 1897, p. 2, col. 6.

116. Mrs Cantlie's diary, 2 November 1896.

cember 1896, may in fact be found in the *Overland China Mail* of the same date. The latter was the overseas edition of the *China Mail*, to which many former residents of Hong Kong subscribed. Having been extremely active in the affairs of the colony,[117] whence they had returned to England only a few months before, the Cantlies appear to have continued to take a great interest in the place,[118] and subscribed to the overseas edition of the local newspaper. This may explain the confusion in the booklet about the two newspapers. After all, the article in the *Overland China Mail* had its origins in the *China Mail*; and Dr Cantlie appears to have thought it better to attribute it to the original paper, forgetting that there was a difference in the dates on which they appeared. This oversight may be taken as yet another piece of corroborating evidence that Dr Cantlie was indeed the author of *Kidnapped in London*.

If Dr Cantlie was the real author of this famous booklet, and there is little evidence to point to the contrary, its contents, on which historians and writers alike have relied so heavily for information, must be seen in a different light, because they probably reflected more of the hopes and fears of Dr Cantlie than those of his former student.

To begin with, I have always been puzzled by certain passages in the booklet. On p. 99, it is alleged that after the release, and on the way from the Legation to Scotland Yard, 'Inspector Jarvis gravely lectured me on my delinquencies, and scolded me as a bad boy, and advised me to have nothing to do any more with revolutions'. If Sun Yatsen was the devoted revolutionary that he was, and had sole control over the writing of the booklet, would he have allowed such a passage to appear in print? On the other hand, the book review in *The Times* echoed the sentiment expressed in the booklet: 'It is to be hoped that Sun profited by the "lecture" he received after his release from Inspector Jarvis, of Scotland Yard. He will probably be less ready after his alarming experiences to take part in any such revolutionary movements as that which necessitated his flight to England and made the

---

117. See Cantlie and Seaver, *Sir James Cantlie*, Chapters 5–6.
118. See the numerous references to Hong Kong in Mrs Cantlie's diary. Dr Cantlie gave at least one lecture about Hong Kong after his return to London (see Wellcome Institute Library, Western MS 1488).

Chinese Legation so anxious to send him back to China'.[119] *The Times* was not alone in echoing such a sentiment. The *Standard* wrote, 'The officials of Scotland Yard undoubtedly gave him sound advice when they counselled him to have nothing more to do with revolutions'.[120] The *London and China Express* repeated this sentence word for word.[121]

Indeed, soon after Sun Yatsen's release, the *Globe*, reporting on yet another interview with Dr Cantlie, wrote,

Sun Yatsen, who is a Christian, attended Divine Service at St Martin's Church yesterday morning. He has no immediate intention of quitting this country, and his services will be placed at the disposal of Dr Cantlie, who is contemplating the establishment of a College of Medicine for Chinese in London, in connection with a similar institution in Hong Kong, of which he is the Dean. Dr Cantlie is also making arrangements to form a committee for the collection of subscriptions in aid of the college in Hong Kong. He points out that the natives who are trained in this college, and who find their way into the houses of the Chinese, have opportunities far more favourable than ever present themselves to foreign missionaries of furthering the cause of education, and spreading Christian knowledge throughout China.[122]

The hopes and fears were quite obvious. The hopes were that Sun Yatsen would disavow revolution and return to the medical profession, and in so doing, would help the sick and spread the Gospel in China. The fears were that Sun Yatsen would not do so and therefore put his life in danger again. The image projected in *Kidnapped in London* was one of an innocent, intelligent, and Western-educated young Christian being persecuted by his own government for having tried to do something about its excesses. It turned out that Sun Yatsen had no intention of abandoning his chosen path in life. Consequently, the image which the booklet succeeded in projecting was very different from the one which Dr Cantlie had hoped to create. Here was a man who rejected the privilege of joining the élite British medical profession, and risked offending his influential teachers, Dr Cantlie and Dr

---

119. *The Times*, 21 January 1897, p. 12, col. 2.
120. *Standard*, 21 January 1897, p. 3, col. 6.
121. *Supplement to the London and China Express*, 22 January 1897, p. 6, col. 2.
122. *Globe*, 26 October 1896, p. 7, col. 2.

Manson,[123] as well as the powerful body of public opinion in Britain[124] and even the British establishment,[125] in favour of continuing to risk his life and to toil, against all odds, for the regeneration of his country. His decision must have been a difficult one, particularly in view of the expectations of those responsible for the 'large number of letters' he received, 'congratulating him upon his release from captivity';[126] and the expectations of those 'Reporters and friends [who came] to congratulate Hamish all day, in troops'.[127]

Thus, the image which the booklet subsequently generated was quite a different one from that which Dr Cantlie had originally intended. In part, his object could have been to consolidate public sympathy for the hero; but, as with all romantic writings, a hero cannot do without a villain. The person whom Dr Cantlie appears to have chosen as the villain of the piece was Sir Halliday Macartney, and not the interpreter of the Legation, who, according to all the accounts attributable to Sun Yatsen, had played the most prominent role in the whole saga.[128] Sun Yatsen would not go so far as to say that Macartney had locked him up in his room inside the Legation.[129] Even the most severe critics of Macartney, such as *The Times*, would only express their surprise that he should have participated in such a transaction.[130] But Dr Cantlie actually accused him of having masterminded the whole operation.[131] It is difficult to explain why Dr Cantlie should have taken this view. Perhaps this was a natural assumption on his

---

123. Dr Cantlie's hopes and fears have just been mentioned. As for Dr Manson, it may be recalled that no sooner had he heard of Sun Yatsen's failed plot at Guangzhou than he told his former student that he 'had better stop that sort of thing'. (FO 17/1718, p. 122, Manson's statement at the Treasury, 4 November 1896, para. 2.)

124. That is, if the book review in *The Times* may be regarded as representing such opinion.

125. That is, if the views of Inspector Jarvis (as well as those of Dr Cantlie and Dr Manson) may be looked upon as typical of the British establishment.

126. *Globe*, 26 October 1896, p. 7, col. 2.

127. Mrs Cantlie's diary, 24 October 1896.

128. See the various newspaper reports on interviews with Sun Yatsen, mentioned in this and the previous three chapters.

129. *Daily Telegraph*, 24 October 1896, p. 7, col. 7: 'Do you know who it was that actually locked you up? — I cannot say'.

130. *The Times*, 24 October 1896, p. 9, cols. 2-3.

131. Sun Yatsen, *Kidnapped in London*, pp. 63-4: 'He little knew that he was going straight to the head centre of all this disgraceful proceeding'.

part, on the grounds that the Chinese minister was seriously ill and Macartney was the most knowledgeable person in the whole Legation. Perhaps Dr Cantlie was so ashamed of the behaviour of his fellow Scot that he allowed himself to be somewhat carried away in his denunciation of Macartney, because in another place he accused him of being insane.[132] It is even possible that Dr Cantlie, in his great annoyance with Macartney, highlighted Macartney's wrongdoings whenever he could in an attempt to impress upon the British public that Sun Yatsen had been wronged by a Briton, hoping that generous donations would be forthcoming to help Sun Yatsen settle his debt with George Cole.[133] Unfortunately, historians and writers alike seem to have been heavily influenced by this view, which, as far as I know, was the first of its kind to appear in print. And the misconception about the actual role played by Macartney has been perpetuated to this day.[134]

In any case, the book reviews show that Dr Cantlie succeeded at the time in creating for Sun Yatsen the sort of heroic image he had envisaged. His ability to convince the press that Sun Yatsen had been kidnapped, and was therefore a victim of Oriental despotism, was reflected in some of the reviews. One reviewer made a straightforward statement: 'On the 11th he was inveigled into the Chinese Legation'.[135] Another was quite cynical: 'The circumstances of his arrest — or, rather, we should say, the two

---

132. Sun Yatsen, *Kidnapped in London*, p. 90: 'In his own mind, I have no doubt, he has reasons for his action; but they seem scarcely consistent with those of a sane man, let alone the importance of the position he occupies'.

133. See Chapter 3, Section V.

134. See, for example, Luo Jialun's influential *Shiliao*, pp. 20, 37, and 49; and Wu Xiangxiang's voluminous *Sun Yixian zhuan*, Vol. 1, pp. 156, 164, and 168. Even Schiffrin, who has done meticulous work on the incident, appears to have been influenced by this view, and assigned to Macartney actions which were in fact not his, as if to give the impression that he plotted the whole thing: 'He also cabled Peking for permission to charter a ship ... He installed an extra lock on the door to Sun's room ...' (*Origins*, pp. 114–15). These statements were not true. It was the interpreter, Deng Tingkeng, and not Macartney, who asked Cole to have an extra lock put on the door (FO 17/1718, pp. 116–19, Cole's statement at the Treasury, 2 November 1896, para. 10). Again, it was the minister, not Macartney, who had the cable sent to Beijing (Beijing Palace Museum Records, Gong Zhaoyuan to Zongli Yamen [cypher], received 15 October 1896, in Luo Jialun, *Shiliao*, pp. 52–3). Schiffrin's book has been translated into Chinese and published, in Beijing in 1981. The full details are: Shi Fulin, *Sun Zhongshan yu Zhongguo geming de qiyuan* (Beijing, Social Sciences Press, 1981).

135. *Graphic*, 6 February 1897, p. 166, col. 3.

versions of the story — are so well known that we need not recapitulate them here ... It is generally understood also that Sir Halliday Macartney denies positively that any arrangement was made for shipping him to China'.[136]

Dr Cantlie also tackled directly the question which Sun Yatsen had tried to avoid during all his news conferences; namely, that of his involvement in revolutionary activities in China.[137] Judging from the reaction in the book reviews, he did so successfully. One reviewer wrote, 'It is clear, from his own account of his alleged misdeeds, that he had been engaged in a movement which might have resulted in the overthrow of the Manchu Dynasty. He is a Christian ... [who] took up with politics, joining what he calls the "Young China" Party, the object of which was the establishment — by the despatch of schemes of reform to the Throne, apparently — of a form of Constitutional Government. Agitation by petition and other documents not being notably successful, Sun Yatsen and others concocted a plan of revolution'.[138] Another reviewer was even sympathetic: 'Sun Yatsen is an enlightened Chinaman, imbued with Western ideas, and is a doctor by profession. He tells his story plainly and briefly, and gives us a sketch of the way in which China is governed. Extortion by officials is, he says, an institution ... The masses are kept in ignorance. No one is allowed on pain of death to invent anything new or to make known any new discovery ... It was to modify this shocking state of affairs that the "Young China" party was formed, and Sun Yatsen became a leading member. A petition for reform was presented to the Throne when the Japanese were threatening Peking. The petitioners were denounced, and the immediate cessation of all suggestions of reform ordered. Then force was resorted to by the Party and foiled, and Sun Yatsen, with others, had to fly'.[139]

Subsequently, the book produced quite a different kind of heroic image in the Orient; an image which Dr Cantlie might not have anticipated at all when he wrote the account. Sun Yatsen's refusal to abandon his revolutionary goals by joining the British medical élite has been noted. The real transformation of the

136. *St James's Gazette*, 30 January 1897, p. 5, col. 2.
137. See Section I of this chapter.
138. *Standard*, 21 January 1897, p. 3, col. 6.
139. *Graphic*, 6 February 1897, p. 166, col. 3.

heroic image came, however, as a result of translations of the book first into Japanese and then into Chinese.

IV The Help of Translators

Despite the success of the Meiji Restoration, and Japan's victory over China in the recent Sino-Japanese War of 1894–5, Japan in 1896 'was still not quite sure of its strength and status, and ... was still smarting under slights from Western imperialist powers'.[140] Paradoxically, therefore, the decline of China became of concern to the Japanese, who feared for the future of the entire yellow race in the face of Western imperialism. Having defeated China and encroached on its territory, Japan now began to 'search for a hero who could arouse patriotism and regenerate China',[141] under Japanese tutelage. Inukai Tsuyoshi, the liberal statesman, gave Miyazaki Torazo, the son of an ex-samurai, secret Foreign Office orders and funds to start such a search.[142]

Miyazaki met Chen Shaobai, who showed him a copy of *Kidnapped in London*[143] which, apparently, had just arrived from England. The book had a picture of Sun Yatsen in it. Miyazaki was so impressed that he could not wait to find out more about Sun Yatsen's revolutionary organization, and immediately went to Hong Kong. There he learnt from one of Sun Yatsen's former teachers that the hero was due to arrive in Japan from London the next day. Miyazaki hurried back to Japan, and met him at Chen Shaobai's lodgings. A very long discussion by pen — the Japanese had adopted the Chinese script — in which Miyazaki probed Sun Yatsen's way of thinking as deeply as he could, convinced Miyazaki that he had found the hero he wanted. Inukai Tsuyoshi and other Japanese leaders took turns to scrutinize the political exile, and found him acceptable. He was provided with a house and all his daily necessities.[144]

When this euphoria was over, Miyazaki settled down to translate *Kidnapped in London*, in May 1898. This Japanese version

---

140. Marius B. Jansen, *The Japanese and Sun Yat-sen*, Harvard Historical Monographs, No. 27 (Cambridge, Mass., Harvard University Press, 1954), p. 59.

141. Jansen, *The Japanese and Sun Yat-sen*, p. 59.

142. Jansen, *The Japanese and Sun Yat-sen*, p. 58.

143. Jansen, *The Japanese and Sun Yat-sen*, p. 65.

144. Schiffrin, *Origins*, pp. 141–7.

appeared in serial form in a local newspaper, the *Kyushu nippo* (*Kyushu Daily*). The title which Miyazaki gave to the Japanese version was *Shinkoku kakumeito shuryo Son Issen yushu roku* (*The Detention of the Chinese Revolutionary Leader Sun Yatsen*).[145] This is important. Whereas in 1895, when news of the plot at Guangzhou reached Japan, the headlines used derogatory terms such as bandits, ruffians, and terrorists to describe Sun Yatsen and his followers;[146] and in 1896, when news of the kidnapping reached Japan, headlines such as 'A Chinese Rebel Arrested in London'[147] were commonplace; Miyazaki now depicted him as a hero. Through Miyazaki, the Japanese people began to learn about Sun Yatsen as a praiseworthy revolutionary leader; about his personality, his ideas, and his noble cause.

Miyazaki's foray into the literary world appears to have been a success, and he attempted something grander: he began writing the now famous *Sanju-sannen no yume* (*A Dream of Thirty-three Years*), which was published in 1902. In it, he devoted a great deal of space to Sun Yatsen's activities up to that time, including, of course, his adventures in London. This immediately attracted the attention of Zhang Shizhao,[148] who lost no time in translating it selectively into Chinese, and published it in Shanghai in 1903. It was widely read in China,[149] where the mood had changed quite dramatically since 1895; witness the preface by Qin Lishan,[150] and the preface by the translator himself.

In the preface, dated 12 October 1903, Qin Lishan began in this way: 'Until four years ago, our impression of Sun Yatsen was

145. Yasui Sankichi, '"Shina kakumeito shuryo Son Issen" ko — Son Bun saisho no raishin ni kansuru jakan no mondai nitsuite', *Kindai*, No. 57, December 1981, p. 73 (hereafter cited as 'Shina'). I am grateful to Professor Jin Chongji for drawing my attention to this article, and to Mr T. Kobayashi for spending hours going through the article together with me.

146. Yasui Sankichi, 'Shina', pp. 62–3, quoting the *Osaka mainichi shinbun*, 5 November 1895, and the *Kobe yushin nippo*, 6 November 1895.

147. Yasui Sankichi, 'Shina', p. 71, quoting the *Kobe yushin nippo*, 1 November 1896.

148. For a short biography of Zhang Shizhao, see Boorman and Howard (eds.), *Biographical Dictionary of Republican China*, Vol. 1, pp. 105–9.

149. Boorman and Howard (eds.), *Biographical Dictionary of Republican China*, p. 105.

150. For a short biography of Qin Lishan, see Chai Degeng, *et al.* (eds.), *Xinhai geming* (Shanghai, 1957; second edition, Shanghai, 1981, 8 vols.), Vol. 1, pp. 282–3.

no more than a pirate in the Bay of Guangzhou'.[151] This opening sentence recalls a similar description by the old China hand who wrote for the Central News in 1896 in London.[152] Qin Lishan went on, 'When the decay of China had not yet been exposed by her defeat in the Sino-Japanese War, Sun Yatsen risked his life in his attempt to capture Guangzhou. At that time, every one thought he was mad. On reflection, we now realise that he was the only one awake, and gifted with unusual courage'.[153]

Zhang Shizhao began his own preface in this way: 'All agree that Sun Yatsen is the originator of recent discussions on revolution, and is the guiding star of all revolutionaries'.[154] Stronger language was to follow: 'The regeneration of China will not be possible without Sun Yatsen'.[155]

Within seven years, therefore, the heroic image had not only changed in character from the one which Dr Cantlie might have intended, but had reached quite unprecedented proportions. I am not suggesting that the heroic image of 1903 did not have anything to do with Sun Yatsen's activities since 1896, such as the Huizhou Uprising of 1900 (albeit a failure); or with the changed mood of the nation as a result of disasters such as the failure of the Hundred Days Reform of 1898 and that of the Hankou Uprising of 1900 (also a failure), of which Qin Lishan himself was a ringleader.[156] I only wish to point out that the origins of that image may be traced back to the treatment of the kidnapping incident by successive writers, popular or serious, such as the as yet unknown correspondent to the *Kobe Chronicle*;[157] the indignant British journalists;[158] the good Samaritan, Dr Cantlie;[159] and the fervent propagandists referred to in this section. And, as we shall see in the next section, Lord Salisbury's intervention may also have played a part.

---

151. Chai Degeng, *et al.* (eds.), *Xinhai geming*, Vol. 1, p. 91.
152. See Section III of this chapter.
153. Chai Degeng, *et al.* (eds.), *Xinhai geming*, Vol. 1, p. 91.
154. Chai Degeng, *et al.* (eds.), *Xinhai geming*, Vol. 1, p. 90.
155. Chai Degeng, *et al.* (eds.), *Xinhai geming*, Vol. 1, p. 90.
156. See my forthcoming article in *Journal of Asian History*, entitled, 'Three Visionaries in Exile: Yung Wing, K'ang Yu-wei and Sun Yatsen 1894–1911'.
157. See Chapter 3, Section I.
158. See Chapter 4, Section II.
159. See Chapter 4, Section III.

Some historians have taken for granted, *ex post facto*, that Sun Yatsen was unquestionably the natural choice as leader of the so-called Revolutionary Alliance which was formed in Tokyo in 1905, uniting the various radical Chinese societies there. The question as to why he was the natural choice, and why unquestionably so, has not been asked often enough. I venture to suggest that his heroic image, as reflected in the unusually adulatory language already used in 1903, was an important contributing factor.

V The Help of Lord Salisbury

Schiffrin seems to think that Lord Salisbury's intervention to save Sun Yatsen's life was regarded by the fugitive as approval or even support for his cause.[160] The signals emanating from almost all sections of the British establishment, such as Inspector Jarvis, the British press, Dr Manson and even Dr Cantlie himself, all pointed to the contrary. Unless Sun Yatsen was blind to all this, and it has yet to be proved that he was insensitive to this degree, it is unlikely that 'his clash with the Legation ... inflated to unrealistic proportions' his conviction that he and the British government had a 'common interest in the anti-dynastic cause'.[161] True, he went on to appeal to the British for benevolent neutrality.[162] I shall deal with this in Chapter 5. It suffices here to say that such an appeal does not necessarily mean that he thought the kidnapping 'had made all the difference in the world' in terms of the attitudes of the British government.[163] Rather, it can be seen as just another example of the ever optimistic and persistent nature which was so typical of the man, and which seems to be the current assessment of him in academic circles.[164]

---

160. Schiffrin, *Origins*, p. 130.
161. Schiffrin, *Origins*, p. 129.
162. Schiffrin, *Origins*, p. 130.
163. Schiffrin, *Origins*, p. 130.
164. At least this is the impression I received, and with which I agree, during the two most recent international conferences on Sun Yatsen, one in Guangzhou in November 1984, and the other in Beijing in March 1985; and when reading some of the recent views such as those expressed in G. Kindermann (ed.), *Sun Yat-sen: Founder and Symbol of China's Revolutionary Nation-Building* (Munich, Gunter Olzog, 1982).

This is not to say that the British actions and attitudes, either positive or negative, had no effect on him. To begin with, Lord Salisbury's intervention did save his life, which appears to have had a decisive effect on him. In a private letter to a friend in Hong Kong, who was a Christian minister, he concluded by saying, 'My survival has made me feel like the prodigal son and the lost sheep, who owe everything to the great favour of God. I do hope that you will write to me regularly, so as to enable me to transform the Rule of God into the Rule of Man, from which I stand to benefit, and all creatures stand to benefit'.[165] Schiffrin has quoted Sharman's translation of the first sentence,[166] and interprets it as follows: 'Most important of all, the kidnapping episode strengthened Sun's self-confidence and sense of dedication. It convinced him that the Supreme Power had forestalled his enemies to preserve him for some high purpose'.[167] This interpretation is reasonable enough, and is made obvious by Sun Yatsen's concluding sentence translated above. Thus, very soon after his release, and in spite of direct lectures such as the one delivered by Inspector Jarvis, and subtle pressures such as those exerted by the British press and Dr Cantlie,[168] Sun Yatsen was quite determined not to abandon his objectives in order to become a Chinese English gentleman. It was determination of this kind which helped generate the sort of image that has persisted to this day.

Less fortunate, however, are some attempts to create, albeit indirectly, an heroic image of him by portraying Salisbury in a poor light, such as those alleging that the Marquis bowed to the public pressure expressed by the newspapers and by fair-minded Londoners, and consequently intervened to save the hero. The earliest account of this kind that I have read is the one by Chen Shaobai. He wrote,

Dr Manson went to see the British Prime Minister and foreign secretary Lord Salisbury. Salisbury was also incredulous, and sent for Macartney, who denied any knowledge of the matter. Having no other recourse, Dr Cantlie [who had approached various newspapers to print the story],

---

165. Sun Yatsen to Qu Fengzhi (*circa* October 1896), in *Sun Zhongshan quanji*, Vol. 1, p. 46. The translation is mine.

166. Schiffrin, *Origins*, p. 129, n.106.

167. Schiffrin, *Origins*, p. 128.

168. See Section III of this chapter.

urged the newspapers to print more. As a result, the newspapers carried more and more details. Even the newsagents erected big posters to attract the attention of passers-by. In the end, the whole of London knew about it. Several thousand shouting Londoners gathered outside the Legation, demanding the release of [the prisoner] on pain of levelling the entire building. The crowd was so angry that even the police were afraid that they might not be able to control it. The Legation staff were frightened. The Marquis also feared the unexpected, and again summoned Macartney to the Foreign Office. Macartney realized that he could no longer deny it, and told the truth. Thereupon, the Foreign Office ordered the release of [the prisoner].[169]

In the light of what has been unearthed in the early parts of the present book, few will disagree that Chen Shaobai's story reads like a fairy tale and is, I believe, the source of subsequent accusations that the Marquis intervened only under the pressure of public opinion. I am not suggesting that Lord Salisbury ever took an active part in the intervention. As narrated in Chapter 1, he merely sanctioned such an action by telegraph from his country estate at Hatfield. Again as narrated in Chapter 1, the Foreign Office intervened partly because it did not want a scandal on its hands — the knowledge that *The Times* had received the story and could publish it at any time appears to have expedited things greatly. But to allege that enormous public opinion, created by the publication of the story in the newspapers, forced the Marquis to take action is factually incorrect. As pointed out before, the police had the Legation surrounded on the evening of 19 October 1896, about three days before the *Globe* first published the news late in the evening of 22 October 1896.[170]

Needless to say, Chen Shaobai also insisted that, despite repeated attempts, Deng Tingkeng failed to obtain a statement from the prisoner.[171] To admit the truth, namely, that Sun Yatsen had made such a statement, as he himself had testified in the British Treasury,[172] or as Dr Cantlie had also written in *Kidnap-*

169. Chen Shaobai, *Xing Zhong Hui*, in *Xinhai geming*, Vol. 1, pp. 37–8. The translation is mine.
170. See Chapter 1, Sections III and IV.
171. Chen Shaobai, *Xing Zhong Hui*, in *Xinhai geming*, Vol. 1, p. 35.
172. FO 17/1718, pp. 119–20, Sun Yatsen's statement at the Treasury, 4 November 1896, para. 13.

ped in London,[173] would have been tantamount to confessing that the hero had done something 'very stupid'.[174]

Chen Shaobai's extraordinary account was published in 1935,[175] posthumously.[176] I am not sure when he actually wrote it, although I am inclined to think that he may have begun the task some time after he retired completely from political life in 1921, when he returned to his native district south of Guangzhou and 'spent his last years in literary pursuits'.[177] I am also tempted to suggest that his motive for writing this account, which constitutes Section 2 in Chapter 2 of a booklet on the draft history of the Xing Zhong Hui, was to put on record past events as he saw them, after the large collection of personal letters he had received from Sun Yatsen over the years was lost in the political upheaval of 1923.[178] If he did begin drafting in 1924 or 1925, he did so at a time when anti-British feelings were running extremely high in China, culminating in the co-ordinated anti-British general strike in both Guangzhou and Hong Kong, in 1925. During one of the anti-British demonstrations in Guangzhou, British troops and the Royal Navy fired on the demonstrators.[179] It is inconceivable that he was not affected by these events, living as he did so close to Guangzhou. This is probably why he abandoned and even contradicted the version contained in *Kidnapped in London*, despite the fact that its Chinese translation had been published in full in 1912.[180]

One other such contradiction is his allegation, attributed to Sun Yatsen, that the hero already knew the exact location of the Chinese Legation in London; that he deliberately changed his name and went there every day to spread the word of

173. Sun Yatsen, *Kidnapped in London*, p. 52.
174. Sun Yatsen, *Kidnapped in London*, p. 53.
175. Luo Jialun, *Shiliao*, p. 43.
176. Luo Jialun, *Shiliao*, p. 43; compare 'Chen Shaobai', in Boorman and Howard (eds.), *Biographical Dictionary of Republican China*, p. 231, and Chen Shaobai, *Xing Zhong Hui*, in *Xinhai geming*, Vol. 1, p. 75.
177. 'Chen Shaobai', in Boorman and Howard (eds.), *Biographical Dictionary of Republican China*, Vol. 1, p. 231.
178. 'Chen Shaobai', in Boorman and Howard (eds.), *Biographical Dictionary of Republican China*, Vol. 1, p. 231.
179. *Zhongguo jinxian dai shi dashi ji* (Shanghai, Knowledge Press, 1982), p. 98.
180. See the note to the Chinese version of *Kidnapped in London* as contained in *Sun Zhongshan quanji*, Vol. 1, p. 86.

200   SUN YATSEN IN LONDON, 1896-1897

revolution.[181] The credibility, or lack of it, of this allegation has been dealt with in Chapter 3, Section I. As for its originator, Schiffrin seems to believe that Sun Yatsen was the man when he writes, 'Chen Shaobai, probably the first close friend he saw upon his return to the East, relates how Sun boasted of having visited the Legation daily'.[182] In the context of the present assessment of the background against which Chen Shaobai wrote his account, which was probably in 1925, one must also remember that his hero died in March of that year.[183] Could he, in his grief over the loss of a lifelong friend and hero, have embellished the story of the kidnapping?

Indeed, his version of events contrasts sharply even with some of the publications on Sun Yatsen in the late 1920s, including one published in 1928 which was specially devoted to the memory of the kidnapping in London and which called on the mass gatherings to commemorate, in particular, Sun Yatsen's courage, perseverance, and alertness as exhibited in that episode.[184] All these publications followed the version in *Kidnapped in London* fairly faithfully. In view of these contrasts, Chen Shaobai's intention in presenting his own version of events may be conjectured. On the one hand, it seems that he was bent on creating an heroic image of Sun Yatsen, regardless of what people might already have learnt about the incident from *Kidnapped in London*, by alleging that the hero had walked fearlessly into the lion's den to convert his enemies. Here, I should like to recall the first account of this kind by the correspondent to the *Kobe Chronicle* in November 1896.[185] That correspondent was, in all likelihood, Chen Shaobai.[186] On the other hand, he appears to have been anxious to create the impression that even the ordinary citizens of London were fair-minded enough to have stood firmly on Sun Yatsen's side and to have forced the hand of their own imperialist chief, Lord Salisbury, to intervene. Such creative writing may be taken as an interesting example of anti-imperialist literature. But

---

181. Chen Shaobai, *Xing Zhong Hui*, in *Xinhai geming*, Vol. 1, p. 35.
182. Schiffrin, *Origins*, p. 112.
183. *Sun Zhongshan nianpu*, p. 372. Even before Sun Yatsen died, Chen Shaobai had become a recluse, so that consultation between the two men about what the latter was writing seems to have been highly unlikely.
184. Wan Xin (ed.), *Zongli Lundun beinan gailue*.
185. See Chapter 3, Section I.
186. See Chapter 3, Section I.

it becomes a different proposition when many Chinese historians after 1935, for one reason or another, appear to have relied heavily on Chen Shaobai's story for information. Even more unfortunate is the fact that very few of them have actually acknowledged their debt to him.[187]

Schiffrin has done meticulous archival research on the kidnapping incident, and therefore has presented the sequence of events accurately. He has also used parts of Chen Shaobai's version critically.[188] However, he could have been more critical when he alleged that Sun Yatsen thought it was British public opinion that 'finally forced Salisbury to press for his release'.[189] The evidence offered to substantiate this allegation was 'Sun, *Collected Works* [205], V.16'.[190] I have checked this source.[191] It turned out to be a letter in Chinese, which Sun Yatsen wrote shortly after his release. Roughly translated, the relevant passage reads: 'London was almost on the boil; some Londoners wanted to gather a crowd to level the Legation. Lord Salisbury sent an official dispatch demanding [my] release, threatening to expel the [Chinese] minister and his staff from England; thereupon, the Legation became afraid and set me free'.[192] Here, Sun Yatsen did not allege that Salisbury had acted under the pressure of public opinion; although, by putting public outbursts before Salisbury's intervention in the sequence of events, his narrative might easily have misled people into thinking that way. Now that Schiffrin's book has been translated into Chinese, will his misinterpretation of Sun Yatsen's letter mislead the Chinese still further?

---

187. See, for example, Shang Mingxuan, *Sun Zhongshan zhuan* (Beijing, 1982), p. 44; and Shao Chuanlie, *Sun Zhongshan* (Shanghai, 1980), p. 39.
188. Schiffrin, *Origins*, p. 112.
189. Schiffrin, *Origins*, p. 129.
190. Schiffrin, *Origins*, p. 129, n. 107.
191. I wish to thank Mrs K. Cherry, assistant librarian in the Fisher Library, University of Sydney, for having obtained for me through an inter-library loan, the 1957 edition of Sun Yatsen's *Collected Works* for checking. I also wish to thank Miss Bronwyn Hutchinson, our department secretary, for having fetched the book from Fisher Library for me while I was laid up in hospital in October 1985.
192. Sun Yatsen to Qu Fengzhi [October 1896], in Sun Yatsen, *Guofu quanji* (Taipei, 1957, revised edition, 6 vols.), Vol. 5, p. 16. The same letter is printed in the Beijing edition of 1981, entitled *Sun Zhongshan quanji*, Vol. 1, pp. 45–6. The translation is mine.

As for the Marquis, if he had lived long enough to read all these accounts, would he not have been pleased to know that his action, albeit somewhat misrepresented, has helped to consolidate an heroic image in distant lands?[193]

---

193. The story goes that when the British Prime Minister, Mrs Margaret Thatcher, visited Beijing in September 1983 to discuss the future of Hong Kong, she told the Chinese that Britain had rendered three significant services to China, one of which was to have saved Sun Yatsen's life. The Chinese rejected her view, insisting that Salisbury had acted only under the pressure of public opinion. I can believe such a story. Nearly all the Chinese historians I have met, whether they are from mainland China or from Taiwan, seem to be quite convinced that Salisbury, in view of the enormous public outbursts, had no choice but to intervene. Such a conviction is reflected in their publications (see, for example, Zhao Huimo, 'Sheji zongli Lundun mengnan jilian shi', in *Zhonghua minguo*, Vol. 2, p. 199; Shang Mingxuan, *Sun Zhongshan zhuan*, p. 44; and Shao Chuanlie, *Sun Zhongshan*, p. 39, and may be traced either to the misleading letter Sun Yatsen wrote shortly after his release in 1896, or to Chen Shaobai's version, published in 1935. It is to be hoped that my research findings have gone some way towards putting the record straight, and towards banishing misunderstanding between Britain and China.

5 Sun Yatsen as Nationalist

After my release in London, I remained in Europe for a while to observe the politics and customs there, and to make friends with distinguished intellects and heroes whether they were in power or not.

Sun Yatsen[1]

I Widening Horizons: Through the Cantlie Connection

After Sun Yatsen's release from the Legation on 23 October 1896, he stayed with the Cantlies until Monday, 2 November 1896, when he took up his lodgings again at 8, Gray's Inn Place.[2] But he continued to visit the Cantlies regularly, according to both Slater's reports and Mrs Cantlie's diary. The frequency of these visits, many of which were apparently unannounced and coincided with meal-times, is an indication of the degree of his intimacy with the Cantlies. In London, nobody would then have turned up for meals uninvited unless he was a member of the family, and Sun Yatsen seems to have been treated as such. Indeed, Sun Yatsen's visits do not appear to have been affected even by the short holidays which the Cantlies took in the country, because Dr Cantlie himself went up to London almost daily during such holidays.[3] Dr Cantlie was obviously a source of comfort and security to the fugitive, and of wisdom to his former student, who spent a lot of time in his study while visiting him.[4] Dr Cantlie himself said that Sun Yatsen read widely while in London, about political, diplomatic, legal, military, and naval matters, as well as on subjects such as mines and mining, agriculture, cattle-rearing, engineering, and political economy.[5] Dr Cantlie's intimate knowledge of what Sun Yatsen read suggests that they must have had constant discussions about the reading matter. Thus, it may be useful to gather some raw statistics about

---

1. *Sun Zhongshan xuanji*, p. 191.
2. Mrs Cantlie's diary, 2 November 1896.
3. See Mrs Cantlie's diary, 1896 and 1897.
4. Sun Yatsen, *Kidnapped in London*, p. 31. See, also, FO 17/1718, pp. 121–2, Cantlie's statement at the Treasury, 4 November 1896, para. 5.
5. Schiffrin, *Origins*, p. 135, quoting Cantlie and Jones, *Sun Yat-sen*, p. 242.

Table 2 Sun Yatsen's Visits to 46, Devonshire Street, as Recorded by Slater, the Private Detective Agency[6]

Date	Time	Duration	Transport
Fri., 23 Oct. 1896	c.19.30–	Overnight	By cab
Sat., 24 Oct. 1896		House guest	
Sun., 25 Oct. 1896		House guest	
Mon., 26 Oct. 1896		House guest	
Tue., 27 Oct. 1896		House guest	
Wed., 28 Oct. 1896		House guest	
29 Oct.–11 Nov. 1896	Not seen to leave or enter 46, Devonshire St.		
Thur., 12 Nov. 1896	Unknown–15.00	Unspecified	
	17.30–unknown	Unspecified	
Fri., 13 Nov. 1896	11.30 left Gray's Inn Place, visited Lincoln's Inn		
Mon., 16 Nov. 1896	11.00–15.00	4 hr	By cab
Tue., 17 Nov. 1896	c.14.45–unknown	Unspecified	By bus
Wed., 18 Nov. 1896	c.11.00–15.30	4 hr 30 min	By cab
Thur., 19 Nov. 1896	Unknown–14.30	Unspecified	Unspecified
	c.16.30–unknown	All evening	Unspecified
Fri., 20 Nov. 1896	Unspecified	Unspecified	Unspecified
Mon., 23 Nov. 1896	c.12.00–14.45	2 hr 45 min	Unspecified

6. Slater's relevant reports were reproduced in Luo Jialun, *Shiliao*, pp. 118–65.

Date	Time	Duration	Mode
Tue., 24 Nov. 1896	c.15.00–evening	Unspecified	Unspecified
Thur., 26 Nov. 1896	c.15.00–evening	Unspecified	Unspecified
Fri., 27 Nov. 1896	c.15.30–unknown	Unspecified	Unspecified
Sat., 28 Nov. 1896	Unspecified	Unspecified	Unspecified
Sat., 5 Dec. 1896	13.00–17.40	4 hr 40 min	By bus
Mon., 7 Dec. 1896	c.15.00–15.20	20 min	Unspecified
Tue., 8 Dec. 1896	c.15.30–16.30	1 hr	By bus
Sat., 12 Dec. 1896	c.12.45–14.15	1 hr 30 min	Unspecified
Tue., 15 Dec. 1896	c.15.30–unknown	Unspecified	Unspecified
Thur., 17 Dec. 1896	13.00–15.00	2 hr	Unspecified
Thur., 24 Dec. 1896	12.00–16.00	4 hr	Unspecified
Sun., 27–Thur., 31 Dec. 1896	To 46, Devonshire St., unspecified number of times		Unspecified
Sat., 2 Jan. 1897	c.12.00–15.00	3 hr	Unspecified
Mon., 4 Jan. 1897	c.14.30–16.00	1 hr 30 min	Unspecified
Tue., 5 Jan. 1897	c.10.30–late hour	Unspecified	Unspecified
Wed., 6 Jan. 1897	c.15.00–17.30	2 hr 30 min	Unspecified
Fri., 8 Jan. 1897	c.11.45–16.00	4 hr 15 min	Unspecified
Tue., 12 Jan. 1897	c.12.30–late hour	Unspecified	Unspecified
Wed., 13 Jan. 1897	c.11.45–14.30	2 hr 45 min	Unspecified
Thur., 14 Jan. 1897	c.15.30–unknown	Unspecified	Unspecified
Sat., 16 Jan. 1897	c.15.30–evening	Unspecified	Unspecified
Mon., 18 Jan. 1897	c.11.00–13.30	2 hr 30 min	Unspecified

Table 2 (continued)

Date	Time	Duration	Transport
Tue., 19 Jan. 1897	c.16.00–evening	Unspecified	Unspecified
Wed., 20 Jan. 1897	c.15.30–17.30	2 hr	Unspecified
Thur., 21 Jan. 1897	c.16.00–17.00	1 hr	Unspecified
Fri., 22 Jan. 1897	c.15.00–unknown	During afternoon	Unspecified
Mon., 25 Jan. 1897	c.14.15–16.00	1 hr 45 min	Unspecified
Tue., 26 Jan. 1897	c.15.00–17.00	2 hr	Unspecified
Wed., 27 Jan. 1897	c.12.00–15.00	3 hr	Unspecified
Thur., 28 Jan. 1897	c.12.00–15.00	3 hr	Unspecified
Mon., 1 Feb. 1897	c.14.00–after 20.00	6 hr +	On foot
Wed., 3 Feb. 1897	c.16.30–unknown	Unspecified	Unspecified
Thur., 4 Feb. 1897	c.12.15–15.30	1 hr 45 min	Unspecified
	c.17.00–evening	Unspecified	Unspecified
Fri., 5 Feb. 1897	c.12.00–15.00	3 hr	Unspecified
Sun., 7 Feb. 1897	c.16.30–evening	Unspecified	Unspecified
Fri., 5 Mar. 1897	c.13.00–c.20.00	7 hr	Bus and on foot
Fri., 12–Mon., 15 Mar. 1897	To 46, Devonshire St., unspecified number of times		
Tue., 16 Mar. 1897	14.45–18.10	3 hr 25 min	Unspecified
Thur., 18 Mar. 1897	c.15.45–unknown	'considerable time'	Bus and on foot
Sat., 20 Mar. 1897	c.16.00–18.30	2 hr 30 min	Bus and on foot

Date	Time	Duration	Mode of transport
Mon., 22 Mar. 1897	c.12.45–15.15	2 hr 30 min	Bus and on foot
Wed., 24 Mar. 1897	c.17.00–unknown	'considerable time'	Unspecified
Sat., 27 Mar. 1897	c.17.00–unknown	Unspecified	Unspecified
Mon., 29 Mar. 1897	c.12.45–17.35	4 hr 50 min	Unspecified
Tue., 6 Apr. 1897	c.17.00–unknown	Unspecified	Unspecified
Wed., 7–Sun., 18 Apr. 1897	'visits nearly every day to the British Museum – No. 46 Devonshire St. – Holborn Post Office'		Unspecified
Thur., 10 Jun. 1897	c.18.30–late hour		Bus and on foot
Thur., 24 Jun. 1897	'He has attended at the British Museum each day as also 46 Devonshire Street ...'		

the number of visits Sun Yatsen paid to 46, Devonshire Street, and the duration of each visit, if only to obtain a rough idea of the number of hours he was in the company of his former teacher and among his books.

The friends of the Cantlies, whom Sun Yatsen met in London, would also have played an important role in widening his horizons. The day after Sun Yatsen was released from the Chinese Legation, Mrs Cantlie entered the following in her diary: 'Reporters and friends to congratulate Hamish all day, in troops. It brought old friends to see us who did not know where we were'.[7] Mrs Cantlie did not specify who those friends were. She simply went on to say that 'Mr Bird (Hong Kong) called & Mrs Boyd. We spent a happy day'.[8] On the basis of this, I can do very little but conjecture that they 'talked of Hong Kong',[9] as Mrs Cantlie so often recalled in her diary after she had received visitors from the colony; and suggest that Sun Yatsen began to gain some idea of the British view of the place through listening to them talking among themselves. This perspective would have been different from those he would have gained through speaking to his Chinese compatriots or talking to the British in Hong Kong. What effect this perspective would have had on his idea of nationalism is an open question, because we do not know the contents of the conversation.

Mrs Cantlie's entry in her diary on the following day, Sunday, 25 October 1896, offers more food for thought. She wrote, 'Hamish & I took Sun Yat Sen to St Martins-in-the-Fields.[10] He is a Christian so it was a thanksgiving service to us. Went to Bruces to dinner & took Sun. Met Mr Weay, a hero of Bulawayo, S. Africa'.[11] This entry touches on two aspects of the man: Sun Yatsen the Christian, and Sun Yatsen the nationalist.

i. Sun Yatsen the Christian

First, Sun Yatsen the Christian. Of all the pertinent entries in Mrs Cantlie's diary, this is the only reference to Sun Yatsen going to church. The private detective's reports made no such reference whatever; but, as I have pointed out, Slater's reports for Sundays

---

7. Mrs Cantlie's diary, 24 October 1896.
8. Mrs Cantlie's diary, 24 October 1896.
9. Mrs Cantlie's diary, 8 October 1896.
10. See Chapter 4, note 85.
11. Mrs Cantlie's diary, 25 October 1896.

were invariably vague throughout the period under review. Nor did Minakata Kumagusu, the Japanese botanist who befriended Sun Yatsen from 16 March 1897 onwards,[12] mention anything in his diary about Sun Yatsen attending divine service. It is not suggested that the absence of evidence for his going to church means that he did not do so. But it is a curious corroboration of a testimony which a close associate was to make later: 'I believe that [Sun Yatsen] became a Christian purely because of the Christian concern for the welfare of mankind. It was the progressive and reformist Christianity, not the conservative and dogmatic Christianity, that attracted his devotion. For years I have accompanied him on his travels in Japan and America, and have seen him hire Christian halls to preach revolution but have never seen him enter a church'.[13]

To return to his days in London, both Mrs Cantlie and the private detective referred to his regular visits to 46, Devonshire Street. But it was only when he was actually staying with the Cantlies that, apparently once, and once only, he went to divine service with them. Thus I am inclined to think that he behaved quite naturally when he was in London. Another person would probably have felt obliged to go to church more often with the Cantlies, who had taken sittings in St Martin's.[14] Going to Sunday service was very much part of the life of the Cantlies,[15] who seem to have been liberal enough not to have tried to encourage Sun Yatsen to do the same. The attitude of the revered former teacher and his wife appears to have had the indirect effect of confirming Sun Yatsen's faith in what he was doing, or at least of not having impeded the natural development of his ideas about Christianity, however unconventional. But then, Sun Yatsen was a Chinese Christian, who happened to regard national salvation as his first priority in life. It is to be expected, therefore, that his thoughts about religion would have been different from those of the British of the late Victorian era.

Sun Yatsen was not alone among the Chinese people in blending national salvation with Christian salvation. One of the church

12. Minakata Kumagusu's diary, 16 March 1897, in *Zenshu*, Supplement, Vol. 2, p. 77.
13. Feng Ziyou, *Geming yishi*, Vol. 2, p. 12. The translation is mine.
14. Mrs Cantlie's diary, 20 September 1896.
15. See the entries for Sundays in Mrs Cantlie's diary.

leaders in China, Bishop Duan Ziheng, later interpreted Sun Yatsen's alias, Dixiang, to mean the 'likeness of God', and consequently to mean that he had been commissioned by God to save China.[16] It is significant that the Bishop was the head of the Episcopal Church of China,[17] which in fact was the Anglican Church in China although it was not known by that name.[18] The Bishop continued, 'The Christian [ideals of] Liberty, Equality and Fraternity are equivalent to Sun Yatsen's Principles of Nationalism, Democracy and the People's Livelihood. Because, Nationalism means the independence of all nations of the world, free from molestation from any Power. Isn't this, therefore, Great Liberty? Democracy means the right of the people to elect or dismiss [officials], and the right to veto or initiate [bills of legislation] ... Isn't this, therefore, Great Equality? The People's Livelihood means that everybody has adequate clothing, food and accommodation. Isn't this, therefore, Great Fraternity?'[19] Coming from a bishop of an oppressed country, these words almost anticipated the so-called Liberation Theology of today.

But Sun Yatsen was not a clergyman; nor would he be addressing Christians in his capacity as a fellow Christian after he left London. His audience would be the ordinary Chinese people, and he would be talking to them as a revolutionary leader. Consequently, and more accurately than the Bishop, he described Liberty, Equality, and Fraternity as the slogans of the French Revolution, and equated his Three Principles of the People with them. His arguments in favour of such an equation were, however, pretty much the same as those of the Bishop.[20] Sun Yatsen made this equation when he delivered his second lecture on the subject of Democracy on 16 March 1924,[21] while the

16. *Sun Zhongshan yishiji* (Shanghai, Sanmin Company, 1926), p. 192.

17. *Sun Zhongshan yishiji*, p. 192. The Chinese name of this denomination was Zhonghua shenggong hui which, according to *Zhongwen da cidian* (Taipei, 1968, 40 vols.), Vol. 27, p. 23, was the Episcopal Church of China.

18. See *Crockford's Clerical Directory* (Oxford, Oxford University Press, 1961), p. 1996. The proper title of the head of the Episcopal Church of China was Chairman of the House of Bishops. I am grateful to my colleague, Professor Ken Cable, for this reference.

19. *Sun Zhongshan yishiji*, p. 192.

20. Sun Yatsen, 'Minquan zhuyi', in *Sun Zhongshan xuanji* (Beijing, 1981), pp. 723–4.

21. Sun Yatsen, 'Minquan zhuyi', in *Sun Zhongshan xuanji*, pp. 615 and 710.

Bishop spoke in 1926, the year after Sun Yatsen's death. I am inclined to think, therefore, that if any attempt had been made to cultivate an heroic image of Sun Yatsen as a great Christian, it must not be attributed to him, but to his fellow Christians such as the Bishop.

But it is remarkable that, extremely grateful though Sun Yatsen might have been to the church-going Cantlies, he should have felt so free to pursue and practise his own ideas about Christianity while he was in London. This must have been related not only to the attitudes of Sun Yatsen himself, but also to those of the Cantlies, particularly those of Dr Cantlie. Hence it will be useful to find out more about the doctor.

Dr Cantlie was born on 17 January 1851.[22] His biographers describe him as 'open-hearted and generous', with a streak of impetuousness which would lead him on occasion to decided but unorthodox opinions'.[23] They continue, 'At the age of fifteen Cantlie ... commenced the Winter Session at Aberdeen University in October 1866. There are, unfortunately, very few records of Cantlie's life during these university days'.[24] A long correspondence with the archivist of Aberdeen University[25] was followed by my visit there in March 1984.[26] The student records[27] show that Cantlie came from the parish of Mortlach, where he had attended the parish school, and had been taught by Mr John Macpherson.[28] The contemporary parochial records show that

---

22. Cantlie and Seaver, *Sir James Cantlie*, p. 3.
23. Cantlie and Seaver, *Sir James Cantlie*, p. 6; see, also, Stewart, *Quality of Mercy*, p. 6.
24. Cantlie and Seaver, *Sir James Cantlie*, p. 6.
25. I wish to record my gratitude to Mr Colin A. McLane, archivist and keeper of manuscripts at Aberdeen University Library, for his patience and help over the years.
26. I also wish to thank Professor Peter Ramsey and Mr Donald J Withrington of the History Department, and Dr Dorothy Johnston of the Library of Aberdeen University, for their hospitality and help during my visit to Aberdeen.
27. Aberdeen University, U1, Student Register, Vol. 1, 1860/61–1890/91, Faculty of Arts, p. 57.
28. William Barclay, *The Schools and Schoolmasters of Banffshire* (Banff, Banffshire Journal, 1925), pp. 134 and 137. Mr John Macpherson was schoolmaster for thirty years, from 1837 to 1866. Therefore, Cantlie's last year as a schoolboy would also have been Macpherson's last year as schoolmaster. I am grateful to Mr Donald Withrington for this information and the reference in the next four footnotes.

Mortlach lay 51 miles north-west of Aberdeen[29] in the presbytery of Strathbogie;[30] that on the whole the inhabitants were 'sedate and religious';[31] that divine service was regularly attended at the parish church; and that there were no dissenting meeting-houses, nor any society for religious purposes, in the parish.[32] Thus, Cantlie was brought up purely under the influence of the Church of Scotland.

From the Mortlach parochial school he went, at the age of 13, as a boarder to Milne's Institution at Fochabers,[33] which prepared him for matriculation at Aberdeen University. Once outside Mortlach, he would have been exposed to all the denominations of the Presbyterian Church in Scotland, of which there were at least three,[34] as well as the Episcopal Church of Scotland and the Catholic Church. These other influences appear to have had a moderating effect on the young Cantlie. King's College in Aberdeen University, where he enrolled in the Arts Faculty,[35] was originally founded by a Papal Bull,[36] as were all medieval universities. Although the lectures began with prayers, at least one professor who taught Cantlie was described as having said prayers 'almost with the chalk in his hand', and his 'Amen' was said to fuse 'completely with his rapid "Yesterday, you will remember, I was dealing with the area of the parabola"'.[37] This rather free religious atmosphere probably explains why Cantlie

29. *The New Statistical Account of Scotland, by the Ministers of the Respective Parishes, under the Superintendence of a Committee of the Society for the Benefit of the Sons and Daughters of the Clergy* (Edinburgh and London, William Blackwood and Sons, 1845), Vol. 13, p. 103 (hereafter cited as *New Statistical Account*).

30. *New Statistical Account*, Vol. 13, p. 103.

31. *New Statistical Account*, Vol. 13, p. 107.

32. *New Statistical Account*, Vol. 13, p. 108.

33. Cantlie and Seaver, *Sir James Cantlie*, p. 4.

34. Apparently, the three Churches were the Free Presbyterian Church, the United Presbyterian Church, and the Church of Scotland. I am grateful to the Revd Dr Hugh Cairns, principal of St Andrew's College in the University of Sydney, for this information.

35. Aberdeen University, U1, Student Register, Vol. 1, 1860/61–1890/91, Faculty of Arts, p. 57.

36. W. Douglas Simpson (ed.), *The Fusion of 1860: A Record of the Centenary Celebrations and a History of the University of Aberdeen 1860–1960* (Edinburgh and London, Oliver and Boyd, 1963), p. 7 (hereafter cited as *The Fusion*).

37. Simpson (ed.), *The Fusion*, p. 198.

had no difficulty in switching to the Anglican Church of St Martin-in-the-Fields when he later went to live in London.[38]

Apart from the relatively free religious atmosphere compared with other places and times, Cantlie's own personality must have had something to do with his attitude towards Sun Yatsen's approach to religion. He was 'unorthodox',[39] and was described by a close friend as having been 'swayed more by his heart than his head'.[40] Here, I am merely suggesting that neither man was dogmatic, and am not expressing any doubt about their sincerity as Christians. On the contrary, I think that concern for the welfare of their fellow human beings[41] in the Christian tradition was probably one of many factors that sealed the friendship between the two men. In 1925, when news of Sun Yatsen's death reached London, Dr Cantlie was invited to deliver a speech at the memorial service organized by the Chinese community in London. With trembling hands and bursting into tears, he said, 'Sun Yatsen's revolutionary ideals, and the relentless efforts he had made to realize these ideals against all odds, may be compared to the spirit with which Jesus had tried to redeem the world'.[42]

Sun Yatsen's ideals were embodied in his Three Principles of the People. Cantlie's obituary reminds us of the words of the Bishop, mentioned above.

In view of the fact that 'for all her talk of justice and fair play',[43] Britain was well known for frustrating the efforts of

---

38. There were, in any case, very few Church of Scotland establishments in London.

39. Cantlie and Seaver, *Sir James Cantlie*, p. 6.

40. Cantlie and Seaver, *Sir James Cantlie*, p. xix: 'Introduction' by Sir Arthur Keith, FRS, FRCS.

41. Cantlie and Seaver, *Sir James Cantlie*, p. xi: '... [Cantlie] captured me body and soul while I was still young, and the passage of years has but served to strengthen the first impression he made on me. Of the good men I have met with in my journey through life there has been none who sought so steadfastly as he to improve the conditions of human life and none so ready to sacrifice self for this end'. I think the same comment applies equally to Sun Yatsen.

42. *Sun Zhongshan pinglunji* (Shanghai, Sanmin Company, 1926), p. 48. I have not been able to locate the English original of Dr Cantlie's speech, and have had to re-translate back into English a report in Chinese.

43. Cantlie and Seaver, *Sir James Cantlie*, p. 118. See, also, Nathan A. Pelcovits, *Old China Hands and the Foreign Office* (New York, American Institute of Pacific Relations, 1948).

Chinese nationalists to regenerate their country, why was Cantlie so sympathetic to Sun Yatsen's cause? I think that this must have had something to do with Cantlie's personality.

Cantlie himself was noted for his own nationalism. As an undergraduate, 'he wore a kilt — which required an exceptional degree of personal courage, for Aberdeen students are merciless critics of modes of speech, dress, and manners with which they are unfamiliar. Cantlie's kilt was an outward expression of his inward feelings; he was proud to have been born in Strathspey'.[44] After graduation, he enrolled for a medical degree at Aberdeen, but actually studied at Charing Cross Medical School in London.[45] 'Cantlie, with the speech, customs, and traditions of Strathspey thick upon him, was plunged amongst English youths living at the very vortex of London life ... Will he ... brush away the most noticeable of his provincialisms, or will he, as does happen in some cases, become ultra-Oxford in speech and manner? Cantlie did none of these things; he remained himself, neither aggressively proud of his Strathspey origin nor ashamed of his nationalisms [sic]'.[46]

As for the rule of law, Cantlie's relentless efforts to save Sun Yatsen from falling victim to oriental despotism, as narrated in Chapter 1, are testimony to his belief in it. Later on, Cantlie demonstrated his faith further. After Sun Yatsen had become provisional president of the Chinese Republic in 1912, and then resigned in favour of Yuan Shikai, Cantlie received a desperate appeal from Sun Yatsen asking for help to stop British banks lending money to Yuan Shikai, who had turned out to be a dictator.[47] Cantlie acted against strong public opinion in Britain by writing to the newspapers, but all his articles were turned down.[48] Mrs Cantlie went to see the Chartered Bank of India, and found it distinctly hostile. 'I felt the insult deeply', she wrote

---

44. Cantlie and Seaver, *Sir James Cantlie*, 'Introduction' by Sir Arthur Keith, p. xix.
45. Cantlie and Seaver, *Sir James Cantlie*, 'Introduction' by Sir Arthur Keith, p. xx.
46. Cantlie and Seaver, *Sir James Cantlie*, 'Introduction' by Sir Arthur Keith, p. xxi.
47. Sun Yatsen to Cantlie [cable], 2 May 1913, reprinted in Cantlie and Seaver, *Sir James Cantlie*, pp. 111–12.
48. Cantlie and Seaver, *Sir James Cantlie*, p. 113.

in her diary.[49] Then she wrote to 'the leading daily papers asking for the prayers of the whole Christian world for Sun'. The response was again reflected in her diary: 'Feel very sad all day about China, for Dr Sun is again a wanderer. A man named Senex wrote a long letter in the *Globe* in a sort of answer to mine saying everything nasty he could of Dr Sun and his party, and saying it was not prayers that China wanted but money. I wrote an answer to him. I felt I must do something for Sun'.[50]

Dr Cantlie's concern for the livelihood and well-being of others is well known. This might have had something to do with his background. He was born into a family of eleven. His father was a farmer. The family could just about make ends meet.[51] His undergraduate records show that he tried unsuccessfully to get a bursary in 1866. He tried again in 1867, against 191 other competitors, and once more failed.[52] But he was moderately provided for compared with his fellow students, some of whom 'had barely enough money to buy salt for their kale. Others, unable to afford candles, were compelled at night to study by the light that entered the window from the street lamp outside'.[53] One of Cantlie's fellow students subsequently wrote, 'Many of us had our constitutions permanently impaired by lack of good and adequate food. Far too large a proportion of my fellow students died early'.[54] According to another account, 'Cantlie described how he knocked up his tutor in the small hours in order to study the classics and how his tutor's bed was then taken by a poor student without lodgings who thus snatched a few hours' sleep'.[55] This sort of experience appears to have had a profound effect on Cantlie, whose subsequent devotion to improving the well-being of mankind, particularly with regard to health, is well documented in his biographies.[56]

The warm and unusually long reviews of his first biography, entitled *Sir James Cantlie*, were signs of the overwhelming approval of the assessment of him by the people who still remem-

49. Cantlie and Seaver, *Sir James Cantlie*, p. 113.
50. Cantlie and Seaver, *Sir James Cantlie*, p. 113.
51. Cantlie and Seaver, *Sir James Cantlie*, pp. xvii–xix.
52. Aberdeen University MS, U11, Bursary Competitors, 1860–1879.
53. Cantlie and Seaver, *Sir James Cantlie*, p. 7.
54. Stewart, *Quality of Mercy*, pp. 6–7.
55. Stewart, *Quality of Mercy*, p. 7.
56. Stewart, *Quality of Mercy*; and Cantlie and Seaver, *Sir James Cantlie*.

bered him well. One writer chose the headline 'Worker for Humanity: Sir James Cantlie's Life', for his review.[57] Another labelled his 'Life of Service: Sir James Cantlie Won All Hearts'.[58] Yet another, 'Romance in Medicine: Civilisation's Debt to Sir James Cantlie'.[59] *Public Opinion* entitled its review 'Sun Yat Sen — and the Good Samaritan: The story of Sir James Cantlie, the eminent doctor who did not pass afflicted humanity on the other side';[60] another paper, 'A Crusader For Good Health: The crowded life of James Cantlie'.[61] The Brisbane *Telegraph* called him 'Dreamer and Doer'.[62]

Sun Yatsen, too, has been described as a dreamer.[63] Comparing the existing biographies of the two men, I am impressed by their similarly unrelenting efforts in pursuit of their sometimes unrealistic, though separate, dreams. I think that the two men had a common language, and that the long hours which Sun Yatsen spent in Cantlie's study may be interpreted as a sign of his attraction to, and the influence upon him of his former teacher. Furthermore, the variety of subjects on which, according to Cantlie, Sun Yatsen had read while in London,[64] may be regarded as evidence that the former student discussed what he had read with his former teacher. Dr Cantlie was not a surgeon with interests confined to his profession. His Arts degree at Aberdeen covered Greek, Latin, Mathematics, Natural Philosophy, Natural History, and Moral Philosophy.[65] He was well-informed and well-travelled, having been to the Far East, South Asia, the Middle East, Hawaii, and North America. While in Hong Kong, he had founded a public library, a hospital and a debating society, and formed a local branch of the St John Ambulance Brigade.[66]

None of the praise for Dr Cantlie in the book reviews was formulated in a Christian context. But at the time, people simply

57. Cantlie Family Papers, p. 62, newspaper cutting, *Otago Daily Times* (New Zealand), n.d.

58. Cantlie Family Papers, p. 40, *New Zealand Herald* (Auckland), n.d.

59. Cantlie Family Papers, p. 38, paper unknown, n.d.

60. Cantlie Family Papers, p. 37, *Public Opinion*, 10 March 1939.

61. Cantlie Family Papers, p. 52, unknown Australian newspaper, n.d.

62. Cantlie Family Papers, p. 39, *Telegraph* (Brisbane), 8 May 1939.

63. C. Martin Wilbur, *Sun Yat-sen: Frustrated Patriot* (New York, Columbia University Press, 1976), p. 5 (hereafter cited as *Sun Yat-sen*).

64. See the opening paragraph of this section.

65. Aberdeen University MS, U1, Student Register, Vol. 1, 1860/66–1890/91.

66. See Cantlie and Seaver, *Sir James Cantlie*; and Stewart, *Quality of Mercy*.

assumed that every Briton was a Christian of some description, and that his good work did not need to be emphasized as Christian. In the same vein, I do not think that we should feel obliged to delineate Sun Yatsen's good work as Christian. Shortly after his release from the Chinese Legation, Sun Yatsen wrote to another of his former teachers and friend, the clergyman Qu Fengzhi, 'I was a prisoner in the Legation for over ten days ... During the first six or seven days, nobody knew that I had been detained ... [Then for the next] six or seven days, I prayed day and night, harder and harder. On the seventh day, I suddenly acquired great peace of mind, and was no longer worried, so much so that I thought my prayers must have been answered'.[67] If Sun Yatsen had set out deliberately to impress his former teacher that he had been a good Christian, he could have claimed that he had begun praying on the very first day of his detention. It was reported that the day before he died, he told those around him that he was a Christian, and had been fighting the devil for more than forty years.[68] Here Sun Yatsen equated racial oppression, political abuse, and economic injustice with the devil.

ii. Sun Yatsen the Nationalist

Second, Sun Yatsen the nationalist. The entry in Mrs Cantlie's diary about taking Sun Yatsen to dinner with the Bruces and meeting a hero of Bulawayo[69] provides much food for thought. On 2 December 1906, Sun Yatsen made a public speech in Tokyo to mark the first anniversary of the founding of his party's organ, the *Minbao*. In it, he briefly outlined his Three Principles of the People. On the subject of Nationalism, he said, '[My idea of] Nationalism does not mean hostility to other nations, but the prevention of other nations' seizing the sovereignty of my nation. We Han people cannot claim that we have a country because we have lost our sovereignty [to the Manchus] ... We are a people without a country! ... A country by the name of Du[70] in Na-

---

67. Sun Yatsen to Qu Fengzhi (*circa* October 1896), in *Sun Zhongshan quanji*, Vol. 1, p. 46. The translation is mine.

68. This report was said to have been contained in a letter from his son to Sun Yatsen's first wife. His son was with him at the time. See *Sun Zhongshan yishiji*, p. 170.

69. Mrs Cantlie's diary, 25 October 1896.

70. The original text was 'Du-guo'. The word 'guo' means a country. As for 'Du', it was spelt out elsewhere as Du-lan-si-wa. See next few notes.

Feizhou[71] consisted of only about 200,000 people. But it took Great Britain three years to conquer it ... We Han people, do we want to take our subjugation lying down!'[72] This speech was printed in the tenth issue of the *Minbao*. In the eleventh issue, on the front page, was printed a large portrait with the caption 'Gu-lu-jia, the Great Leader of the Republic of Du-lan-si-wa'.[73]

Not only Sun Yatsen, but also many of his party faithful wrote numerous articles in the various revolutionary publications both inside and outside China, using the comparison between China and this mysterious nation in Africa to whip up nationalism among the Chinese.[74] But what was this African nation? When and where had Sun Yatsen begun his interest in African affairs? Mrs Cantlie's reference to having taken Sun Yatsen to dinner at the Bruces', where the subject of the evening's conversation appears to have been the story of Bulawayo,[75] goes some way towards answering these questions.

Bulawayo was the capital of the state of Ndebele whose chief was Lobengula. In 1887, the British had induced Lobengula to sign a treaty pledging him not to cede territory without leave of the British high commissioner. Then Cecil John Rhodes made haste to stake his claims therein by sending his agents to secure the now famous Rudd Concession of 1888, in which Lobengula gave away the monopoly of the minerals in his kingdom. This Concession became the basis of Rhodes' South Africa Company. Meanwhile, Rhodes tried to keep the wavering chief to his bargain by sending Leander Starr Jameson to '"keep Lobengula

---

71. 'Feizhou' means Africa. 'Na' does not make any sense at all unless it has been mistaken for 'Nan' which means 'South', so that the whole term means 'South Africa'. Sun Yatsen's speech was subsequently printed from notes taken by Hu Hanmin (*Sun Zhongshan quanji*, Vol. 1, p. 331). It is possible that Hu Hanmin misheard the speaker.

72. *Minbao*, No. 10, p. 84; reprinted in *Sun Zhongshan quanji*, Vol. 1, pp. 323–31.

73. I am grateful to Professor Jin Chongji for drawing my attention to this information.

74. See, for example, Anon., 'Lun Zhongguo zhi qiantu ji guomin yinjin zhi zeren', in *Hubei xuesheng jie*, No. 3, 29 March 1903, p. 7; Han Ju, 'Xin zhengfu zhi jianshe', in *Jiangsu*, No. 6, 21 September 1903, 'Xueshuo', p. 4; and Wang Zhengwei, 'Bo geming keyi zhao guafeng shuo', in *Minbao*, No. 6, 25 July 1906, p. 33. I am grateful to Professor Jin Chongji for these references.

75. Mrs Cantlie's diary, 25 October 1896.

sweet" with that elusive charm and bantering tongue of his'.[76] The first armed attack on Bulawayo by the British South Africa Company was contemplated in December 1889.[77] Lobengula 'bought another three years of Home Rule'[78] by making further concessions. The Company used that time to consolidate its position. In October 1893, the necessary incident of Ndebele firing on British troops was manufactured; Jameson's machine-gun fire broke Ndebele resistance; and Bulawayo was burnt down.[79]

Mr Weay, whom Mrs Cantlie described as a hero of Bulawayo, must have been a lively and imaginative talker, whose story captured the attention of all those who dined with him. It has not been possible to find out any information about him in the standard references and biographical dictionaries.[80] Nor can it be said with any certainty that Sun Yatsen's knowledge about the Ndelebe war came entirely from him; although I should imagine that it would have been too late for Sun Yatsen to have read about the final conquest of Bulawayo in 1893 in the daily newspapers in 1896, and too early for formal accounts such as books and articles to have been made available to him in London. When in 1906, as mentioned at the beginning of this section, he talked about Du-lan-si-wa and Gu-lu-jia (Gu-lu-ger in Cantonese), he was probably referring to the Transvaal and Kruger of the Boer War (1900–2), and not Ndebele and Lobengula. But some of the key British actors were the same. Jameson's role in the annexation of Ndebeleland has been noted. The Jameson Raid into the Transvaal on 29 December 1895 with the clear

76. Eric A. Walker, *A History of Southern Africa* (London, Longman, 1957), p. 413 (hereafter cited as *Southern Africa*). I am grateful to my retired colleague, Emeritus Professor Marjorie Jacobs, for lending me this book.

77. T. O. Ranger, 'The Nineteeth Century in Southern Rhodesia', in T. O. Ranger (ed.), *Aspects of Central African History* (London, Heinemann, 1968), p. 135 (hereafter cited as 'The Nineteeth Century in Southern Rhodesia'). I am grateful to my colleague. Professor Deryck Schreuder, for lending me his books on Africa.

78. Ranger, 'The Nineteeth Century in Southern Rhodesia', p. 136.

79. Ranger, 'The Nineteenth Century in Southern Rhodesia', p. 137. Walker, *Southern Africa*, pp. 426–30. For more details, see T. O. Ranger, *Revolt in Rhodesia* (London, Heinemann, 1967); and Stafford Glass, *The Matabele War* (London, Longman, 1968).

80. These include the *South African Dictionary of National Biography*, edited by Eric Rosenthale (London, Frederick Warne, 1966), and the *Dictionary of South African Biography*, edited by W. J. de Kock *et al.* (Nasionale Boekhandel, Cape Town, Johannesburg, Durban, and Pretoria, 1968–81), Vols. 1–4.

intention of precipitating another war of annexation, and his
subsequent surrender to Kruger's forces on 2 January 1896,[81]
created a scandal of such magnitude in London that public debate
and official inquiries went on throughout and beyond Sun Yatsen's sojourn in London.[82] Sun Yatsen could not have failed to
take note of it. The subsequent Boer War has been regarded as
one of the greatest struggles of nationalism against imperialism.
Thus, Sun Yatsen's background knowledge of African affairs,
probably originating from the briefing in 1896 by Mr Weay, is of
particular interest in the context of the present analysis. It
appears that Sun Yatsen subsequently came across to his followers as somebody who was knowledgeable not only about the
West but also about Africa. To those who had journeyed only to
Japan, not to mention those who had never left China, Sun
Yatsen seems to have succeeded in cultivating an heroic image of
a revolutionary leader who was well-travelled and well-informed.
In addition, the knowledge he gained in London about nationalism in Africa, with which he later propagated his Principle of
Nationalism, partially substantiates his claim that he finalized the
formulation of his Three Principles of the People while he was in
London in 1896–7. This claim will be examined further in the
next section.

II Widening Horizons:
Through the Kidnapping Sensation

It is not clear whether or not Sun Yatsen, after his release from
the Chinese Legation on 23 October 1896, subsequently read the
London papers of that day and of the next day. If he was
interested in them, it seems that quite a collection of them would
have been readily available at the Cantlies. This is made obvious
by the diary of Mrs Cantlie, who, as late as 27 October 1896,
wrote, 'Still much talk in the newspapers about Sun'.[83] Even if it
had not occurred to him that he might be interested, the Cantlies
would most probably have drawn his attention to them as fine
examples of British public opinion that had concerned him in-

81. Walker, *Southern Africa*, pp. 452–3.
82. Walker, *Southern Africa*, pp. 454–71.
83. Mrs Cantlie's diary, 27 October 1896.

timately. On the assumption that he did read those newspapers, he would have been duly impressed by, among other things, the expression therein of strong British nationalism aroused by the kidnapping incident,[84] the kind of nationalism which he found had been so sadly lacking in China and which he subsequently tried so hard to arouse among his fellow countrymen.[85]

But Sun Yatsen's idea of Nationalism went beyond the national pride, unity, and even the degree of prejudice exhibited in the British press of October 1896. He lectured to his followers, 'Great Britain is developed, and is developed basically by the Anglo-Saxon people who number 38,000,000, within an area that is composed basically of England and Wales. This people, therefore, may be called a *purely* [*my italics*] British race. This race is now the most powerful race on earth, and the country it has built is the most powerful country on earth'.[86] Apart from the obvious errors about the composition of the British people and the United Kingdom, Sun Yatsen seems to have thought that the 'purity' of the British people was a major contributing factor to its greatness. But all was not lost for China, he insisted. In the same lecture, which was delivered on 27 January 1924, when the emphasis was on conciliation with, rather than hostility towards, the Manchus, he said, 'The Chinese people totals four hundred million. In it, impurities include only a few million Mongols, just over a million Manchus, a few million Tibetans, and just over a million Moslem Turks. Thus, the alien elements do not exceed ten million, so that, on the whole, the four hundred million Chinese people can be described as complete Han'.[87] He suggested that the weakness of China was not caused by the impurity of her people but by the absence of Nationalism.[88]

What a strange idea about the relationship between the purity of race and the greatness of power! Even in one of the most glorious periods of Chinese history, the Tang dynasty (618–907

---

84. For an account and assessment of British nationalism as expressed in the London newspapers, see Chapter 4, Section II.

85. Sun Yatsen, 'Minzu zhuyi: diwujiang', in *Sun Zhongshan xuanji*, pp. 674–5.

86. Sun Yatsen, 'Minzu zhuyi: diyijiang', in *Sun Zhongshan xuanji*, pp. 621–2.

87. Sun Yatsen, 'Minzu zhuyi: diyijiang', p. 621.

88. Sun Yatsen, 'Minzu zhuyi: diyijiang', p. 621.

AD), China was inhabited not just by one people but by very many.

Where did Sun Yatsen get this strange idea? If we are to believe his claim that he finalized the formulation of his Three Principles of the People while he was in London in 1896–7, we must look closely at what, in his own words, he had seen and heard.

Of his known contacts, which have been established mainly by Professor Harold Schiffrin,[89] none would seem to have influenced him in that direction. Is it because we do not know enough about these contacts, or are there more contacts to be discovered?

Schiffrin has pointed out one serious gap in our knowledge. 'Had Slater's been more efficient', he wrote, 'we might have a better idea as to whom Sun was meeting during this period besides Dr Cantlie. His frequent and lengthy visits to 12 Albert Road from the end of October through December aroused the detectives' curiosity, but they were unable to satisfy it'.[90] I have checked the detectives' reports, and feel that Schiffrin's remark is quite justified, although Sun Yatsen continued to call at that address even after December 1896. Therefore, it is of some importance to prepare the necessary statistics about these visits.

Table 3 shows some raw figures about Sun Yatsen's visits to 12, Albert Road, which were made roughly once a week from the end of October 1896 to the beginning of April 1897. It is not clear whether or not the visits continued after 2 April 1897; and if they did, whether or not they were made on the same regular basis. Slater's report on Sun Yatsen during the Easter holidays, which began on Thursday, 15 April 1897, is extremely vague; and then the reports between 23 April and 9 June 1897 are apparently missing.[91] Even on the basis of the available statistics alone, it is interesting to know that Sun Yatsen visited 12, Albert Road, so regularly, sometimes going to the expense of calling a cab when he was not exactly rich.

The first visit took place on Tuesday, 27 October 1896, four days after Sun Yatsen's release from the Legation late on Friday, 23 October 1896. Mrs Cantlie wrote on 24 October 1896 that

89. Schiffrin, *Origins*, pp. 125–39.
90. Schiffrin, *Origins*, p. 134, n. 120.
91. There are indications that the visits continued after 2 April 1897. See Section V for some further evidence on this question.

Table 3 Sun Yatsen's Visits to 12, Albert Road, as Recorded by
Slater, the Private Detective Agency[92]

Date	Time	Duration	Transport
Tue., 27 Oct. 1896		1 hr	
Mon., 16 Nov. 1896		30 min	
Tue., 17 Nov. 1896	10.30–14.30	4 hr	By cab
Thur., 19 Nov. 1896	15.00–16.00	1 hr	By bus
Tue., 24 Nov. 1896	10.50–12.30	1 hr 40 min	By cab
Fri., 27 Nov. 1896	11.15–15.00	3 hr 45 min	By bus
Sat., 28 Nov. 1896	Unspecified	Unspecified	
Sun., 29 Nov. 1896	Unspecified	Unspecified	
Mon., 30 Nov. 1896	15.00–17.30	2 hr 30 min	
Wed., 2 Dec. 1896	13.00–16.15	3 hr 15 min	
Mon., 7 Dec. 1896	15.50–18.50	3 hr	
Sat., 19 Dec. 1896	13.15–17.00	3 hr 45 min	By bus
Sat., 2 Jan. 1897	15.20–18.00	2 hr 40 min	By bus
Sat., 9 Jan. 1897	14.45–16.45	2 hr	
Fri., 15 Jan. 1897	14.30–17.30	3 hr	
Wed., 27 Jan. 1897	15.20–17.30	2 hr 10 min	
Fri., 29 Jan. 1897	15.00–16.30	1 hr 30 min	
Thur., 4 Feb. 1897	15.50–16.50	1 hr	
Fri., 2 Apr. 1897	11.20–13.50	2 hr 30 min	
Total: 19 known visits		39 hr 25 min+	

reporters and friends came all day in troops. It is quite possible
that the occupant of 12, Albert Road (which was not far away
from the Cantlies), was among these visitors; and that Sun Yatsen returned the visit shortly after. Very likely, therefore, the
kidnapping sensation was instrumental in starting the friendship.

It is obviously important to find out who the occupant of 12,
Albert Road, was. I looked up the *London A–Z*. 'Albert Road'
was not listed. I went to the Greater London Council Record
Office in May 1983, and with the help of Mr R. Hart there, dug
up two old maps. One of them was printed in 1890,[93] the other in

92. These records have been reprinted in Luo Jialun, *Shiliao*, pp. 111–65.
93. Greater London Council, Map 1495 J St M 1890.

1869.[94] Both maps confirmed that what had been known as 'Albert Road' is now 'Prince Albert Road'. Then I went to inspect what should have been 12, Albert Road, and found it to be a free-standing and palatial house of the Victorian era. Nearly all the houses in that road are of about the same style and size, and all face the lovely lawns and shady trees of Regent's Park. It is indeed an exclusive area. I conclude that the occupant of that house, whom Sun Yatsen saw so regularly during his sojourn in London, must have been quite well off to have been either the owner or the tenant.

Then I looked up *Kelly's*. The 1896 directory indicated that the premises were unoccupied. The 1897 directory listed a certain Mrs Roscoe as the occupant; and the 1898 directory, Mr Edwin Collins.

One of Professor Schiffrin's contributions to Sun Yatsen studies was his discovery of an article entitled 'China's Present and Future', which Sun Yatsen had written 'with the assistance of one Edwin Collins', and which had appeared in a London publication called the *Fortnightly Review* on 1 March 1897.[95] Later, Professor Nakamura Tadashi[96] found another, also written in collaboration with Edwin Collins, published in London in July 1897, and entitled 'Judicial Reform in China'.[97] It did cross my mind, therefore, that Sun Yatsen could have been seeing Edwin Collins at 12, Albert Road; but according to *Kelly's*, Edwin Collins did not begin occupying the premises until 1898, and Sun Yatsen left London on 30 June 1897.[98]

A scholar has suggested that Mrs Roscoe could have been the knowledgeable mother of one of the leading lawyers in London, as there were a few prominent lawyers by the name of Roscoe listed in the legal directories; and that Sun Yatsen could have been seeking some free legal advice from her as to the wisdom of suing the Chinese Legation for damages. As has been pointed out before, some British newspapers had urged him to seek

94. Greater London Council, Map 2113 J St M 1869.
95. Schiffrin, *Origins*, p. 130.
96. See his articles, 'East Asia nitsuite', in *Shingaikakumei kenkyu*, No. 2, March 1982, pp. 44–8; and 'Kikan zenshu mishuroku no Son Bun ronbun: Judicial Reform in China', in *Shingaikakumei kenkyu*, No. 3, March 1983, pp. 99–104.
97. *East Asia*, Vol. 1, No. 1, July 1897, pp. 3–13.
98. See Section I of the Conclusion.

compensation,[99] and Sun Yatsen had gone so far as to consult the Treasury solicitor about it.[100] But the hard evidence is simply not there to proceed any further with the suggestion.

Instead, my thoughts turned to *Kelly's* itself. If, according to the 1896 directory, 12, Albert Road, was unoccupied, why should Sun Yatsen have called at an empty house so regularly from 27 October 1896? The key was to find out the manner in which the directories were compiled. With an introduction from Mr J. A. Tomlin of the Senate of the Inns of Court and the Bar, I sought assistance from the authorities of *Kelly's*, who confirmed my thinking that any particular directory 'was compiled during the Summer of the year and published on the last day of the year, bearing the date of the following year'.[101] Furthermore, 'All entries were, and still are, checked by personal call'.[102]

Thus, if Edwin Collins did move into 12, Albert Road, in the autumn of 1896, he would have missed the call from *Kelly's* made in the summer of 1896 and his name would therefore not have appeared in the 1897 directory. I may safely conclude that apart from the Cantlies, Edwin Collins was another Briton whom Sun Yatsen visited regularly and for long hours. Since the visits were made roughly on a weekly basis, I suggest that Sun Yatsen told his story to Edwin Collins by instalments. Collins then wrote up the story, also by instalments, and read them to Sun Yatsen on subsequent occasions, whereupon some further suggestions and revisions might have been made. As mentioned, at least two articles were written in this way.

It is difficult to imagine that the two men used all their meetings solely for writing these articles, and that they did not talk about other things as well. In particular, Sun Yatsen appears to have been quite preoccupied with the final formulation of his Three Principles of the People. What influence could Edwin Collins have had on him?

But to begin with, who was Edwin Collins? He has not been listed in the standard biographical dictionaries. In Guangzhou, I

99. See, for example, *Sun*, 24 October 1896, p. 3, col. 2.
100. FO 17/1718, pp. 151–2, Cuffe to Sanderson (with enclosure), 31 December 1896.
101. D. W. Lee to Wong, 23 November 1983. Mr Lee is a director of Information Services Ltd., which has taken over *Kelly's*.
102. D. W. Lee to Wong, 23 November 1983.

was shown a copy of the *Sun Yatsen University Journal*, in which appeared a Chinese translation of the article 'Judicial Reform in China', mentioned above. The Preface to the translation referred to Edwin Collins as a newspaper reporter.[103] I asked the senior of the two translators about the source of his information. He said that he had read about it in the Preface to the Japanese reproduction of the English original.

I checked the Japanese journal, in which Professor Nakamura Tadashi had reproduced his xerox copy of the article. There was no such reference in the Japanese Preface.[104] In November 1984 I took another month of study leave, which enabled me to consult Professor Nakamura in person. He told me that Edwin Collins was the editor of *East Asia*, saying that such information was printed in the journal itself. By that time it was too late for me to go back to London; but with the help of an old friend, Mr Howard Nelson, I was able to establish that the editor of *East Asia* was not Edwin Collins, but somebody by the name of Henry Faulds.[105] Then another Chinese historian alleged that Edwin Collins was the editor of the *Fortnightly Review*.[106] I checked the journal and discovered that the editor was in fact W. L. Courtney. These incidents go some way towards illustrating what Professor Martin Wilbur has described as the difficulties involved in studying Sun Yatsen;[107] and highlight some of the obstacles encountered particularly by historians in China and Japan.

I scrutinized the two articles in an attempt to detect what influence, if any, Edwin Collins might have had on Sun Yatsen. It was not a rewarding exercise, but turned out to be useful in another way. Each article bore a footnote to the effect that it would probably form part of a book which the two men were hoping to write. It occurred to me that Edwin Collins might have published some books, which in turn might offer some clues for further investigation. The British Library Catalogue lists a certain Edwin Collins as having translated, with an Introduction, *The Duties of the Heart, by Rabbi Bachye*,[108] and *The Wisdom of*

---

103. *Zhongshan daxue xuebao*, No. 1, 1984, p. 7.
104. Nakamura Tadashi, 'Kikan zenshu mishuroku no Son Bun ronbun: Judicial Reform in China', p. 99.
105. *East Asia*, Vol. 1, No. 1, front cover.
106. Wu Xiangxiang, *Sun Yixian zhuan*, Vol. 1, p. 191.
107. Wilbur, *Sun Yat-sen*, p. 1.
108. British Library reference 14003.a.2. Published in London in 1904.

Israel: being extracts from the Babylonian Talmud and Midrash Rabboth.[109] It also lists him as having written an Introduction to Marie Trevelyan's *Britain's Greatness Foretold.*[110] The place (London) and the dates (between 1900 and 1906) of publication of these books suggested that this Edwin Collins might have been the same man as the one that I was looking for. But was he?

Again, with the help of my friend Mr Howard Nelson, who called up for me *Britain's Greatness Foretold* from the Woolwich store of the British Library, I found that Edwin Collins was described as the 'Author of "China's Present and Future", etc'. This article, it will be recalled, was written in collaboration with Sun Yatsen. But the question of Edwin Collins' identity remained.

The other two books, mentioned above, may be found in the Public Library of New South Wales in Sydney.[111] Both refer to the translator as 'Hollier Hebrew Scholar of University College London'. The College records show that Edwin Collins attended classes in Hebrew in the Faculty of Arts in 1876–7, and was awarded the Hollier Scholarship in Hebrew in 1876.[112] The records do not contain any information about his age, address, or other family details,[113] but the conditions governing the award of the Scholarship stipulated that no candidate would be eligible unless, on the first day of October next following the examination for the Scholarship in July, he was less than 22 years of age.[114] Thus we know that on 1 October 1876, Edwin Collins was not older than 21; and that he was not older than 41 on 1 October 1896. In other words, he would have been about ten years Sun Yatsen's senior.

In addition, Sun Yatsen visited him during the weekdays a lot of the time. This may suggest that he was not a professional man, but a gentleman of means and leisure, who could afford to live in

109. British Library reference 14003.a.10. Published in London around 1906.
110. British Library reference 12631.m.11. Published in London in 1900.
111. Their references are S296.5/27 and S296.6/1 respectively.
112. C. M. Budden to Wong, 8 November 1984. University College London Fee Receipt Book, Faculty of Arts and Law, Session 1876–77, *University College London Calendar, 1877–1878*, p. 132. I am most grateful to Mrs Budden, records officer at University College, London, for her help in my attempts to find out more information about Edwin Collins.
113. *University College London Calendar 1877–1878*, p. 132.
114. *University College London Calendar, 1877–1878*, p. 64.

comfort and to help Sun Yatsen write articles about the Far East; and later, to translate and publish extracts from the Babylonian Talmud and Midrash Rabboth from Aramaic and Hebrew. But it is the Introduction he wrote for Marie Trevelyan's book that is most revealing. The full title of the book is *Britain's Greatness Foretold: The Story of Boadicea, the British Warrior-Queen*. The title of the Introduction which he wrote for it is 'The Prediction Fulfilled'. The Introduction is quite long (pp. xv–lxiv). In it, he set out to demonstrate the manner in which Boadicea prefigured Queen Victoria. Right at the end, he anticipated that the civilizing influence of Europe and America would one day benefit China, despite 'the fact that England once helped to stifle the noble revolt of the Taiping, and to save the cruel and corrupt Tartar dynasty from deposition'.

Edwin Collins exhibited all the characteristics of a British Israelite.[115] The British Israelites represent a complex historical phenomenon,[116] which is beyond the scope of this book. For the purpose of the present study, I shall restrict myself to identifying certain facets which appear to have captured Sun Yatsen's attention.

First, in the words of one of the best-known expositors of the group, 'British Israel Truth ... account[s], as nothing else can, for the growth, power, and influence of the British Empire'.[117] The reason for this, so claimed the British Israelites, was that the Anglo-Saxons were migrants from Israel, who had started their journeys about a thousand years or more before Christ, in several waves.[118] Not only Anglo-Saxons, but Celts, Gauls, Jutes, Danes, Normans, in short, all the inhabitants of the British Isles were descendants of Israel, albeit having arrived at the

---

115. As soon as I told my colleague, Professor Ken Cable, an expert on church history and Christian religious sects, he concluded that Edwin Collins was a British Israelite. Thus began a completely new line of enquiry about Sun Yatsen and the origins of his ideas. Such is the advantage of belonging to a large History Department.

116. Perhaps the best exponent of the views of British Israelites is the book by M. H. Gayer, himself an Israelite, entitled *The Heritage of the Anglo-Saxon Race* (Haverhill, Mass., Destiny Publishers, 1941). I am grateful to Professor Lawrence Foster, Visiting Fullbright Scholar to my Department in 1985, for this reference.

117. Gayer, *The Heritage of the Anglo-Saxon Race*, pp. 139 and 142.

118. Charles Braden, *These also Believe* (New York, Macmillan, 1957), pp. 392–3. This book gives a very good assessment of the British Israelites in Chapter 11. Again, I wish to thank Professor Lawrence Foster for this reference.

'Appointed Place' (2 Sam. 7:10) at different times.[119] As such, the British people, more commonly known as the Anglo-Saxons in this particular context, were God's chosen race.[120] To Abraham, God said, 'I will make of thee a great nation' (Gen. 17.6). To Jacob He said, 'And thou shalt be called by a new name' (Isa. 62:2). 'Wherefore glorify ye Jehovah in the east, even the name of Jehovah, the God of Israel, in the isles of the sea' (Isa. 24:15). All these prophecies, and many more, the British Israelites believed, had been fulfilled 'in Britain or the Anglo-Saxon people'.[121] If Sun Yatsen had not known it already, Edwin Collins would have assured him that the Anglo-Saxons were the greatest people on earth, who had built the the world's greatest country — a view which, as mentioned, was subsequently reflected in Sun Yatsen's lecture on Nationalism.[122]

Second, the American connection. 'The first Anglo-Saxon Association was founded in 1879 in England. A periodical, *Heirs of the World*, was published in America as early as 1880 (in New York), so the idea was evidently spreading'.[123] Initially, it was 'British Israel', not 'Anglo-Saxon Israel'. But because the dominant race in the United States of America was Anglo-Saxon a change in name to Anglo-Saxon meant that a large part of the American people and perhaps even the American nation might share whatever responsibilities and benefits there were that grew out of their identification with Israel.[124] This probably explains why Edwin Collins included America as a country that might ultimately civilize China.[125]

Third, the purity of a particular race. 'Interesting light is thrown on the question by a pamphlet *The Bible Answers the Race Question*'.[126] The author asserted that intermarriage of disparate races had evil results and *weakened the race*. The Biblical curse on Ham was defended, and the care of Abraham, Isaac,

119. Braden, *These also Believe*, pp. 397–8.
120. Braden, *These also Believe*, p. 357.
121. Braden, *These also Believe*, p. 390.
122. Sun Yatsen, 'Minzu zhuyi: diyijiang', p. 622.
123. Braden, *These also Believe*, p. 389.
124. Braden, *These also Believe*, p. 398.
125. Edwin Collins, 'The Prediction Fulfilled', which, as mentioned, was the Introduction to Marie Trevelyan's book, *Britain's Greatness Foretold*.
126. Braden, *These also Believe*, p. 400.

and Jacob to maintain the purity of the race was applauded.[127]
The strange logic which Sun Yatsen subsequently used to argue
that the Chinese people were a pure race, namely, that the Han
overwhelmingly outnumbered the Mongols, Manchus, Tibetans,
and so on,[128] is reminiscent of such a view.

It is difficult to measure the extent to which Sun Yatsen was
influenced by Edwin Collins. If we are to believe his claim that
what he had seen and heard in London enabled him to finalize
the formulation of his Three Principles of the People (and so far
there is no evidence to suggest the contrary) then we do know that
he saw a lot of, and heard a great deal from, Edwin Collins.

When put in the Chinese context, Anglo-Saxon 'Israel' presented a fundamental difficulty for Sun Yatsen, who was seeking
desperately to strengthen China. No attempt had been made by
any Christian Israelite to suggest that the Chinese were the descendants of 'Israel', although one Israelite did try to prove that
the 'ruling families of the White Japanese — the Samurai — are
our own people of Joseph's seed who took their names from
Samaria', the capital of Northern Israel.[129] It seems that Sun
Yatsen tried to overcome this difficulty in three ways. First, he
emphasized that the Chinese people, like the Anglo-Saxons and
the Japanese, were a pure race. Second, he argued that sheer
numbers might count, saying that the Chinese were by far the
largest race on earth, much larger than the Anglo-Saxons and the
Japanese.[130] Third, he completely omitted 'Israel' — the central
theme of all Israelites — and replaced it with a supreme national
spirit which he called the Principle of Nationalism, that had made
both Britain and Japan such powerful nations.[131]

III Attempts to Accommodate British Might

If Sun Yatsen recognized that Great Britain was the world's most
powerful nation, which had important vested interests in China,

---

127. Braden, *These also Believe*, pp. 400–1.

128. Sun Yatsen, 'Minzu zhuyi: diyijiang', p. 621.

129. See Braden's treatment of this particular case in *These also Believe*,
p. 399.

130. He argued that the Anglo-Saxons had trebled in the past hundred years
or so and now totalled merely 38,000,000; and that the Japanese had also trebled
in the last hundred years or so and now totalled about 56,000,000; but the
Chinese were by far the largest race on earth! See note 131.

131. Sun Yatsen, 'Minzu zhuyi: diyijiang', p. 622.

how would he go about regaining for China her national independence, which, after all, was the crux of his Principle of Nationalism? In any case, why would he have wanted to be so involved with, of all people, a British Israelite? Conversely, why should a British Israelite such as Edwin Collins have wished to spend so much time with a 'Chinaman'?[132] Some clues to the answers may be found in the two known articles which the two men wrote jointly, and in Edwin Collins' own publications.

First, the possible motives of Edwin Collins. The two published translations by Edwin Collins belonged to a series entitled 'Wisdom of the East'. The Editorial Note reads:

The object of the Editors of this series is a very definite one. They desire above all things that, in their humble way, these books shall be the ambassadors of good-will and understanding between East and West — the old world of Thought and the new of Action. In this endeavour, and in their own sphere, they are but followers of the highest example in the land. They are confident that a deeper knowledge of the great ideals and lofty philosophy of Oriental thought may help to a revival of that true spirit of Charity which neither despises nor fears the nations of another creed and colour.

L. Cranmer-Byng
S. Kapadia
Northbrook Society
185 Piccadilly, W.

It seems that while Edwin Collins was upholding 'Israel' (formerly of the East), he was at the same time promoting understanding among races by helping Sun Yatsen of the Far East write those articles about the wickedness that existed in pagan China. As for the Northbrook Society, it was listed in the London telephone

---

132. As noted before, Sun Yatsen himself used the word 'Chinaman'. It is not clear whether or not he realized the racial connotations of such a word when he used it. '"Chinaman" itself, a designation much disliked by Chinese when they learned English (still more its shorter form "Chink"), conveyed a suggestion of wiliness or artfulness, which might be engaging, as in Bret Harte's playful verse, or in the cricketing parlance of recent years, or might have a more unpleasant flavour. It lent itself to epigrams like Halliday Macartney's after a tour in 1873, "the Chinaman is a low animal"'. V. G. Kiernan, *The Lords of Human Kind: European attitudes towards the outside world in the Imperial Age* (London, Weidenfeld and Nicolson, 1969), p. 160 (hereafter cited as *Lords of Human Kind*).

directory as late as 1983, the address being given as 59, Doughty Street, London WC1.[133] In the *Directory of Grant Making Trusts 1983*, there is an entry for the Northbrook Trust, whose address is also given as 59, Doughty Street. This Trust was founded in 1961. Its object was 'The advancement of education in general and in particular, education in the U.K. of Nationals of India, Burma, Ceylon, Pakistan and other Countries of the East'. Its income in 1983 was only £1,150, so perhaps the Society was discontinued through a shortage of funds.[134] But this is further evidence to suggest that it was in keeping with the philosophy of Edwin Collins to help Sun Yatsen write those articles. Edwin Collins described his role thus, 'This article, which will probably form part of a book we are writing together, is the result of a collaboration between Dr Sun Yatsen and myself, in which he is responsible for the facts and for the opinions expressed; I, only for their selection from the mass of material, for their arrangement, and for the form in which they now appear'.[135]

As for Sun Yatsen's motives, some idea may be obtained from the contents of the articles themselves. The first article, entitled 'China's Present and Future', had its object clearly set out in the first paragraph. It was to deal with the question of corruption in China, because, '... I venture to think, no European has yet fully realised the extent and far-reaching consequences of the *corruption* [*my italics*] which makes China a reproach and danger among nations, or knows the extent of her latent recuperative forces, and of the possibilities that exist for her salvation from within'.[136] The article was highly organized, and concentrated on four serious problems in China, problems which were well-known to foreigners. They were famine, flood, pestilence, and banditti. Throughout, graphic details were given to prove that corruption was the sole cause of them all. Such universal corruption was entirely the work of the Manchus, who had conquered the 'pure Chinese'.[137] Therefore, the Manchus had to go; and it would be

---

133. Budden to Wong, 28 February 1985.
134. Budden to Wong, 29 May 1985.
135. Note to Sun Yatsen, 'China's Present and Future: The Reform Party's Plea for British Benevolent Neutrality', in *Fortnightly Review*, New Series, Vol. 61, 1 March 1897, p. 424 (hereafter cited as 'China's Present and Future').
136. Sun Yatsen, 'China's Present and Future', p. 424.
137. Sun Yatsen, 'China's Present and Future', pp. 424 and 440.

'in the interests of Europe generally, and of England in particular, to allow us to succeed',[138] because the Manchus had been extremely anti-foreign, anti-Christian, and anti-free trade.[139] He did not ask for material assistance, only 'the benevolent neutrality of Great Britain and the other Powers'.[140]

In making such a request, Sun Yatsen felt obliged to repudiate the policy, often recommended to the British government by old China hands, of protecting the present regime from every attack native or foreign. He singled out for comment such a recommendation contained in an article in the August issue of the *Fortnightly Review*, whose author used the pseudonym 'L'.[141]

The main thrust of the second article was the gruesome picture of the various cases of torture which he had treated as a medical practitioner, or witnessed, or learnt about personally as a native of the land. Again, the argument was that universal corruption was the sole cause of such sickening injustice, 'the cleansing of which would be so absolutely impossible without an entire change of the system of official life, which, in turn, can never improve until the Manchu or Tartar dynasty ceases to rule China'.[142] Recalling the recent massacre of a dozen English missionaries, men, women, and children in China, he concluded, '... no lesson seems sufficient to bring home to the Government or the people of Great Britain that the laws of China, as enforced with the sanction and support of England, are a blot upon Creation and a disgrace to our common humanity. If England could realise this, the Reform Party of Young China might hope for at least freedom from molestation in its attempt to make possible the introduction of a Europeanised judicial system into our country'.[143] Here again, benevolent neutrality was all he asked of Britain.

Despite his statement to the contrary,[144] Edwin Collins prob-

---

138. Sun Yatsen, 'China's Present and Future', p. 440.
139. Sun Yatsen, 'China's Present and Future', p. 439.
140. Sun Yatsen, 'China's Present and Future', p. 440.
141. Sun Yatsen, 'China's Present and Future', p. 440. Upon checking the issue, it is found that the pertinent details are: 'L', 'The Future of China', *Fortnightly Review*, New Series, Vol. 60, 1 August 1896, pp. 159–74. For my assessment of this article, see the last section of this chapter.
142. Sun Yatsen, 'Judicial Reform in China', p. 3.
143. Sun Yatsen, 'Judicial Reform in China', p. 3.
144. See the footnote to the first article, mentioned above.

ably did contribute some of his own ideas to both articles, such as the purity of the Chinese race, and the questions of Christianity and free trade. It is also likely that it was his curiosity about certain 'things Chinese', such as the subject of torture which had been mentioned by several London newspapers during Sun Yatsen's detention, that led to the writing of the second article. It is even possible that in the course of their friendship, he was to some extent influenced by Sun Yatsen's views. At a time when very few Englishmen still sympathized with the Taipings, for example, Edwin Collins, as mentioned, later blamed his own government for having 'helped to stifle the noble revolt of the Taiping' and for having saved 'the cruel and corrupt Tartar dynasty from deposition'.[145] In fact, it is difficult to see how the two men could have put together articles containing views about which they seriously disagreed. The collaboration was probably a process of exchange of views and learning from each other, both about Britain and China.

Without the benefit of any information about Edwin Collins, or the advantage of having the second article for comparison, Schiffrin made an assessment of the first and concluded that it was the result of Sun Yatsen's attempt to translate his triumph over the Legation into official British endorsement of his revolutionary movement.[146] 'One of the basic premises of the Canton [Guangzhou] plot had been that the West, and especially Britain, would recognise its common interest in the anti-dynastic cause', he wrote. 'Sun's clash with the Legation not only reinforced this conviction but inflated it to unrealistic proportions'.[147] Omitting what seems to have been the main thrust of the first article, which was on corruption, Schiffrin concentrated on the suggested remedy to such an evil, which was the replacement of the Manchu government with 'a pure administration by native Chinese with, at first, European advice, and, for some years, European administrative assistance'.[148]

In view of the analysis of Sun Yatsen's behaviour in this and the preceeding chapters, it is doubtful if the first article can be

---

145. Edwin Collins' Introduction, entitled 'The Prediction Fulfilled', in Marie Trevelyan, *Britain's Greatness Foretold*.
146. Schiffrin, *Origins*, p. 129.
147. Schiffrin, *Origins*, p. 129.
148. Schiffrin, *Origins*, p. 131.

seen in that light any longer. But the article did contain the suggestion on European advice and administrative assistance which, by today's standards, is an unusual one for a nationalist to have made. This is a facet which cannot be ignored in the investigation of the origins of Sun Yatsen's heroic image, particularly his image as a nationalist. Schiffrin thought that Sun Yatsen's appeal as contained in the first article was, 'essentially the same as Ho Kai's'.[149] Ho Kai (or He Qi, 1859–1914) was one of Sun Yatsen's former teachers at the College of Medicine in Hong Kong. Like Sun Yatsen, he had studied at the Government Central School in Hong Kong. Like Dr Cantlie, he was a medical graduate of Aberdeen. He later read law as well and was called to the Bar in London. Upon his return to Hong Kong, he became one of the colony's most distinguished civic leaders.[150] Thus, it becomes necessary to investigate the colony.

IV The Hong Kong Connection

On 21 May 1895,[151] the *China Mail* in Hong Kong published a summary of He Qi's scheme for reform in China, which had appeared in serial form in the *China Mail*'s Chinese counterpart, by the name of *Wah Tsz Yat Po* (*Chinese Mail*).[152] Schiffrin has encapsulated this summary very well.[153] It suffices here to say that it was a blueprint for a constitutional monarchy in China. The question as to whether Sun Yatsen had at any stage of his life been a constitutional monarchist or whether he was a republican throughout will be explored in Section V of this chapter. As far as the examination of Sun Yatsen as a nationalist is concerned, one aspect of He Qi's scheme for reform is directly relevant to the present analysis. The scheme proposed that 'an Inland Customs Service should be created on lines similar to the Imperial Chinese Maritime Customs, with the administration centralised in the same manner'.[154] The Chinese Maritime Customs

149. Schiffrin, *Origins*, p. 131.
150. Schiffrin, *Origins*, pp. 20–1.
151. Schiffrin referred to a different date, 23 May 1895 (*Origins*, p. 75). Upon checking his footnote, I found that he had used the *Overland China Mail*, which, as mentioned, was the overseas weekly edition of the *China Mail*.
152. *China Mail*, 21 May 1895, p. 3, cols. 5–7.
153. Schiffrin, *Origins*, pp. 75–6.
154. *China Mail*, 21 May 1895, p. 3, col. 6.

at this time was controlled by the British. To suggest that the Inland Customs should follow the same model was to concede yet another vital area of Chinese sovereignty. Sun Yatsen's idea of foreign administrative advice and assistance to his projected new government might have invited some modern criticism on his lack of confidence, as a nationalist, in his own people to run their own country properly, but certainly not accusations of a sell-out of sovereign rights. He merely sought Western managerial expertise. At least in 1896-7,[155] he merely asked Great Britain not to interfere with what he hoped to do with his own country. Therefore, the interpretation that Sun Yatsen's appeal for British benevolent neutrality was 'essentially the same as Ho Kai's',[156] cannot stand.

The question remains as to why Sun Yatsen suggested European administrative advice and assistance. Schiffrin thought that this was designed to assure his readers that 'British influence would help to shape the new administration'.[157] But why was this assurance even necessary? Was it the result of a 'conviction' that 'the West, and especially Britain, would recognise its common interest in the anti-dynastic cause'?[158] If so, how did this 'conviction' come about (if a conviction it was)? On this, we need to examine the attitudes of the British in Hong Kong towards Chinese politics, because it was in Hong Kong that Sun Yatsen had received his secondary and tertiary education; and it was also from Hong Kong that he had plotted to overthrow the provincial government at Guangzhou in 1895.

It has been suggested that He Qi, having taught Sun Yatsen medicine in Hong Kong, served as a model for him and influenced his thinking beyond his formative years in the colony.[159] This may well have been the case. But we have just seen the difference in the concessions the two men were prepared to make to Britain, which may be interpreted as a difference in the degree of faith in, and commitment to, Britain. This difference, in turn, may be explained partly by the fact that He Qi had read medicine

155. Later in his life, Sun Yatsen is said to have made promises of significant concessions to the Powers. But that is outside the scope of the present analysis.
156. Schiffrin, *Origins*, p. 131.
157. Schiffrin, *Origins*, p. 131.
158. Schiffrin, *Origins*, p. 129.
159. Schiffrin, *Origins*, p. 24.

and then law in Britain and had married a British lady,[160] while
Sun Yatsen's tertiary education had been confined to the colony.
In this regard, the attitudes of British colonists may have produced different responses from the two men. These attitudes
were best reflected in the local press, such as the *China Mail* and
the *Hongkong Telegraph*. But since the relevant issues of only
the *China Mail* have survived to this day, we have to be content
with the evidence preserved in one newspaper alone.

According to Xie Zuantai (who was one of the secret few
within the Xing Zhong Hui and who knew all the details of the
plot to seize Guangzhou), both the editor of the *China Mail*,
Thomas A. Reid, and the editor of the *Hongkong Telegraph*,
Chesney Duncan, had promised help.[161] Reid, in particular,
pledged 'to do his best to work for the sympathy and support of
the British Government and people of England'.[162] Xie Zuantai's
version is corroborated by various editorials in the *China Mail*
beginning on 12 March 1895, in which Manchu misrule was
condemned, the possibility of an organized rebellion in South
China was predicted, and an appeal for sympathy for the 'patriots'
was made. The most telling editorial appeared on 29 October
1895, after the plot had failed. In it, the editor professed to have
had full knowledge of the plot and to have respected that confidence to date. Now, however, he decided to release the details
because the 'stories that are going about are in some cases grossly
misleading'.[163]

Schiffrin has assessed the editorials of 12, 16, and 18 March
1895 in some detail.[164] For the purpose of the present analysis,
the point should be made that these editorials repeatedly stressed
the importance of foreign advisers in terms of what they could
offer 'to reconstitute the [Chinese] Government on modern lines
to the benefit of the whole population'.[165] The fact that Sun
Yatsen made the same point in his two London articles may

160. Schiffrin, *Origins*, pp. 20–1.
161. Schiffrin, *Origins*, p. 71, n. 52, and p. 79, n. 66, quoting Tse Tsan Tai,
The Chinese Republic, p. 9.
162. Schiffrin, *Origins*, p. 71, n. 52, and p. 79, n. 66, quoting Tse Tsan Tai,
The Chinese Republic, p. 9.
163. *China Mail*, 29 October 1895, p. 3, col. 6.
164. Schiffrin, *Origins*, pp. 72–5.
165. *China Mail*, 18 March 1895, p. 3, col. 7. See, also, *China Mail*, 12 March
1895, p. 3, col. 7.

suggest that he agreed with it. And his omission of the business of handing over the collection of China's inland revenue to the British, first suggested in the *China Mail* editorial of 18 March 1895,[166] and then formally publicized by He Qi in May,[167] may be interpreted as his disagreement with it.

In any case, the available evidence does not enable an equation to be drawn between Sun Yatsen's views and those expressed in the *China Mail* and by He Qi. Hence there is an obvious fallacy in the opinion that the proposition concerning the Inland Customs, though inconsistent with the accepted image of Sun Yatsen as a young nationalist, was nevertheless compatible with his low social origins and Westernized intellectual orientations.[168] This opinion, expressed under the subtitle 'Nationalists or "Running Dogs of Imperialism"?', simply makes the fallacy more conspicuous. In the same vein, the views of the *China Mail* and of He Qi cannot be used as the basis for an assertion that Sun Yatsen had a 'conviction' about Britain identifying her interest with the anti-dynastic cause.[169] Furthermore, it is doubtful whether Sun Yatsen's two London articles can be taken as evidence that such a 'conviction' had been inflated to unrealistic proportions by his 'clash with the Legation'.[170] After all, Sun Yatsen only appealed to British neutrality, which was no more, if not less, than what the *China Mail* and He Qi had asked for.

Far from being an Anglophile like He Qi, there is evidence to suggest that Sun Yatsen sought foreign aid from others than the British. On 16 March 1895, Xie Zuantai entered the following in his diary: 'We obtained the secret support of the Japanese Government through the Japanese Consul'.[171] He did not name the person who had approached the Japanese consul. The author of the article, which was originally published in the *Kobe Chronicle*, and which was subsequently reprinted in the *China Mail*, also wrote, '. . . attempts were made, without tangible result, to secure the co-operation of the Japanese Government. What would have been the result if the verbal sympathy of Japanese under-

---

166. *China Mail*, 18 March 1895, p. 3, col. 7.
167. See *China Mail*, 21 May 1895, p. 3, col. 6.
168. Schiffrin, *Origins*, pp. 77–8.
169. Schiffrin, *Origins*, p. 129.
170. Schiffrin, *Origins*, p. 129.
171. Tse Tsan Tai, *The Chinese Republic*, p. 9.

officials had been followed by active sympathy in higher quarters, none can tell'.[172] As speculated before,[173] the mysterious author was most probably Chen Shaobai. And as mentioned before,[174] Chen Shaobai and Xie Zuantai belonged to two rival factions within the Xing Zhong Hui. Thus, important representatives from the two opposing factions agreed that the Japanese had been approached.

But concrete evidence was not available until quite recently, when Professor Hazama Naoki of Kyoto University was shown a collection of neglected old papers. Amongst them was a hand-written confidential report by the Japanese consul in Hong Kong, Nakagawa Tsunejiro, to Hara Takashi, the Japanese vice-minister for foreign affairs.[175] The consul referred to a visit by Sun Yatsen to the Consulate on 1 March 1895.[176] On this occasion, Sun Yatsen requested Japanese aid to the order of 25,000 guns and 1,000 pistols. On subsequent visits, Sun Yatsen continued to press for Japanese aid, albeit on a small scale.[177] Of special interest is the confidential statement by the Japanese consul that He Qi was opposed to the move to seek Japanese aid.[178] Although Sun Yatsen's pains were never rewarded materially, nothing stopped him and his party faithful from declaring that the Japanese were secretly involved in the plot.

It appears that Sun Yatsen also approached the German consul in Hong Kong, Dr Knappe, for assistance, according to a British intelligence report.[179] Although corroborative evidence from German sources is still wanting, and although Sun Yatsen does not

---

172. *China Mail*, 26 November 1896, p. 2, col. 6.
173. See Chapter 4, Section I.
174. See Chapter 4, Section I.
175. For a short biography of Hara Takashi (1856–1921), see the relevant entry in Seiichi Iwao (ed.), *Biographical Dictionary of Japanese History*, translated by Burton Watson (Tokyo, Kodansha International Ltd., 1978), pp. 337–9.
176. I am grateful to Professor Hazama Naoki for a photocopy of the letter, and to my colleague Mr Kobayashi Toshihiko for having helped me read it. This letter, dated 4 March 1895, is now published in *Hara Takashi kankei bunsho* (Tokyo, Nihon hoso shuppan kyokai, 1984), pp. 392–3.
177. Nakagawa Tsunejiro to Hara Takashi, 17 April 1895, in *Hara Takashi kankei bunsho*, pp. 395–6.
178. Nakagawa Tsunejiro to Hara Takashi, 4 March 1895, in *Hara Takashi kankei bunsho*, p. 393.
179. Schiffrin, *Origins*, p. 79, n. 63, referring to CO 129/274, MacDonald to Salisbury, 19 October 1896, enclosure, extract from Fraser's intelligence report, October 1896.

appear to have had better luck in this area, there is no reason to doubt the reliability of the report.

Thus, it seems that the available evidence consolidates, rather than impairs, the accepted image of Sun Yatsen as a young nationalist.

V The Cultivation of the Heroic Image

A recurrent theme in the pertinent editorials of the *China Mail* prior to the plot in Guangzhou was the lack of 'a leader of outstanding quality'.[180] Not only the editor, but also the satirist Brownie made the same point when he wrote, 'I see you speak seriously of possible demonstrations in China in favour of reform ... the great desiderata of such a movement would be organisation and leadership'.[181] The *Shanghai Mercury*, as reprinted in the *China Mail*, voiced the same opinion, 'Is no leader of the people ever going to arise who will, with staggering blows, set this poor and oppressed population free!'[182] What would have been the effect of these British colonial views on Sun Yatsen, the leader of the revolutionary party who was busy organizing an uprising? His approaches to the Japanese and the German consuls in Hong Kong, in the face of opposition from He Qi, may be regarded partly as his reaction at the time. His London articles may be interpreted as his subsequent attempt to establish himself as the spokesman and leader of a movement which was devoted to the regeneration of China. Put in this perspective, the action of writing and publishing those English articles was more important than the content. Here Sun Yatsen was consciously trying to cultivate an heroic image of himself in the eyes of the British public in Great Britain itself.

Nor was he content with simply writing and then publishing those articles. There is evidence to suggest that he used at least one of them to give public lectures. On 16 January 1897, Mrs Cantlie entered the following in her diary, 'Dr Sun is to lecture at Oxford [at] the end of the month so he brought his written MS to

---

180. *China Mail*, 12 March 1895, p. 3, col. 6; and *China Mail*, 16 March 1895, p. 3, col. 6.

181. *China Mail*, 16 March 1895, p. 4, col. 4.

182. *China Mail*, 15 March 1895, p. 4, col. 3, quoting the *Shanghai Mercury*.

show Hamish. It is very good'.[183] By this time, Sun Yatsen would have been visiting Edwin Collins regularly for about two and a half months. Consequently, at least a draft of the first article would have been ready. It is not clear on which day he went to Oxford, or which society he addressed. Such information could have been provided by the private detective shadowing him. But, as on other occasions, the detective's reports are disappointing. In any case, it was a very rare honour to have been invited to speak at Oxford; and Sun Yatsen must have felt greatly gratified to have been offered the opportunity to cultivate his public image at that sort of level.

On 11 March 1897, Mrs Cantlie again wrote, 'The Lecture on "Things Chinese" at St Martin's Town Hall came off tonight for the benefit of Charing Cross Hospital. Dr Sun read an *article* [*my italics*] on the Government of China and Hamish talked about different things. It was attended by 260 people'.[184] Those who had the leisure to go to St Martin's Town Hall, the money to donate to Charing Cross, and the interest to listen to 'Things Chinese', were most probably middle- and upper-class Londoners. Here again, Sun Yatsen would have had the satisfaction of addressing a relatively distinguished gathering.

Mrs Cantlie referred to an *article* which he read on this occasion, and to the fact that this article was on the government of China. His first London article had been published on 1 March 1897,[185] and was in substance about the government of China, while the second was not published until July 1897.[186] It is likely, therefore, that Sun Yatsen would have read the first, rather than the second, piece of work. This, in turn, may suggest that Sun Yatsen continued to visit Edwin Collins after 2 April 1897, if only to write the second article, and thereby received more doses of *Pax Britannica* from the British Israelite.[187] This again raises the question of the Principle of Nationalism. Sun Yatsen may have nurtured nationalist, anti-Manchu sentiments since his schooldays in Hawaii.[188] But to have felt the need for, and hence to

183. Mrs Cantlie's diary, 16 January 1897.
184. Mrs Cantlie's diary, 11 March 1897.
185. Sun Yatsen, 'China's Present and Future', pp. 424–40.
186. Sun Yatsen, 'Judicial Reform in China', pp. 3–13.
187. For details about the importance of Sun Yatsen's visits to Edwin Collins, see Section III of this chapter.
188. Schiffrin, *Origins*, p. 13.

have tried to formulate and then promote the Principle of Nationalism among his fellow countrymen, was a different matter which involved conceptualizing his experiences and his knowledge. As for the attitude of the Cantlies towards the collaboration between Sun Yatsen and Edwin Collins, Mrs Cantlie's aforementioned remarks about one of the two articles may be regarded as an indication of approval.

It would have been quite an experience for Sun Yatsen to have read the *China Mail*'s constant lament not only over the absence of 'an outstanding leader' within the movement he led, but also over the lack of patriotism among the Chinese people. In its very first pertinent editorial, the *China Mail* wrote, '... there is a lamentable lack of that spontaneity of action, of that intellectual vigour which enables races like men to rise on the stepping stones of dead selves to higher things'.[189] If Sun Yatsen had wondered what that 'spontaneity of action' meant in real life, he would have had an opportunity to witness it during the kidnapping incident in London. And if subsequently he had any difficulty conceptualizing it, Edwin Collins was there to assist him.[190] Thus, by helping him write those articles, the British Israelite also played a role in cultivating Sun Yatsen's heroic image as a 'patriot', the kind of person, the British colonists consistently complained, so sadly lacking in China.[191]

The two London articles were also a political statement. In both articles he insisted on a complete overthrow of Manchu rule by his so-called Reform Party. Such a statement may be seen to contain a contradiction in terms. Reform usually means an improvement of the existing system; but Sun Yatsen wanted to do away with the existing system altogether. A similar contradiction may be found in the pertinent editorials of the *China Mail*, in which a revolution by the Reform Party was predicted. One possible explanation for this apparent contradiction may be that they both meant the elimination of the Manchu government and everything it represented, with its replacement by a completely

---

189. *China Mail*, 12 March 1895, p. 3, col. 6. See, also, *China Mail*, 15 March 1895, p. 4, col. 4, quoting the *Shanghai Mercury*; and *China Mail*, 18 March 1895, p. 3, col. 6.

190. See Section III of this chapter.

191. See, for example, *China Mail*, 15 March 1895, p. 4, col. 4, quoting the *Shanghai Mercury*.

new form of government, modelled on Western lines. Such an explanation cannot be applied to He Qi's reform programme, which was aimed at establishing a constitutional monarchy and which, as the *China Mail* commented, depended for its success on 'the Emperor-Mother and Li Hung-chang [Li Hongzhang]'.[192] But this explanation is made all the more plausible by another report prepared by the Japanese consul, who said that Sun Yatsen had planned to set up a republic once he had forcibly secured the independence of the two southern provinces of Guangdong and Guangxi from the Manchu government.[193] Sun Yatsen did not repeat the same view in his London articles, probably because he thought it would be politically unwise to offend the British constitutional monarchy, to whose benevolent neutrality he was appealing.

It is to be hoped that this interpretation of Sun Yatsen's London articles, reinforced by the aforementioned new Japanese sources, has gone some way towards settling the great controversy among Chinese experts as to whether the Sun Yatsen of 1895–7 was a reformer who aimed at constitutional monarchy, or a revolutionary who wanted nothing short of a republic.[194]

But in the context of the present study of Sun Yatsen's heroic image, his repudiation of 'L' in the first of his two London articles deserves some consideration. 'L''s article denounced the ruling élite in China, the education that produced it, and the corruption that plagued it. The author called for British tutelage. In essence, the article was rather similar to that of Sun Yatsen. The major difference lay in its call for British support to prop up the Manchu dynasty.[195] The author spoke with power and authority, and it is to Sun Yatsen's credit that he had the courage to argue against him. Professor Wu Xiangxiang has speculated that 'L' could very well have been the famous missionary, Timothy

---

192. *China Mail*, 21 May 1895, p. 3, col. 7.
193. Nakagawa Tsunejiro to Hara Takashi, 17 April 1895, in *Hara Takashi kankei bunsho*, p. 396.
194. This controversy arose during an international conference on Sun Yatsen, held near Beijing in March 1985, and was sparked off by a well-argued paper by Professor Lin Zengping, who took the view that the Sun Yatsen of this period was a reformer. That paper, jointly authored with Li Yumin, was entitled 'Sun Zhongshan zaoqi sixiang shuping'.
195. 'L', 'The Future of China', pp. 159–74.

Richard.[196] Although Professor Wu does not seem to have read the article itself, and the article does not appear to take the stand of a missionary, the speculation is none the less interesting. Timothy Richard himself said that, shortly after the kidnapping incident, Sun Yatsen went to see him.[197] Slater reported that on 11 February 1897, Sun Yatsen went to the Foreign Missions Club at 151, Highbury Park Road.[198] The Club had been opened in December 1893 to offer temporary accommodation to missionaries on furlough.[199] Field-work shows that the Club had since moved to 26, Aberdeen Park,[200] but the Visitors' Book has survived. Sun Yatsen's signature was dated 18 February 1897.[201] Miss G.M. Dawe, retired manageress of the Club, told me that, as a rule, only those who had spent at least one night as a resident of the Club would sign the Visitors' Book.[202] It seems, therefore, that Sun Yatsen visited Timothy Richard first on 11 February, and that he returned a week later to spend a longer period of time with this famous missionary. Richard's recollection of a lengthy debate with Sun Yatsen corroborates this.[203] Thus, if Professor Wu's speculation is correct, then it appears that the verbal debate turned into written exchanges, and further testifies to Sun Yatsen's courage and hence his keenness to establish himself in the eyes of the world by taking on somebody of Timothy Richard's standing.

In addition to the London articles, there is other evidence to support the interpretation that part of Sun Yatsen's preoccupation in London was to attract the attention of influential Britons. One such piece of evidence is his translation of Dr Osborne's work on first aid. In the Preface to his Chinese translation, Sun

196. Wu Xiangxiang, *Sun Yixian zhuan*, Vol. 1, p. 194. Among other things, Professor Wu thought that 'L' could have stood for the first letter of Richard's Chinese name, Li.

197. Timothy Richard, *Forty-five Years in China* (New York, Stokes, 1916), p. 350. Professor Schiffrin was the first to use this source (*Origins*, p. 128, n. 101).

198. Chinese Legation Archives, Slater to Chinese minister, 30 January to 14 February 1897, in Luo Jialun, *Shiliao*, p. 143.

199. Phyllis Thompson, *A Place for Pilgrims: The Story of the Foreign Missions Club in Highbury, London* (London, 1983), pp. 2-3.

200. My research note of 15 May 1983.

201. Foreign Missions Club Visitors' Book, 18 February 1897.

202. My researcn notes of 21 May 1983. I am most grateful to Miss Dawe for seeing me, and to Mr Robert West for arranging the interview.

203. Richard, *Forty-five Years in China*, p. 350.

Yatsen wrote that the work had been rendered into French, German, Italian, and Japanese, and had been held in high esteem by the heads of these states. Then in the winter of 1896–7, he toured Windsor Castle with Dr Osborne, who invited him to translate it into Chinese as a tribute to the Diamond Jubilee of Queen Victoria's reign. He further wrote that subsequently Dr Osborne reported the plan to Her Majesty, who was greatly pleased and who declared that such a translation would benefit the millions of Chinese living under the Union Jack all over the world. Dr Osborne also planned to send copies of the Chinese version to the governors of Hong Kong and of the various British possessions in South-east Asia.[204] Thus, it seems reasonable to assume that Sun Yatsen's motives for translating the work were not only to benefit the overseas Chinese, but also to attract the attention of the Queen and Her Majesty's representatives throughout the British Empire.[205]

Sun Yatsen's statement is corroborated by other evidence. On Saturday, 31 October 1896, Mrs Cantlie wrote, 'Sun Yat Sen went to stay till Monday with Dr Osborne at Datchet'.[206] On Monday, 2 November 1896, she wrote, 'Sun came back & went to live again with Miss Pollard'.[207] On Monday, 28 June 1897, Minakata Kumagusu wrote in his diary that Sun Yatsen had given him three copies of the Chinese version of the work on first aid; and that Sun Yatsen had also presented a copy to the Queen and to Lord Salisbury, the binding of which alone cost £5 each.[208] It may be assumed that the fugitive would not have spent that amount of money unless he was quite determined to impress the recipients.

Another opportunity for Sun Yatsen to cultivate his public image came when Professor Herbert Giles of Cambridge wrote to

---

204. Sun Yatsen, 'Hongshizihui jiusheng diyifa yixu', in *Sun Zhongshan quanji*, Vol. 1, pp. 107–8.
205. Professor Chen Xiqi thought that Sun Yatsen's motive for translating the work was the need for first aid in his envisaged armed uprisings. See his article entitled 'Guanyu Sun Zhongshan de daxue shidai', in *Sun Zhongshan yanjiu luncong*, Vol. 1, 1983, p. 3. This may well have been the case, but his statement in the Preface of the Chinese version should not be overlooked either.
206. Mrs Cantlie's diary, 31 October 1896.
207. Mrs Cantlie's diary, 2 November 1896. It will be recalled that Miss Lucy Pollard was the landlady of 8, Gray's Inn Place.
208. Minakata Kumagusu, *Zenshu*, Supplement, Vol. 2, p. 92.

Dr Cantlie for information about Sun Yatsen so as to prepare an entry for the *Chinese Biographical Dictionary* which he was compiling.[209] To Professor Giles Sun Yatsen replied that he was prepared to go through 'burning fire and boiling oil' in order to collect like-minded heroes to overthrow Manchu misrule and regenerate China; and that his narrow escape from death at the hands of the Legation was not only his own good fortune but also the good fortune of the four hundred million Chinese people.[210] No plainer language could have been chosen to proclaim to the world that he was the leader, and that he was destined to create a new China.

---

209. Sun Yatsen to Giles, n.d., in *Sun Zhongshan quanji*, Vol. 1, p. 46.
210. Sun Yatsen to Giles, n.d., in *Sun Zhongshan quanji*, Vol. 1, pp. 46-7.

6 Sun Yatsen as Observer

'Youzhi jingcheng' ['The Ambition Fulfilled']

Sun Yatsen

I The Power

Sun Yatsen once said that the survival of China was dependent on her successful diplomatic relations with Great Britain.[2] Where could he have got this idea? No doubt he would have read about the power of the British Empire; and, of course, he would have seen evidence of it in the Far East. But this was greatly over-shadowed by what he saw and experienced in England itself. While he was in London, something happened there to which no historian so far seems to have paid any attention. This was the Jubilee celebrations to mark the sixtieth year of Queen Victoria's reign.

On 27 June 1897, Minakata Kumagusu wrote, 'Sun [Yatsen] and Tajima saw the Naval Review yesterday, but Sun said that because of the rain he could not see anything'.[3] This information shows that Sun Yatsen went to watch the Naval Review at Spit-head in Portsmouth. Although this evidence is not corroborated by other sources, such as the private detective's report, there is no reason to doubt its reliability because it has been proved often enough that the detective could have been more vigilant in watching his subject. In addition, the Naval Review took place on a Saturday, and the detective was generally more slack on weekends than on weekdays. It is possible, however, to verify the reference to the rain, about which Sun Yatsen complained. 'To the end', reported *The Times*, 'fortune has smiled on the splen-dours of the Jubilee ... on Saturday the weather was glorious during the Review, and it was not until all was over that a thunderstorm broke over Portsmouth, which, though it wetted

---

1. Sun Yatsen, 'Jianguo fanglue zhiyi', p. 196.
2. Sun Yatsen, 'Jianguo fanglue zhiyi', p. 210.
3. Minakata Kumagusu's diary, 27 June 1897, in *Zenshu*, Supplement, Vol. 2, p. 92.

thousands to the skin, passed off before night, and enhanced rather than detracted from the brilliant effect of the orderly illumination of the long array of ships'.[4] Thus, there is a direct contradiction between Kumagusu's diary and *The Times*. In this case, *The Times* is to be believed. To begin with, Kumagusu himself was not at Portsmouth. His information about the weather was merely second-hand. Furthermore, Kumagusu did not speak Chinese; and Sun Yatsen did not speak Japanese. The two men conversed in bad English. Sun Yatsen could very well have said that it rained so heavily he could not see anything, referring to the heavy rain rather than the Review. It is, of course, possible that Sun Yatsen arrived at Portsmouth in time for the rain but not the Review. But given his great eagerness to learn about Britain, it is unlikely that he would have been so slack as to have missed something so important. In any case, the Review did not begin until 2 p.m.,[5] and it is most improbable that Sun Yatsen would have missed it.

The experience of being at Spithead in the midst of a vast crowd, and in sight of the 165 British ships partaking in the Review, could not have failed to leave a deep impression on him. In addition to the British men-of-war there were fourteen foreign warships 'representing the sea Powers of the world'.[6] They had come from Austria-Hungary, Denmark, France, Germany, Italy, Japan, Holland, Norway, Portugal, Russia, Spain, Sweden, and the United States of America.[7] The day before the Review, *The Times* printed an official chart showing the positions of the various ships in five lines.[8] On the actual day, 'Our Special Correspondent, indeed, observes this morning that the spectacle is almost too vast to be seen as a whole. The main lines in which the Fleet is disposed are more than five nautical miles in length, and the width ... nearly one mile. Five square miles of sea covered with ships moored as close together as safety will permit are rather more than any but a well trained eye can pretend to see at once'.[9] The five lines of ships, if joined together, would

4. *The Times*, 28 June 1897, p. 11, col. 3.
5. *The Times*, 25 June 1897, p. 13, cols. 5–6.
6. *The Times*, 25 June 1897, p. 15, col. 2.
7. *The Times*, 25 June 1897, p. 15, cols. 2–3.
8. *The Times*, 25 June 1897, p. 13, right across the top of the page.
9. *The Times*, 26 June 1897, p. 11, col. 3.

have stretched for some thirty miles, and were as symmetrically arrayed and daintily dressed as the finest regiment of Guards on parade in Hyde Park on some gala day.[10] The countless flags supplied the tone of rejoicing.[11]

At 2 p.m., the *Victoria and Albert*, flying the Royal Standard and with the Prince of Wales on board, left Portsmouth harbour for Spithead to inspect the Fleet on behalf of the Queen. Guns on board ships from designated divisions fired a salute as he sailed past. In addition, officers and men gave three cheers as he passed each ship; and, in those which possessed bands, the National Anthem was played. When the yacht came to anchor, a signal was made from the *Renown* and three cheers were given throughout the Fleet.[12] The cheers of some 40,000 officers and men[13] would have sounded very impressive indeed. The available records show that Sun Yatsen had never in his life seen or heard anything remotely similar in grandeur and magnitude to this demonstration of national strength and solidarity.

The Fleet he saw 'is certainly the most formidable in all its elements and qualities that has ever been brought together, and such as no combination of other nations can rival. It is at once the most powerful and far-reaching weapon which the world has ever seen. Proud as all Britons must be of this unexampled exhibition of national strength, skill, and ingenuity ...',[14] yet, this 'unique naval display has not entailed the withdrawal of a single ship from the foreign stations, whither indeed two vessels have very lately been despatched', wrote *The Times*. 'Nor is it by any means a full presentation of the British Navy in home waters. Other ships could have been commissioned without extraordinary effort, and some here present have men considerably in excess of their complements'. That paper continued, 'The spectacle was witnessed by the ships sent by all the Great Powers of the world, and, without unseemly boasting, we may assume that they have taken its lessons to heart ... It is unnecessary to dwell on the impression produced by this unparalleled scene on the imagination of the spectators ... That supremacy at sea belongs to Great

10. *The Times*, 28 June 1897, p. 11, col. 2.
11. *The Times*, 28 June 1897, p. 15, col. 1.
12. *The Times*, 25 June 1897, p. 13, cols. 5–6.
13. *The Times*, 28 June 1897, p. 11, col. 2.
14. *The Times*, 25 June 1897, p. 13, col. 1.

Britain, and that she has no intention of abandoning it, is a great fact which no man with his eyes open, whether he be an Englishman or not, can pretend to dispute'.[15] It may be assumed that he was one of those who had learnt the 'great object lesson'.[16]

Such an object lesson may indeed help to throw some light on at least one historical phenomenon. When the 1911 Revolution broke out in China, Sun Yatsen was in Denver, Colorado.[17] He wanted to return to China as quickly as he could, and the fastest route would have been to cross the Pacific. But he went via London instead. Before leaving New York, he telegraphed his friend Homer Lea, expressing his confidence that no viable government could be formed in China before his return.[18] When he reached London, Mrs Cantlie handed him a copy of a telegram which the revolutionaries in China had sent him, and in which they asked him to be the president of the newly established Republic.[19] To the British reporters, therefore, he said that he would be pleased to form a new government and to head it when called upon to do so by his fellow countrymen.[20] But on 16 November 1911, when he was still in Europe, he cabled China suggesting that Yuan Shikai should be the new president.[21] Historians have found this sudden change of attitude inexplicable. It transpires that on 13 November 1911, he and Homer Lea had signed a statement and had had it submitted to the British Foreign Office. In it, he sought British support and promised, among other things, to place the Chinese navy under the command of British officers subject to his own orders, confident that he was to become the president.[22] The reaction of the foreign secretary, Sir

15. *The Times*, 28 June 1897, p. 11, cols. 2–3.
16. *The Times*, 28 June 1897, p. 15, col. 1. .
17. Harold Z. Schiffrin, *Sun Yat-sen: Reluctant Revolutionary* (Boston, Little Brown, 1980), p. 155 (hereafter cited as *Reluctant Revolutionary*).
18. Sun Yatsen to Homer Lea (telegram), 31 October 1911, in *Sun Zhongshan quanji*, Vol. 1, p. 544.
19. Cantlie and Seaver, *Sir James Cantlie*, pp. 108–9.
20. See the report by British journalists, as collected in *Sun Zhongshan quanji*, Vol. 1, p. 559.
21. Sun Yatsen to Revolutionary Government in China, care of *Minlibao*, 16 November 1911, in *Sun Zhongshan quanji*, Vol. 1, p. 546.
22. Harold Z. Schiffrin, 'The Enigma of Sun Yat-sen', in Mary Wright (ed.), *China in Revolution: The First Phase, 1900–1903* (New Haven, Yale University Press, 1968), p. 471 (hereafter cited as 'Enigma'), quoting FO 371/1905, Grey to Jordan, Dispatch 45661, 14 November 1911, encl. Dawson to Grey, 13 November 1911.

Edward Grey, was that Yuan Shikai was best qualified to lead China.[23] Consequently, on his arrival back at Guangzhou, he tried hard to persuade his followers that it would be expedient for the time being to use Yuan Shikai to terminate 260 years of Manchu tyranny, although the strong man was not trustworthy and might even continue to abuse power just as the Manchus had done.[24]

In his submission to the British Foreign Office, Sun Yatsen also said that he wanted to form an alliance with Britain and the United States, and claimed that 'Senators [sic] Knox and Root were interested, and prepared to lend the revolutionaries one million pounds if Britain agreed'.[25] Professor Schiffrin describes this as 'desperate bluff', and interprets it as 'Sun's long-shot gamble for personal success'.[26] Professor Wilbur also believes that Sun Yatsen's claim was 'truly'[27] desperate, and interprets it as his single-minded concentration on 'the overthrow of the hated Manchus and the establishment of a progressive regime to benefit the Chinese nation'.[28] In the context of the present analysis, Sun Yatsen's action substantiates his expressed view that the survival of China depended on her successful diplomatic relations with Great Britain. The view appears to have been formed while he was in London, particularly during the Jubilee celebrations, when he witnessed an unprecedented show of British might.

The Naval Review on Saturday, 26 June 1897, was only part of the celebrations. The Queen's Procession in London on 22 June 1897 had been just as, if not more, spectacular. There are no references to Sun Yatsen having watched the Procession. But since he had gone as far as Portsmouth to see the Naval Review, there is no reason to suppose that he would not have watched the Queen's Procession in London four days before. Months of meticulous preparations had preceded this day, and the map showing the route of the Procession was repeatedly printed in the newspapers for weeks beforehand.

---

23. Schiffrin, 'Enigma', p. 472.
24. Record of a conversation between Sun Yatsen and Hu Hanmin, 21 December 1911, in *Sun Zhongshan quanji*, Vol. 1, p. 569.
25. Schiffrin, 'Enigma', p. 471.
26. Schiffrin, 'Enigma', p. 472.
27. Wilbur, *Sun Yat-sen*, p. 74.
28. Wilbur, *Sun Yat-sen*, p. 75.

On the day itself, a total of 46,943 troops were employed in the Procession, lining the streets and as guards of honour.[29] Every place to which the general public was admitted was thronged, because people from the outlying districts had been travelling up to London 'and murdering the sleep of the inhabitants on their lines of march all night'.[30] At midnight, men and women began taking their places at the south end of London Bridge as soon as it had been closed to traffic; and by early dawn, Trafalgar Square was overspilling with people.[31]

Shortly after 9 a.m., the Procession began.[32] First came the Royal Horse Guards, with the band of the same regiment. Next came the colonial mounted troops with the colonial premiers: the Canadian Hussars, Dragoons, and Mounted Police; the New South Wales Lancers and Mounted Rifles, the Victorian Mounted Rifles, the Queensland Mounted Rifles, and the South Australian Lancers and Mounted Rifles; the New Zealand Mounted Troops; the Cape Mounted Rifles and Natal Carabiniers; the Umvoti, Natal, and Border Mounted Rifles; the Mounted Troops of the Crown Colonies, Zaptiehs from Cyprus, and the Trinidad Mounted Rifles; and a few Rhodesian Horse.[33]

Third, and heralded by the band of the 1st Middlesex, came the colonial infantry: the Malta Militia and Artillery, the Canadian Active Militia, the 48th Canadian Highlanders, the West Australian Artillery Volunteers, the Trinidad Field Artillery, the West Australian Infantry, the Trinidad Infantry, the Borneo Police, and the Trinidad Police. And the band of the London Scottish headed the Jamaica Artillery, the Sierra Leone Artillery and Frontier Police, the Royal Niger Hausas, the Gold Coast Hausas, the British Guiana Police, the Ceylon Light Infantry and Artillery Volunteers, the Chinese Police from Hong Kong, and the Straits Settlements Police.[34]

At 9.45, the Jubilee pageant itself began,[35] with the appearance of four troopers of the 2nd Life Guards. The cavalry, with

29. *The Times*, 23 June 1897, p. 9, col. 2.
30. *The Times*, 23 June 1897, p. 9, col. 1.
31. *The Times*, 23 June 1897, p. 9, col. 1.
32. *The Times*, 23 June 1897, p. 9, col. 4.
33. *The Times*, 23 June 1897, p. 9, col. 1.
34. *The Times*, 23 June 1897, p. 9, cols. 1–2.
35. *The Times*, 23 June 1897, p. 9, col. 4.

its bands playing the National Anthem, were followed by the bluejackets; Dragoons by Artillery, Hussars by Lancers, 'in such numbers that the eye got dazzled with the brilliant uniforms'. As the pageant moved in stately majesty along its appointed course, 'Guns boomed in Hyde Park, the bells changed from St Paul's, and it seemed as though the laggard sun had come to the conclusion that it was time for him to be up and doing. He was roused as by a signal, and he did his duty nobly all day', wrote *The Times*. 'Huge cheers rose on every side, and the waving of white handkerchiefs was a pretty spectacle'.[36]

Next came the carriages of the foreign envoys, among whom was seen the new Chinese minister, carrying a fan and seated next to the papal nuncio. Next came the carriages of the princesses of the royal families from all over the world, among them Empress Frederick, Princess Charles of Denmark, Princess Frederica of Hanover, the Princess of Bulgaria, and the Princess of Naples. There followed forty foreign princes. 'Every uniform that is worn under the sun seemed to be represented'.[37]

Then the signal was given that Her Majesty was leaving the Palace. Guns were fired and the massed bands thundered forth the National Anthem. The crowd roared with cheers, which seemed to increase in volume at every moment, and long after the procession ceased to be in view, the acclamations of the multitude reached the ear like the sound of a tumultuous sea.[38]

What would have been Sun Yatsen's impression had he been in the midst of all this? The first part of the Procession, representing the political and military strength of dominions, colonies, and dependencies should have given him a realistic sense of the size and power of the British Empire. The pageant itself would not have failed to impress upon him Britain's military might and all the infrastructure that went with it, which had created the Empire. The enthusiasm of the crowd for 'Queen and Country' would have left everlasting memories of the wonders that nationalism could bring about.

36. *The Times*, 23 June 1897, p. 9, cols. 2–3.
37. *The Times*, 23 June 1897, p. 9, col. 4. It was the custom in Europe for the wife of a member of royalty to be called by her husband's name. Empress Frederick, for example, was the widow of Frederick II of Germany. She was the eldest daughter of Queen Victoria.
38. *The Times*, 23 June 1897, p. 9, col. 5.

The Queen's Procession and the Naval Review were of course the highlights. There were, however, nation-wide celebrations which did not attract as much attention from the press. Even with the Queen's Procession itself, numerous civilians had been involved for quite some time in its preparations. The degree of national fervour involved could not but have impressed Sun Yatsen. Mrs Cantlie, for example, had been elected honorary secretary of the Jubilee Committee of Charing Cross.[39] On 17 June, she 'went to Hospital & began the decorations'. By this time, the City was already 'looking very gay'.[40] On Saturday, 19 June, all the Cantlies 'went down to Barnes on the top of an omnibus & saw all the decorations on the way'.[41] On 22 June, Mrs Cantlie wrote, 'The Queen's Jubilee. God save the Queen'. Then she went with her children to Charing Cross Hospital to watch the Procession. 'We saw splendidly & the who [whole] procession was a glorious one. Everything well arranged & no accidents to speak of & only a few faints'. Dr Cantlie was on duty first at Trafalgar Square and then at Scotland Yard with an ambulance company. He treated one such case. 'He was called to the Hon Balfour's house in Downing St where Miss Balfour had taken in a fainting woman'. The Cantlies stayed to watch the illuminations at night and did not go to bed until 11 p.m.[42]

The Cantlies went to the Naval Review, too, but not as ordinary spectators on the shore. 'We went (Hamish & I) to the Royal Engineers Submarine Station by invitation of Col. Wilkinson where we embarked on a steamer & went up & down the lines. There were 5 lines of battleships 5 miles long. Truly the most magnificent sight ever seen in these waters … In the evening we went on the roof & from there saw all the ships illuminated by electricity at 9.15 p.m. Suddenly every ship stood out in brilliant relief'.[43]

As mentioned, Sun Yatsen was almost part of the Cantlie family. His regular visits and meals there would have given him

---

39. See, for example, the entry in her diary on 5 and 24 May, and on 4 and 10 June 1897. The meetings took place at Mrs Kitto's — St Martin's Vicarage — which suggests that the committee was for the Charing Cross area, and not merely for Charing Cross Hospital.
40. Mrs Cantlie's diary, 17 June 1897.
41. Mrs Cantlie's diary, 19 June 1897.
42. Mrs Cantlie's diary, 22 June 1897.
43. Mrs Cantlie's diary, 26 June 1897.

plenty of opportunity to listen to what Dr and Mrs Cantlie had to say. And although he had not been privileged enough to have inspected all the men-of-war one by one during the Naval Review, they would have shared their experience with him. Even if he had not read *The Times* editorial about it, they might have done so and would have told him that not the least remarkable feature about the fleet was that by far the larger part of it had been built within the previous ten years.[44] This was concrete evidence of Britain's vitality and her extraordinary capacity for self-regeneration, in view of the fact that the Royal Navy had been enjoying naval supremacy for a very long time, certainly since the beginning of the nineteenth century. In addition, 'when constructors and engineers have done their best, it is still upon her seamanship and her fighting instincts that she must rely in whatever struggles the future may bring', and *The Times* believed that British sailors were superior to those of any other nation.[45] What Sun Yatsen heard and personally experienced during the Jubilee celebrations could only have reinforced what Edwin Collins had been telling him all along about the Anglo-Saxons and nationalism. After all, Dr Cantlie himself called London 'the very centre of the universe'.[46]

II The Glory

The Jubilee celebrations may be described as the climax of Sun Yatsen's lessons in London. There were numerous others he would have learnt in everyday life in the nine months since he had set foot on British soil.

To begin with, the place where he lived, 8, Gray's Inn Place, was affiliated to Gray's Inn. Contrary to the belief of many Chinese historians, Gray's Inn was no ordinary 'inn',[47] but was one of the major Inns of Court that trained all the barristers for

---

44. *The Times*, 26 June 1897, p. 11, col. 3.

45. *The Times*, 26 June 1897, p. 11, col. 3.

46. Sun Yatsen, *Kidnapped in London*, p. 30. As analysed in Chapter 4, Section III, Dr Cantlie was the true author of this booklet.

47. Luo Jialun, *Shiliao*, p. 20. Shang Mingxuan, *Sun Zhongshan zhuan*, p. 41; Hu Qufei, *Sun Zhongshan xiansheng zhuan* (Taipei, 1968, second edition), p. 25; Wu Xiangxiang, *Sun Yixian zhuan*, Vol. 1, p. 152; and *Sun Zhongshan quanji*, Vol. 1, p. 55.

Britain as well as the Empire. Sun Yatsen also made a point of visiting the other Inns of Court. On 13 November 1896, he was reported to have gone to No. 7, Stone Buildings, in Chancery Lane.[48] The Stone Buildings were of course part of Lincoln's Inn.[49] Slater said that Sun Yatsen went to the Stone Buildings accompanied by 'a Chinaman'. This person has yet to be identified; but there are some clues. No. 7, Stone Buildings, had been used by the Masters of the Exchequer until about 1880, when the offices therein were converted into common-rooms of the Inn.[50] Thus, the 'Chinaman' was probably a member of Lincoln's Inn, very likely a student.

The detective continued, 'They remained here half an hour when they went to the Hall and Library Stone Buildings remaining half an hour'.[51] This reference had led a modern historian to allege that Sun Yatsen went to a certain Stone Building Library (Shishi tushuguan) for books, in addition to those in the British Museum.[52] Little does he realize that in those days, Stone Buildings was a synonym for Lincoln's Inn,[53] and therefore the Library in Stone Buildings simply meant the Library of Lincoln's Inn. Spending half an hour in both the Hall and the Library would suggest that Sun Yatsen was given an introduction to the most prominent features of that Honourable Society.

The detective went on, 'They then proceeded to the Hall and Library of the Inner Temple after which he returned home'.[54] No historian who has used the detective's report seems to have commented on this particular entry. Perhaps no relevance may be

---

48. Chinese Legation Archives, Slater to Chinese minister, 21 November 1896, in Luo Jialun, *Shiliao*, p. 123.

49. I am grateful to Mr Roderick Walker, librarian of Lincoln's Inn, for receiving me on 17 May 1983, and presenting me with the pertinent literature on that Honourable Society. I asked him about a visitors' book, if only to attempt to find corroborative evidence for the detective's report. Unfortunately, the present visitors' book dates back to 1946 only.

50. Sir Ronald Roxburgh (ed.), *The Records of the Honourable Society of Lincoln's Inn: The Black Books, Vol. 5, A.D. 1845–A.D. 1914* (London, 1968), p. xxxvii.

51. Chinese Legation Archives, Slater to Chinese minister, 21 November 1896, in Luo Jialun, *Shiliao*, p. 123.

52. Wu Xiangxiang, *Sun Yixian zhuan*, Vol. 1, p. 186.

53. Roxburgh (ed.), *The Records of the Honourable Society of Lincoln's Inn: The Black Books, Vol. 5, A.D. 1845–A.D. 1914*, p. xxxvii.

54. Chinese Legation Archives, Slater to Chinese minister, 21 November 1896, in Luo Jialun, *Shiliao*, p. 123.

seen in the fact that Sun Yatsen visited a 'temple'. But like Gray's Inn, the Inner Temple was no ordinary 'temple'. It was another of the Inns of Court that trained all the British barristers. Not only did these Inns train barristers, many of whom later became judges, but they also provided chambers for the barristers and judges. Indeed, each Inn was a very high-powered legal community, with its own educational and professional facilities, such as a library, dining-hall, chapel, common-rooms, lecture-rooms, chambers for the senior members, and residential quarters for the junior members, just like a college at Oxford or Cambridge.

The Inner Temple derived its name from the religious and military order of the Templars, founded in 1118, whose headquarters in Jerusalem were located near the church known as the Temple of Solomon. In 1308, the Templars in England were arrested and their land seized; and by 1381 it is certain that the lawyers had moved in. They have been there ever since.[55] The original Hall and Library were destroyed during the Second World War.[56] Fortunately, a tracing of the Library has survived, which has made it possible to reconstruct, to some extent, a mental picture of the sort of environment that greeted Sun Yatsen.[57] Right next to the Inner Temple was the Middle Temple (there was never an Outer Temple); and the two Temples jointly owned the Chapel, the Hall, and the Library.

As for Gray's Inn, although the detective never referred to his visiting the Hall and Library of that Honourable Society, it is difficult to believe that he visited the other Inns and not the one which was within one minute's walk of his lodgings. Thus, it is very likely that he visited all four Inns of Court in London.

In fact, it appears that Sun Yatsen had more to do with Gray's Inn than any of the other three. The detective constantly referred to Sun Yatsen's visits to 5, South Square. No. 5, South Square, was indeed No. 5 staircase in the South Square of Gray's Inn. Table 4 provides some statistics on these visits.

---

55. *Notes on the Constitution, Administration, History and Buildings of the Inner Temple* (London, 1962), p. 4.
56. *Notes on the Constitution, Administration, History and Buildings of the Inner Temple*, pp. 8–9.
57. I am most grateful to the librarian of the Inner Temple, Mr W. W. S. Breem, for receiving me on 17 May 1983, and for showing me the precious tracing and the grounds.

Table 4 Sun Yatsen's Visits to 5, South Square, as Recorded by Slater, the Private Detective Agency[58]

Date	Time	Duration
Mon., 23 Nov. 1896	9.30	10 min
Sat., 19 Dec. 1896	10.30	10 min
Tue., 22 Dec. 1896	Morning	10 min
Wed., 23 Dec. 1896	9.45	A few minutes
Sat., 2 Jan. 1897	Unspecified	Unspecified
Mon., 4 Jan. 1897	10.30	Unspecified
Thur., 7 Jan. 1897	Unspecified	Unspecified
Sat., 9 Jan. 1897	11.30	Unspecified
Mon., 11 Jan. 1897	11.00	Unspecified
Tue., 12 Jan. 1897	10.30	Unspecified
Mon., 18 Jan. 1897	10.30	Unspecified
Fri., 29 Jan. 1897	9.50	10 min
Mon., 1 Feb. 1897	10.15	A few minutes
(*Reports missing between 23 April and 9 June 1897*)		
Thur., 17 Jun. 1897	Unspecified	Unspecified
(*Reports blank on Sun Yatsen thereafter*)		

These visits appear to have been extraordinarily frequent and brief. How can they be interpreted? To begin with, finding out the occupants of 5, South Square, may help. Unfortunately, the pertinent records of Gray's Inn were destroyed by bombing during the Second World War.[59] The *Law Lists* of 1896 and 1897 were checked in vain.[60] Again, *Kelly's* came to the rescue; the authorities helped to find out that the tenants of 5, South Square, were Frederick Dredge, Henry George Hibbert, Charles Hugh Horniman, and James Charles Marse.[61]

---

58. Slater's relevant reports were reproduced in Luo Jialun, *Shiliao*, pp. 118–65.
59. I wish to thank Mrs C. Butters of Gray's Inn Library, for receiving me on 16 May 1983 and offering this information.
60. I am indebted to Mr J. A. Tomlin and Miss Donna Robinson of the Senate of the Inns of Court and the Bar for having helped me check the *Law Lists*.
61. D. W. Lee to Wong, 23 November 1983, and encl. For a moment the name Henry George caused a great deal of excitement in me, because Sun Yatsen is alleged to have been greatly influenced by him. But unfortunately the surname of this Henry George was Hibbert.

With this information, another trip to Gray's Inn was made. The newly appointed librarian, Mrs Teresa Thom, was most helpful. Numerous references were checked.[62] There was no information whatever about Marse. Two records on Dredge have survived, both concerning his application to have 'the House Chambers in his occupation at No. 5 in South Square' enlarged. His application was rejected.[63] As for Hibbert, if he was the same person as listed in *Men-at-the-Bar* and *Alumni Cantabrigiensis*, then he was a 56-year-old barrister,[64] who would have been too busy to see anybody in prime office hours unless he was paid to do so. And there is no evidence to suggest that Sun Yatsen was involved in legal matters so important as to warrant such expense. Even if he were, he would have dealt with a solicitor, and not a barrister direct.

An extensive search yielded some most interesting information about Horniman. His application to be a student of Gray's Inn has been preserved. In the document, dated 16 January 1895, Horniman stated that he was 22 years old and the third son of William Horniman, who was a retired paymaster-in-chief of the Royal Navy living in Hampshire. He described himself as a journalist. He was admitted on 6 November 1895.[65] There is no record of his being called to the Bar, which suggests that he either discontinued or failed.[66]

Thus, Hugh Horniman is most likely to have been the person

62. They included the *Law List, 1897*; *Gray's Inn Book of Orders, March 1894 to April 1899*; *Admissions Register of Middle Temple*; *Admissions Register of Lincoln's Inn*; a list of manuscript documents in the custody or control of the Library of the Honourable Society of Gray's Inn from *circa* mid-sixteenth century to *circa* 1900, by R. A. Rontledge, 1975 (typescript); Joseph Foster, *Alumni Oxoniensis (Ser. 2) 1715–1886*; and *Dictionary of National Biography*, Index 1901–21.

63. Gray's Inn MSS, Pension, 4 November 1890, *Gray's Inn Book of Orders*, Vol. 28 (May 1888–March 1894), pp. 284 and 323.

64. Joseph Foster (comp.), *Men-at-the-Bar* (London, Hazell, Watson and Viney, 1889, second edition), p. 216; and J. A. Venn (comp.), *Alumni Cantabrigiensis: A biographical list of all known students, graduates, and holders of office at the University of Cambridge from the earliest times to 1900. Part 2, from 1752–1900* (Cambridge, Cambridge University Press, 1947), Vol. 3, p. 356.

65. Gray's Inn MSS, Admission Document, 16 January 1895. This document is corroborated by an entry in another collection of Gray's Inn MSS, entitled 'Gray's Inn Admissions and Calls Etc.'

66. Both the *Gray's Inn Call Register* and the contemporary *Law Lists* have been searched for his name, in vain.

to whom Sun Yatsen paid those regular, albeit brief, visits which
seem to have continued throughout his sojourn in London.
Horniman was a student, and therefore was perhaps more inclined to give his time free. He had been a journalist, and would
have been interested in someone like Sun Yatsen, if only because
of the great sensation caused by the kidnapping saga. In 1906,
and for the first time in his life, Sun Yatsen voiced publicly his
views on the question of a constitution. He said that he had made
a study of the various constitutions of the world, and had found
that of all the unwritten constitutions, the British was the best.
However, the British constitution could not be copied because it
had evolved over a period of six to seven hundred years, so that
much of it was convention.[67] It seems that the only occasion on
which Sun Yatsen had the opportunity to study the British constitution in some detail was during his sojourn in London. It is
quite possible, therefore, that he made an attempt to understand
the British constitution and British law under the supervision of
the young law student. The brief but frequent visits may mean
that Sun Yatsen went to Hugh Horniman either to borrow and
return books, or to seek quick advice on problems arising out of
his reading. Horniman, as a student of Gray's Inn, might have
given him an outline of the history of the Inn as well.[68]

In 1921, when Sun Yatsen again spoke publicly on the subject
of a constitution, he no longer insisted that the British constitution could not be copied, even if partially.[69] A plausible explanation lies in the fact that the British constitution was that of a
monarchy, and what Sun Yatsen wanted to do in 1906 was to rid
China of its monarchy. By 1921, however, the Chinese Republic
had existed for a decade, with less threat of a revival of the
monarchy. As a result, Sun Yatsen probably had fewer reservations about praising the British system. But to return to 1896-7,
when Sun Yatsen seems to have been trying hard to understand
the Westminster system, it is inconceivable that he did not visit
the Houses of Parliament. The private detective referred to his

---

67. Sun Yatsen, 'Zai Dongjing *Minbao* Chuangkan zhounian qingzhu dahui
de yanshuo', in *Sun Zhongshan quanji*, Vol. 1, pp. 329-30.
68. For details about the Inn, see *The Honourable Society of Gray's Inn*
(London, 1976, second edition), pp. 18-26.
69. Sun Yatsen, 'Wuquan xianfa', in *Sun Zhongshan xuanji*, pp. 485-98.

doing so on Saturday, 9 October 1896.[70] Although the timing of the visit as contained in the report is suspect,[71] it is most likely that he would have done so at some point during his sojourn in London.

The detective also reported that on 18 January 1897, Sun Yatsen went at 1.30 p.m. from 46, Devonshire Street, by cab to the Constitutional Club in Northumberland Avenue. He left the Club at 5.30 p.m.[72] It has not been possible to find out what happened in the Club. Very probably, Sun Yatsen had been telling the Cantlies about his efforts to understand the British constitution, was informed on this occasion that a particular function was going to take place in the Club, and left in a hurry to attend it.

Agriculture and husbandry had interested Sun Yatsen greatly even before he went to England. One essay written around 1891 on modernizing Chinese agriculture along Western lines has been attributed to him.[73] Similar proposals were contained in two important memorials he wrote to the Chinese authorities in 1890[74] and 1894[75] respectively. With good reason, these interests have been hailed as evidence of his great concern for the economy of the nation and the livelihood of the people.[76] While in London, he went on 8 December 1896 to the Royal Agricultural Hall at Islington.[77] There, he saw the full glory of British husbandry. 'The largest and most important of the shows of Christmas fat stock held annually in England' had opened at the Royal Agricultural Hall the day before. The show had been instituted by the Smithfield Club, principally for the purpose of 'supplying the cattle markets of Smithfield and other places with the cheapest and best meat'. The 1896 show was the ninety-ninth of

70. Chinese Legation Archives, Slater to Macartney, 12 October 1896, in Luo Jialun, *Shiliao*, p. 115.
71. See Chapter 3, Section II.
72. Chinese Legation Archives, Slater to Chinese minister, 3–21 January 1897, in Luo Jialun, *Shiliao*, pp. 137–8.
73. Sun Yatsen, 'Nunggong', in *Sun Zhongshan quanji*, Vol. 1, pp. 3–6.
74. Sun Yatsen, 'Zhi Zheng Zaoru shu', in *Sun Zhongshan quanji*, Vol. 1, pp. 1–3.
75. Sun Yatsen, 'Shang Li Hongzhang shu', in *Sun Zhongshan quanji*, Vol. 1, pp. 8–18.
76. Chen Xiqu, 'Guanyu Sun Zhongshan de daxue shidai', Vol. 1, pp. 10–11.
77. Chinese Legation Archives, Slater to Chinese minister, 16 December 1896, in Luo Jialun, *Shiliao*, pp. 129–30.

the series, and the total value of the prizes offered for competition on this occasion was £3,822. Among the contestants were 334 head of cattle, 220 pens of sheep, and 102 pens of pigs. In addition, 23 cattle and 33 sheep were entered for the carcass competition.[78] The Devon, Hereford, Shorthorn, Sussex, Red Polled, Aberdeen, Galloway, Welsh, Highland, and Cross-bred breeds of cattle were amongst those on show. Breeds of sheep on show included the Leicester, Border Leicester, Cotswold, Lincoln, Romney Marsh, Devon, Southdown, Hampshire, Suffolk, Shropshire, Oxford, Cross-bred, Cheviot, Mountain, Dorset, and so on. The breeds of pig included Small White, Middle White, Black, Berkshire, Tamworth, and Cross-bred.[79] How much Sun Yatsen would have absorbed is an open question. But the display could not have failed to impress him with its variety, richness, and good organization.

For the third year in succession, the show of dead table poultry was held in conjunction with the cattle show: 884 chickens, 138 ducks, 102 geese, 54 turkeys, 16 guinea fowl, 40 pigeons, and 15 rabbits and hares. Among these entries were 229 home-bred fowl and 165 foreign fowl (French and Belgian). The 153 entries of French poultry comprised representatives of the Faverolles, La Fleche, Bresse, Houdan, Gascogue, Gatinais, and other breeds. The Belgian poultry industry was represented by 24 specimens of the Coucon de Malines breed. 'The inclusion of this foreign section should prove an instructive novelty', wrote The Times.[80]

In the miscellaneous section of the show, all the available space was occupied. The root and seed stands were described as particularly attractive. Heaps of mangels, swedes, potatoes, seed corn, and vegetable seeds of all varieties were exhibited. Heavy machinery, including dairy implements and appliances, was shown in the bays on the ground floor, where all the leading firms were represented. Altogether, there were about 250 exhibitors in the miscellaneous section.[81]

These details, and others which follow, are of much more than anecdotal interest. The demonstration of the great wealth and

---

78. The Times, 7 December 1896, p. 4, col. 1.
79. The Times, 8 December 1896, p. 12, cols. 1–2.
80. The Times, 8 December 1896, p. 12, col. 2.
81. The Times, 8 December 1896, p. 12, col. 2.

variety of British pastoral and agricultural produce, with prizes designed to stimulate improvements, and public display which provided a medium for spreading new ideas and techniques, might well have left a deep impression on Sun Yatsen, who was so keenly aware of the need to modernize Chinese agriculture. His great eagerness to see the show may be gleaned from the fact that he went to it the very afternoon it was opened to the public, on 8 December 1896, when the charge for admission was 5 shillings, as against the normal entrance fee of 1 shilling.[82]

The detective also reported that on 11 December 1896, Sun Yatsen went to the Crystal Palace. He spent the whole day there.[83] The Palace was originally built at Hyde Park in the centre of London in 1851 to house the Great Exhibition. Some 100,000 objects were sent by 5,000 exhibitors from all over the world.[84] China had been invited to participate,[85] but declined, saying that the Chinese government could not publicize the British invitation, although Chinese artisans might do what they liked.[86] Sun Yatsen's visit to the Crystal Palace represented a complete change of attitude among some Chinese from the conservative to the progressive.

After the Great Exhibition, the Palace was dismantled and re-erected in 1854 as a centre for popular entertainment on a large scale at Sydenham in south London, with an extension of 50 per cent more cubic space.[87] It seems highly unlikely that this

---

82. *The Times*, 8 December 1896, p. 12, col. 2.

83. Chinese Legation Archives, Slater to Chinese minister, 2–11 December 1896, in Luo Jialun, *Shiliao*, p. 130.

84. D. A. Girling (ed.), *Everyman's Encyclopaedia* (London, J.M. Dent & Sons, 1978, sixth edition), Vol. 3, pp. 750–1. The Crystal Palace was subsequently burnt down in 1936, so a mental picture of the environment in which Sun Yatsen found himself may be recreated only from existing literature about this example of British achievement.

85. FO 677/26, Bonham to Xu Guangjin, 11 June 1850, as summarized in J. Y. Wong, *Anglo-Chinese Relations, 1839–1860 : A Calendar of Chinese documents in the British Foreign Office Records* (London, Oxford University Press, 1983), p. 207 (hereafter cited as *Anglo-Chinese Relations*).

86. FO 677/26, Xu Guangjin to Bonham, 22 June 1850, as summarized in Wong, *Anglo-Chinese Relations*, p. 208.

87. Girling (ed.), *Everyman's Encyclopaedia*, pp. 750–1. The economy, lightness, and elegance of the building marked an architectural revolution. It was the first prefabricated building in the world. Ninety-five per cent of it was built of glass, supported by thin iron frames. The glass roof covered an area of 7.2 hectares. The sheet glass panels, 25.4 cm by 124.4 cm, were the largest yet

extraordinary place would have failed to make a deep impression upon a man who had come from a country where nothing of the kind existed.

What was happening at the Crystal Palace when Sun Yatsen went there on 8 December 1896? It transpired that this was the penultimate day of the fifth annual National Bicycle Show. The display was described as a remarkable one and had not been exceeded in the extent and variety of entries by any previous exhibition.[88] Surely, it is no coincidence that Sun Yatsen, coming from a country where the vast majority had to depend on their feet for travelling, showed such interest in this relatively new and cheap form of transport that was giving mobility to millions of Europeans. Mrs Cantlie, for example, had lessons in bicycle riding after she returned to England from Hong Kong.[89] Then she received £5 from her mother as a present for her new bicycle,[90] which she tried on 17 April 1897;[91] but soon had to have some repairs done to it.[92]

As for ocean transport, Sun Yatsen went to see some samples of the spectacular achievements of this seafaring nation on 10 March 1897, 'accompanied by another gentleman', at the Royal Albert Dock in East London, 'viewing various vessels therein'.[93] The Royal Albert Dock was among many docks constructed along the lower reaches of the River Thames.[94] To this dock came great ocean-going steamers to unload their cargoes, consisting mainly of grain, tobacco, and frozen meat.[95] It must be

---

(87. *continued*)
manufactured. And the glass alone amounted to 83,612 square metres. The whole structure was erected between July 1850 and January 1851. This phenomenal speed was accomplished by the use of standardized, interchangeable, mass-produced components, the use of steam-driven machinery, the division of labour, and general rationalization.

88. *The Times*, 5 December 1896, p. 13, cols. 2–3.

89. Mrs Cantlie's diary, 30–1 December 1896 and 1–5 January 1897.

90. Mrs Cantlie's diary, 31 March 1897.

91. Mrs Cantlie's diary, 17 April 1897.

92. Mrs Cantlie's diary, 21 April 1897.

93. Chinese Legation Archives, Slater to Chinese minister, 4–10 March 1897, in Luo Jialun, *Shiliao*, p. 147.

94. H.M. Tomlinson, 'Down in Dockland', in St John Adcock (ed.), *Wonderful London: The world's greatest city described by its best writers and pictured by its finest photographers* (London, Fleetway House, n.d.), Vol. 1, p. 148 (hereafter cited as *Wonderful London*).

95. Tomlinson, 'Down in Dockland', p. 151.

remembered that this was a time when the traffic at the London docks in terms of both ships and cargoes was among the greatest in the world.

It is not clear whether Sun Yatsen boarded any of the vessels which he viewed at the Royal Albert Dock, but there is evidence to show that subsequently he did have the opportunity to examine in detail at least one of the latest products of the British ship-building industry. The private detective reported that on 13 April 1897, 'a Chinaman accompanied by an Englishman' went with Sun Yatsen to Tilbury Docks and boarded a Japanese naval vessel, the *Fuji*, where they 'remained three hours and half [*sic*]'.[96] The so-called 'Chinaman' was in fact the Japanese botanist, Minakata Kumagusu, and the 'Englishman' was indeed the Irish nationalist, Rowland J. Mulkern. 'While we were being shown around by a sailor, Mr Tsuda came and showed us everything in detail. After that we went to the dining-room and were served drinks and soda water', wrote Minakata in his diary.[97] Neither the detective's report nor this entry in Minakata's diary offered any information about the origin of the *Fuji*. But *The Times* gave the secret away. She had just been built by the Thames Ironworks Company, and was to represent Japan in the Naval Review on 26 June 1897. She resembled in many respects the *Sovereign* class and in a few the *Majestic*. Her armament consisted of four 12-inch guns, ten 6-inch quick-firers, and twenty-four other guns.[98]

Sun Yatsen had had the opportunity to inspect, at least in part, what lay behind this British technology. On 23 December 1896, at 10.15 a.m., he went to the Imperial Institute for an hour, after which he went immediately to the nearby South Kensington Museum, remaining until 3.30 p.m.[99] Then on 26 January 1897, he toured the Regent Street Polytechnic.[100]

96. Chinese Legation Archives, Slater to Chinese minister, 7–15 April 1897, in Luo Jialun, *Shiliao*, p. 158. There is a misprint in this source. The date should have been Tuesday, 13 April, not Tuesday, 15 April. See note 97.

97. Minakata Kumagusu's diary, 13 April 1897, in his *Zenshu*, Supplement, Vol. 2, p. 80. The translation is mine, with the help of my colleague Mr Toshihiko Kobayashi.

98. *The Times*, 25 June 1897, p. 15, col. 2.

99. Chinese Legation Archives, Slater to Macartney, 23 December 1896, in Luo Jialun, *Shiliao*, p. 133.

100. Chinese Legation Archives, Slater to Macartney, 22–9 January 1897, in Luo Jialun, *Shiliao*, p. 140.

The foundation stone of the Imperial Institute was laid by Queen Victoria in 1887, with the twofold object of marking the fiftieth year of her reign and cementing the British Empire. She declared it open in 1893. The architect, T. E. Colcutt, was inspired by Tennyson's words, 'Raise a stately memorial, Make it really gorgeous. Some Imperial Institute, Rich in symbol, in ornament, Which may speak to the centuries'.[101] In the galleries therein were important exhibits from the British dominions and colonies displaying their various products, manufactures, and natural features.[102]

The South Kensington Museum was the unofficial name of the Victoria and Albert Museum, which was designed to serve a similar purpose to the galleries of the Imperial Institute. It was founded in 1857 'as an exhibition of decorative and applied art intended especially for the instruction of craftsmen and students'. Numerous special guides, handbooks, and monographs to the contents of the 145 rooms were available. The collections were arranged in eight general departments: Architecture and Sculpture; Ceramics, Glass, and Enamels; Engraving, Illustration, and Design; Library and Book Production; Metal Work; Paintings; Textiles; Woodwork, Furniture, and Leather Work. 'Art as applied to industry had no finer demonstration than is to be found here, for where famous originals were not available their place has been supplied by notable reproductions'.[103] Apparently Sun Yatsen found that one visit was not sufficient to view all the exhibits or to absorb the lessons therein. He returned on 17 March 1897 for another four hours or so.[104]

The Regent Street Polytechnic has an interesting history.[105] It seems that the 'Poly' had dual origins. In 1838, the Polytechnic Institution was founded at 309, Regent Street, by Sir George Cayley. 'The objects of this truly valuable institution are', wrote an author in 1839, 'the advancement of practical science in con-

101. *Queen's London*, Vol. 1, p. 21.

102. W. Francis Aitken, 'The Museums and Their Treasures', in Adcock (ed.), *Wonderful London*, Vol. 1, p. 1105.

103. Adcock (ed.), *Wonderful London*, Vol. 3, pp. 1104–5.

104. Chinese Legation Archives, Slater to Chinese minister, 16–23 March 1897, in Luo Jialun, *Shiliao*, pp. 149–50.

105. I am grateful to Mr M. Collier, deputy head of library services of the Polytechnic, for receiving me on 3 April 1984, and for drawing my attention to some relevant literature which is not commonly known.

nection with agriculture, the arts and manufactures; the demonstration, by the most simple and interesting methods of illustrations of those principles upon which every science is based, and processes employed in the most useful arts and manufactures affected'.[106] It aimed to draw public attention to new discoveries in these fields by holding formal educational courses as well as popular public lectures. In 1881, Quintin Hogg purchased the premises in order to extend his work among the poorer classes of young people in Central London, which he had begun in 1864. What would have been Sun Yatsen's impression of the 'Poly'?[107]

On 25 March 1897, he was seen to have spent a whole day in the Zoo.[108] On 19 June 1897, he went to Kew Gardens; and the next day he visited the Natural History Museum.[109] The Zoo in Regent's Park was one of the show-pieces in London. Opened in 1828, it had a collection of over 4,000 animals and birds, and was intended to be a sort of living library for the learned Zoological Society.[110] Kew, on the other hand, 'has been a botanical garden since the end of the seventeenth century ... It is a fairyland of flowers ... not merely clumps and tufts of flowers, but great mounds and lakes of lovely colour; mounds of azaleas and rhododendrons, lakes of daffodils and narcissi, ponds of tulips, showers of white and pink cherry-blossom, fountains of hawthorn, lilac and magnolia. Throughout its seasons it is a paradise of changing bloom and greenery'.[111] The Natural History Museum was opened in 1881 to provide room for the natural history

106. Ethel M. Wood, *A History of the Polytechnic* (London, Macdonald, 1965), p. 17. (hereafter cited as *Polytechnic*).

107. The 'Poly' published a weekly by the name of *The Polytechnic Magazine*, which has been preserved in bound volumes. I thought it plausible that Sun Yatsen's visit might have been reported therein. A search through the pertinent volumes, however, failed to yield any information. The volumes checked were Vol. 29, 1 July 1896–30 December 1896; Vol. 30, 13 January 1897–30 June 1897; and Vol. 31, 14 July 1897–29 December 1897.

108. Chinese Legation Archives, Slater to Chinese minister, 25 March 1897, in Luo Jialun, *Shiliao*, p. 152.

109. Minakata Kumagusu's diary, 19 and 20 June 1897, in *Zenshu*, Supplement, Vol. 2, p. 91.

110. H.J. Massingham, 'A Look at the Zoo', in Adcock (ed.), *Wonderful London*, Vol. 1, p. 162.

111. Martin Armstrong, 'Leafy London: In Park and Pleasaunce', in Adcock (ed.), *Wonderful London*, Vol. 1, p. 377.

exhibits from the British Museum. Different sections dealt with botany, entomology, zoology, mineralogy, and geology.[112]

Sun Yatsen's cultural life in London included a visit to Madame Tussaud's Waxwork Exhibition on 13 January 1897, and to Queen's Hall on 3 February 1897.[113] Madame Tussaud's was, and still is, 'one of the sights of London, especially dear to country cousins; and the spacious building . . . is visited by many thousands of both old and young folk annually'.[114] On the day of Sun Yatsen's visit, the exhibits on display included 'King John signing the Magna Charta'.[115] Queen's Hall no longer exists, but field-work shows that it was situated at the north end of Regent Street, almost directly opposite the 'Poly'. It was a 'handsome temple of music erected in 1893', and was the principal point of attraction in this neighbourhood, consisting of a spacious hall some 21,000 square feet in area, including its double galleries, and which seated 3,000 people. A permanent orchestra was formed at this hall, under the directorship of Mr (later Sir) Henry Wood.[116] The Sir Henry Wood Promenade Concerts of today, held annually in the Royal Albert Hall and broadcast world-wide, date back to the time of Queen's Hall. When Sun Yatsen went and stayed there on 3 February 1897 for two and a half hours, he was probably there for a function of some kind,[117] because an ordinary tour of inspection would not have taken that long.

What is there left to say except that Sun Yatsen saw and heard some of the most impressive specimens of British glory in the Victorian era?

---

112. Aitken, 'The Museums and Their Treasures', in Adcock (ed.), *Wonderful London*, Vol. 2, p. 1103.

113. Chinese Legation Archives, Slater to Chinese minister, 3–21 January 1897, and 30 January–14 February 1897, in Luo Jialun, *Shiliao*, pp. 137 and 142.

114. *Queen's London*, Vol. 2, p. 265.

115. *The Times*, 13 January 1897, p. 1, col. 5.

116. *Queen's London*, Vol. 2, p. 395.

117. Unfortunately, the advertised programme for that day mentioned only the evening, 'Queen's (small) Hall — Tonight, at 8 o'clock — The Grimson Family. This very remarkable family will play the Gade Octet, the Dvorak Piano Quintet, with piano, violin, and cello, solos by Misses Amy and Jessie and Master Robert Grimson. Tickets 5s., 3s., and 1s.' *The Times*, 3 February 1897, p. 1, col. 4.

III The Poverty

In the shadow of glory lay poverty. While in Hong Kong, the Cantlies had servants, Chinese and Japanese. Some of their Japanese servants accompanied them back to England so as to look after them on the way.[118] It probably had not occurred to Sun Yatsen, until his arrival in London, that back home, the Cantlies would then have servants who were British. The first thing that Mrs Cantlie did, when moving into 46, Devonshire Street, was to make arrangements for Jessie, the cook, to live there.[119] And within days, the 'new boy Fritz came'.[120] Very quickly she regretted that Fritz was not a success, and sent him away as he was too naughty.[121] He was replaced by a new boy, Giles, five days later.[122] Giles stayed for six months before he too was dismissed,[123] and within four days, 'Gillett's mother brought him up yesterday from Cottered & we have decided to take him at 12 pounds per year'.[124] It would have been difficult for Sun Yatsen to imagine that white men, too, could be servants.

During his detention at the Chinese Legation, Sun Yatsen came into contact daily with two English servants who took turns to guard him twenty-four hours a day. They were George Cole, the porter, and Henry Mulliner, the footman. It seems that he spoke to both of them each day, if only to beg them to take messages to either Dr Cantlie or Dr Manson. Because the pertinent documents are overwhelmingly concerned with the kidnapping, relatively little is revealed about the background of the servants. But there is sufficient information to form some idea. On the second card, which Cole took to Dr Cantlie appealing for help, Sun Yatsen included the following message; 'Please take care of the Messenger for me at present, he is very poor and will

---

118. See, for example, Cantlie and Seaver, *Sir James Cantlie*, p. 100; and Mrs Cantlie's diary, 14, 16, 17, 19, and 25 July 1896.
119. Mrs Cantlie's diary, 3, 18, 19, and 21 May 1896.
120. Mrs Cantlie's diary, 1 June 1896.
121. Mrs Cantlie's diary, 10 June and 10 July 1896.
122. Mrs Cantlie's diary, 15 July 1896.
123. Mrs Cantlie's diary, 12 February 1897.
124. Mrs Cantlie's diary, 16 February 1897.

lose his work by doing for me [*sic*]'.[125] Cole stated that he lived at
36, Little Albany Street, Regent's Park.[126] All the old houses in
that and the neighbouring streets have disappeared and have
been replaced by multi-storey council blocks. The narrow streets,
the congested lodgings, and one or two derelict factories all
testify to the area having been a slum. Both 36, Little Albany
Street, and 12, Albert Road, were situated in the suburb of
Regent's Park. Presumably, the masters lived in mansions and
the servants in slums. 'I am 29 years of age', Cole testified. 'I had
no special duties in the Legation; I simply had to make myself
generally useful. I generally took my immediate orders from the
housekeeper, Mrs Howe, an English woman'.[127] Cole is reminiscent of the boys Fritz, Giles, and Gillett, who were employed one
after another at 46, Devonshire Street. In time, each would
become another Cole.

As mentioned in the previous section of this chapter, field-
work has shown that the Regent Street Polytechnic was physically
located across the street from Queen's Hall. Metaphorically, it
might also be said that the 'Poly' lived under the shadow of
Queen's Hall. While the élite of London went to concerts per-
formed by gentlemen in tails, 'young castaways' of Victorian
London went to the 'Poly' on the other side of the street for 'the
merest minima of literacy and decency', wrote the grandson of
Quintin Hogg. 'I am just old enough to remember some of the
progeny of that heroic period, the products of the ragged school
who stayed on and became part of the permanent tradition of the
Institute or the Technical College'.[128] Going up Regent Street to
visit the Cantlies, Sun Yatsen passed the 'Poly' on his left and
Queen's Hall on his right, and vice versa on his way back to his
lodgings at 8, Gray's Inn Place.

Gray's Inn Place seems to have offered cheap student lodgings.
When Cantlie studied at Charing Cross Medical School, he
shared lodgings there with a fellow student, Mitchell Bruce.[129]

---

125. FO 17/1718, p. 30, Sun Yatsen to Cantlie, n.d., enclosed in Cantlie's
affidavit of 22 October 1896.
126. FO 17/1718, pp. 116–19, Cole's statement at the Treasury, 2 November
1896, para. 1.
127. FO 17/1718, pp. 116–19, Cole's statement at the Treasury, 2 November
1896, para. 1.
128. Wood, *Polytechnic*, p. 13.
129. Cantlie and Seaver, *Sir James Cantlie*, p. 9.

This is probably why Cantlie found accommodation for Sun Yat-sen at 8, Gray's Inn Place.[130] The glorious Inns of Court were not without their shadows in the slums of Holborn and the Strand. Some areas of the Strand were described as crowded, and the population mixed, with a large proportion of Irish people, including many rough characters. A good deal of poverty existed in the back streets, where many labourers, costers, porters, printers, and carmen lived. A lot of the houses were in bad repair, but were let at high rents. Some streets in Holborn were alleged to be among the worst in London, containing low common lodging-houses and brothels, and inhabited by tramps, sandwich men, and others, who were noisy and drunk at night.[131] The government had demolished some of the worst and poorest streets there, but the inhabitants remained. 'Houses built for one family are used by two families, or perhaps three, or even more of the very poor, and the great "models" are filled up by the new comers.'[132]

During the Queen's Jubilee Procession, the stands on both sides of the route were of course filled only by the well-to-do, on account of the prodigious prices their owner exacted.[133] The women in the parks near Buckingham Palace, though they could not compete with their richer sisters who filled the stands, were nonetheless 'dressed as becomingly as they could, so that the coup d'oeil was not marred by anything unsightly', commented The Times.[134]

The Fuji at Tilbury Dock, and the ocean liners at the Royal Albert Dock, which Sun Yatsen inspected either on board or from the shore, were of course grand.[135] The dockland itself was depressing. But, after all, commented a contemporary writer, what a visitor to the dockland should have wanted was the reality, not romance. He should be prepared to walk and walk till he

---

130. FO 17/1718, p. 121, Cantlie's statement at the Treasury, 4 November 1896, para. 3.
131. Charles Booth (ed.), Labour and Life of the People in London (London, Williams and Norgate, 1891–1902, 8 vols.), Vol. 2 Appendix, pp. 1–2 and 18–19. For a good description of poverty in Central London and of the common lodging-houses, see the text of Vol. 2 itself (pp. 293–304, and 335–49).
132. Booth (ed.), Labour and Life of the People in London, Vol. 2, p. 303.
133. The Times, 23 June 1897, p. 9, col. 1.
134. The Times, 23 June 1897, p. 9, col. 3.
135. See previous section of this chapter.

was ready to drop with fatigue. 'The gloom of the region, which even sunlight relieves only into dinginess, requires as stout a heart to carry its depressing influence as ever was needed by a traveller in a country unremitting in its opposition of grey rock and sullen light'.[136]

The British press reported on and analysed the problems of the legal poor (those eligible for financial assistance from the authorities) of London,[137] the sick and aged poor in workhouses,[138] the Poor Law children,[139] and the like quite unreservedly. According to the private detective, Sun Yatsen bought newspapers regularly. It may be assumed, therefore, that Sun Yatsen would not only have seen and heard about the poor in Britain, but would also have read systematic reports on the problem.

Not just the legal poor, but ordinary self-sufficient people might find a wide trough between themselves and the well-to-do. One August vacation, for example, the Cantlies took their holidays at Flatford Mill.[140] 'We bathed and spent the day on the sands, but it was very overrun with common folks & so we did not care to take the children'.[141]

Subsequently, Sun Yatsen wrote that the experiences he gained at this time made him realize that although the European Powers were rich and powerful, not all their people were happy. Having given the question a great deal of thought, Sun Yatsen continued, he invented the Principle of the People's Livelihood. This, together with the Principle of Nationalism and the Principle of Democracy, should, he thought, provide a permanent solution to China's problems.[142] If his experiences had made him aware of the importance of the People's Livelihood, how could he ever have hoped to solve a problem which even the great Western Powers had failed to solve? For a long time, historians have had

136. Tomlinson, 'Down in Dockland', Vol. 1, p. 153. See, also, Beatrice Potter, 'The Docks', in Booth (ed.), Labour and Life of the People in London, Vol. 1, pp. 184–209.
137. See, for example, The Times, 26 December 1896, p. 8, col. 2, to p. 9, col. 1.
138. The Times, 8 April 1897, p. 3, col. 1.
139. The Times, 18 January 1897, p. 8, col. 6.
140. Mrs Cantlie's diary, 1 August 1896.
141. Mrs Cantlie's diary, 12 August 1896.
142. Sun Yatsen, 'Youzhi jingcheng', in Sun Zhongshan xuanji, p. 196.

their eyes fixed on the Library of the British Museum.[143] So let us look at what hope that noble institution might have offered him.

IV The Hope

There is no concrete evidence to show exactly what books Sun Yatsen read in the British Museum. The British Museum has not kept the order forms of readers; and if it had, a second museum would have had to be built to house them. Therefore, historians have had to search through Sun Yatsen's writings, particularly his Three Principles of the People, for names. As a result, those of Karl Marx, Henry George, John Stuart Mill, Peter Kropotkin, Charles Montesquieu, and others, have been mentioned.[144] I do not propose to rake over old coals. And since my research has not broken new ground in this respect, a different approach may prove slightly more rewarding and may even suggest new ways in which future historians might usefully employ their time.

One aspect of Sun Yatsen's activities in the British Museum that has yet to be established is some idea of the amount of time he spent there. Table 5 gives some statistics.

Table 5 Sun Yatsen's Visits to the British Museum, as Recorded by Slater, the Private Detective Agency[145]

Date	Time	Duration
Sat., 5 Dec. 1896	11.40–13.00	1 hr 20 min
Mon., 7 Dec. 1896	10.30–14.30	4 hr
Tue., 8 Dec. 1896	10.30–14.30	4 hr
Wed., 9 Dec. 1896	11.55–unspecified	(3 hr)
Thur., 10 Dec. 1896	Unspecified	(3 hr)
Fri., 11 Dec. 1896	Unspecified	(3 hr)
Tue., 15 Dec. 1896	Unspecified–14.15	(3 hr)
Thur., 17 Dec. 1896	Unspecified–12.40	(2 hr)

---

143. Schiffrin, *Origins*, p. 134; Shang Mingxuan, *Sun Zhongshan zhuan*, p. 45; and Wu Xiangxiang, *Sun Yixian zhuan*, Vol. 1, pp. 185–207.

144. Schiffrin, *Origins*, p. 135; and Wu Xiangxiang, *Sun Yixian zhuan*, Vol. 1, pp. 187 and 201–3.

145. These records have been reprinted in Luo Jialun, *Shiliao*, pp. 129–64.

Table 5 (*continued*)

Date	Time	Duration
Tue., 22 Dec. 1896	11.45–15.45	4 hr
Sun., 27 Dec. 1896	Unspecified	
Mon., 28 Dec. 1896	Unspecified	
Tue., 29 Dec. 1896	Unspecified	
Wed., 30 Dec. 1896	Unspecified	
Thur., 31 Dec. 1896	Unspecified	
Fri., 1 Jan. 1897	Unspecified	
Wed., 6 Jan. 1897	11.10–14.30	3 hr 20 min
Mon., 11 Jan. 1897	13.40–15.30	1 hr 50 min
Thur., 14 Jan. 1897	12.00–15.00	3 hr
Sat., 16 Jan. 1897	11.00–15.00	4 hr
Tue., 19 Jan. 1897	11.40–15.30	3 hr 50 min
Wed., 20 Jan. 1897	12.00–15.00	4 hr
Thur., 21 Jan. 1897	12.00–15.00	3 hr
Tue., 26 Jan. 1897	Unspecified	1 hr
Sat., 30 Jan. 1897	13.00–18.00	5 hr
Sat., 6 Feb. 1897	10.50–15.00	4 hr 10 min
Mon., 8 Feb. 1897	11.30–16.00	4 hr 30 min
Tue., 9 Feb. 1897	13.00–18.00	5 hr
Fri., 12 Feb, 1897	11.30–18.00	6 hr 30 min
Sat., 13 Feb. 1897	13.00–18.10	5 hr 10 min
Wed., 17 Feb. 1897	Unspecified	
Thur., 18 Feb. 1897	Unspecified	
Fri., 19 Feb. 1897	Unspecified	
Sat., 20 Feb. 1897	Unspecified	
Sun., 21 Feb. 1897	Unspecified	
Mon., 22 Feb. 1897	Unspecified	
Tue., 23 Feb. 1897	Unspecified–18.40	
Thur., 4 Mar. 1897	11.00–18.00	7 hr
Sat., 6 Mar. 1897	Unspecified	
Sun., 7 Mar. 1897	Unspecified	
Mon., 8 Mar. 1897	Unspecified	
Tue., 9 Mar. 1897	Unspecified	
Thur., 18 Mar. 1897	11.50–15.15	3 hr 25 min
Fri., 19 Mar. 1897	12.05–19.30	7 hr 25 min
Sat., 20 Mar. 1897	12.15–15.25	3 hr 10 min
Mon., 22 Mar. 1897	15.45–20.00	4 hr 15 min

Table 5 (*continued*)

Date	Time	Duration
Tue., 23 Mar. 1897	12.00–18.30	6 hr 30 min
Wed., 24 Mar. 1897	10.45–16.15	5 hr 30 min
Fri., 26 Mar. 1897	14.10–19.30	5 hr 20 min
Sat., 27 Mar. 1897	Unspecified–16.45	
Tue., 30 Mar. 1897	12.00–18.40	6 hr 40 min
Fri., 2 Apr. 1897	14.20–18.30	4 hr 10 min
Sat., 3 Apr. 1897	11.30–17.30	6 hr
Mon., 5 Apr. 1897	12.40–19.15	6 hr 35 min
Tue., 6 Apr. 1897	12.00–16.35	4 hr 35 min
Wed., 7 Apr. 1897	11.35–18.10	6 hr 35 min
Fri., 9 Apr. 1897	11.45–14.00	2 hr 15 min
	15.00–19.00	4 hr
Sat., 10 Apr. 1897	13.30–19.30	6 hr
Wed., 14 Apr. 1897	13.30–19.00	5 hr 30 min
(*Detective's reports missing between 22 April and 10 June*)		
Thur., 10 Jun. 1897	11.40–18.00	6 hr 20 min
Wed., 16 Jun. 1897	Unspecified	
Thur., 17 Jun. 1897	15.00–19.00	4 hr
Fri., 18 Jun. 1897	Unspecified	
Sat., 19 Jun. 1897	Unspecified	
Sun., 20 Jun. 1897	Unspecified	
Mon., 21 Jun. 1897	Unspecified	
Tue., 22 Jun. 1897	Unspecified	
Wed., 23 Jun. 1897	Unspecified	
Thur., 24 Jun. 1897	Unspecified	

According to this table, the figures of which can only be rough, it may at least be said that Sun Yatsen was very studious and persistent. This table lends support to Dr Cantlie's remark that Sun Yatsen read widely, on all sorts of subjects, such as politics, diplomacy, mines and mining, agriculture, cattle-rearing, engineering, and political economy, as well as legal, military, and naval matters.[146] We must remember that Sun Yatsen visited Dr

---

146. Schiffrin, *Origins*, pp. 134–5, quoting Cantlie and Jones, *Sun Yat-sen*, p. 242.

Cantlie very regularly, and that he seems to have been in the habit of discussing with his former teacher what he had been reading. If Sun Yatsen read only one or two books pertinent to each subject, it is quite conceivable that he could have covered all the subjects mentioned by Cantlie. Whether he managed to 'digest'[147] all he read, however, is a different matter.

Since he spent so much time in the British Museum, it might be useful to find out who he might have met there. Generally speaking, these people may be divided into three groups: the British establishment, some Russian exiles, and a Japanese Pan-Asianist.

The British establishment was represented by Mr (later Sir) Robert Kennaway Douglas, who was the keeper in the Department of Oriental Printed Books and MSS at the British Museum.[148] It seems that Sun Yatsen met him soon after his release from the Chinese Legation and had kept in touch since.[149] According to the detective's report, Sun Yatsen went to the British Museum for the first time on 5 December 1896,[150] twenty-five days after he was said to have met Douglas (on 10 November 1896).[151] The detective's report is corroborated by the Museum's records.[152] If all three sources are accurate, then Sun Yatsen must have been introduced to Douglas outside the Museum, perhaps on a social occasion and even by the Cantlies. Then on 16 March 1897, Minakata Kumagusu met Sun Yatsen for the first time in Douglas' office; and on 30 March 1897, he and Sun Yatsen went together to see Douglas.[153]

It seems, therefore, that Sun Yatsen saw Douglas from time to

147. Schiffrin, *Origins*, p. 135.

148. *Who was Who, Vol. 1: 1897–1915* (London, A. & C. Black, 1920), p. 205.

149. Wu Xiangxiang, *Sun Yixian zhuan*, Vol. 1, p. 195. Professor Wu has not given a specific reference for the source of his information. Therefore, I am not in a position to check its accuracy. See note 150.

150. Chinese Legation Archives, Slater to Chinese minister, 2–11 December 1896, in Luo Jialun, *Shiliao*, p. 129. Wu Xiangxiang, *Sun Yixian zhuan*, p. 186, alleges that Sun Yatsen went for the first time on 4 December 1896. Professor Wu must have misread the report, the relevant parts of which are: 'On the 4th inst. he was not seen to leave throughout the day, but on Saturday 5th inst. he left No. 8 Gray's Inn Place at 11 a.m. and went ... to the British Museum where he remained an hour and twenty minutes'. See note 151.

151. Wu Xiangxiang, *Sun Yixian zhuan*, Vol. 1, p. 195.

152. British Museum, Readers' Register, 5 December 1896.

153. Minakata Kumagusu's diary, 16 and 30 March 1897, in *Zenshu*, Supplement, Vol. 2, pp. 77 and 79.

time. Who was Douglas? He was born in 1838, and was the son
of the Revd Philip W. Douglas.[154] In 1858, he was appointed as a
student interpreter in Her Majesty's Consular Service in China,
and studied Chinese in Guangzhou and then Beijing.[155] Guangzhou in 1858 was, of course, under the occupation of the Allied
British and French Forces; and the man with real power was the
head of the Allied Commission, the bellicose Harry Parkes.[156]
Thus, the 20-year-old Douglas began his career by studying the
language and culture of a conquered people in an occupied city.
What effect this had on him is an open question. When the Allied
Forces marched on Beijing and occupied that city too, Douglas
continued his studies there. In 1861, he was appointed as inter-
preter to the British Force of Occupation of Tianjin, under
General Staveley. In 1862, he became acting vice-consul at Dagu.
In 1864, he returned to England on sick-leave.[157] The next year,
he applied successfully to be first-class assistant in the Depart-
ment of Oriental Printed Books and MSS in the British
Museum,[158] rising to the headship of that Department in 1892.[159]
In 1873, he was elected professor of Chinese at King's College,
London.[160] This position he held concurrently with his appoint-
ment at the British Museum. Subsequently, he was knighted in
1903. He retired in 1907, and died in 1913.[161]

Thus, when he met Sun Yatsen in 1896, Douglas was professor
of Chinese at King's College, London, and keeper of the Department of Oriental Printed Books and MSS in the British Museum.
Like Professor Herbert Giles of Cambridge, Douglas had been in
the Consular Service in China; and, on his return to England,

---

154. *Who was Who, Vol. 1: 1897–1915*, p. 205.
155. British Museum Central Archives, Establishment Lists, Douglas' application to be First Class Assistant in the Museum's Department of Oriental Printed
Books and MSS, 1 February 1865. I am most grateful to Miss Janet Wallace for
her help in locating this valuable document.
156. See Wong, *Anglo-Chinese Relations*, pp. 263–310.
157. King's College, London, MSS, KA/1C/D60, Douglas' application for the
Chair of Chinese, 1 November 1896.
158. British Museum Central Archives, Establishment Lists, Douglas' application to be First Class Assistant in the Museum's Department of Oriental Printed
Books and MSS, 1 February 1865.
159. *Who was Who, Vol. 1: 1897–1915*, p. 205.
160. King's College, London, MSS, KA/1C/D60, Douglas' application for the
Chair of Chinese, 1 November 1873; and KA/C/M11, Council Minutes 488, p.
270, in which was recorded the decision to elect Douglas to the Chair of Chinese.
161. *Who was Who, Vol. 1: 1897–1915*, p. 205.

subsequently held a Chair of Chinese. It will be remembered that Professor Giles had asked Sun Yatsen, through Dr Cantlie, for a draft entry for the *Chinese Biographical Dictionary* which he was compiling. This may be interpreted as Giles' recognition of Sun Yatsen as somebody of potential importance. The fact that Douglas was prepared to spend time with Sun Yatsen, when he would turn down a request from 'Prince' Tokugawa to rent a room in his mansion,[162] may be interpreted in the same way.

If a letter from Douglas to *The Times* is any guide,[163] it may be said that he and Sun Yatsen had at least two things in common. They both hated the officialdom then governing China, and they both attributed anti-Christian riots in China to incitement by officials. When Douglas' letter to *The Times* was published, it received a lengthy commentary in the *China Mail* when Sun Yatsen was still in Guangzhou in October 1895. The letter concerned the massacre of some English missionaries in Fujian. The *China Mail* urged that the Chinese officials responsible should be exiled to India. 'The historical deportation of Viceroy Yeh from Canton to Calcutta establishes a good precedent', wrote the paper.[164] The viceroy in question was the imperial commissioner for foreign affairs, who was stationed at Guangzhou, and who fought the British and the French during the *Arrow* War (1856–60).[165] Dr Cantlie later mentioned diplomatic and military matters as two of the subjects on which Sun Yatsen had read in London. As a former member of the British Consular Service working with the British Army, and as the author of such books as *Europe and the Far East*, and *The Life of Li Hung-chang*,[166] it is possible that Douglas guided Sun Yatsen through the pertinent literature. If so, Douglas' action may have been seen by Sun Yatsen as an endorsement of what he had done and of what he planned to do in the future, and may even have been a source of encouragement to him, like that of Dr Cantlie.

---

162. Minakata Kumagusu's diary, 3, 26, and 28 May 1897, in *Zenshu*, Supplement, Vol. 2, pp. 83 and 87.

163. Douglas' letter to the editor, 17 September 1895, in *The Times*, 18 September 1895, p. 4, col. 4.

164. *China Mail*, 22 October 1895, p. 3, col. 5.

165. See my books *Yeh Ming-ch'en: Viceroy of Liang-Kuang, 1852–1858* (Cambridge, Cambridge University Press, 1976), and *Anglo-Chinese Relations*.

166. *Who Was Who, Vol. 1: 1897–1915*, p. 205.

In addition, it is interesting to note the referees who supported Douglas in his application for the Chair of Chinese. They included Major-General Sir Charles Staveley, KCB, and Sir Anthony Panizzi, KCB, LLD, formerly principal librarian and secretary of the British Museum. He also attached a testimonial from the late Hon. Sir Frederick Bruce, GCB, formerly minister plenipotentiary and envoy extraordinary of Her British Majesty in China.[167] It is not clear whether Douglas introduced Sun Yatsen to any of his friends and patrons in high circles. I have found a photograph in the BBC Hulton Picture Library, with Sun Yatsen on the left, a little girl in the middle, and Admiral Sir Percy Scott on the right. I have not discovered any information pertinent to what may turn out to be a very important photograph, but do hope that future historians may have better luck.[168]

The second group of people whom Sun Yatsen met in the British Museum consisted of some Russian exiles. Sun Yatsen recalled twenty-eight years later that when he was in England shortly after the failure of his first uprising, he met some Russians in a library. It transpired that they were fellow revolutionaries. The Russians asked him how long it would take for the Chinese Revolution to succeed. Secretly he had planned another uprising in a year or two; but to be conservative, he said thirty years. The Russians expressed astonishment, whereupon he asked them how long it would take them. The Russians said a hundred years; but they had to start working on it there and then, in the hope that it would ultimately succeed. Sun Yatsen was very impressed. And when he was subsequently teased about his successive failures, he repeated the words of the Russians about perseverance.[169] It seems, therefore, that the Russians were likewise a source of encouragement to him.

Schiffrin has identified one of the Russians in the group. He was Felix Volkhovsky (1846–1914), editor of *Free Russia*, the monthly organ of the English 'Society of Friends of Russian Freedom'. He had spent seven years in solitary confinement in the Schlusselburg fortress in St Petersburg, then eleven years of

167. King's College, London, MSS, KA/1C/D60, Douglas' application for the Chair of Chinese, 1 November 1896; and enclosures.
    168. BBC Hulton Picture Library, P.2482. *Who Was Who, Vol. 2: 1916–1928* has an entry on Admiral Sir Percy Scott (pp. 941–2).
    169. Sun Yatsen, 'Zhuyi shengguo wuli', in *Guofu quanji*, Vol. 2, pp. 620–3.

exile in Siberia, before escaping first to Canada and then to Britain.[170] I toured the Schlusselburg fortress in 1972, and can testify to the solitary nature of such confinement. Thus, I fully agree with Professor Schiffrin's assessment that meeting 'a man of Volkhovsky's courage and determination must have been an enlightening and inspiring experience'.[171] Furthermore, there is evidence to suggest that Sun Yatsen also met these Russian exiles outside the Museum at least once. On this occasion, it was said that the meeting took place in the home of a Briton by the name of Greg. It was also reported that Sun Yatsen took the opportunity to recommend *Kidnapped in London* to those present, of whom there were five. *Kidnapped in London* was published on 21 January 1897,[172] so the meeting must have taken place after that date. He also expressed the view that the Manchu regime could not be reformed, it could only be overthrown; that a responsible and representative government would replace it; that most of the inhabitants of Central China belonged to secret societies; that a general uprising was only a matter of time; and that the time would come when the necessary arms and ammunition were available.[173] The reference to weapons may be interpreted as Sun Yatsen's attempt to explore the possibility of aid from the Russian exiles. If so, what he got was the Russian translation of *Kidnapped in London*, which was published at the end of 1897.[174]

The third category consisted of a lone Japanese Pan-Asianist temporarily resident in London, Minakata Kumagusu. In his diary, Minakata merely said that he met Sun Yatsen for the first time in Douglas' office on 16 March 1897.[175] In a letter to a friend, he went into more detail about this encounter. He said that Sun Yatsen asked him what his life's ambition was. He answered, 'My wish is that we Asians will drive out [of Asia] all

170. Schiffrin, *Origins*, p. 135.
171. Schiffrin, *Origins*, p. 135.
172. See Chapter 4, Section III.
173. Record of an interview between Sun Yatsen and a gathering of five in London in 1897, in *Sun Zhongshan quanji*, Vol. 1, pp. 86-7.
174. Record of an interview between Sun Yatsen and a gathering of five in London in 1897, in *Sun Zhongshan quanji*, Vol. 1, pp. 86-7.
175. Minakata Kumagusu, *Zenshu*, Supplement, Vol. 2, p. 77.

Westerners once and for all'.[176] Referring to the same occasion, he told another friend that he had said this in the presence of both Douglas and Sun Yatsen, when Douglas introduced Sun Yatsen to him. Both Douglas and Sun Yatsen were said to have been taken by surprise.[177] Minakata was employed at the time as a temporary assistant to help Douglas compile a catalogue of Oriental printed books.

It was plain rudeness on the part of Minakata to have said what he did in front of Douglas, who was both his superior and a Westerner. But such behaviour seems to have been consistent with his conduct on a different occasion. He was walking from Fenchurch Street to Cannon Street, when apparently a British woman mocked him. He lost control of himself. 'I had a scuffle with her', he wrote. 'Four policemen came and I was taken to a nearby police station. A few more scuffles followed (probably after 6 p.m.). [I] went home at 2 a.m. (because the policemen did not know what to do with me — they found it impossible to handle me)'.[178]

But Sun Yatsen seems to have been quite taken with him, and subsequently spent a fair amount of time in his company, as Table 6 shows.

Table 6 Meetings between Sun Yatsen and Minakata Kumagusu According to Minakata's Diary,[179] 16 March to 3 July 1897

Date	Time	Comments
Tue., 16 Mar.		Met in Douglas' office.
Thur., 18 Mar.		Sat in British Museum (BM) talking.

---

176. Kasai Kiyoshi, *Minakata Kumagusu* (Tokyo, 1967), p. 131, quoting Minakata's letter to Yanagita. I am grateful to Mr T. Kobayashi for his help in translating the Japanese text. See notes 177 and 178.

177. Kasai, *Minakata Kumagusu*, pp. 131–2, quoting Minakata's letter to Uematsu.

178. Minakata Kumagusu's diary, 28 April 1897, in *Zenshu*, Supplement, Vol. 2, pp. 82–3.

179. Minakata Kumagusu's diary, *Zenshu*, Supplement, Vol. 2, pp. 77–93.

Table 6 (*continued*)

Date	Time	Comments
Fri., 19 Mar.	18.00–22.00	Left BM with Sun. To Maria Restaurant, to Hyde Park, bus to Sun's home till 22.00.
Sat., 20 Mar.		Spoke to Sun in BM.
Fri., 26 Mar.	Evening	With Sun to Vienna Restaurant, then to Saisho's, then BM.
Sat., 27 Mar.	Evening–22.00	With Sun to Shora Restaurant, then to Sun's.
Tue., 30 Mar.	Afternoon	With Sun to Douglas' office.
Mon., 5 Apr.	Till 21.00	With Sun to Shora Restaurant, then to Sun's.
Wed., 7 Apr.	Afternoon	Spoke with Sun at BM.
	Evening	To Sun's, Sun not at home.
Thur., 8 Apr.		Spoke to Sun in BM.
Sat., 10 Apr.		Spoke to Sun in BM.
Tue., 13 Apr.	*c*.12.00–*c*.16.30	With Mulkern to visit Sun, all 3 to Tilbury to see Tsuda.
Mon., 19 Apr.	Evening–22.00	With Sun to Vienna Restaurant, then to Sun's.
Tue., 20 Apr.		Sun in BM.
Sat., 8 May		Asked Mr Read to show Sun alum tea.
Mon., 24 May	Evening	Dined with Sun, then to see various people, none at home.
Wed., 26 May	Afternoon	Spoke to Sun in BM.
Wed., 16 Jun.	Afternoon–24.00	With Sun visited Kamada, then to Minakata's, then to restaurant, then Hyde Park.

Table 6 (*continued*)

Date	Time	Comments
Fri., 18 Jun.		Waited for Sun, who did not come.
Sat., 19 Jun.	p.m.–evening	Sun came, to Kew, to Tajima's in West Kensington till 21.00, to High St. by bus, then dinner.
Sun., 20 Jun.	p.m.–evening	Sun came, to Museum of Natural History; dinner at Maria Restaurant.
Fri., 25 Jun.		Sun came, arranged meeting day after tomorrow.
Sat., 26 Jun.		Sun and Tajima see Naval Review.
Sun., 27 Jun.	c.16.00–24.00	Sun came. After 19.00 to Tajima's. After 22.00 to Maria Restaurant. After 23.00 to Hyde Park.
Mon., 28 Jun.		Letter to Kamada re Sun.
	After 17.00	Saw Sun at Museum.
Tue., 29 Jun.	After 16.00	Saw Sun at BM, gave him letter.
Wed., 30 Jun.	c.11.00	Visited Sun by cab, handed him letter . . . At 11.00 parted in front of Sun's residence.

What did they talk about during the long hours that they spent together? Given Minakata's views and personal sentiments, it may be assumed that the central theme of their conversations was Pan-Asianism. Sun Yatsen was one year older then Mina-kata, and both men may be regarded as belonging to the same generation, sharing much of the experience typical of their times. Minakata claimed that 'the unfortunate Sun Yatsen could count on merely Mr Mulkern, who was a member of the "Restoration Party" in Ireland, and myself, as his only two close friends in London'.[180] Mulkern is not listed in any of the standard biographical dictionaries, although it can be shown that he accompanied Sun Yatsen to the Royal Albert Dock and again to Tilbury Dock,[181] almost as his bodyguard in case the Chinese Legation staff should scheme to use the Chinese community there to lay their hands on him again. Subsequently, he played a similar role by accompanying Sun Yatsen to Singapore in 1900,[182] and participated in the Huizhou Uprising in China later in the same year.[183] When Sun Yatsen revisited London in 1905, he was a house-guest at Mulkern's,[184] amidst newspaper reports that the Manchu authorities wanted him dead or alive for a reward of £10,000. 'He will be beheaded on sight without trial if detected by the spies of the Empress', wrote a reporter.[185] As for the so-called 'Restoration Party', it could have been any one of the numerous nationalist parties in Ireland at this time. In 1895, the Bill for Home Rule in Ireland was defeated again in the House of Lords, and the Home Rule Party, Gaelic League, and so on, immediately became active again.[186]

During the last few meetings between Minakata and Sun Yatsen, it is obvious that they were preoccupied with letters of introduction for Sun Yatsen to, it appears, people of some in-

---

180. Kasai, *Minakata Kumagusu*, p. 131, quoting Minakata's letter to Uematsu. This indicates that either Minakata was exaggerating, or Sun Yatsen had not told him about the Cantlies (which seems unlikely).

181. See Chinese Legation Archives, Slater to Chinese minister, 10 March and 14 April 1897, in Luo Jialun, *Shiliao*, pp. 147 and 158–9; and Minakata Kumagusu's diary, 13 and 15 April 1897, in *Zenshu*, Supplement, Vol. 2, pp. 80–1.

182. FO 17/1718, pp. 351–2, Record of interview between Sun Yatsen and Sir Alexander Swettenham *et al.*, 10 July 1900.

183. Schiffrin, *Origins*, p. 128.

184. On this visit, Sun Yatsen applied for a new reader's ticket at the British Museum. The address he gave was 66, Clarendon Road, Holland Park (British Museum Central Archives, Reading Room Register 1905, 13 March 1905 — I am grateful to Miss Janet Wallace and Mr Howard Nelson for their help in locating this information). No. 66, Clarendon Road, Holland Park, was, of course, the place where Mulkern lived (Minakata Kumagusu's diary, 15 April 1897, in *Zenshu*, Supplement, Vol. 2, p. 81).

185. FO 17/1718, p. 509, Newspaper cutting, *Daily Mirror*, 12 January 1905.

186. See D. George, *Nationalism in Ireland* (London, Croom Helm, 1982), pp. 159–94. I am grateful to my colleague, Professor D. M. Schreuder, for lending me the book.

fluence in Japan. Increasingly, it seems that Sun Yatsen was beginning to place his hopes on Japanese patronage as well as British benevolent neutrality.

How realistic were his hopes? The most important of all the letters of introduction was that written by Kamata Eikichi, who was visiting London at the time,[187] to a certain Okamoto Ryunosuke. The latter had been born in the same prefecture as Minakata, and was a dismissed soldier and ardent Pan-Asianist who subsequently took part in the Wuchang Uprising in 1911 as a Japanese adventurer.[188] Kamata was never really important in Japanese politics; and it seems that Minakata managed to get him to write a letter of introduction on the basis of their having been born in the same district in Japan and, in that sense, being fellow clansmen. The irony is that, when Sun Yatsen finally reached Japan again later in the year, he was sought out by Miyazaki Torazo and was introduced to people who really mattered in Japanese politics;[189] and when Minakata himself returned to Japan, Sun Yatsen wrote letters of introduction for him so as to help him settle down in his homeland.[190]

But the discovery of Sun Yatsen's friendship with Minakata in London is important in a different sense. It is commonly believed in academic circles that Sun Yatsen's contacts with Japanese Pan-Asianists did not begin until he revisited Japan in the second half of 1897.[191] Now we may safely say that such contacts had begun earlier, on 16 March 1897 in the British Museum.

V The Projection of the Heroic Image

In 1919, Sun Yatsen published Part One of his famous *Jianguo fanglue* (*A Plan to Reconstruct China*). The last chapter of this work was entitled 'Youzhi jingcheng' ('The Ambition Fulfilled'). In it, he gives a brief history of his revolutionary activities until

---

187. I am grateful to Professor Junji Banno of Tokyo University for helping me locate the three volumes of *Kamata Eikichi zenshu* (Tokyo, 1935), which contain a chronological biography of the man.

188. 'Okamoto Ryunosuke', in *Kokushi daijiten* (Tokyo, 1980), Vol. 2, p. 759. I am grateful to Mr Kobayashi for this reference.

189. Schiffrin, *Origins*, pp. 146–7.

190. Kasai, *Minakata Kumagusu*, p. 136ff.

191. See, for example, Jansen, *The Japanese and Sun Yat-sen*, pp. 64–8; and Schiffrin, *Origins*, pp. 140–8. See, also, Section I of my Conclusion.

the establishment of the Chinese Republic and his assuming office as its first president on 1 January 1912. The language and contents of his chapter leave little doubt that he was deliberately projecting his own heroic image. Indeed, it was here that he made his well-known statement, parts of which have been quoted earlier, that during his two-year sojourn in Europe he made friends with the most distinguished Britons; and that what he saw and heard gave him much food for thought, as a result of which he finalized the formulation of his Three Principles of the People.[192]

There are several issues involved in this short statement. First, the duration of the sojourn; second, the location of the sojourn; third, the people he befriended; fourth, what he saw and heard; and fifth, the finalizing of the formulation of the Three Principles of the People.

Schiffrin has taken him to task for his claim that he stayed in Europe for two years; 'Sun's *memory* [*my italics*] failed him . . . he was not in England for two years nor did he visit any other European country'.[193] In the context of the present analysis, it is, of course, not Sun Yatsen's memory that is the focal point of interest, but his claim that he stayed two years instead of the actual nine months. Schiffrin's criticism is based on Slater's reports about Sun Yatsen's movements, which show that Sun Yatsen arrived at Liverpool on 30 September 1896, and left around 2 July 1897. These dates are corroborated to some extent by other sources. An evening newspaper in Liverpool, for example, confirmed the arrival of the SS *Majestic* on 30 September 1896, and printed the names of several of the more notable cabin passengers. Sun Yatsen's name was not among them;[194] but one would not expect it to have been, because he was not yet notable. Information about his departure from London is corroborated by the diaries of Mrs Cantlie and Minakata.[195] Thus, it can be stated categorically that Sun Yatsen spent nine, and not twenty-four,

---

192. *Sun Zhongshan xuanji*, p. 196.
193. Schiffrin, *Origins*, p. 137.
194. *Liverpool Echo*, 30 September 1896, p. 3, col. 4. I am grateful to Dr Frank Taylor of the John Rylands Library, Manchester, and Miss Janet Smith of the City Library of Liverpool, for their help in locating this information.
195. Mrs Cantlie's diary, 30 June 1897; and Minakata Kumagusu's diary, 3 July 1897, in *Zenshu*, Supplement, Vol. 2, p. 93. See Conclusion for further details.

months in England. Although it was quite acceptable in Chinese convention to refer vaguely as being two years what was actually a short period of time stretching over two calendar years, the fact that the Westernized Sun Yatsen should have resorted to such a usage may be interpreted as an exaggeration on his part to boost the period of his learning on Western soil, and thus a projection of his heroic image as a pioneer in Western learning with a view to regenerating China.

As for his use of the word 'Europe' rather than England, it is true that Slater's reports, as reproduced by Luo Jialun, make no mention of his ever going to the Continent. However, historians have generally overlooked the fact that the reports are missing for forty-eight days between 23 April and 10 June 1897. But during the period, Minakata said in his diary that he saw Sun Yatsen on 8, 24, and 26 May 1897,[196] while Mrs Cantlie's diary contained no reference to him at all. On balance, it is unlikely that he would have been on the Continent at this time. Ordinary courtesy would have required him to inform the Cantlies of such a trip; and Minakata's reference to having seen him on 8, 24, and 26 May breaks up the period under consideration into three small parts, making any extended visit to the Continent improbable. Absolute certainty on this point cannot be reached, however, on the basis of the evidence available so far. In any case, it was quite acceptable in Chinese custom to say that one had been to Europe, even if the trip had been restricted to England. What is important in the context of the present analysis is, again, the fact that the Westernized Sun Yatsen should have resorted to this Chinese custom at all, which may, once again, be interpreted as his eagerness to impress upon his compatriots that his experience was not limited to England alone.

The Chinese term he used for describing the people who had befriended him — *chaoye xianhao* ('distinguished intellects and heroes') — was also designed to impress, perhaps even to mislead. With due respect, I would not have considered an ex-Hong Kong doctor (at least not the Dr Cantlie of 1896–7), an ex-interpreter of the Consular Service, an obscure British Israelite, a journalist cum first-year law student who was never to be called

---

196. Minakata Kumagusu's diary, 8, 24, and 26 May 1897, in *Zenshu*, Supplement, Vol. 2, pp. 74 and 87.

to the Bar, Russian exiles, an Irish nationalist, and a Japanese Pan-Asian extremist, among others, as particularly distinguished or heroic. In some ways, they might all be described as members of fringe groups. Despite the fact that he had gone to the expense of having two copies of his Chinese translation of Dr Osborne's work on first aid bound for £10, there is no evidence to show that Lord Salisbury, not to mention the Queen, ever paid any attention to it when they received their copies. Nor is there any indication that Sir Thomas Sanderson or any of his colleagues in the Foreign Office, who had worked hard to rescue him from the Legation, ever took any interest in him subsequently. Not even the Treasury solicitor, who painstakingly interviewed him about the kidnapping and wrote a very favourable report about him, ever took any notice of him afterwards. As for other eminent Britons of the time, such as prominent thinkers or literary figures, there is no evidence to suggest that any of them paid the slightest attention to him.

Sun Yatsen's experience was not unique. In 1904, his arch-rival, the reformer Kang Youwei, reached London and persistently tried for a few months to see Mr Balfour at the Foreign Office, but found that he was either out of town or 'busy with state affairs'. In the end he tried to force his hand by sending him a piece of ancient Chinese porcelain.[197] The reaction of one of the Foreign Office personnel was: '. . . it is I think rather impertinent of him'.[198] But this is by the way. The point is that Sun Yatsen could hardly claim to have made friends with some of the most distinguished intellects and heroes in Europe. The fact that he nonetheless did so may be regarded as testimony to his determination to project his heroic image in 1919.

As for the relationship between what he saw and heard, and the formulation of his Three Principles of the People, Sun Yatsen was never specific about it. Consequently, some historians have felt obliged to make amends, even if only to continue the projection of his heroic image. Using a textbook on modern history prepared in Moscow, one historian has accused British capitalists of oppressing the British workers — and Sun Yatsen the observer has been described as being greatly angered by this. Instances of

---

197. FO 17/1718, pp. 695-6, Kang Youwei to Balfour, 28 October 1904.
198. FO 17/1718, pp. 697-8, Barrington to Short, 8 November 1904.

industrial dispute were cited: the strike by workers in the 'machine-manufacturing' industry in London, the miners' strike in South Wales, and the slate workers' strike in North Wales.[199] To make the same point, another historian repeated the same instances without checking the details.[200]

The free press in London reported practically every industrial dispute in the country. There *was* such a thing as a strike by slate workers in North Wales — not in all of North Wales, only at Penrhyn. It started in December 1896, and was not settled before Sun Yatsen left London.[201] The dispute had nothing to do with pay and working conditions. Indeed, the workers were quite well-off in these respects. The real issue was Lord Penrhyn's refusal to recognize the committee elected by the workers to negotiate on their behalf.[202] The question, therefore, was not so much one of livelihood, as one of the right to form a trade union.

Indeed, the London press was full of reports of industrial disputes of all descriptions: the cab-drivers and railwaymen in London, the miners in Wales, engineers and workers at shipyards in the north. But apart from the quarrymen at Penrhyn, all of them were concerned with pay rises over and above the existing wages, which were either substantial or subsistent, depending on the level of skill. Certainly the workers did not live as well as their employers, but whether or not 'oppressed' is the word to describe them depends on the political stance of the writer.

In addition, the description of the strike by the so-called workers of the 'machine-manufacturing' industry in London fits the well-known Engineering Lock-out of 1897,[203] but the strike

199. Chen Xiqi, *Tongmenghui chengliqian de Sun Zhongshan* (Guangzhou, People's Press, 1984, second edition), pp. 44–5.
200. Wu Xiangxiang, *Sun Yixian zhuan*, Vol. 1, pp. 200–1.
201. *The Times*, 29 December 1896, p. 4, cols. 1–2; 1 January 1897, p. 8, cols. 4–5; 4 January 1897, p. 8, col. 3; 5 January 1897, p. 8, cols. 1–3, and p. 9, cols. 4–5; 6 January 1897, p. 9, cols. 1–2; 9 January 1897, p. 6, col. 6; 16 January 1897, p. 10, cols. 5–6; 18 January 1897, p. 9, col. 6; 29 January 1897, p. 9, cols. 2–3 and cols. 4–5; 15 February 1897, p. 11, col. 1; 1 March 1897, p. 7, col. 6; 19 March 1897, p. 11, col. 6; 20 March 1897, p. 12, col. 6; 22 March 1897, p. 9, col. 5; 5 April 1897, p. 3, col. 4; 18 May 1897, p. 10, col. 3; 29 May 1897, p. 11, col. 6; and 31 May 1897, p. 10, col. 1.
202. *The Times*, 29 January 1897, p. 9, cols. 4–5.
203. See H. A. Clegg, Alan Fox, and A.F. Thompson, *A History of British Trade Unions since 1889, Vol. 1, 1889–1910* (Oxford, Oxford University Press, 1964), p. 163 (hereafter cited as *British Trade Unions 1889–1910*).

did not start until July of that year, well and truly after Sun Yatsen had left London. Indeed, the engineers were fighting for an eight-hour day. But the major concern of the employers was the union's objection to technical change and its consequences.[204]

Instead of resorting to indirect evidence such as reports about the industrial unrest in Britain, I have decided to concentrate as much as I can on events in which Sun Yatsen appears to have been directly involved. Judging from what he, in his own words, 'saw and heard', it is clear that he was impressed with the outbursts of British nationalism over the kidnapping saga and during the Jubilee celebrations, and with British justice which rescued him from the Chinese Legation, and was distressed by the gross unequal distribution of wealth. Without being able to be any more specific than Sun Yatsen himself, I *do* think that his experiences in London had a profound effect on the formulation of his Three Principles of the People.

Such an effect was not without its limitations, due perhaps not so much to what he saw and heard but to his own perception of them. He saw the demonstration of British power, particularly during the Naval Review and the Queen's Procession. But he does not seem to have perceived the real source of that power, which was industrialization. Instead, it appears that he mistook the scenes of 'all classes [being] drunk with sightseeing and hysterical loyalty'[205] as the source of that power. The views of a British Israelite, such as those of Edwin Collins, would probably have confirmed such a mistaken notion. Consequently, Sun Yatsen emphasized the importance of nationalism far more often than he talked about industrialization. And when he spoke about economic matters, his central theme was to tax the growing value of land rather than industrialization. His preoccupation with this tax has been attributed to his reading of the works of Henry George. This may have been the case. But his possible misconception about the real source of British power should not be overlooked either. He might have read about the strikes and heard about the socialist revolutionary movements, and blamed them on the unequal distribution of wealth. But these disruptions were only some of the many facets of industrial and concomitant

---

204. Clegg, *et al.*, *British Trade Unions 1889–1910*, p. 164.
205. James Morris, *Pax Britannica: The climax of an empire* (London, Faber and Faber, 1968), p. 26, quoting the diary of Beatrice Webb.

developments. Other facets, such as the generation of wealth and power, Sun Yatsen appears to have failed to investigate. The available records do not suggest that Sun Yatsen visited a factory while he was in London. If it were true that he had not done so, then it is not surprising that he left Britain with an imperfect knowledge of the real source of Britain's might.

Conclusion

I The Farewell

On 30 June 1897, Mrs Cantlie wrote, 'I went to see Sun Yatsen off to Japan where he has gone to live for the present. We sent a notice to that effect to the *Globe*, & they put it in'.[1] The notice read:

Sir,
    As you have all along taken a kindly interest in my welfare, I consider it only courteous to the *Globe* and to the public to state that I start for the Far East by steamer leaving Liverpool Thursday 1 July. I travel by the Canadian Pacific route across America. With grateful remembrance of your prompt action on my behalf when imprisoned in the Chinese Legation.

Yours truly,
Sun Yat Sen
46 Devonshire Street
Portland Place W
29 June[2]

On 30 June 1897, Minakata Kumagusu also wrote that he took a cab to see Sun Yatsen at his lodgings, and found that R. J. Mulkern was already there. At 11 a.m., Mulkern left, while Minakata accompanied Sun Yatsen to St Pancras Station to see him off. Then Minakata went to see R. K. Douglas in the British Museum with a farewell message from Sun Yatsen.[3] Thus Sun Yatsen left by the same route whereby he had arrived, via St Pancras Station[4] and Liverpool, from the land of glory to the land of hope.

---

1. Mrs Cantlie's diary, 30 June 1897.
2. *Globe*, 30 June 1897, p. 3, col. 5.
3. Minakata Kumagusu's diary, 30 June 1897, in *Zenshu*, Supplement, Vol. 2, p. 92.
4. It is probable that Mrs Cantlie saw him off at St Pancras Station also, because it would have been quite unnecessary for her to have gone with him to Liverpool to do so. If this were true, and there is no evidence to the contrary, the claim that she saw him off on the dockside (Stewart, *Quality of Mercy*, p. 95) must have been made on the assumption that Sun Yatsen sailed from London. I

He was well prepared for his new adventures. The available evidence does not suggest that he had been inclined towards Pan-Asianism until he met Minakata Kumagusu. Whether or not he was enthused with what was to him a new way of thinking is an open question. Given the long hours he had spent with Minakata, he probably was. What is significant, in the context of the present study, is that he said the right things when he was subsequently sought out by another ardent Japanese Pan-Asianist, Miyazaki Torazo, who then introduced him to very influential politicians in Tokyo. For the next ten years or so, Japan was to be the land of his hope.[5]

II Sun Yatsen, the Man

Minakata's diary and other pertinent writing were not available to Professor Schiffrin when he wrote his book on Sun Yatsen, published in 1968. Consequently, his interpretation of Sun Yatsen's impressive answers to Miyazaki's questions was that Sun Yatsen was 'endowed with radar-like sensitivity in adjusting to his targets'.[6] This interpretation can no longer stand, in view of Sun Yatsen's close association with the fervent Pan-Asianist, Minakata, before he met Miyazaki.

With regard to the kidnapping saga, Professor Schiffrin's belief that 'the truth would have to be modified', in order to blacken the Manchu regime, was something Sun Yatsen '*intuitively* [*my italics*] grasped when he told his story to the British'.[7] I suggest

---

(4. *continued*)
have checked all the departures listed in *The Times* for this period. The SS *Numidian*, on which Sun Yatsen travelled (Chinese Legation Archives, Slater to Chinese minister, 11–24 July 1897, in Luo Jialun, *Shiliao*, p. 166), was not listed. This may be regarded as indirect evidence that Sun Yatsen did not set sail from London, and thus corroborates the information in the *Globe* to the effect that he left England via Liverpool. Absolute certainty on this point was finally established with the help of the archivist of the Liverpool Record Office, who informed me that the *Liverpool Mercury* of 1 July 1897 announced that the *Numidian* was to sail on that day, and that the 'shipping — sailed' column of the same paper for 2 July 1897 reported that the *Numidian* had sailed for Montreal on 1 July 1897 (Evetts to Wong, 16 May 1986).

5. Jansen, *The Japanese and Sun Yat-sen*, p. 64ff.; Schiffrin, *Origins*, p. 140ff.

6. Schiffrin, *Origins*, p. 144. Professor Schiffrin does not seem to have changed his views when he published his *Reluctant Revolutionary* in 1980. See note 7.

7. Schiffrin, *Origins*, p. 115. Professor Schiffrin has not changed this view in his 1980 publication either. See note 6.

that this is not the case at all. Studying the available records on the subject, particularly those written by the keenly inquisitive journalists who had put him under public scrutiny, I think that he behaved quite naturally, without exaggerating his injuries in any way. More often than not, he had to be prodded by the reporters into saying things which another person would have said quite spontaneously.

On the crucial question as to whether or not he walked into the Legation of his own free will, Professor Luo Jialun suggests, and Professor Schiffrin asserts, that he did so. In the light of the present assessment of the evidence on which they have based their views, in particular, the circumstances under which such evidence was produced, I cannot agree with them. My own interpretation is reinforced by the new evidence which I have discovered in London, Beijing, Hong Kong, and Japan; and by extensive field-work.

For all my pains, I may still be wrong, since all the evidence that I have assembled so far has not enabled me to reach absolute certainty on this point. I cannot emphasize more strongly that, without the meticulous research conducted by both Professor Luo Jialun and Professor Schiffrin, I could never have hoped to reach my present stage of understanding of the subject. I very much hope that some future historian will build on the work we have done. Before that happens, I am more than inclined to believe that Sun Yatsen *did not lie* on this point.

To look at the question from a different angle, Professor Luo Jialun suggests, and Professor Schiffrin asserts, that Sun Yatsen twisted the story. Therefore, the onus is on them to prove that Sun Yatsen actually did so. I have not been convinced by their arguments or by their supporting evidence. Until I am so convinced, I prefer to believe Sun Yatsen's own words as stated publicly, recorded publicly, circulated publicly and scrutinized publicly at the time. I am inclined to regard with caution indirect reports about what he was alleged to have said quite some time after the event, when all the circumstances had changed. Indeed, such oral reports are only part of a sea of adulatory literature about the man who was being sanctified as 'Father of the Nation'.

'Where in this mass of materials should we find the real Sun Yatsen?', Professor Martin Wilbur has asked.[8] There was a

---

8. Wilbur, *Sun Yat-sen*, p. 1.

period of nine months in Sun Yatsen's life, before he became
important politically, when his activities were recorded by three
people who might be described as disinterested parties. They
were Slater, Mrs Cantlie, and Minakata Kumagusu. Then for
about two weeks in this period, his behaviour was closely watched and documented, and his words and actions judiciously recorded. And for two or three days thereafter, he was hotly
pursued by journalists who reported practically everything he
did, everything he said, and everything that was said about him.
These materials differ from the massive collection of adulatory
essays, reminiscences, and commemorative speeches about him;
they differ even from his own subsequent writings, speeches,
letters, and telegrams, all of which appear to have been intended
to serve a particular purpose at a particular time.

In this regard, it is hoped that the present study has enabled us
to catch a glimpse of 'the intimate and esoteric aspects of Sun
Yatsen, the man'.[9]

III The Creation of the Heroic Image by Others

But even those nine months were not entirely free from adulatory
literature of some kind. One discovery in the present study is that
the very first claim that Sun Yatsen had walked fearlessly into the
Chinese Legation to preach revolution was made by somebody in
Japan as soon as news of the kidnapping reached that country.
As suggested, the writer was most probably Chen Shaobai, who
was a devoted follower of Sun Yatsen and who was most anxious
to create an heroic image for him, in the wake of the struggle for
leadership within the Xing Zhong Hui, and the subsequent dis-
mal failure of the plot at Guangzhou. Thus began a deliberate
attempt to create an heroic image, without the hero himself
knowing anything about it.

The late Professor Luo Jialun was a very serious scholar; so is
Professor Schiffrin. But their respective speculations and assertions have simply consolidated this image.

There were others who made their contributions, directly or
indirectly, such as Dr Cantlie, the British press, translators of

9. Wilbur, *Sun Yat-sen*, p. 2.

Kidnapped in London, and even Lord Salisbury. There was a host of favourable circumstances to which the origins of the heroic image may be traced. This image has varied according to these circumstances. Sometimes it was created and projected for political purposes, and at other times it is described historically.

IV The Cultivation and Projection of the Heroic Image

Apart from others' efforts, Sun Yatsen also had a role in cultivating and projecting his own heroic image. The writing of the two London articles was perhaps one of the most important actions in this regard. In these articles he tried to establish himself as the spokesman and leader of the progressive elements in China. They were designed almost as an answer to the constant lament of the *China Mail* (and hence also of the *Overland China Mail*, destined largely for Britain) that China lacked an outstanding leader. He refuted the arguments of a well-written, persuasive, and powerful article by an anonymous British author who favoured British official support of China, and who wanted to prop up the Manchu dynasty.

His translation of Dr Osborne's work on first aid, and his presentation of two copies bound at great expense to Queen Victoria and Lord Salisbury, may be interpreted as an attempt to impress the recipients.

More important was the entry he prepared for Professor Giles' *Chinese Biographical Dictionary*. In it, he proclaimed to the world that he was the man destined to save China.

V The Hero's Image of Himself

What made Sun Yatsen think that he was the man destined to save China? In this, the last section of my Conclusion, I may be allowed to throw open a few ideas which are bound to provoke some comment and stimulate further discussions.

It is said, and is generally believed, that when Sun Yatsen was a child of 11, he used to listen with great interest to the stories told by former soldiers of the Taiping Army, who had returned to his village; that he was full of admiration for the Taiping leader, Hong Xiuquan;[10] and that he regarded himself as Hong Xiu-

---

10. Luo Jialun, *Guofu nianpu*, Vol. 1, p. 18.

quan's successor.[11] Specialists on Sun Yatsen have invariably emphasized the anti-Manchu aspect of the Taiping leader, but seldom if ever the other side of the coin, which was the Christian facet of the man, who was convinced that he had been chosen by God to save China and rid her of all evils.

At the age of 13, Sun Yatsen went to Hawaii and studied at Iolani School, an Anglican establishment. Thus began his association with Christianity, 'which was to exert a powerful influence in shaping his political *career* [*my italics*]'.[12] By this, it was probably meant that the clergy and churches subsequently offered him cover and protection while he conducted his subversive activities, particularly during the plot at Guangzhou.[13] But the Christian influence on his political *thinking* has been glossed over.

Had there not been opposition from his 'heathen relatives', it has been alleged, Sun Yatsen would have been baptized at Iolani School.[14] After graduating from this school at the age of 17, he entered Oahu College, which was run by the Hawaiian Evangelical Association (Congregationalist and Presbyterian).[15] Sun Yatsen's conversion appeared imminent, and his brother sent him back to China.[16] Returning to his native village, he went about desecrating the wooden image of the local deity while talking enthusiastically about the Taipings. Again, the comment has been made that his secular and religious education in Hawaii were incompatible with peasant mores and beliefs,[17] but no attempt has been made to relate Sun Yatsen's behaviour to that of the Taiping leader, Hong Xiuquan, who had done the same thing to his village idols.[18] Both men were forced to leave their villages as a result.

Sun Yatsen went to Hong Kong, and attended another Anglican school, the Diocesan Home. At the same time, he also studied the Chinese classics with Qu Fengzhi, a minister asso-

11. Schiffrin, *Reluctant Revolutionary*, p. 23.
12. Schiffrin, *Origins*, p. 14.
13. Schiffrin, *Origins*, pp. 80 and 89–92.
14. Schiffrin, *Origins*, p. 14, quoting Henry B. Restarick, *Sun Yat Sen, Liberator of China* (New Haven, 1931).
15. Schiffrin, *Origins*, pp. 14–15, quoting Kuykendall, *Hawaiian Kingdom*, pp. 105 and 110.
16. Schiffrin, *Origins*, p. 15.
17. Schiffrin, *Origins*, p. 15.
18. Franz Michael, *The Taiping Rebellion: History and Documents, Vol. 1 History* (Seattle, University of Washington Press, 1966), p. 28.

ciated with the London Missionary Society. In 1884, at the age of 18, he was baptized by Dr Charles Hager, an American Congregationalist missionary.[19] In 1887, he entered the College of Medicine for Chinese in Hong Kong. It was here that he earned himself the nickname of 'Hong Xiuquan'.[20] Why did his classmates call him by the name of the Taiping leader? Was it simply because of his anti-Manchu sentiments, as alleged;[21] or was it also because his personal outlook as a Christian was similar to that of the Taiping leader, namely, that he regarded himself as the saviour of China?

If Sun Yatsen had designated himself as another Hong Xiuquan since he was a child, the formal grounding in the Bible that he received as a youth would have forestalled anything like Hong Xiuquan's claim to be the younger brother of Jesus. Probably, his case was one of transposing a somewhat religious image to the world of politics; and instead of seeing himself as a spiritual cum political leader as Hong Xiuquan had done, he looked upon himself simply as a saviour of his people downtrodden by the Manchus. His experiences in London reinforced the sense of his destiny. Having, it seems, worked out in his mind the Three Principles of the People, he was all the more confident about his ability to lead; and he returned to the Far East with a much clearer idea of the direction in which China was going to move.

---

19. Schiffrin, *Origins*, p. 16.
20. Chen Shaobai, *Xing Zhong Hui*, in *Xinhai geming*, Vol. 1, p. 24.
21. Chen Shaobai, *Xing Zhong Hui*, in *Xinhai geming*, Vol. 1, p. 24.

Selected Bibliography

Archives

British Foreign Office Archives, Public Record Office, London.
> FO 17/1718, Chinese Revolutionaries in British Dominions, 1896–1905.
> FO 17/1158, O'Conor to Foreign Office, 1893.
> FO 17/1286, Domestic Various, 1896.
> FO 17/1327, Domestic Various, 1897.

Boothe Papers, Hoover Institution on War, Revolution and Peace, Stanford, California.

British Manuscripts, Aberdeen University, Aberdeen.
> U1 Student Register, Vol.1, 1860/1–1890/1.
> U11 Bursary Competitors, 1860–79.
> Medical Schedule, 1873.

British Manuscripts, British Museum, London.
> BL Add. 39168/138–141, Sun Yatsen's letters to G.E. Musgrove, 1908–10.
> Central Archives, Reading Room Register.
> Central Archives, Minutes of the Standing Committee of the British Museum Trustees, 10 October 1914.
> Central Archives, Douglas' application to be First-Class Assistant in the Department of Oriental Printed Books and MSS, 1 February 1865.

British Manuscripts, of the Cantlie family, England.
> Mrs (later Lady) Mabel Cantlie's diary.
> The Cantlie Family Papers, including newspaper cuttings, and so on.
> Sir Keith Cantlie's memoirs (typescript).

British Manuscripts, Charing Cross Hospital.
> A brief history of the Hospital (typescript).
> A résumé of Sir James Cantlie's history and achievements (typescript).

British Manuscripts, Foreign Missions Club, London.
> Visitors' Book: entries for 1896.

British Manuscripts, Gray's Inn, London.
> Gray's Inn Admissions and Calls, etc., 1625–1900.
> Gray's Inn Book of Orders, Vol. 18, May 1888–March 1894.
> Gray's Inn Book of Orders, Vol. 20, April 1899–April 1903.
> Gray's Inn Admission Document.

British Manuscripts, King's College, London.
 KA/1C/D60, Papers relating to Douglas' application to be Professor of Chinese in 1873.
 KA/C/M11, Council Minutes, Vol. 50, entry 488, Douglas elected Professor of Chinese.
British Manuscripts, Modern Records Centre, Maritime House, Liverpool.
 Voyage Book of the SS *Glenfarg*.
 Wage Book of the SS *Glenfarg*.
British Manuscripts, University College, London.
 Fee Receipt Book, Faculty of Arts and Law, Session 1876–7.
British Manuscripts, Wellcome Institute, London.
 Western ms 1488, Dr James Cantlie's lecture on Hong Kong (incomplete).
 Western ms 2934, Sun Yatsen's examination script, 1887.
 Western ms 2935, Examination scripts for 1887: names of students.
Chinese Legation (London) Archives, reprinted in Luo Jialun, *Shiliao*.
 Reports by Slater's Detective Association.
 Letters and telegrams to and from the Legation.
Chinese Palace Museum Records, Palace Museum, Beijing.
 Waiwubu 536, documents *re* Minister Gong Zhaoyuan.
 Waiwubu 870, financial reports of the Legation in London.
 Waiwubu 871, documents *re* Minister Zhang Deyi.

Works in Western Languages

Aberdeen University Calendar, 1870–1871, and *1871–1872*.
Aberdeen University, Preliminary Record of the Arts Class, 1866–1870 (Murray, Aberdeen, 1901).
Aberdeen University, Records of the Arts Class, 1868–1872, edited by P. J. Anderson (Aberdeen University Press, 1892, first edition); edited by Stephen Ree (Aberdeen University Press, 1930, second edition).
Aberdeen University Review, Vol. 13, 1925–1926.
Aberdeen University, Roll of Graduates 1860–1900, edited by Col. William Johnston (Aberdeen University Press, 1906).
Aberdeen University, Roll of Service (Aberdeen University Press, 1921).
Adcock, St John (ed.), *Wonderful London: The world's greatest city described by its best writers and pictured by its finest photographers* (London, Fleetway House, n.d., 3 vols.).
Adelaide Advertiser (Adelaide).
Age, The (Melbourne).
Aitken, W. Francis, 'The Museums and Their Treasures', in Adcock (ed.), *Wonderful London*, Vol. 3, pp. 1096–109.

Alcock, Leslie, *Arthur's Britain: History and Archaeology*, A.D. *367–634* (London, Allen Lane, 1971).
Altman, A. A., and Schiffrin, H. Z., 'Sun Yat-sen and the Japanese, 1914–1916', *Modern Asian Studies*, Vol. 6, April 1972, pp. 129–49.
Anon., *A Brief History of the Metropolitan Police* (London, 1983).
Armstrong, Martin, 'Leafy London: In Park and Pleasaunce', in Adcock (ed.), *Wonderful London*, Vol. 1, pp. 367–78.
Arrowsmith, 1854–1954, 1954–1979 (Bristol, J. W. Arrowsmith, 1979, second edition).
Aurora Borealis Academica: Aberdeen University Appreciations, 1860–1889 (Aberdeen University Press, 1889).
Bahya Ibn Yusuf, *The Duties of the Heart* ..., translated and with an introduction by Edwin Collins (London, Oriental Press, 1904).
Baildon, W. Paley, *The Quin-Centenary of Lincoln's Inn, 1422–1922* (London, 1922).
Baines, T., *History of the Commerce and Town of Liverpool* (London, Longman, 1852).
Balme, Harold, *China and Modern Medicine* (London, United Society for Mission Education, 1921).
Banffshire Journal (Banffshire).
Barclay, William, *The Schools and Schoolmasters of Banffshire* (Banff, Banffshire Journal, 1925).
Bible, The Holy (Oxford, Oxford University Press, 1896).
Birmingham Post (Birmingham).
Black and White (London).
Blake, Robert, Lord, *A History of Rhodesia* (London, Eyre Methuen, 1977).
Bland, J. O. P., *Li Hung-chang* (London, Constable, 1917).
—— and Backhouse, E., *China Under the Empress Dowager* (London, Heinemann, 1910).
Bolt, Christine, *Victorian Attitudes to Race* (London, Routledge & Kegan Paul, 1971).
Boorman, Howard L., and Howard, Richard C. (eds.), *Biographical Dictionary of Republican China* (New York, Columbia University Press, 1967–71, 4 vols.).
Booth, Charles (ed.), *Labour and Life of the People in London* (London, Williams and Norgate, 1891–1902, 8 vols.).
Boulger, Demetrius C., *The Life of Sir Halliday Macartney K.C.M.G.* (London, John Lane, 1908).
Boyce, D. George, *Nationalism in Ireland* (London, Croom Helm, 1982).
Braden, Charles, *These also Believe* (New York, Macmillan and Company, 1957).

Brinton, Crane, *English Political Thought in the Nineteenth Century* (London, Ernest Benn, 1933).

———— *The Anatomy of Revolution* (New York, Vintage Books, 1957).

Brisbane Courier (Brisbane).

Brisbane Telegraph (Brisbane).

British Review (London).

Britton, Roswell S., *The Chinese Periodical Press, 1800–1912* (Shanghai, Kelly & Walsh, 1933).

Brunnert, H. S., and Hagelstrom, V. V., *Present Day Political Organization of China*, translated by A. Beltchenko and E. E. Moran (Shanghai, Kelly & Walsh, 1912).

Bruun, Geoffrey, *Nineteenth Century European Civilization, 1815–1914* (New York, Oxford University Press, 1960).

Bunker, Gerald E., 'The Kidnapping of Sun Yatsen in London, 1896', seminar paper, Harvard University, 1963.

Cadbury, W. W., and Jones, M. H., *At the Point of a Lancet: One Hundred Years of the Canton Hospital, 1835–1935* (Shanghai, Kelly and Walsh, 1935).

'Cantlie, James', *Aberdeen University Preliminary Record of the Arts Class, 1866–70* (Aberdeen, Murray, 1901), p. 10.

'Cantlie, James', *Aberdeen University Records of Arts Class, 1866–1870* (Aberdeen University Press, 1930), pp. 19–20.

'Cantlie, James: An Obituary', *Aberdeen University Review*, Vol. 13, 1925–6, pp. 283–4.

'Cantlie, James', *Aberdeen University Roll of Graduates 1860–1900*, edited by Col. William Johnston (Aberdeen, 1906), p. 76.

'Cantlie, James', *Aberdeen University Roll of Service* (Aberdeen University Press, 1921), p. 147.

Cantlie, James, and Jones, C. Sheridan, *Sun Yat-sen and the Awakening of China* (London, Jarrold & Sons, 1912).

Cantlie, Neil, and Seaver, George, *Sir James Cantlie: A Romance in Medicine* (London, John Murray, 1939).

Cape Argus (Cape Town).

Carter, C. H., *The Western European Powers, 1500–1700* (London, Hodder & Stoughton, 1971).

Chan, Mary Man-yue, 'Chinese Revolutionaries in Hong Kong, 1895–1911', Master's thesis, University of Hong Kong, 1963.

Chandler, George, *Liverpool Shipping: A Short History* (London, Phoenix House, 1960).

Chang Hao, 'Liang Ch'i-ch'ao and Intellectual Changes in the Late Nineteenth Century', *Journal of Asian Studies*, Vol. 29, No. 1, November 1969.

Chen, Stephen, and Payne, Robert, *Sun Yat-sen, a Portrait* (New York, John Day, 1946).

Chen Yuan-chuan, 'Elements of an East-West Synthesis in Dr Sun Yatsen's Concept of the "Five-Power Constitution" and in the Chinese Constitution of 1946' in Kindermann (ed.), *Sun Yat-sen: Founder and Symbol of China's Revolutionary Nation-Building*, pp. 143–72.

Ch'en, Jerome, *Yuan Shih-k'ai, 1859–1916: Brutus Assumes the Purple* (London, George Allen & Unwin, 1961).

Chin Hsiao-yi, 'The Influence of Chinese Confucian Political Theory and Cultural Tradition on Sun Yatsen's Ideology of Synthesis' in Kindermann (ed.), *Sun Yat-sen: Founder and Symbol of China's Revolutionary Nation-Building*, pp. 97–110.

China Mail (Hong Kong).

Chinese Biographical Dictionary, compiled by H. A. Giles (London, B. Quaritch, 1898).

Christchurch Press (Christchurch).

Clegg, H. A., Fox, Alan, and Thompson, A. F., *A History of British Trade Unions since 1889, Vol. 1, 1889–1910* (Oxford, Oxford University Press, 1964).

Cohn, Norman, *The Pursuit of the Millenium: Revolutionary Millenarians and Mystical Anarchists of the Middle Ages* (London, Temple Smith, 1970).

Concise Dictionary of National Biography, 1901–1970 (Oxford, Oxford University Press, 1982).

Crockford's Clerical Directory (Oxford, Oxford University Press, 1961).

Daily Chronicle (London).

Daily Graphic (London).

Daily Mail (London).

Daily News (London).

Daily Telegraph (London).

Diplomaticus, 'Lord Salisbury's New China Policy', *Fortnightly Review*, new series, 65.388, 1 April 1899, pp. 539–50.

'Douglas, Sir Robert Kennaway', in *Who Was Who, Vol. 1: 1897–1915*, p. 205.

Echo (London).

Eddey, Keith, *The English Legal System* (London, Sweet & Maxwell, 1982, third edition).

Ellison, T., *Reminiscences* (Liverpool, Henry Young, 1905).

Endacott, G. B., *A History of Hong Kong* (London, Oxford University Press, 1958).

English and Empire Digest, replacement volume 16, 1981 reissue (London, Butterworth & Co., 1981).

Ensor, R. C. K., *England 1870–1914* (Oxford, Oxford University Press, 1936).

Evening News (London).

Evening Standard (London).

'Finlay, Robert Bannatyne', in *Who Was Who, Vol. 3: 1929–1940*, p. 446.

Ford, J. F., 'An Account of England, 1895–1996 — By Fung Ling, Naval Attaché at the Imperial Chinese Legation in London', China Society Occasional Papers, No. 22 (London, 1982).

Foreign Office List, 1896 (London, Harrison and Sons, 1896).

Foreign Office List, 1897 (London, Harrison and Sons, 1897).

Foster, Joseph, *Men-at-the-Bar* (London, Hazell, Watson and Viney, 1889, second edition).

Franke, Wolfgang, *The Reform and Abolition of the Traditional Chinese Examination System* (Cambridge, Mass., Harvard University, Centre for East Asian Studies, 1960).

Fried, Albert, and Elman, Richard M. (eds.), *Charles Booth* (London, Hutchinson, 1969).

Gayer, M. H., *The Heritage of the Anglo-Saxon Race* (Haverhill, Mass., Destiny Publishers, 1941).

George, D., *Nationalism in Ireland* (London, Croom Helm, 1982).

George, Henry, Jr., *The Life of Henry George* (Toronto, Poole Publishing Co., 1900).

'Giles, Herbert Allen', in Venn (comp.), *Alumni Cantabrigienses: A biographical list of all known students, graduates, and holders of office at the University of Cambridge from the earliest times to 1900. Part 2, from 1752–1900*, Vol. 3, p. 49.

'Giles, Herbert Allen', in *Who Was Who, Vol. 3: 1929–1940*, p. 512.

Girling, D. A. (ed.), *Everyman's Encyclopaedia* (London, J. M. Dent & Sons, 1978, sixth edition).

Glasgow Herald (Glasgow).

Glass, Stafford, *The Matabele War* (London, Longman, 1968).

Globe (London).

Gore's Official Directory, 1897.

Graphic (London).

Gray, Richard (ed.), *American Verse of the Nineteenth Century* (London, Dent & Totowa; New Jersey, Rowman & Littlefield, 1973).

Hackett, Roger F., 'Chinese Students in Japan, 1900–1910', *Papers on China*, Harvard University, Committee on International and Regional Studies, No. 3, 1949, pp. 134–69.

Hager, Charles R., 'Dr Sun Yat Sen: Some Personal Reminiscences', *The Missionary Herald* (Boston, April 1912), reprinted in Sharman, *Sun Yat-sen: His Life and its Meaning*, pp. 382–7.

Harnack, E. P., 'Glen Line to the Orient', *Sea Breezes*, new series, Vol. 19 [April 1955], pp. 268–92.

Hartt, Julian, 'Americans' Plot for Chinese Revolt Revealed: Letters at Hoover Tower Tell of 1908 Conspiracy', *Los Angeles Times*, 13 October 1966.

Hastings, James (ed.), *Encyclopaedia of Religions and Ethics* (Edinburgh, T&T Clarke, 1915, 11 vols.).

Hayne, M. B., 'The Quai D'Orsay and French Foreign Policy, 1891–1914', unpublished Ph.D. thesis, University of Sydney, 1985.

Hearnshaw, E. J. C., *The Centenary History of King's College, London, 1828–1928* (London, George Harrap & Co., 1929).

Heuston, R. F. V., *Lives of the Lord Chancellors 1885 to 1940* (Oxford, Oxford University Press, 1964).

Hobart Mercury (Hobart).

Hocking, Charles, *Dictionary of Disasters at Sea, 1824–1962* (London, Lloyd's Register of Shipping, 1969, 2 vols.).

Honourable Society of Gray's Inn, The (London, 1976, second edition).

Howard, Richard C., 'K'ang Yu-wei (1858–1927): His Intellectual Background and Early Thought', in Wright and Twitchett (eds.), *Confucian Personalities*, pp. 294–316.

_____ 'The Chinese Reform Movement of the 1890s: A Symposium', *Journal of Asian Studies*, Vol. 29, No. 1, November 1969.

Hsiao Kung-chuan, 'K'ang Yu-wei and Confucianism', *Monumenta Serica*, Vol. 18, 1959, pp. 96–212.

_____ *A Modern China and a New World: K'ang Yu-wei, Reformer and Utopian, 1858–1927* (Seattle, University of Washington Press, 1975).

_____ *Rural China: Imperial Control in the Nineteenth Century* (Seattle, University of Washington Press, 1960).

Hsu Chi-wei, 'The Influence of Western Political Thought and Revolutionary History on the Goals and Self-Image of Sun Yatsen and the Republican Revolutionary Movement in China', in Kindermann (ed.), *Sun Yat-sen: Founder and Symbol of China's Revolutionary Nation-Building*, pp. 111–27.

Hsu, I. C. Y., *The Ili Crisis* (New York, Oxford University Press, 1966).

Hsueh Chun-tu, 'Sun Yat-sen, Yang Ch'u-yun, and the Early Revolutionary Movement in China', *Journal of Asian Studies*, Vol. 19, No. 3, May 1960, pp. 317–18.

Hu Sheng, *Imperialism and Chinese Politics* (English translation) (Beijing, Foreign Languages Press, 1955).

Huang, Philip C., *Liang Ch'i-Ch'ao and Modern Chinese Liberalism* (Seattle, University of Washington Press, 1972).

Huddersfield Examiner (Huddersfield).

Hummel, Arthur W. (ed.), *Eminent Chinese of the Ch'ing Period* (Washington, DC, Government Printing Office, 1944, 2 vols.).

Illustrated London News (London).

Irish Times (Dublin).

Iwao Seiichi (ed.), *Biographical Dictionary of Japanese History*, translated by Burton Watson (Tokyo, Kodansha International Ltd., 1978).

Jansen, Marius B., *The Japanese and Sun Yat-sen*, Harvard Historical Monographs, No. 27 (Cambridge, Mass., Harvard University Press, 1954).

Judges and Law Officers, 1897.

Kelly's Post Office London Directory, 1896 (London, Kelly & Co., 1896).

Kelly's Post Office London Directory, 1897 (London, Kelly & Co., 1897).

Kelly's Post Office London Directory, 1898 (London, Kelly & Co., 1898).

Kiernan, V. G., *The Lords of Human Kind: European attitudes towards the outside world in the Imperial Age* (London, Weidenfeld and Nicolson, 1969).

Kindermann, G. (ed.), *Sun Yat-sen: Founder and Symbol of China's Revolutionary Nation-Building* (Munich, Gunter Olzog, 1982).

———— 'Sunyatsenism — Prototype of a Syncretistic Third World Ideology', in Kindermann (ed.), *Sun Yat-sen: Founder and Symbol of China's Revolutionary Nation-Building*, pp. 79–96.

'Kitto, The Late Reverend Prebendary', in *St Martin-in-the-Fields Monthly Messenger*, No. 158, May 1903, pp. 9–13.

Kock, W. J. de, *et al.* (eds.), *Dictionary of South African Biography* (Nasionale Boekhandel, Cape Town, Johannesburg, Durban, and Pretoria, 1968–81, 4 vols.).

Kwong, Luke S. K., *A Mosaic of the Hundred Days: Personalities, Politics, and Ideas of 1898*, Harvard East Asian Monographs, No. 112 (Cambridge, Mass., Harvard University, Centre for East Asian Studies, 1984).

L., 'The Future of China', *Fortnightly Review*, new series, Vol. 60, 1 August 1896, pp. 159–74.

Lauterpacht, Hersh (ed.), *L.F.L. Oppenheim, International Law: A Treatise* (London, Longman, 1957, eighth edition).

Levenson, Joseph R., *Liang Ch'i-ch'ao and the Mind of Modern China*, Harvard Historical Monographs, No. 26 (Cambridge, Mass., Harvard University Press, 1953).

Li Chien-nung, *The Political History of China, 1840–1928*, translated by Teng Ssu-yu and Jeremy Ingalls (Princeton, New Jersey, Van Nostrand, 1956).

Linebarger, Paul, *Sun Yat-sen and the Chinese Republic* (New York, Century, 1925).

Liverpool Echo (Liverpool).

Liverpool Mercury (Liverpool).

Lo Hui-min (ed.), *The Correspondence of G. E. Morrison, Vol. 1, 1895–1912* (Cambridge, Cambridge University Press, 1976), *Vol. 2: 1912–1920* (Cambridge, Cambridge University Press, 1978).

London and China Express (London).

MacNaghten, Sir Melville L., *The Days of My Years* (London, Edward Arnold, 1914).

Manchester Guardian (Manchester).

Mao Tse-tung, Soong Ching-ling, *et al.*, *Dr Sun Yat-sen: Commemorative Articles and Speeches* (Beijing, 1957).

Martin, Bernard, *Strange Vigour: A Biography of Sun Yat-sen* (London, William Heinemann, 1944).

——— 'Sun Yat-sen's Vision for China', China Society Occasional Papers, No. 15 (London, 1966).

Massingham, H. J., 'A Look at the Zoo', in Adcock (ed.), *Wonderful London*, Vol. 1, pp. 154–65.

Megarry, Rt. Hon. Sir Robert, *An Introduction to Lincoln's Inn* (London, 1980, revised edition).

Michael, Franz, *The Taiping Rebellion: History and Documents, Vol. 1 History* (Seattle, University of Washington Press, 1966).

Miltoun, Francis, *All About Ships and Shipping. A Handbook of Popular Nautical Information*, revised and edited by E. P. Harnack (London, Alexander Moring, 1930, fourth edition).

Morning (London).

Morning Advertiser (London).

Morning Leader (London).

Morning Post (London).

Morris, James, *Pax Britannica: The climax of an empire* (London, Faber and Faber, 1968).

Morrison, G. E., *An Australian in China* (London, H. Cox, 1902).

Morse, Hosea Ballou, *The Trade and Administration of the Chinese Empire* (London, Longman, 1908; reprinted in Taipei, 1966).

——— *The International Relations of the Chinese Empire* (London, Longman, 1910–18, 3 vols.).

Mortimer, J. E., *History of the Boilermakers' Society. Volume 1: 1834–1906* (London, George Allen & Unwin, 1973).

Muramatsu Yuji, 'Some Themes in Chinese Rebel Ideologies', in Wright (ed.), *The Confucian Persuasion*, pp. 241–67.

Nath, Marie-Luise, 'China in World Politics: Sun Yatsen's Views on International Relations', in Kindermann (ed.), *Sun Yat-sen: Founder and Symbol of China's Revolutionary Nation-Building*, pp. 301–9.

New Catholic Encyclopedia (Washington, DC, Catholic University of America, 1967, 15 vols.).

New Issue of the Abridged Statistical History of Scotland Illustrative of its Physical, Industrial, Moral, and Social Aspects, and Civil and Religious Institutions, from the Most Authentic Sources, arranged Parochially with Biographical, Historical, and Descriptive Notices, edited by James Hooper Dawson (Edinburgh, W. H. Lizars, 1857).

New Statistical Account of Scotland, by the Ministers of the Respective Parishes, under the Superintendence of a Committee of the Society for the Benefit of the Sons and Daughters of the Clergy (Edinburgh and London, William Blackwood and Sons, 1845), Vol. 13.

New York Times (New York).

New Zealand Herald (Auckland).

Nikiforov, V. N., *Sun Iat-sen, Oktiabr 1896; dve nedeli iz zhizni kitaisko-go revoliutsionera* (*Sun Yatsen, October 1896; Two Weeks in the Life of a Chinese Revolutionary*) (Moscow, Nauka, 1977).

Nivison, David S., and Wright, Arthur F. (eds.), *Confucianism in Action* (Stanford, Stanford University Press, 1959).

Notes on the Constitution, Administration, History and Buildings of the Inner Temple (London, 1962).

Observer (London).

Otago Press (Otago).

Overland China Mail (Hong Kong).

Overland Mail (London).

Pall Mall Gazette (London).

Pelcovits, Nathan A., *Old China Hands and the Foreign Office* (New York, American Institute of Pacific Relations, 1948).

Pelling, Henry, *A History of British Trade Unionism* (Harmondsworth, Penguin, 1963).

Potter, Beatrice, 'The Docks', in Booth (ed.), *Labour and Life of the People in London*, Vol. 1, pp. 184–209.

Public Opinion (London).

Pugh, Edwin, 'Outcasts in the Great City', in Adcock (ed.), *Wonderful London*, Vol. 3, pp. 1089–96.

Queen's London: A pictorial and descriptive record of the great metropolis in the last year of Queen Victoria's reign (London, Cassell, 1902, 2 vols.).

Ranger, T. O., 'The Nineteenth Century in Southern Rhodesia', in T. O. Ranger (ed.), *Aspects of Central African History* (London, Heinemann, 1968), pp. 112–53.

――――― *Revolt in Rhodesia* (London, Heinemann, 1967).

Restarick, Henry B., *Sun Yat Sen, Liberator of China* (New Haven, Yale University Press, 1931).

Richard, Timothy, *Forty-five Years in China* (New York, Stokes, 1916).

Rosenthale, Eric (ed.), *South African Dictionary of National Biography* (London, Frederick Warne, 1966).

Roxburgh, Sir Ronald (ed.), *The Records of the Honourable Society of Lincoln's Inn: The Black Books, Vol. 5, A.D. 1845–A.D. 1914* (London, 1968).

Royal Court of Justice (London, 1983).

St James's Gazette (London).

St Martin-in-the-Fields Monthly Messenger, No. 82, October 1896; No. 83, November 1896; No. 84, December 1896; No. 90, June 1897; and No. 158, May 1903.

Scalapino, Robert A., and Yu, George T., *The Chinese Anarchist Movement*, University of California, Centre for Chinese Studies, Research Series No. 1 (1961).

───── and Schiffrin, Harold Z., 'Early Socialist Currents in the Chinese Revolutionary Movement: Sun Yat-sen versus Liang Ch'i-ch'ao', *Journal of Asian Studies*, Vol. 18, No. 3, May 1959.

Schiffrin, Harold Z., 'The Enigma of Sun Yat-sen' in M. Wright (ed.), *China in Revolution: The First Phase, 1900–1903* (New Haven, Yale University Press, 1968), pp. 443–74.

───── 'Sun Yat-sen's Early Land Policy: The Origin and Meaning of "Equalization of Land Rights"', *Journal of Asian Studies*, Vol. 16, August 1957, pp. 549–64.

───── and Sohn Pow-key, 'Henry George on Two Continents: A Comparative Study in the Diffusion of Ideas', *Comparative Studies in Society and History*, Vol. 2, October 1959, pp. 85–108.

───── *Sun Yat-sen and the Origins of the Chinese Revolution* (Berkeley & Los Angeles, University of California Press, 1968).

───── *Sun Yat-sen: Reluctant Revolutionary* (Boston, Little Brown, 1980).

Schreuder, D. M., *Gladstone and Kruger: Liberal Government and Colonial 'Home Rule' 1880–85* (London, Routledge & Kegan Paul, 1969).

Schwartz, Benjamin, *In Search of Wealth and Power: Yen Fu and the West* (Cambridge, Mass., Harvard University Press, 1964).

Scott, Carolyn, *Betwixt Heaven and Charing Cross: The Story of St Martin-in-the-Fields* (London, Robert Hale, 1971).

Sell's Dictionary of the World's Press, 1897 (London, 1897).

Sharman, Lyon, *Sun Yat-sen: His Life and its Meaning* (New York, John Day, 1934).

Sheppard, Francis, 'London and the Nation in the Nineteenth Century', *Royal Historical Society Transactions*, No. 35 (London, 1985), pp. 51–74.

Simpson, W. Douglas (ed.), *The Fusion of 1860: A Record of the Centenary Celebrations and a History of the University of Aberdeen 1860–1960* (Edinburgh and London, Oliver and Boyd, 1963).

Smith, Richard J., *Mercenaries and Mandarins: The Ever-Victorious Army in Nineteenth-century China* (New York, KTO Press, 1978).

Soothill, William E., *Timothy Richard of China* (London, Seeley, Service & Co., 1924).

Speaker (London).

Standard (London).

Star (London).

Stevens, Sylvester K., *American Expansion in Hawaii, 1842–1898* (Harrisburg, Penn., Archive Publishing, 1945).

Stewart, Jean C., *The Quality of Mercy: The Lives of Sir James and Lady Cantlie* (London, George Allen & Unwin, 1983).

Straits Times (Singapore).

Strand Magazine (London).

Sun (London).

Sun Yatsen, *Kidnapped in London: Being the story of my capture by, detention at, and release from the Chinese Legation, London* (Bristol, Arrowsmith, 1897).

——— 'China's Present and Future: The Reform Party's Plea for British Benevolent Neutrality', *Fortnightly Review*, new series, Vol. 61, No. 363, 1 March 1897, pp. 424–40.

——— 'Judicial Reform in China', *East Asia*, Vol. 1, No. 1, July 1897, pp. 3–13.

——— 'My Reminiscences', *Strand Magazine*, March 1912, pp. 301–7.

Sydney Morning Herald (Sydney).

Talmud, *The Wisdom of Israel: being extracts from the Babylonian Talmud and Midrash Rabboth*, translated from the Aramaic and Hebrew with an introduction by Edwin Collins (London, Orient Press, 1904).

Tatler (London).

Taylor, A. J. P., *English History, 1914–1945* (Oxford, Oxford University Press, 1965).

Teng Ssu-yu and Fairbank, John K., *China's Response to the West: A Documentary Survey, 1839–1923* (Cambridge, Mass., Harvard University Press, 1954).

Thompson, Phyllis, *A Place for Pilgrims: The Story of the Foreign Missions Club in Highbury, London* (London, 1983).

The Times (London).

Time and Tide (London).

Tomlinson, H. M., 'Down in Dockland', in Adcock (ed.), *Wonderful London*, Vol. 1, pp. 147–54.

Toronto Star (Toronto).

Trevelyan, Marie, *Britain's Greatness Foretold. The Story of Boadicea, the British Warrior Queen . . .*, with an introduction, 'The Prediction Fulfilled', by Edwin Collins, etc. (London, J. Hogg, 1900).

Tse Tsan Tai, *The Chinese Republic: Secret History of the Revolution* (Hong Kong, 1924).

University College London Calendar, 1877–1878.

Venn, J. A. (comp.), *Alumni Cantabrigienses: A biographical list of all known students, graduates, and holders of office at the University of*

Cambridge from the earliest times to 1900. Part 2, from 1752–1900 (Cambridge, Cambridge University Press, 1947), Vol. 3.

Wakeman, Frederic Jr., *Strangers at the Gate: Social Disorder in South China, 1839–1861* (Berkeley and Los Angeles, University of California Press, 1966).

Walker, D. M., *The Oxford Companion to Law* (Oxford, Oxford University Press, 1980).

Walker, Eric A., *A History of Southern Africa* (London, Longman, 1957).

Wang Gungwu, 'Sun Yatsen and Singapore', *Journal of the South Seas Society*, No. 15, December 1959, pp. 55–68.

Wang, Y. C., *Chinese Intellectuals and the West: 1872–1949* (Chapel Hill, North Carolina University Press, 1966).

Weale, B. L. Putnam, *The Fight for the Republic in China* (New York, Dodd, Meads & Co., 1917).

Weber, Timothy P., *Living in the Shadow of the Second Coming: American Premillenialism 1875–1925* (New York, Oxford University Press, 1979).

'Webster, Richard Everard', in *Concise Dictionary of National Biography, 1901–1970*, p. 710.

Western Daily Press (Bristol).

Westminster Gazette (London).

Who Was Who, Vol 1: 1897–1915 (London, A. & C. Black, 1920); *Vol. 2: 1916–1928* (London, A. & C. Black, 1947, second edition); and *Vol. 3: 1929–1940* (London, A. & C. Black, 1947).

Wilbur, C. Martin, *Sun Yat-sen: Frustrated Patriot* (New York, Columbia University Press, 1976).

Williams, Ann (ed.), *Prophesy and Millenarianism: Essays in Honour of Marjorie Reeves* (Burnt Hill, Essex, Longman, 1980).

Wong, J. Y., *Yeh Ming-ch'en: Viceroy of Liang-Kuang, 1852–1858* (Cambridge, Cambridge University Press, 1976).

———— *Anglo-Chinese-Relations, 1839–1860: A Calendar of Chinese Documents in the British Foreign Office Records* (London, Oxford University Press, 1983).

———— 'Three Visionaries in Exile: Yung Wing, K'ang Yu-wei and Sun Yatsen, 1894–1911', *Journal of Asian History*, 1986 forthcoming.

Wood, Ethel M., *A History of the Polytechnic* (London, Macdonald, 1965).

Wright, Arthur F. (ed.), *The Confucian Persuasion* (Stanford, Stanford University Press, 1960).

———— and Twitchett, D. (eds.), *Confucian Personalities* (Stanford, Stanford University Press, 1962).

'Wright, Sir Robert Samuel', in *Who Was Who, Vol. 1: 1897–1915*, pp. 782–3.

Young, Ernest P., 'Ch'en T'ien-hua (1875–1905): A Chinese Nationalist', *Papers on China*, Harvard University, East Asian Research Centre, No. 13, 1959, pp. 113–62.

———— *The Presidency of Yuan Shih-k'ai, 1859–1916* (Ann Arbor, University of Michigan Press, 1977).

Yung Wing, *My Life in China and America* (New York, Henry Holt, 1909).

Works in Chinese and Japanese

Anon., 'Lun Zhongguo zhi qiantu ji guomin yingjin zhi zeren' 論中國之前途及國民應盡之責任 ('The Future of China and Duty of a Citizen'), *Hubei xueshengjie* 湖北學生界 (*Hubei Students*), No. 3, 29 March 1903.

Cai Nanqiao 蔡南橋, *Zhongshan xiansheng zhuanji* 中山先生傳記 (*Biography of Sun Yatsen*) (Shanghai, Commercial Press, 1937).

Chai Degeng, *et al.* (eds.) 柴德賡, *Xinhai geming* 辛亥革命 (*The 1911 Revolution*) (Shanghai, 1957; second, edition, Shanghai, People's Press, 1981).

Chen Jianan 陳劍安, 'Guangdong huidang yu xinhai geming' 廣東會黨與辛亥革命 ('The Relationship between the Secret Societies in Guangdong and the 1911 Revolution'), in *Jinian Xinhai geming qishi zhounian qingnian xueshu taolunhui lunwen xuan*, pp. 23–72.

Chen Shaobai 陳少白, *Xing Zhong Hui geming shiyao* 興中會革命史要 (*An Outline of the Revolutionary History of the Xing Zhong Hui*) (Nanjing, 1935), reprinted in Chai Degeng, *et al.* (eds.), *Xinhai geming*, pp. 21–75.

Chen Xiqi 陳錫祺, *Tongmenghui chengliqian de Sun Zhongshan* 同盟會成立前的孫中山 (*Sun Yatsen prior to the Founding of the Tongmenghui*) (Guangzhou, People's Press, 1984, second edition).

———— 'Guanyu Sun Zhongshan de daxue shidai' 關於孫中山的大學時代 ('On Sun Yatsen's University Days'), in *Sun Zhongshan yanjiu luncong* 孫中山研究論叢 (*Sun Yatsen Studies*), Vol. 1, 1983, pp. 1–16.

Dangdai Zhongguo mingren zhuan 當代中國名人傳 (*Eminent Chinese of the Contemporary Period*) (1931).

Feng Ziyou 馮自由, *Zhonghua minguo kaiguo qian geming shi* 中華民國開國前革命史 (*History of the Revolution prior to the Founding of the Chinese Republic*) (Shanghai. 1928).

———— *Geming yishi* 革命逸史 (*Reminiscences of the Revolution*) (Beijing, 1981, reprint, 6 vols.).

Fengling 鳳凌, *Youyu jinzhi* 遊餘僅誌 (*Records of My Travels*) (1929).

'Gong Xinzhan' 龔心湛, in *Dangdai Zhongguo mingren zhuan*, p. 458.

'Gong Zhaoyuan' 龔照瑗, in *Zhongguo jinshi mingren xiaoshi*, p. 102.

Guo Songtao 郭嵩燾, *Guo Songtao riji* 郭嵩燾日記 (*Diary of Guo Songtao*) (Changsha, People's Press, 1980, 4 vols.).

Guo Tingyi 郭廷以, *Jintai Zhongguo shishi rizhi* 近代中國史事日誌 (*Chronology of Modern Chinese History*) (Taipei, 1963, 2 vols.).

―――― *Guo Songtao nianpu* 郭嵩燾年譜 (*Chronological Biography of Guo Songtao*) (Taipei, 1971, 2 vols.).

Han Ju 漢駒, 'Xin zhengfu zhi jianshe' 新政府之建設 ('The Construction of a New Government'), *Jiangsu* 江蘇 (*Jiangsu Province*), No. 6, 21 September 1903, 'Xueshuo', p. 4.

Hara Takashi kankei bunsho 原敬關係文書 (*The Papers of Takashi Hara*) (Tokyo, Nihon hoso shuppan kyokai, 日本放送出版協會, 1984).

He Qi (Ho Kai) and Hu Liyuan 何啟，胡禮垣, 'Xinzheng zhenquan' 新政眞詮 (Excerpt) ('The True Meaning of Modern Government'), in *Zhonghua minguo kaiguo wushinian wenxian: Xing Zhong Hui, shang*, pp. 149–73.

Hu Hanmin 胡漢民, 'Hu Hanmin zizhuan' 胡漢民自傳 ('Autobiography of Hu Hanmin'), in *Jindaishi ziliao* 近代史資料 (*Sources in Modern History*), No. 2, 1981 (Beijing, China Press).

Hu Qufei 胡去非, *Sun Zhongshan xiansheng zhuan* 孫中山先生傳 (*Biography of Sun Yatsen*) (Taipei, 1968, second edition).

Hu Shengwu and Jin Chongji 胡繩武，金冲及, 'Xinhai geming shiqi Zhang Binglin de zhengzhi sixiang'辛亥革命時期章炳麟的政治思想('The Political Thought of Zhang Binglin during the Period of the 1911 Revolution'), in *Xinhai geming wushi zhounian jinian lunwen ji* 辛亥革命五十週年紀念論文集 (*Essays to Commemorate the 50th Anniversary of the 1911 Revolution*) (Beijing, China Press, 1983, 3 vols.), Vol. 1, pp. 323–53.

Hu Shengwu 胡繩武, 'Sun Zhongshan minchu huodong yanjiu shuping' 孫中山民初活動研究述評 ('A Critique of Sun Yatsen's Activities in the Early Republican Period'), paper presented at the Sun Yatsen International Conference, held near Beijing between 22 and 28 March 1985.

Huang Yuhe 黃宇和, 'Fenxi Lundun baojie dui Sun Zhongshan beinan zhi baodao yu pinglun' 分析倫敦報界對孫中山被難之報導與評論 ('An Analysis of the Reports and Comments by the London Press on Sun Yatsen's Kidnapping'), *Sun Zhongshan yanjiu* 孫中山研究 (*Studies on Sun Yatsen*) (Guangzhou, People's Press, 1986), pp. 10–30.

―――― 'Sun Zhongshan Lundun beinan yanjiu shuping' 孫中山倫敦被難研究述評 ('An Assessment of the Current Scholarship on the Kidnapping of Sun Yatsen in London'), in *Huigu yu zhanwang: guoneiwai yanjiu Sun Zhongshan shuping* 回顧與展望：國內外孫中山研究述評 (*An Assessment of the Current Scholarship on Sun Yatsen both inside and outside China*) (Beijing, China Press, 1986), pp. 474–500.

Jin Liang (ed.) 金樑, *Jinshi renwu zhi* 近世人物誌 (*Biographies of Recent Dignitaries*) (Taipei, 1955).

Jindaishi jiaocheng 近代史教程 (*A Textbook on Modern History*), translated from Russian (Beijing, People's Press, 1953).

Jing Chongji and Hu Shengwu 金冲及，胡繩武, 'Lun Sun Zhongshan geming sixiang de xingcheng he Xing Zhong Hui de chengli' 論孫中山革命思想的形成和興中會的成立 ('The Formation of Sun Yatsen's Revolutionary Ideas and the Establishment of the Xing Zhong Hui'), *Lishi yanjiu* 歷史研究 (*Historical Research*), Vol. 5, 1960, pp. 49–58.

Jinian Xinhai geming qishi zhounian qingnian xueshu taolunhui lunwenxuan 紀念辛亥革命七十周年青年學術討論會論文選 (*Papers Selected from a Junior Scholars' Conference Held to Commemorate the 1911 Revolution*), edited by the Central and South China 1911 Revolution Society and the Hunan Historical Society (Beijing, China Press, 1983, 2 vols.).

Kasai Kiyoshi 笠井清, *Minakata Kumagusu* 南方熊楠 (*Biography of Minakata Kumagusu*) (Tokyo, 1967).

Kōbe yushin nippō 神戸又新日報 (*New Kobe Daily*) (Kobe).

Kokka gakkai zasshi 國家學會雜誌 (*Journal of the Association of Political and Social Sciences*) (Tokyo).

Lai Xinxia 來新夏, 'Shilun Qing Guangxu monian de Guangxi renmin daqiyi' 試論清光緒末年的廣西人民大起義 ('An Inquiry into the Great Popular Risings in Guangxi during the Last Years of the Guangxu Reign in the Qing Period'), *Lishi yanjiu* (*Historical Research*), Vol. 11, 1957, pp. 57–77.

Lebao 叻報 (Singapore).

Li Enhan 李恩涵, 'Qingmo Jinling jiqiju de chuangjian yu fazhan' 清末金陵機器局的創建與發展 ('The Establishment and Development of the Nanjing Arsenal'), in *Jindai Zhongguo shishi yanjiu lunji* 近代中國史事研究論集 (*Studies on Modern Chinese History*) (Taipei, 1982).

——— *Zeng Jize de waijiao* 曾紀澤的外交 (*The Diplomacy of Zeng Jize*) (Taipei, 1966).

Li Hongzhang 李鴻章, *Li Wenzhong gong wenshu: zougao* 李文忠公文書：奏稿 (*Papers of Li Hongzhang: Memorials*), juan 79, p. 36.

Li Wenhai 李文海, 'Xinhai geming yu huidang' 辛亥革命與會黨 ('The 1911 Revolution and the Secret Societies'), in *Xinhai geming wushi zhounian jinian lunwen ji* 辛亥革命五十週年紀念論文集 (*Essays to Commemorate the 50th Anniversary of the 1911 Revolution*) (Beijing, China Press, reprinted 1980, 2 vols.), Vol. 1, pp. 166–87.

Li Yunhan 李雲漢 (ed.), *Yanjiu Sun Zhongshan xiansheng de shiliao yu shixue* 研究孫中山先生的史料與史學 (*Sources and Methodology on the Study of Sun Yatsen*) (Taipei, 1975).

Lin Zengping and Li Yumin 林增平，李育民，'Sun Zhongshan zaoqi sixiang shuping' 孫中山早期思想述評 ('A Critique on Sun Yatsen's Way of Thinking in His Early Days'), paper presented at the Sun Yatsen International Conference, held near Beijing between 22 and 28 March 1985.

Liu Chengyu 劉成禺，'Xian Zongli jiuzhilu' 先總理舊誌錄 ('Records of the Late President'), *Guoshiguan guankan* 國史館館刊 (*Journal of the National Academy of History*), Vol. 1, December 1947.

Liu Danian 劉大年, 'Xinhai geming yu fan-Man wenti' 辛亥革命與反滿問題 ('The 1911 Revolution and the Anti-Manchu Question'), *Lishi yanjiu* 歷史研究 (*Historical Research*), Vol. 5, 1961, pp. 1–10.

Luo Jialun 羅家倫, *Zhongshan xiansheng Lundun mengnan shiliao kaoding* 中山先生倫敦蒙難史料考訂 (*An Assessment of the Records on Sun Yatsen's Kidnapping in London*) (Nanjing, 1935, second edition).

——— (ed.), *Guofu nianpu* 國父年譜 (*Chronological Biography of Sun Yatsen*), enlarged by Huang Jilu 黃季陸 (Taipei, 1969, 2 vols.).

Luo Xianglin 羅香林, *Guofu yu Ou Mei zhi youhao* 國父與歐美之友好 (*Sun Yatsen and his Western Friends*) (Taipei, 1951).

——— *Guofu zhi daxue shidai* 國父之大學時代 (*Sun Yatsen's University Days*) (Taipei, 1954).

Ma Meibo 馬眉伯, *Zhongshan gushi* 中山故事 (*Stories about Sun Yatsen*) (Shanghai, Commercial Press, 1928).

Minakata Kumagusu 南方熊楠, *Minakata Kumagusu zenshu* 南方熊楠全集 (*The Complete Works of Minakata Kumagusu*) (Tokyo, 1975), Supplement 2.

Miyazaki Torazō (Tōten) 宮崎寅藏（滔天）, *Sanjū-sannen no yume* 三十三年の夢 (*Thirty-three Years' Dream*) (Tokyo, 1902, 1926, 1943).

Nakamura Tadashi 中川義, '"East Asia" nitsuite' *East Asia* について ('On East Asia'), in *Shingaikakumei kenkyu* 辛亥革命研究 (*Studies on the 1911 Revolution*), No. 2, March 1982, pp. 44–8.

——— 'Kikan zenshu mishuroku no Son Bun ronbun: Judicial Reform in China' 既刊全集未收錄の孫文論文 Judicial Reform in China' ('"Judicial Reform in China": An Article Which Has Not Been Included in Any of the Published Collected Works of Sun Yatsen'), in *Shingaikakumei kenkyu* 辛亥革命研究 (*Studies on the 1911 Revolution*), No. 3, March 1983, pp. 99–104.

'Okamoto Ryūnosuke' 岡本柳之助 ('Short Biography of Okamoto Ryunosuke'), in *Kokushi daijiten* 國史大辭典 (*Dictionary of National Biography*) (Tokyo, 1980), Vol. 2, p. 759.

Osaka asahi shinbun 大阪朝日新聞 (*Osaka Daily News*) (Osaka).

Peng Guoxing 彭國興, 'Lun Qin Lishan' 論秦力山 ('On Qin Lishan'), *Jinian Xinhai geming qishi zhounian qingnian xueshu taolunhui lunwen xuan*, pp. 225–48.

Qian Shifu 錢實甫, *Qingji xinshe zhiguan nianbiao* 清季新設職官年表 (*A Chronological Table of New Positions Created in the [late] Qing Period*) (Beijing, China Press, 1977).

Qing shilu, Guangxu 光緒朝清實錄 (*Veritable Records of the Qing Dynasty, Guangxu Period*), juan 354, p. 12a.

Shang Mingxuan 尚明軒, *Sun Zhongshan zhuan* 孫中山傳 (*Biography of Sun Yatsen*) (Beijing, Beijing Press, 1982).

Shao Chuanlie 邵傳烈, *Sun Zhongshan* 孫中山 (*Sun Yatsen*) (Shanghai, 1980).

Shi Fulin 史扶鄰 (Schiffrin), *Sun Zhongshan yu Zhongguo geming de qiyuan* 孫中山與中國革命的起源 (*Sun Yatsen and the Origins of the Chinese Revolution*) (Beijing, Social Sciences Press, 1981).

Shiwubao 時務報 (*Current Affairs*) (Shanghai).

Sun Yatsen 孫中山, *Guofu quanji* 國父全集 (*Collected Works of Sun Yatsen*), edited by the Guomindang (Taipei, 1957, revised edition, 6 vols.).

——— 'Hongshizihui jiushang diyifa yixu' 紅十字會救傷第一法譯序 ('Preface to the Translation of the Red Cross First Aid'), in *Sun Zhongshan quanji*, Vol. 1, pp. 107–8.

——— 'Jianguo fanglue zhiyi' 建國方略之一 ('A Plan to Reconstruct China, Part 1'), in *Sun Zhongshan quanji*, Vol. 1, pp. 115–211.

——— 'Minzu zhuyi diwujiang' 民族主義第五講 ('On Nationalism, Lecture 5'), in *Sun Zhongshan xuanji*, pp. 667–8.

——— 'Minzu zhuyi diyijiang' 民族主義第一講 ('On Nationalism, Lecture 1'), in *Sun Zhongshan xuanji*, pp. 616–30.

——— 'Nunggong' 農功 ('On Agriculture'), in *Sun Zhongshan quanji*, Vol. 1, pp. 3–6.

——— 'Shang Li Hongzhang shu' 上李鴻章書 ('A petition to Li Hongzhang'), in *Sun Zhongshan quanji*, Vol. 1, pp. 8–18.

——— *Sun Zhongshan quanji* 孫中山全集 (*Collected Works of Sun Yatsen*) (Vol. 1, Beijing, China Press, 1981; Vol. 2, Beijing, China Press, 1982; Vol. 3, Beijing, China Press, 1984).

——— *Sun Zhongshan xuanji* 孫中山選集 (*Selected Works of Sun Yatsen*) (Beijing, China Press, 1981, second edition).

——— 'Wuquan xianfa' 五權憲法 ('The Five Power Constitution'), in *Sun Zhongshan xuanji*, pp. 485–98.

——— 'Youzhi jingcheng' 有志竟成 ('The Ambition Fulfilled'), in *Sun Zhongshan xuanji*, pp. 191–211.

——— 'Zai Dongjing *Minbao* Chuangkan zhounian qingzhu dahui de yanshuo' 在東京《民報》創刊週年慶祝大會的演說 ('An Address in

Tokyo Made on the Anniversary of the Founding of the *Minbao*'),
in *Sun Zhongshan quanji*, Vol. 1, pp. 329–30.

——— 'Zhi Zheng Zaoru shu' 致鄭藻如書 ('A Letter to Zheng Zaoru'),
in *Sun Zhongshan quanji*, Vol. 1, pp. 1–3.

——— 'Zhi Qu Fengzhi han' 致區鳳墀函 ('A Letter to Qu Fengzhi'), in
Sun Zhongshan quanji, Vol. 1, pp. 45–6.

——— 'Zhongguo zhi sifa gaige' 中國之司法改革 ('Judicial Reform in
China'), *Zhongshan daxue xuebao* 中山大學學報 (*Sun Yatsen University Journal*), No. 1, 1984, pp. 7–13.

——— 'Zhuyi shengguo wuli' 主義勝過武力 ('Principles Will Overcome
Brute Force'), in *Guofu quanji*, Vol. 2, pp. 620–30.

Sun Zhongshan nianpu 孫中山年譜 (*Chronological Biography of Sun
Yatsen*), compiled by the History Department of the Guangdong
Academy of Social Sciences, *et al.* (Beijing, China Press, 1980).

Sun Zhongshan pinglunji 孫中山評論集 (*Essays on Sun Yatsen*) (Shanghai, Sanmin Company, 1926).

Sun Zhongshan xiansheng danchen jiushi zhounian jinian shiji
孫中山先生誕辰九十週年紀念詩集 (*Poems Composed on the Occasion
of the 90th Anniversary of Sun Yatsen's Birth*), compiled and
published by the Shanghai Branch of the Guomindang Revolutionary Committee (Shanghai, 1956).

Sun Zhongshan xiansheng shishi zhounian jiniance 孫中山先生逝世
週年紀念冊 (*A Volume Devoted to the Anniversary of Sun Yatsen's
Death*), compiled and published by the Chaomei Committee
潮梅支部 (Guangdong, 1926).

Sun Zhongshan yishiji 孫中山軼事集 (*Anecdotes about Sun Yatsen*)
(Shanghai, Sanmin Company, 1926).

Tang Zhijun 湯志鈞 (ed.), *Zhang Taiyan nianpu changbian* 章太炎
年譜長編 (*Chronological Biography of Zhang Taiyan*) (Beijing,
China Press, 1979, 2 vols.).

Wanguo gongbao 萬國公報 (*International Affairs*) (Shanghai).

Wan Xin 萬新 (ed.), *Zongli Lundun beinan gailue* 總理倫敦被難概略
(*An Outline of Sun Yatsen's Kidnapping in London*) (Guangzhou,
9 October 1928).

Wang Chonghui 王寵惠, 'Zongli Lundun mengnan shiliao' 總理倫敦
蒙難史料 ('Sources on Sun Yatsen's Kidnapping in London'), in
*Zhonghua minguo kaiguo wushinian wenxian: Xing Zhong Hui,
xia*, Vol. 2, pp. 187–99.

Wang Haoli 王好立, 'Cong Wuxu dao Xinhai Liang Qichao de minzhu
zhengzhi sixiang' 從戊戌到辛亥梁啟超的民主政治思想 ('Liang Qichao's
Democratic Ideas from the Hundred Days Reform to the 1911
Revolution'), in *Jinian Xinhai geming qishi zhounian qingnian
xueshu taolunhui lunwen xuan*, pp. 73–105.

Wang Jingwei 汪精衛, 'Bo geming keyi zhao guafen lun' 駁革命可以召瓜分論 ('A Refutation of the Idea that a Revolution Could Lead to the Partition of China'), *Minbao* 民報 (*The People's Newspaper*), No. 6, 25 July 1906.

Wong, J. Y., *see* Huang Yuhe 黃宇和.

Wu Deduo 吳德鐸, 'Sun Zhongshan Lundun mengnan ...' 孫中山倫敦蒙難 ('The Kidnapping of Sun Yatsen in London ...'), in *Renmin ribao* 人民日報 (*People's Daily*), 14 September 1981, p. 8.

Wu Xiangxiang 吳相湘, 'Haiwai xinjian Zhongguo xiandaishi shiliao' 海外新見中國現代史史料, ('New Overseas Sources on the Study of Modern Chinese History'), in Wu Xiangxiang (ed.), *Zhongguo xiandaishi congkan* 中國現代史叢刊 (*Essays on Modern Chinese History*) (Taipei, 1962), Vol. 1, pp. 47–63.

———— ''Lundun mengnan" zhenxiang bixu chengqing' 「倫敦蒙難」眞相必須澄清 ('What Happened during the Kidnapping Incident Must Be Clarified'), in *Lianhe bao* (Taipei, 12 November 1964); reprinted in Li Yunhan (ed.) 李雲漢, *Yanjiu Sun Zhongshan xiansheng de shiliao yu shixue* 研究孫中山的史料與史學 (Taipei, 1975), pp. 223–35.

———— *Sun Yixian xiansheng* 孫逸仙先生 (*Biography of Sun Yatsen*) (Vol. 1, Taipei, 1970; Vol. 2, Taipei, 1972).

———— *Sun Yixian xiansheng zhuan* 孫逸仙先生傳 (*Biography of Sun Yatsen*) (Taipei, 1982, 2 vols.).

Wu Ya 無涯, 'Sun Zhongshan zai Aomen suo chuangban de baozhi' 孫中山在澳門所創辦的報紙 ('The Newspaper Founded by Sun Yatsen in Macau'), in *Da gong bao* 大公報 (*Great Justice Daily*), 29 January 1956, p. 1 (Hong Kong).

Wu Zonglian 吳宗濂, *Suiyao biji sizhong* 隨軺筆記四種 (*Four Kinds of Notes Made While Accompanying the Minister on His Foreign Missions*) (1902).

Xiao Gongquan 蕭公權, *Zhongguo zhengzhi sixiang shi* 中國政治思想史 (*The History of Chinese Political Thought*) (Taipei, 1961, 6 vols.).

Xiong Yuezhi 熊月之, 'Lun Xinhai geming zhunbei shiqi de zichan jieji minzhu sixiang', 論辛亥革命准備時期的資産階級民主思想 ('On the Bourgeois Democratic Ideas during the Preparatory Stage of the 1911 Revolution'), in *Jinian Xinhai geming qishi zhounian qingnian xueshu taolunhui lunwen xuan*, pp. 149–83.

Xu Quxuan 徐蘧軒, *Sun Zhongshan shenghuo* 孫中山生活 (*The Life of Sun Yatsen*) (Shanghai, World Press, 1929).

Xue Fucheng 薛福成, *Yongan quanji xubian* 庸盦全集續編 (*Yongan Collection*): *Riji* 日記 (*Diary*) (Shanghai, 1897).

Yasui Sankichi 安井三吉, ''Shina kakumeitō shuryō Son Issen" ko — Son Bun saisho no raishin ni kansuru jakan no mondai nitsuite'

「支那革命黨首領孫逸仙」 考—孫文最初の来神に関する若干の問題について ('A Study of "The Chinese Revolutionary Leader Sun Yatsen" — Certain Questions Regarding His Arrival at Kobe'), *Kindai* 近代 (*Modern Times*), No. 57, December 1981, pp. 49–78.

Yuan Honglin 袁鴻林, 'Xing Zhong Hui shiqi de Sun Yang liangpai guanxi' 興中會時期的孫楊兩派關係 ('The Relations Between the Sun and Yang Factions during the Period of the Xing Zhong Hui'), in *Jinian Xinhai geming qishi zhounian qingnian xueshu taolunhui lunwen xuan*, Vol. 1, pp. 1–22.

Zhang Shizhao (pseud. Huang Zhonghuang) 章士釗 (黃中黃), *Sun Yixian* 孫逸仙 (*Sun Yatsen*) (Shanghai, 1903), reprinted in Chai Degeng, *et al.* 柴德賡 (eds.), *Xinhai geming*, Vol. 1, pp. 90–132.

Zhao Huimo 趙惠謨, 'Sheji zongli Lundun mengnan jinian shi' 攝記總理倫敦蒙難紀念室 ('Notes on Photographing the Room in which Sun Yatsen was Kept Prisoner'), *Zhonghua minguo kaiguo wushinian wenxian Xing Zhong Hui, xia*, Vol. 2, pp. 199–202.

Zhongguo jinshi mingren xiaoshi 中國近世名人小史 (*Short Biographies of Eminent Chinese in the Modern Period*) (1927).

Zhongguo jinxian dai shi dashi ji 中國近現代史大事記 (*Major Events in Modern Chinese History*) (Shanghai, Knowledge Press, 1982).

Zhonghua minguo kaiguo wushinian wenxian: Xing Zhong Hui, shangxia 中華民國開國五十年文献：興中會, 上, 下 (*The Establishment of the Chinese Republic: Documents Compiled on its 50th Anniversary — Xing Zhong Hui, Vols. 1–2*) (Taipei, 1964).

Zhongwen da cidian 中文大辭典 (*Chinese Dictionary*) (Taipei, 1968, 40 vols.).

Zhou Hongran 周弘然, 'Guofu "Shang Li Hongzhang shu" zhi shidai beijing' 國父 "上李鴻章書" 之時代背境 ('Background and times of "Sun Yatsen's letter to Li Hongzhang"'), in *Zhonghua minguo kaiguo wushinian wenxian: Xing Zhong Hui, shang*, pp. 270–80.

Zhongli danchen jinian zhuankan 總理誕辰紀念專刊 (*A Volume Devoted to the Memory of Sun Yatsen's Birth*), edited and published by the Guomindang Central Committee (1931).

Glossary

Arrow War 亞羅戰爭
Banno Junji 坂野潤治
baoxing 寶星
Beijing 北京
Cantlie, Dr James 康德黎醫生
chaoye xianhao 朝野賢豪
Chen Shaobai 陳少白
Chen Yongsheng 陳永生
Chen Zaizhi 陳載之
Chiang Kaishek 蔣介石
China Mail 德臣西報
Dagu 大沽
Dai Jitao 戴季陶
daotai 道台
Deng Muhan 鄧慕韓
Deng Tingkeng 鄧廷鏗
Dixiang 帝象
Dou-na-le 竇納樂
Du-guo 杜國
Du-lan-si-wa 杜蘭斯哇
Duan Ziheng 段子恒
Episcopal Church of China
　　中華聖公會
equality 平等
Feizhou 非洲
Feng Yongheng 馮詠蘅
Fengling 鳳凌
fraternity 博愛
Fuji 富士
Fujian 福建
Gaosheng 高陞
Gong Xinzhan 龔心湛
Gong Zhaoyu 龔照嶼
Gong Zhaoyuan 龔照瑗
Gong Zhiqiang 龔志强
Gu-lu-jia 古魯加
Guan Xiaoqing 關笑卿
Guangdong 廣東
Guangxi 廣西

Guangzhou 廣州
Guo Songtao 郭嵩燾
Guofu 國父
Guomindang 國民黨
Han 漢
Hara Takashi 原敬
Hazama Naoki 狹間直樹
He Qi (Ho Kai) 何啟
He Yuefu 賀躍夫
Hong Kong 香港
Hong Xiuquan 洪秀全
Hu Hanmin 胡漢民
Hu Shouwei 胡守爲
Huang Yuhe 黃宇和
Huizhou 惠州
Hunan 湖南
Inukai Tsuyoshi 犬養毅
jianguo fanglue 建國方略
Jin Chongji 金冲及
Ju Deyuan 鞠德源
Kamata Eikichi 鎌田榮吉
Kang Youwei 康有爲
Kobayashi Toshihiko 小林壽彦
Kōbe yushin nippo 神戶又新日報
Kokka gakkai zasshi
　　國家學會雜誌
Kolao 哥老 (會)
Kowshing, see Gaosheng
Kubota Bunji 久保田文次
Kwan Siu-hing, *see* Guan
　　Xiaoqing
Kyushu nippo 九州日報
Lau Yun-woo, *see* Liu Runhe
Lebao 叻報
Lee Lai-to, *see* Li Litu
Li Hongzhang 李鴻章
Li Lianying 李蓮英
Li Litu 李勵圖
Li Shengzhong 李盛鐘

Li Yumin 李育民
liberty 自由
Lin Zengping 林增平
Liu Jingren 劉鏡人
Liu Guilin 劉桂林
Liu Ruifen 劉瑞芬
Liu Runhe 劉潤和
Luo Fenglu 羅豐祿
Luo Jialun 羅家倫
Macau 澳門
Macartney, Sir Halliday 馬格里
Manchu 滿州
Manson, Dr Patrick 孟森醫生
Meiji 明治
Meiji Shinbun Zasshi Bunko
　明治新聞雜誌文庫
Minakata Kumagusu 南方熊楠
Minbao 民報
Minquan 民權
Minsheng 民生
Minzu 民族
Miyazaki Torazō 宮崎寅藏
Na 那
Nakagawa Tsunejiro 中川恒次郎
Nakamura Tadashi 中川義
nan 南
Nanjing 南京
Osaka asahi shinbun
　大阪朝日新聞
Osaka mainichi shinbun
　大阪毎日新聞
Osborne, Dr 柯士賓醫生
Pan Chenglie 潘承烈
Parkes, Harry 巴夏禮
Peng Yuxin 彭雨新
Qing 清
Qu Fengzhi 區鳳墀
quzhi 去職
Richard, Timothy 李提摩太
Rixin 日新
Salisbury, Lord 沙士勃雷侯爵
Sanderson, Sir Thomas 山德森
Sang Bing 桑兵
Schiffrin, Harold 史扶邻

Shamian 沙面
Shao Yuanchong 邵元冲
Shi Jingqiang 施景強
Shingaikakumei kenkyu
　辛亥革命研究
*Shinkuko kakumeito shuryo Son
　Issen yushu roku*
　清國革命首領孫逸仙幽囚錄
Shishi tushuguan 石室圖書館
Shiwubao 時務報
Sichuan 四川
Singapore 星加坡
Song Yuren 宋育仁
Song Zhitian 宋芝田
Songjiang 松江
Sun Wen 孫文
Sun Yatsen 孫逸仙
Suzhou 蘇州
Taiping 太平
Tajima 田島
Tang 唐
Tang Zhijun 湯志鈞
taotai, see daotai
Tianjin 天津
Tokugawa Yorimichi 德川賴倫
Triads 三合會
Tsuda Saburo 津田三郎
Uematsu 上松
Wah Tsz Yat Po 華字日報
Wang Chonghui 王寵惠
Wang Fengchang 王鳳長
Wang Gungwu 王賡武
Wang Pengjiu 王鵬九
Wang Xigeng 王錫庚
Wanguo gongbao 萬國公報
Watanabe Hiroshi 渡邊浩
White Lily Society 白蓮教
Wong, J. Y., *see* Huang Yuhe
Wu Deduo 吳德鐸
Wu Xiangxiang 吳相湘
Wu Zonglian 吳宗濂
Xiangshan 香山
Xianshan 先生
Xiao Zhizhi 蕭致治

Xie Bangqing 謝邦清
Xie Zuantai 謝纘泰
Xing Zhong Hui 興中會
Xue Fucheng 薛福成
Yamaguchi Ichiro 山口一郎
Yanagita 柳田
Yang Guoxiong 楊國雄
Yang Quyun 楊衢雲
Yang Ru 楊儒
Yeh Mingchen 葉名琛
Yeung, Peter, *see* Yang Guoxiong
Yokohama 横濱
youzhi jingcheng 有志竟成
Yuan Shikai 袁世凱

Zeng Guangquan (Jingyi)
曾廣銓（景沂）
Zeng Jize 曾紀澤
Zhang Binglin, *see* Zhang
Taiyan
Zhang Deyi 張德彝
Zhang Kaiyuan 章開沅
Zhang Taiyan (Binglin)
章太炎（炳麟）
Zheng Shiliang 鄭士良
Zhongshan 中山
Zhu Shouci 朱壽慈
Zongli Yamen 總理衙門

Index

ABERDEEN PARK, 244
Aberdeen University, 211ff.
Abraham, 229
Ackroyd, Judge, 26
affidavits, 39, 40, 41, 42, 44
agriculture, 261ff.
Albert Road, 17, 222ff.
American Congregationalist, 298
anecdotal interest, 262
Anglican Church, 213
Anglican Church of China, 210
Anglo-Saxon, 221ff., 228ff., 255
Anglo-Turkish Contingent, 67
Anglophile, 238
anti-British feelings, 199
anti-British strike, 199
anti-Christian, 278
Armenian, 66, 165
arrest, 110
Arrow War, 278
Arrowsmith, 186
Attorney-General, 42
Australia, 121, 122
'Awkins, 178

BABYLONIAN TALMUD, 228
baggage, 104
bait, 146
Balfour, 288
ballots, 176ff.
Banno, Junji, 18
Barclay-Brown, Mrs, 185
Barnes, 143, 254
Basinghall Street, 30
Bay of Guangzhou, 195
bedclothes, 102
Beijing, 65, 88ff.
Bertie, Hon. Francis L., 34, 43
Bible, 298
Bird, Mr, 208
Blacker, Dr Carmen, 18
Boadicea, 228
boast, 117, 118
Boer War, 220
bon vivant, 85
Boulger, 9
Bow Street, 53

Boyd, Mrs, 208
bread, 101
breakfast, 152
British Israelite, 228ff.
British Library, 273
British Museum, 256, 268, 273ff.
British nationalism, 177, 178, 221ff.,
    253–4, 290
British neutrality, 238
British South Africa Company, 218ff.,
    219
Brownie, 240
Bruce, Hon. Sir Frederick, 279
Bruce, Dr Mitchell, 217, 218, 270
Buckingham Palace, 271
Bulawayo, 208, 217, 218, 219ff.
Burgevine, Henry, 68–9
burglary, 25, 27

CABLE, 89, 90, 91, 133, 137ff.; *see, also*,
    cyphers
Calcutta, 278
Calvo, 98
Canada, 280
Canadian Pacific, 292
Cantlie, Dr James, 1, 7, 8, 9, 21, 59,
    120, 183ff.; background, 211ff.;
    bursary, 215; dreamer, 216; Good
    Samaritan, 216; nationalism, 214
Cantlie, Kenneth, 187
Cantlie, Mrs Mabel, 24, 27; bicycle,
    264; warning Sun Yatsen, 135, 195,
    291
Cantlie, Sir Colin, 143
Cantlie, Sir Keith, 143, 187
Cantlie, Sir Neil, 143
Canton Christian College, 119
Canton plot, 65, 121, 170–1, 173, 234,
    237, 240, 243
Cantonese, 93, 128–9, 134, 145–6
Carlill, 143
castaways, 270
Catholic Church, 212
Catholic missionaries, 69
Cavendish, Mr, 53
Cayley, Sir George, 266
cemetery, 143

tracings, 11
Trafalgar Square, 254
Transvaal, 219–20
travel journals, 85
treason, 99, 130–1
Triads, 174
trick, 29
Tsuda, 265
Turkey, 6
Turkish Ambassador, 66

UNION JACK, 245

VERBIEST, 69
Victoria and Albert, 249
Victoria and Albert Museum, 266
visa, 6
Volkhovsky, Felix, 17, 279ff.

WAH TSZ YAT PO, 235
Wang Chonghui, 11
Wang Fengchang, 37n. 100
Wang Xigeng, 74, 131
Ward, Frederick, 68
Washington, 50, 118, 123, 126, 133, 134, 154
Weay, Mr, 209, 217
West End, 30
Westminster Bridge, 26
Westminster Gazette, 50
Wheaton, 98
white Japanese, 230
White Lily Society, 172, 174, 183
White Star Line, 73
Whitehall, 34, 35, 58, 84, 92
Wilbur, Martin C., 226, 251

Wilkinson, Col., 254
Windsor Castle, 245
Wood, Sir Henry, 268
Woods Pasha, 65
Wright, Judge R.S., 39, 42
Wu Xiangxiang, 5, 6, 7, 9, 10, 13, 112–13, 243–4
Wu Zonglian, 3, 11, 73, 74, 79, 83, 87, 125ff., 150ff.
Wuchang Uprising, 285; see, also, Revolution (1911)

XIANGSHAN, 116
Xiansheng, 5
Xie Bangqing, 79
Xie Zuantai, 122ff., 170, 237, 238, 239
Xing Zhong Hui, 116, 199, 237, 239, 295
Xue Fucheng, 77

YANG QUYUN, 121ff.
Yang Ru, 72–3
Yeh Mingchen, 278
Young China Party, 192
'Youzhi jingcheng', 285
Yuan Shikai, 20, 214, 250–1

ZENG GUANQUAN, 56, 79
Zeng Jize, 71
Zhang Shizhao, 194–5
Zhang Taiyan, 63
Zheng Shiliang, 119ff., 170
Zhu Shouci, 79
Zongli Yamen, 88
Zoo, 267
Zoological Society, 267